THE OBJECTIONABLE LI ZHI

THE OBJECTIONABLE LI ZHI

FICTION, CRITICISM, AND DISSENT IN LATE MING CHINA

Edited by
Rivi Handler-Spitz, Pauline C. Lee, and Haun Saussy

UNIVERSITY OF WASHINGTON PRESS
Seattle

The Objectionable Li Zhi was published with the support of a grant from the Joseph and Lauren Allen Fund for Books on Asian Literature, Art, and Culture.

GEISS HSU FOUNDATION

This publication was also made possible in part by an award from the James P. Geiss and Margaret Y. Hsu Foundation.

Additional support was provided by the Wallace Scholarly Activities Fund at Macalester College, the Division of the Humanities at the University of Chicago, and the Office of the Vice President for Research and the Department of Theological Studies at St. Louis University.

Composed in Warnock Pro, typeface designed by Robert Slimbach

24 23 22 21 20 5 4 3 2 1

Printed and bound in the United States of America

UNIVERSITY OF WASHINGTON PRESS
uwapress.uw.edu

LIBRARY OF CONGRESS CATALOGING-IN-PUBLICATION DATA

Names: Handler-Spitz, Rivi, editor. | Lee, Pauline C., editor. | Saussy, Haun, 1960–, editor.
Title: The objectionable Li Zhi : fiction, criticism, and dissent in late Ming China / edited by Rivi Handler-Spitz, Pauline C. Lee, and Haun Saussy.
Description: Seattle : University of Washington Press, 2021. | Includes bibliographical references and index.
Identifiers: LCCN 2020020100 (print) | LCCN 2020020101 (ebook) | ISBN 9780295748375 (hardcover) | ISBN 9780295748382 (paperback) | ISBN 9780295748399 (ebook)
Subjects: LCSH: Li, Zhi, 1527–1602.
Classification: LCC B128.L454 O25 2020 (print) | LCC B128.L454 (ebook) | DDC 181/.11—dc23
LC record available at https://lccn.loc.gov/2020020100
LC ebook record available at https://lccn.loc.gov/2020020101

The paper used in this publication is acid free and meets the minimum requirements of American National Standard for Information Sciences—Permanence of Paper for Printed Library Materials, ANSI Z39.48–1984.∞

CONTENTS

ACKNOWLEDGMENTS

This book began in the fall of 2013 as a workshop on Li Zhi titled "Writing, Virtues, and Social Change in Sixteenth-Century China." We gratefully acknowledge the friends and colleagues who participated; their ideas can be found everywhere in these pages. We thank the Division of the Humanities at the University of Chicago for generously sponsoring the workshop. During the long journey between that gathering and the shaping of this book's chapters, we benefited from the comments and criticism of our external reviewers. We are grateful to Yuhang Li for suggesting the cover image, Li Haiyang for granting us permission to use his artwork, and Katrina Noble for designing a cover that so aptly expresses Li Zhi's impishness. Cho-Chien Feng provided thoughtful and meticulous assistance on the glossary and bibliography. The project would not have been possible without the encouraging guidance of our editor, Lorri Hagman, and the skill of our copyeditor, Judith Hoover. Finally, we would like to acknowledge the financial support of the Office of the Vice President for Research and the Department of Theological Studies at St. Louis University, the Division of the Humanities at the University of Chicago, and the Wallace Scholarly Activities Fund at Macalester College, the Joseph and Lauren Allen Fund, and the James P. Geiss and Margaret Y. Hsu Foundation.

This book is dedicated to provocative intellectuals the world over, in gratitude for the bold intellectual exchanges they engage in and inspire.

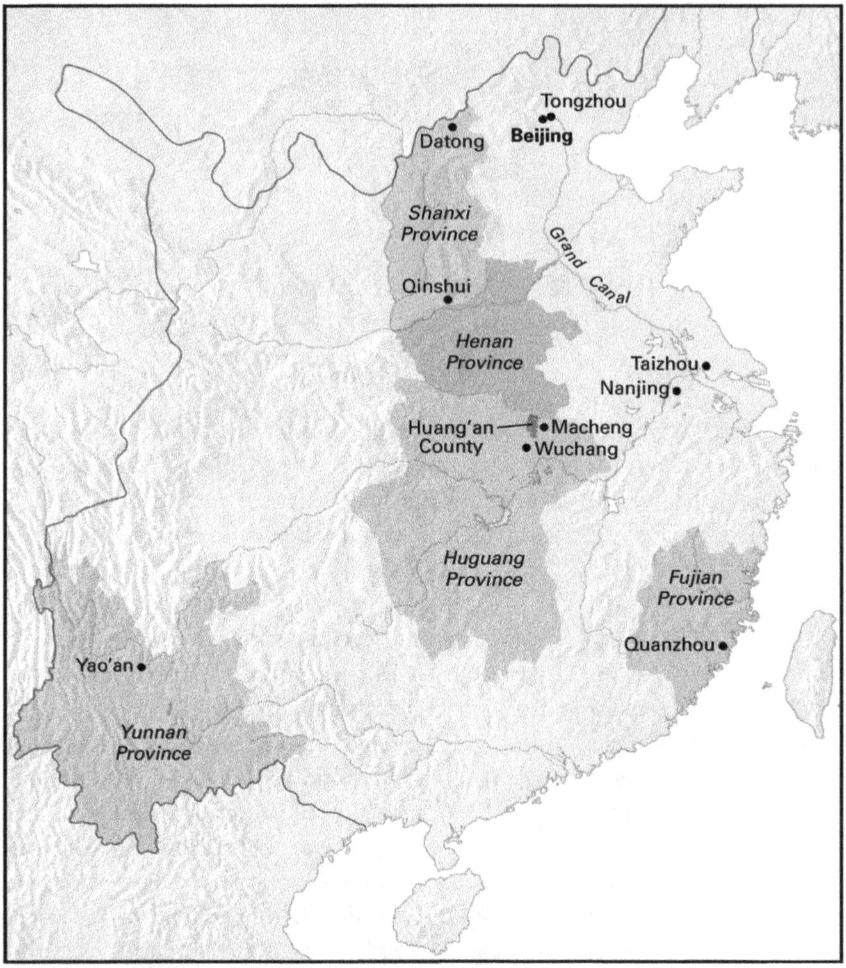

Late-Ming China, highlighting cities and regions significant to Li Zhi. Reprinted from *A Book to Burn and A Book to Keep (Hidden)*.

THE OBJECTIONABLE LI ZHI

INTRODUCTION

RIVI HANDLER-SPITZ, PAULINE C. LEE,
AND HAUN SAUSSY

ICONOCLAST, ECCENTRIC, HERO, INDIVIDUALIST. THESE WORDS have all been used to describe Li Zhi (1527–1602; style name Zhuowu), the "Confucian monk" whose provocative actions and inflammatory writings captivated readers in the waning years of the Ming dynasty. Li Zhi's life and books exemplify many of the social, ethical, metaphysical, economic, and linguistic concerns emblematic of his era. Never a systematic thinker, he delighted in poking holes in respected doctrines, upending traditions, subverting norms, and decrying the hypocrisies of the social class into which he had risen. Fearlessly irreverent and unremittingly creative, he embraced paradox and, oscillating between sincerity and irony, charted a zigzag course strewn with self-contradictions. His writings in many genres—essays, letters, poems, aesthetic criticism, historical annotation, and philosophical commentary—showcase his keen powers of observation and his incisive interpretations of popular and classical texts spanning the Confucian, Buddhist, and Daoist traditions.

The internal inconsistencies found everywhere in Li Zhi's writings have generated widely divergent interpretations. Some scholars have labeled him a steadfast anti-Confucian. Others have portrayed him as a devout Buddhist, a Daoist, a nihilist, or a relativist. One of the earliest Western scholars to write on Li Zhi, William Theodore de Bary, regarded him as an "arch-individualist."[1] This volume aims to probe beyond two-dimensional explanations of Li Zhi that would cast him simply as an adherent to (or opponent of) any one school. Rather, the contributors to this volume maintain that deep-seated contradictions and inherent ambiguities lie at the core of Li Zhi's literary and philosophical oeuvre and inform his polyvalent identities as a lay Buddhist, an example of mercantile-literati values, and a new type of Confucian contending for a place in the orthodox lineage.

Given Li Zhi's penchant for celebrating contradictory positions, the chapters in this book correspondingly provide arguments that sometimes clash, sometimes converge. What emerges in these pages is not a uniform image of Li Zhi but a kaleidoscopic array of opposing perspectives. Approaching his life and work from heterogeneous disciplinary perspectives—literary studies, intellectual history, social and cultural history, religious studies, and book history—each chapter focuses on a single type of contribution he made to late-Ming culture: his theory of authenticity, displays of filial piety, practice of friendship, pedagogical strategies, performances of masculinity, revaluation of women's roles in society, participation in examination culture, involvement in Buddhist self-cultivation, commentaries on popular drama and fiction, and views on the afterlife. And just as Li Zhi adopted the pedagogical method of withholding answers to students' questions—at times hoping thereby to spark independent, critical thought and at other times perhaps believing answers could be found only within the heart and mind of each student—so too does this book refrain from neatly reconciling discrepant views.

Arranged in five sections—"Authenticity and Filiality," "Friends and Teachers," "Manipulations of Gender," "Textual Communities," and "Afterlives"—these chapters analyze the relationship between Li Zhi's much-touted celebration of genuineness and the fragmented sense of self conveyed in his autobiographical writings. They question the autonomy of his understanding of selfhood and inquire into its dependence on social networks. They seek the meanings underlying his inconsistent use of language and the seriousness of his attacks on Confucian officialdom. They examine the relative malleability and intransigence of his public persona and its dependence on and diffusion via print media. They explore his intense devotion to friendship and letter-writing. And they analyze his attitudes toward "eight-legged" examination essays, filial piety, Confucian orthodoxy, women's self-realization, and metaphysics. In doing so, they reflect the complexity and internal diversity of Li Zhi's corpus and demonstrate its ability to crystallize debates of central importance in the late Ming. Moreover, they establish Li Zhi as a pivotal figure in the history of dissent in China.

LI ZHI'S LIFE

Born into a Muslim merchant family in the port city of Quanzhou in the southern province of Fujian, Li Zhi was schooled by his father in the

Confucian classics. As a young man, he hired himself out as a tutor, and in 1552, at the age of twenty-six, he passed the first level of the imperial examinations. Due to his obligation to support his only living parent, his father, along with his siblings, he decided in 1555 to settle for a government position immediately rather than sit for the metropolitan examination in hopes of attaining a better placement. He was assigned to serve as a lecturer at the government school in Huixian, Henan. This marked the beginning of his more than twenty-year-long official career.[2]

In 1566 he was promoted to a coveted post in the Ministry of Rites serving in the southern capital, Nanjing. Four years later, he accepted the position of secretary of the Ministry of Punishments (1570–77). Across the Yangzi River and a little less than a hundred miles east of Nanjing was the city of Taizhou, birthplace of Wang Gen (1483–1541), founder of what would later be referred to as the Taizhou School, a branch of Wang Yangming's (1472–1529) School of the Mind, which blended Confucian ethics with Buddhist teachings and celebrated each individual's innate ethical knowledge. While serving in Nanjing, Li Zhi became deeply influenced by disciples of Wang Yangming who shaped the Taizhou School. These included Wang Bi (1511–1587), son of Wang Gen, as well as two great teachers whom Li Zhi deeply admired, Wang Ji (1498–1583) and Luo Rufang (1515–1588). Li Zhi's final official post (1577–80) was as prefect in the remote region of Yao'an, Yunnan.

Beginning in the 1570s, Li Zhi enjoyed the patronage and close friendship of the Geng family, which occupied a leading position in Huang'an County, Huguang Province. He sustained a lengthy and spirited epistolary correspondence with the successful older brother, Geng Dingxiang (1524–1596), who rose to national prominence as a vice censor in chief. Yet the younger brother, Geng Dingli (1534–1584), was Li Zhi's more cherished friend. Having failed the provincial examinations, Dingli devoted himself to ethical and spiritual cultivation, including the study of Chan Buddhism and the teachings of Wang Yangming. Inspired in part by Dingli's example, Li Zhi stepped down from his post in Yunnan, drawing harsh criticism from the conservative Geng Dingxiang, who viewed Li's act as an abdication of Confucian duty to society. The differences between Geng Dingxiang and Li Zhi led to a highly publicized epistolary quarrel between the two in which Geng strove to position himself as the embodiment of orthodoxy and to discredit Li as a deviant.[3] For his part, Li cast Geng as a careerist hypocrite and portrayed himself as an authentic truth-seeker.

Li Zhi esteemed those who, unlike Geng Dingxiang, unwaveringly adhered to their ideals and made personal sacrifices to realize them. One of his greatest heroes was He Xinyin (1517–1579), an adherent of the Taizhou School, who believed that moral truth resided in the heart of each individual. Though friendly with Geng Dingxiang, He Xinyin turned his back on an official career and forsook his family in order to cultivate moral and spiritual growth alongside like-minded soul-friends. A passionate social reformer, He Xinyin also organized local communities to resist official corruption and predatory tax collecting. Li Zhi revered this bold reformer and was aghast that Geng Dingxiang, who held considerable political influence on the national stage, refused to intervene when He Xinyin was later arrested for sedition and beaten to death in prison. Li publicly condemned Geng for moral weakness and excoriated him as a disloyal friend. It was probably with Geng in mind that Li wrote, "He Xinyin's intimates and fellow students calmly observed his death as if they were throwing stones down a well."[4] Li Zhi regarded He Xinyin as an ethical model deserving emulation; Geng Dingxiang, lamentably, as a compromised friend who could not be brought back to the Way.

The gulf between Li Zhi and Geng Dingxiang only widened in 1587 when Li sent his wife of over forty years, Madame Huang (1533–1588), as well as their daughter, sole survivor among their seven children, back to their hometown in Fujian while he espoused a monastic life of study and contemplation. Greatly attracted by Buddhist teachings, Li Zhi moved first to the Vimalakīrti Monastery and then to the Zhifoyuan Monastery on Dragon Lake, just outside of the city of Macheng. The year 1588 was particularly eventful for Li Zhi: having abandoned his family and taken up residence in an unlicensed monastery, he shaved his head as if entering Buddhist orders, an act that provoked scandal and outrage. Geng Dingxiang considered it a repudiation of Confucianism, but Li Zhi himself wrote that he shaved his head merely to unburden himself of familial obligations and show his family and clan that he was determined never to return home.[5] His wife died that same year; Li Zhi learned of her burial only later and never did return to his hometown.

Nestled in his mountain retreat on the shores of Dragon Lake, a place often mentioned in his writings, Li Zhi devoted his days to study and composed his most influential works during this period. He also took part in Buddhist rituals, all the while carrying on a lively correspondence with prominent Ming literati, including Jiao Hong (1540–1620), the Yuan brothers Zhongdao (1570–1623), Hongdao (1568–1610), and Zongdao (1560–1600), and many others. Friendship among like-minded individuals was central to Li Zhi's vision of a good life, and his conversation partners further included those both nearby—such as his patron Ma Jinglun

(1562–1605)—and far away, including the Jesuit Matteo Ricci (whom Li met for the first time in 1599). Li Zhi's friends and acquaintances also included Buddhist monks, such as the abbot of the Cloister, Wunian (secular name, Xiong Shenyou, 1544–1627), and women, including Li's most controversial disciple, Mei Danran, daughter of the statesman Mei Guozhen.

The publication, wide dissemination, and even falsification of Li Zhi's writings confirmed his towering status in the burgeoning print culture of the late Ming. Yet responses to his works were mixed. Some contemporaries heralded him as a fearless champion of authenticity and self-expression, while others condemned him as a threat to public order. In 1602, the chief supervising secretary of the Ministry of Rites, Zhang Wenda (d. 1625), presented a memorial to the emperor accusing Li Zhi of heretical beliefs, heterodox writings, and outlandish behavior. Li was condemned for praising tyranny (exemplified by the first emperor of China, Qin Shihuang) and applauding unfilial acts like elopement (exemplified by the second century BCE widowed poet Zhuo Wenjun)—two unorthodox judgments among many expressed in his writings. Zhang also relayed gossip about Li's questionable behavior, including bathing with prostitutes and inviting the daughters of respectable Macheng families to spend the night at the monastery. These allegations, although unproved, caused serious trouble for Li.

In the years leading up to Zhang Wenda's memorial, Li Zhi's critics had threatened and harassed him. In 1591, while sightseeing with his friend and disciple Yuan Zhongdao at the Yellow Crane Pavilion in Wuchang, Li Zhi was attacked by a mob, possibly set on him by Geng Dingxiang. A few years later, he was accused of undermining public order by the Huguang provincial surveillance commissioner, Shi Jingxian, who threatened to have Li Zhi sent back to his native province of Fujian. A few years later, Li Zhi's quarters at the Zhifoyuan Monastery were burned down and the gravesite he had been preparing for himself was desecrated. He fled from Macheng to Tongzhou, a dozen or so miles from Beijing, and was received by his friend and staunch supporter Ma Jinglun.

Several months later, imperial marshals sent in response to Zhang Wenda's memorial arrested Li Zhi at Ma Jinglun's home and took him to prison. Once there, Li asked a prison guard for a razor; with it he cut his throat, committing suicide at the age of seventy-six. His dramatic death seems only to have fed his fame. Although an imperial edict issued the same year banned his books and ordered them burned along with the wooden blocks for printing them, his writings continued to circulate widely, inciting scandal and shaping aesthetic tastes for generations.

AN OVERVIEW OF THIS BOOK

Part I: Authenticity and Filiality

The opening chapters address Li Zhi's repeated attempts to express his genuine self. Chapter 1, by Wai-yee Li, argues that Li Zhi characterizes "genuineness" (*zhen*) as the return to an original essence, a pure state of selfhood untainted by external influences. The "genuine" self to which he alludes in his celebrated essay "On the Childlike Mind" (Tongxin shuo) is a unitary entity that admits no divided or conflicted loyalties. Yet as Wai-yee Li points out, Li Zhi's autobiographical writings rarely portray their author engaging in such spontaneous, unselfconscious acts of "genuine" self-expression. Indeed, autobiographical writings by their very nature tend to bifurcate the self: a present, writing self reflects upon a past, narrated self. Accordingly, his writings cast him simultaneously in the roles of subject and object, highlighting his theatrical flair and his struggles to make sense of conflicting desires. He was aware, as Ying Zhang argues in chapter 6, that he could not control the reception of his writings. Thus Wai-yee Li examines the rhetorical strategies he undertook to square the circle—to reconcile the multiplicity of perspectives his writings embody with their bid for pure, "genuine" self-expression. The chapter concludes by suggesting that despite relentless self-questioning, Li Zhi never succeeded in attaining his ideal of a "genuine," unitary self.

Chapter 2, by Maram Epstein, connects Li Zhi's struggle for authentic self-expression to Confucian understandings of filial piety. Anticipating Miaw-fen Lu's more detailed historiographical account in chapter 11, Epstein focuses on one pivotal moment in the reception history of Li Zhi's works, the May Fourth Movement. Epstein argues against May Fourth understandings of Li Zhi as a brazen iconoclast and an apostate from Confucian values. Instead, she foregrounds his efforts to present himself as a model filial son and exemplar of Confucian masculinity. Paying close attention to the paired concepts of *gong*, "the appropriate or ritually sanctioned," and *si*, "the improper, selfish, or biased," Epstein exposes the lengths to which Li Zhi went to cultivate the image of a Confucian man cleaving to his ethical values and consistently prioritizing obligations to his patriline over responsibilities to his wife and children. Epstein's conclusion, that May Fourth intellectuals overemphasized the subversiveness of Li Zhi's thought, resonates with Kai-Wing Chow's investigation into Li's advocacy for the conservative Confucian "eight-legged" examination essay genre (chapter 8). Although his efforts to project the public image of an exemplary Confucian man were not very successful (chapter 6), Epstein maintains that his posture as both a rebel and a filial son—or as a rebel who yearned to be regarded as a filial son—unsettles May Fourth conceptions of filial piety as antithetical to modern individualism.

Part II: Friends and Teachers

Li Zhi adopted the rhetorical stance of a filial son, but he departed from classical precedent by ranking friendship, not political or familial relationships, first among the five Confucian bonds (*wulun*): ruler-minister, father-son, husband-wife, elder brother–younger brother, and friend-friend. The chapters in part II examine Li Zhi's attitudes toward and relationships with friends and, by extension, teachers and students. In chapter 3, Martin Huang examines Li Zhi's commitment to friendship in both theory and practice, as well as the censure this devotion drew. Enthusiasm for friendship reached a new peak in the Ming dynasty, as exemplified by the writings and actions of Li's heroes He Xinyin and Deng Huoqu (1498–ca. 1569), who left behind family and career and, disregarding four of the five relationships, dedicated themselves to friendship. Li Zhi not only defended these men verbally but also emulated their unorthodox deeds, choosing to live away from his family for long stretches and refusing to take a concubine after his wife's death, even though he had no heir.

The portrait of Li Zhi that Huang sketches differs starkly from the image Epstein paints: Huang casts him as an iconoclast whose decision to reject familial obligations and instead seek a "soul-friend" with whom to pursue enlightenment and investigate questions of life and death scandalized contemporaries. Huang's chapter anticipates Jiang Wu's discussion of Li Zhi's spiritual seeking in chapter 9 and paves the way for Miaw-fen Lu's analysis of Li's attitudes toward the afterlife in chapter 11. Tragically, although Li Zhi never found the ideal friend he sought, he did alienate many contemporaries by daring to question the orthodox Confucian hierarchy of human relationships that would place family over friends.

No one criticized Li Zhi more harshly than did his sometime friend Geng Dingxiang. In a widely publicized series of open letters that circulated both as manuscript copies and in redacted, printed form, each man accused the other of straying from the ethical path. In chapter 4, Timothy Brook analyzes this epistolary exchange in light of two shaping factors: the history of postal delivery—including personal and commercial courier services—and the expansion of print culture in the late Ming. These widely circulated letters contributed substantially to Li Zhi's growing image problem, the topic of chapter 6. Brook shows that despite the deepening ideological rift between Li and Geng, both men agreed to publish their differences, providing a highly visible example of a friendship forged and contested publicly in print. In published letters, each friend earnestly strove to correct and admonish, guide and reform the other, thus taking on the role of teacher. And, as Brook argues, it was their shared commitment to this type of rigorous ethical transformation that prompted them to bring their philosophical disagreements before the court of public opinion. In doing so, they contributed to the late-Ming "public sphere of letters," a forum for publicly voicing unauthorized opinions.

Although Geng Dingxiang's remonstrations failed to move Li Zhi, the latter did develop close relationships with teachers and students, several of whom he described as "teacher-friends" (*shiyou*). As Rivi Handler-Spitz demonstrates in chapter 5, even though Li Zhi abjured the formal role of pedagogue, he willingly mentored students and embraced the role of student, studying under prominent neo-Confucians such as Luo Rufang and Wang Ji. Analyzing Li Zhi's funerary tributes to these masters, Handler-Spitz traces his recorded impressions of and interactions with these two influential teachers. This chapter demonstrates that just as Li Zhi strove to present himself in print as a filial son (chapter 2) and a model Confucian man (chapter 6), so too did he endeavor to create the public image of himself as a loyal friend to his teachers and a worthy transmitter of their teachings. Yet his teachers prized personal self-discovery and self-reliance over strict adherence to doctrine. The question thus arises how, or even whether, students trained in this school could acknowledge and honor their mentors: would striking out on their own and rejecting their teacher's doctrines paradoxically preserve the teacher's legacy? Li Zhi encouraged intellectual autonomy and goaded his students to think critically. His pedagogical strategies thus echo rhetorical strategies evident in his commentaries on the classics (chapter 7), and these in turn resonate with comments attributed to the fiction and drama commentator "Li Zhuowu," an alias designed to impersonate Li Zhi. As Robert Hegel suggests in chapter 10, the persona of Li Zhuowu employed an arsenal of commentarial strategies consonant with the anti-authoritarian pedagogical style of the historical Li Zhi.

Part III: Manipulations of Gender

One reason Li Zhi was considered such a controversial figure was that he unsettled conventional Confucian gender norms. Part III examines his attitudes toward women and his performance of his own masculinity. In chapter 6, Ying Zhang builds on Epstein's argument (chapter 2) to illuminate Li Zhi's efforts to present himself as the embodiment of exemplary masculinity. Highlighting Li Zhi's artful combination of neo-Confucian and Buddhist vocabularies, a theme elaborated by Wu in chapter 9, Zhang demonstrates that the nuances of Li's position often eluded readers. For in the late-Ming world of promiscuous printing, Li Zhi's words were frequently torn from their original contexts; readers excerpted them at will, co-opting them for their own polemical purposes. As unpredictable interpretations proliferated, questions arose regarding who had the authority to determine the meaning of a printed text: the author, the state through its educational institutions, or individual readers? The multiplication of opinions regarding Li Zhi generated what Zhang terms Li's "image problem." Although he consistently and unflinchingly criticized the moral decline of his era, readers attacked him for exemplifying that very moral decline, especially with respect to women. Thus, while his enemies saw him as a threat to established gender norms, his defenders, especially his patron Ma Jinglun, praised him as a model of manly self-restraint and the embodiment of Confucian values. The coexistence of these opposing interpretations attests to the impossibility of controlling one's public image in an era of increasingly widespread print media.

Pauline Lee in chapter 7 also focuses on the subject of gender. But in marked contrast to Zhang's analysis of loss of control, Lee focuses on the masterful control Li exhibits in his writings. Picking out seemingly insignificant lines from poems, historical essays, letters, and philosophical commentaries, Lee argues that what emerges in bits and pieces is a rather consistent effort to nudge or provoke the reader to reimagine conventional conceptions of women's roles in society. Li Zhi envisions women as fully actualized human beings who travel freely, read and write, choose their own marriage partners, and participate in government. Juxtaposing this view of women's roles in society with more radical developments in the late Qing, Lee stresses Li Zhi's commitment to anchoring his progressive ideas in the classical texts of the Confucian canon. This chapter adumbrates the deviously creative strategies Li Zhi developed to achieve his aim of inserting women into central positions in the Confucian tradition: he redefined the meaning of words, "misremembered" passages from classical texts, and recast anecdotes from antiquity. These strategies, which showcase his own virtuosity as a reader and critic, anticipate the irreverent tone and iconoclastic opinions characteristic of the "Zhuowu" fiction and drama commentator (chapter 10).

Part IV: Textual Communities

Part IV emphasizes the internally diverse textual communities in which Li Zhi participated. In chapter 8, Kai-wing Chow highlights Li's contributions to a newly emerging class of "mercantile-literati" (*shishang*), while Wu, in chapter 9, addresses Li's role as a Dao learner (*xuedaoren*), a "spiritual seeker" who used Buddhism to pursue self-cultivation across sectarian and doctrinal lines. Chow highlights Li's central role in a social network that was expanding to include writers who identified as literati but relied on both patronage and commercial publication. The glue holding this network together was print. Like Epstein, Chow argues against the widespread view that Li was an "individualist" out of step with his time. Instead, Chow deems him exemplary of a newly emerging merchant-literati culture, whose materialist values—including self-interest and care of the self—he articulated and publicized. He not only expressed merchant-literati values; he also courted readers belonging to this social class by addressing subjects of interest to them. His comments on friends' eight-legged examination essays, annotations on the *Four Books*, and paratextual advertisements aimed at examination candidates can all be interpreted in this light. These various methods, Chow argues, permitted Li to redefine ethical relationships in material terms, legitimate worldly concerns, and chip away at the social hierarchy that would maintain the traditional dominance of literati over merchants.

If Chow regards Li Zhi as a representative of the mercantile literati, Wu identifies him as a standard-bearer of a very different community, "Dao learners" who, drawing eclectically on Daoist, Buddhist, and Confucian teachings, attempted to cultivate themselves ethically and spiritually. Relying on the concept of "textual spirituality," spirituality cultivated through reading and writing, Wu examines Li Zhi's interpretations of Buddhist texts and shows how he and the community of Dao learners not only read and wrote but also performed, witnessed, and reenacted one another's performances of Chan encounter dialogues. Through eccentric actions such as rolling on the ground, Dao learners both demonstrated and taught their conceptions of "authenticity." Harking back to Wai-yee Li's discussions of authenticity (chapter 1) and Lee's analysis of Li Zhi as a reader (chapter 7), this chapter concludes by inviting us to consider how Li Zhi's interpretations of Buddhist texts shaped his understanding and enactment of authenticity.

Part V: Afterlives

The final section provides two complementary interpretations of the afterlives of Li Zhi's writings. In chapter 10, Robert Hegel approaches the subject of afterlives from a metaphorical perspective and examines the renowned fiction commentator "Li Zhuowu," the fictitious persona created by ghostwriters, primarily Ye Zhou, in imitation of Li Zhi. In chapter 11, Miaw-fen Lu takes as her subject Li Zhi's metaphysical reflections on transcendence after death and the relevance of these ideas to the reception of his works from the Qing dynasty on.

As Hegel shows, Li Zhi's name was pinned to commentaries on several of the most popular Ming dynasty works of long fiction in the *xiaoshuo* genre: *The Water Margin* (Shuihu zhuan), *The Romance of the Three Kingdoms* (Sanguo zhi yanyi), and *The Journey to the West* (Xiyou ji), as well as several dramatic works. Situating the "Li Zhuowu" commentaries in the history of seventeenth-century fiction commentary, Hegel notes the tremendous influence these commentaries exerted on the development of Chinese vernacular fiction. He shows that in these commentaries, which took the form of brief interlinear remarks as well as lengthier prefatory or concluding statements, Li Zhuowu comes across as an astute, discerning, impish, and emotionally keen reader. The authenticity of these commentaries, let alone their connection to views held by the historical Li Zhi, cannot be verified. Nonetheless, they unquestionably reflect values associated with Li Zhi: affirmation of individuality, celebration of subjectivity, and passionate expression of emotion. Moreover, Hegel argues, these renowned commentaries provide glimpses of the image projected upon Li Zhi by his contemporaries.

Expanding on the theme of reception history, Lu demonstrates that although many scholars have characterized Confucian thought as unconcerned with the afterlife and matters of transcendence, Confucians from the late Ming through the Qing cared deeply about these subjects. She situates Li Zhi's preoccupation with death and his changing attitudes toward it in the context of diverse neo-Confucian approaches to moral cultivation. Her discussion opens onto a larger question: If after death all humans shed their individual identity and return to the cosmos, why should anyone engage in self-cultivation at all? Outlining various responses to this question, this chapter provides a fitting conclusion to the volume by demonstrating the shifting values that stimulated widely varying responses to Li Zhi's writings. In his own time, Li Zhi was considered a highly controversial figure; in the seventeenth and eighteenth centuries, as Wang Yangming's teachings receded and evidential scholarship rose to the fore, interest in Li Zhi waned; in the twentieth century, scholars approached him with renewed interest, heralding him as a harbinger of the Chinese Enlightenment; and following on the twenty-first century's discoveries of new aspects of his writings, this volume attests to the complexity and continued relevance of Li's thought.

NOTES

1 De Bary, "Individualism and Humanitarianism," 145–48.

2 Li Zhi, "Da Geng Sikou," in *LZ* 1:77.

3 See chapters 4 and 6.

4 Li Zhi, "He Xinyin lun," in *LZ* 1:246 and *A Book to Burn*, 87.

5 On contending interpretations of this action, see Handler-Spitz, *Symptoms*, esp. ch. 3.

PART ONE

AUTHENTICITY AND FILIALITY

CHAPTER 1

THE PARADOXES OF GENUINENESS

Problematic Self-Revelation in Li Zhi's Autobiographical Writings

WAI-YEE LI

LI ZHI ONCE COMPARED THE QUEST FOR "TRUE NATURE" WITH Daoist alchemy, the assembly and refinement of secret ingredients to produce the elixir of immortality (external alchemy, *waidan*) as well as the physical, mental, and spiritual discipline that turns the body into the "laboratory" of "internal alchemy" (*neidan*) and nourishes the "holy embryo" (*shengtai*), "the avatar of the realized state of immortality in the adept's body."[1] In a letter dated 1591 he wrote, "As soon as there is a glimmer, apply a strong flame, so that once true gold emerges from the ore, it will not be reabsorbed by the ore again. Isn't that grand! The level of burning power having been reached, true nature will naturally be revealed. This is not the time to let go.... It's all a matter of daily applying fire; it is no different from cherishing and nourishing the Holy Embryo."[2]

In this model, "true nature" is attained through relentless, measured, and gradual moral and spiritual self-cultivation. The image mirrors similar formulations in the writings of thinkers on the learning of the heart and mind (*xinxue*). In *Records of Transmission and Practice* (Chuanxi lu), Wang Yangming (1472–1529) describes the "focus of intent" (*lizhi*) on "heavenly principles" (*tianli*) as a process of "condensation in the heart" (*xin zhong ningju*) comparable to the formation of the Holy Embryo in Daoist alchemy.[3] According to Wang Yangming's disciple Wang Ji, "Emotions return to moral nature: this is called 'recovering the cinnabar.'"[4] ("Recovering the cinnabar" refers to the successful creation of the elixir for immortality as well as the attainment of inner truth and inner renewal.) Wang Ji also compares the recovery of one's "true original nature" (*benlai zhenxing*) from the crust of worldly concerns and desires to the process of smelting metal. Just as gold buried in ore requires the application of a strong flame, one's true nature can be liberated from worldly desires only by self-examination and self-cultivation.[5]

By far the more typical stance in Li Zhi's writings, however, presents "true nature" or "genuine core" as something that needs to be expressed rather than attained—that is, the trajectory is outward rather than inward. Expression comes with the burden of confronting potential misunderstanding. It is not surprising, therefore, that Li Zhi's most frequently cited formulation of the subject, "On the Childlike Mind" (Tongxin shuo),[6] should focus on questions of evaluation and misjudgment (rather than self-cultivation). The essay begins with an apologetic statement from Li Zhi's friend Jiao Hong (1540–1620) (under the pseudonym "Mountain Farmer of the Dragon Cave"), who wrote in his 1582 preface to the Yuan play *The Western Chamber* (Xixiang ji; ca. fourteenth century), "It will be great if those with real understanding do not say that I still have a childlike mind." Here "childlike mind" is negative: the reader may recall examples of classical usage, such as the dire prediction for Lord Zhao of Lu in *Zuozhuan* as one who "would not be able to come to a good end" because he "still had a childlike mind" even at the age of nineteen, as evinced by his ritual impropriety during his mother's funeral.[7] Li Zhi refutes this implicit denigration of "the childlike mind" by upholding it as "the genuine mind" (*zhenxin*), the untarnished beginning of consciousness: "The childlike mind cuts off all fakery and is pure genuineness—it is the original mind behind the first glimmer of consciousness. If one loses the childlike mind, then one loses the genuine mind. To lose the genuine mind is to lose the genuine person. If a person is not genuine, then he will no longer recover his beginning."

At first glance, "the childlike mind" echoes "the heart and mind of the newborn child" (*chizi zhi xin*) in *Mengzi* (ca. fourth–third century BCE) or "the pristine moral consciousness" (*liangzhi*) valorized by Wang Yangming and his followers, notably Wang Gen (1483–1541), Wang Ji, and Luo Rufang (1515–1588).[8] But it soon becomes obvious that Li Zhi is not interested in "the childlike mind" as the goal of a quest or as the impetus for moral action. Elsewhere he links sensual desires and the desire for gain to "the original heart and mind" (*benxin*) and "simple and immediate words" (*eryan*).[9] He also affirms self-interest (*si*) and "the heart and mind of power and profit" (*shi li zhi xin*) as "endowed nature" (*bingfu zhi ziran*).[10] If the childlike mind gives rise to works that celebrate desire and rancor such as *The Western Chamber* and *Water Margin* (Shuihu zhuan), then by definition it encompasses emotions and impulses beyond pristine moral consciousness.

The beginning polemical stance (arguing against a negative understanding of "the childlike mind") persists throughout the essay. This oppositional mood underlies the diatribes against "fake people" (*jiaren*), "fake words" (*jiayan*), "fake deeds" (*jiashi*), and "fake writings" (*jiawen*). Li Zhi does not explain how one reaches the childlike mind, although he implies that removing obstacles such as acquired principles and information and the desire to earn a good name or to avoid a bad one would be instrumental. This elision comes about because his prime concern is the manifestation of "the childlike mind" and its opposite as well as the authority to elevate one and decry the other.

Li Zhi's essay is famous for valorizing *The Western Chamber, The Water Margin,* and Ming examination essays as being rooted in "the childlike mind" and for heretically rejecting the canonical classics as "topics and excuses for Confucian scholars, a gathering place for fake people." (The inclusion of examination essays may seem incongruous, but it fits into his argument pitting contemporary and recent genres against hallowed ancient ones. See chapter 8.) While the praise of fiction and drama recurs in his oeuvre, his condemnation of canonical classics is obviously belied by his extensive commentaries on these works. Why, then, did he strike this pose? Perhaps contemporary hypocrisy drove him to extremes. Perhaps he obeyed the dictate of his oppositional stance vis-à-vis society. While being genuine seems to imply the spontaneous manifestation of "the childlike mind," its expression is inevitably mediated by the anticipation of how one's words and actions are perceived. It also involves a sense of radical difference, the awareness of the gap between one's views and "consensual opinion" and of the corollary struggle to claim the authority of judgment.

In that sense Li Zhi's essay is intensely dialogic and proleptic: the argument proceeds by refuting its imagined detractors. It is an act of communication that presumes misunderstanding, hence the concluding line: "Alas, how can I get to have a word about writing with a true great sage who has not yet lost his childlike mind?" It echoes the last line of "External Things" (Waiwu) in *Zhuangzi*: "How can I get to have a word with one who has forgotten words?"[11] The paradox of transcending language through language in *Zhuangzi* becomes the paradox of spontaneity and mediation, individual difference and authority in Li Zhi's essay. The question becomes: How can the genuine core that defies external constraints seek external validation?

This version of genuineness makes it problematic as the goal of quest, for Li Zhi associates deliberation (*youxin*) with pretense (*zuowei*; literally, "creating falsehood").[12] Instead it seems tied to the notion of spontaneous expression. Li Zhi describes the process whereby this childlike mind produces great works through the "natural generation of finely patterned writing" (*ziwen*). His other discussions of literary creation are likewise dominated by images of spontaneous and involuntary creation.[13] Yet even as there are unexplained mediatory steps between the "childlike mind" and formal perfection, the quest for genuineness is bound to be somewhat self-contradictory.

The problem is compounded by self-division. If one is torn by conflicting motives and desires, which "genuine self" does one express? To what extent can "genuineness" accommodate inconstancy, inconsistency, or contradictions? One can of course characterize (or even dramatize) the process of conflict as itself the "stuff" of genuine expression, but that is not admissible if the genuine is valorized as something pristine, indivisible, and "expressible," as in Li Zhi's essay on the childlike mind. Further, does the awareness of one's audience compromise genuineness? Li Zhi often declares that he is following his own inclinations as he defies conventions or that he is writing for his own pleasure,[14] yet the obsession with how he will be judged or understood is never far from the surface. Sometimes there is a distinct sense of performance. In what follows I will focus on Li Zhi's autobiographical writings to ponder the tensions and contradictions in the idea of genuineness ("expressing the genuine" and "genuine expression") in his writings, beginning with his short "Self-Summation" (Zizan) from 1588.

THE LIAR'S PARADOX

> His nature is intolerant and impatient. His appearance is self-possessed and arrogant. His words are outlandish and vulgar. His heart is wild and deluded. His actions are careless and reckless. His friends are few and yet he shows great warmth. As for whether he approves of others—he is eager to seek their faults and takes no pleasure in their strengths. As for how he hates others—having cut ties with them, he would to the end of his life want to harm them. His ambition is the warmth and satisfaction of material wellbeing, but he calls himself Boyi or Shuqi.[15] His character is that of the shameless, boastful man from Qi,[16] but he presents himself as being sated with virtues and the Way. Obviously unwilling to "give away even a blade of grass," he nevertheless appeals to Yi Yin as an excuse.[17] Obviously unwilling to "pull out even a hair," he yet denounces Yang Zhu

> for destroying humaneness.[18] His actions go against the multitude; his mouth contradicts his heart. That being the way he is, all the men in his community abhor him. Formerly Zigong asked the Master, "What if all the men in his community abhor him?" The Master said, "One cannot judge him yet." As for the Layman, perhaps one can!

The "Self-Summation" is written in the third person, and Li Zhi refers to himself as "the Layman" (Jushi), the usual designation for a man who embraces Buddhist or Daoist ideals without belonging to a religious order. In Li Zhi's writings the term seems to invoke his liminal state and his defiance of categorical distinctions. The modern editors of Li Zhi's collected writings (*Li Zhi quanji zhu*) tentatively date this piece to 1588, when attacks from his erstwhile friend Geng Dingxiang (1524–1596) might have accounted for its bitterly ironic tone.[19] They read this negative self-portrait as transparently tongue-in-cheek: "Not only does it indicate his lofty and pure character that places him far above the mundane crowd, it also contains barbs directed against Confucian scholars."[20] According to this reading, Li Zhi is simply affecting the venomous tone of his critics as they denounce his arrogance, perversity, vindictiveness, and hypocrisy. However, closer examination reveals distinctions in the string of negative epithets. To describe oneself as proud, impatient, obsessed, or reckless is a common way to affirm one's defiant character in the late Ming. Being unforgiving and given to fault-finding points to a relentless need to go beyond the polite veneer of society.[21] Elsewhere Li Zhi claims to glory in exposing his own flaws (although we see him often bristling at criticism and being intolerant of disagreement): "I take pleasure not in being without faults but in having my faults pointed out by others, I do not worry about having faults so much as not having my faults made manifest."[22] The first half of "Self-Summation" may thus be taken "straight" as a conventionally unconventional mode of self-validation.

The picture becomes murkier with self-accusations of hypocrisy and false claims. Is it possible to read at least part of this diatribe as being rooted in unease? Is Li Zhi at all troubled by the margin between "not giving away a blade of grass" and "not giving away a blade of grass to those not upholding the Way," following the example of Yi Yin (*Mengzi* 5A.7)? We are landed in the liar's paradox. His critics no doubt charge him with being concerned with material well-being even as he professes disdain of gain and power as if he were Boyi or Shuqi, who, according to Sima Qian, vie to give up kingship and eventually die of starvation because they cannot approve of the Zhou leader's (the future King Wu of Zhou) campaign against Shang (*Shiji* 61). Does Li Zhi feel any self-doubt as he relies on his friends' patronage and financial support even as he abjures worldly gain?[23] The man of Qi from *Mengzi* hides the truth of how he begs at gravesides for offerings and instead boasts about grand friends in front of his wife and concubine (*Mengzi* 4B.61). Was Li Zhi aware enough of his own desire for fame or the indignities of dependence to contemplate a possible analogy? In a letter (1585) defending the Confucian-scholar-turned-Buddhist-monk Deng Huoqu, Li Zhi writes, "Now everybody knows that those who seek wealth and profit beg at gravesides, but how could they know that the multitude with gourds and bamboo hats wandering among clouds and rivers (i.e., recluses or monks) are also begging at gravesides? . . . I am but a man of Qi, how can I laugh at Huoqu?"[24] To style himself "a man of Qi" is to aggressively refute the expectation that he should rise above worldly cares; it conveys both rueful recognition of the contradictions of his situation and disdain of his critics.

Li Zhi ends this piece with an equivocal reversal of the exchange between Confucius and his disciple Zigong in the *Analects* (13.24). The Master says that the condemnation of the community (or more literally, people from the same hometown or region) does not suffice as grounds for judgment: only when we evaluate the men offering judgment can we trust the judgment. In the case of Li Zhi, "perhaps one can [rely on the judgment of his community]": this seems to be a perverse affirmative implying negation; it echoes the sentiment Li Zhi expresses in a letter (1586) to Jiao Hong, where he compares heroes to "big fish" destined to be rejected by their communities: "Now if one were to seek heroes among those loved by everybody in the community, it would be like angling for fish in a well, how can that be possible? . . . Heroes are certainly not loved by their communities, and certainly no heroes will emerge from those belonging to their communities."[25] In this passage Li Zhi categorically rejects consensual judgments, while in "Self-Summation" he adopts the voice of his critics to embrace such judgments or posit them as plausible. If Li Zhi dons a mask to unmask the fatuousness of his critics, does he consider whether the self-division endemic to masking poses problems for the ideal of genuineness?

EMOTIONS AND REPRESSION, SELF AND OTHER

Perhaps all attempts to give an account of oneself are doomed to be caught in self-division, inasmuch as it involves a basic separation of the self as observer and as observed. The gap between the self as the source of judgment and its object is heightened with the incorporation of a fictive chronicler and narrator, as in the case of "A Sketch of Zhuowu [Li Zhi]" (Zhuowu lunlüe), written in 1578 when Li Zhi was fifty-two.[26] Here the narrator, Kong Ruogu, is a supposed friend who explains Li Zhi's life. The name does not appear elsewhere in Li Zhi's writings, and it seems transparently allegorical. Wu Pei-yi glosses Kong's name as "an aperture as large as a valley."[27] The possibility of an unreliable narrator can bracket the whole account as mere fiction. Alternatively, "Kong Ruogu" may also imply the voice of wisdom (with Kong suggesting Confucius) and humility (as in the expression "keeping the mind empty [of preconceptions] as if it were a valley [encompassing all things]," *xuhuai ruogu*). Is Li Zhi positing an ideal interlocutor who can understand his struggles? Is he using the idea of a fictive or unreliable narrator to distance himself from his own story? Does the narrator's implied judgment provide the prism for self-criticism or for self-justification? Does this dialogue dramatize his inner conflicts?

"A Sketch of Zhuowu" begins with Li Zhi's different names, and the proliferation of his cognomens becomes a persisting theme, a way for him to consider the gap between name and reality, intention and execution, emotions and self-restraint, self-perception and judgment by others. "The Layman calls himself 'Zhuo,' but he is called 'Du' in the official records. Even in his hometown, some call him 'Zhuo'; others call him 'Du.' There is no uniformity." "Zhuo" and "Du" sound similar enough in Li Zhi's local dialect; hence the confusion. "Kong Ruogu" suggests that Li Zhi should resolve the confusion, but he refuses: "Do you want me to replace something useful with something useless? Also, 'Zhuo' (eminent, outstanding, distinctive) is of course me, and 'Du' (steadfast, sincere) is also me. Yet if you call me 'outstanding,' I am not yet capable of it; and if you call me 'steadfast,' I am not yet capable of it. Why should I replace what I am not yet capable of with what I am not yet capable of?" "Something useful" is "functional naming," the ascertainable connection between Li Zhi and the names "Zhuo" and "Du." "Something useless" is the quest for absolute correspondence between name and reality. "Zhuo" and "Du" are both names Li Zhi gladly answers to, but both announce ideals that he claims to fulfill insufficiently.

Li Zhi's protestation of being "not yet capable" of the qualities encoded by the names "Zhuo" and "Du" may be no more than conventional modesty, but it also points to the gap between intention and execution in all the acts of naming in this essay. He calls himself Layman of Wenling (Wenling Jushi) after the Song Chan Master Wenling (twelfth century), who was famous for his commentary on the *Lotus Sutra* and who lived in Quanzhou, Li Zhi's hometown. The verbal connection between the name of Li

Zhi's birthplace and that of Hundred Springs Mountain (Baiquan Shan), a famous landmark in northwest Henan, seems almost providential; hence the cognomen Layman of Hundred Springs (Baiquan Jushi). With this name Li Zhi also marks his aspiration to achieve moral and spiritual self-cultivation like the Song Confucian thinker Shao Yong (1011–1077), who made his home, the Abode of Bliss (Anle Wo), at Hundred Springs Mountain. Yet Li Zhi comes no closer to Buddhist enlightenment or Confucian spiritual self-discipline. Unlike Shao Yong, who found an inspiring teacher of the *Changes* in Li Zhicai (980–1045),[28] "Li, proud and independent, finally did not hear of the Way after staying at Hundred Springs for five years."

"Wenling" or "Hundred Springs" marks the distance between aspiration and mundane toil. Looking back in 1566 on the first ten years of his official career, Li Zhi exclaims, "For ten years I rushed north and south, all for the sake of family affairs. I have completely forgotten about the thinking behind Wenling or the Abode of Bliss at the Hundred Springs!" In 1566, Li Zhi began working in the Ministry of Rites in Beijing. Responding to criticism that he was prone to find faults in others and should "broaden" himself by studying the Way, he adopted the moniker Hongfu (Broad-Minded Elder), a name at odds with his nature. The name was intended to encourage him to "broaden" himself, but all evidence suggests that he remained unforgiving of himself and others.[29] The last name Li Zhi mentions in "A Sketch of Zhuowu" is "Layman Sizhai" (Sizhai Jushi; Yearning for My Father, Master Baizhai), signaling his regret at not being able to share with his deceased father the joy of "immersion in the wonders of the Way." The acts of naming here suggest absence, longing, and disappointment.

Several important acts of naming are notable for their elision. Li Zhi's ancestors, for reasons unexplained, changed their surname from Li to Lin. Li Zhi seemed to have changed his name from Lin to Li around age sixteen. In his writings he gave no explanation for this change.[30] Also, he was originally named Zaizhi. He dropped the "Zai" when it became a "tabooed character" with the ascension of the Longqing emperor (r. 1567–72), whose personal name was Zhu Zaihou. While these changes may be ignored because they have no bearing on Li Zhi's character in this text, the same cannot be said of the widely used name Zhuowu, which appears in the title. According to Shen Fu's biography, Li Zhi adopted this name when he was serving at the Ministry of Rites in Beijing: "He [Li Zhi] parsed moral ideas with Li Cai of Yuzhang and Xu Yongjian of Lanxi at the capital. After a few days of discussion, both gentlemen admired him for his early receptivity to the Way and his outstanding [*zhuo*] understanding of it. That was why he called himself 'Zhuowu.' What he meant was: Yan Yuan once lamented that Confucius' eminence [*zhuo*] is unattainable,[31] but the eminence of the Way is fully in each of us, what need is there for lamentation?"[32]

The name Zhuowu is thus a confident proclamation that the perfection of the Way can be attained within oneself. Biographies of Li Zhi single out moments of intellectual and spiritual awakening.[33] In his "Sketch of Zhuowu," he describes his years in Beijing (1566–70) as a period of "immersion in the wonders of the Way." Its culmination, however, is not confident mastery (as announced by the name Zhuowu) but a new sense of loss, for at this juncture he mourns his father's passing ever more and calls himself "Layman Sizhai." Li Zhi thus draws attention not to enlightenment but to an unfulfilled quest, as symbolized by imagined communion with his dead father. The highlighted names signal the slippage between the ideal and the real; the one name that could have resolved a sense of uncertainty, Zhuowu, is not mentioned. Eighteen years later, Li Zhi reveled in the notion of transcending names: "I am a person from everywhere, one without name and surname. It is only that when I hear myself called Li Zhuowu, I consider myself Li Zhuowu. Coming to Pingshang, upon hearing myself called the seventy-one-year-old Li Laozi [Old Master], I should perhaps consider myself Li Laozi."[34]

The gap between intention and execution is echoed in the struggle between emotions and spiritual discipline. The ideal of genuineness calls for spontaneous expression of emotions, but controlling emotions is the intermittent refrain in "A Sketch of Zhuowu." Comparing himself to Shao Yong, he feels ashamed. Shao did not marry until after he had attained "true understanding," while Li Zhi is mired in human attachments and mundane concerns. Grief over the loss of his son threatened his focus on attaining the Way. The tension between emotions and the perceived need to control or transcend them underlies many of his writings.

The fictive interlocutor Kong Ruogu clarifies or mediates this conflict. Kong is filled with pity when Li Zhi's second son dies the same day that he receives news of his grandfather's death. But when Kong visits him to offer condolences, Li "appeared unchanged." Li explains that his most urgent concern is to arrange for "three generations to return to earth." Interment of his great-grandparents and father has been delayed because of the quest for auspicious burial grounds; he plans to bury them along with his grandfather, ignoring the convention of abiding by geomantic prescription in the interest of timely burial. To facilitate this he divides the "condolence money," leaving half to his wife for supporting the family in Gongcheng (in Henan) and using the other half for his homeward journey and the burial.

Li Zhi explains to Kong Ruogu, "My only fear is that my wife will not agree. I will go in, but if she does not heed me, I beg you, Sir, to take up the case."

> The Layman entered, and spoke to her again and again. Lady Huang said, "It's not as if this is not right. But my mother is old. She has lived as a widow only to bring me up. Even now, when I am fortunate to be here, she longs for me and weeps day in and day out, so much so that she has become blind in both eyes. If she sees that I am not returning, she will die for sure." Her tears streamed down before she could finish speaking. The Layman, looking stern, paid no heed. She also knew that ultimately she could not go against him. Stopping her tears, she calmed down and apologized, "Fine, fine. All I ask is that when you see my mother, say that all is well, as usual. Tell her she should not be too sad, nor should she long for me too much. The day will come when she will see me. Do your best with the funeral. Even though I am not going back, I dare not complain."

Kong Ruogu expects great grief, but apparently Li Zhi is unmoved. Kong draws attention to the calmness as evidence of emotions controlled rather than absent. Li solicits Kong's assistance to persuade his wife, but no such help is needed since she realizes she must obey. Li Zhi places his filial duty above the needs of his wife and children, and the sequence of the narrative suggests that this choice represents triumph over his earlier moment of "weakness," when grief over the death of his eldest son shows that he is "concerned only with emotions." As Maram Epstein points out in chapter 2, Li Zhi takes pains to emphasize his role as a filial son. Fulfilling his filial duty toward dead ancestors, however, means that his wife cannot be a filial daughter to her mother.[35] Is Li Zhi aware of the irony? His stated respect for women's mental capacity notwithstanding (see chapter 7), he seems unyielding in the conviction of his own superior judgment. Does the inclusion of her speech, presented as reported to Kong Ruogu, indicate residual disquiet on Li Zhi's part?

The logic that prompts Li Zhi to accept patrilineal duty as a moral imperative that should override personal emotions also gives unequivocal priority to public welfare over possible protection for his own family. Before he returns to Fujian, he arranges the purchase of land that is supposed to supply the needs of his family in Henan. At that time a corrupt official, after failing to extort money from a rich family, tries vindictively to divert water from irrigation waterways to the Grand Canal. Li Zhi tries in vain to oppose this policy and also refuses to seek a reprieve for his personal property, even though such a request might well have been granted—he cannot accept such selective mercy when others are suffering.

Li Zhi's second and third daughters become sick and die as a result of the famine. Does he hold himself responsible for these tragedies? Rejecting private succor in the name of upholding public justice is an honorable principle, but does this justify the sacrifice of one's children? If he can foresee the famine, why does he still decide to leave his family in Henan? Does he question his decision? His wife and eldest daughter survive through the good offices of Deng Lincai, Li Zhi's friend serving in Henan. The narrator makes a point of reporting an exchange between Lady Huang and an interlocutor who suggests that she seek Deng's help. Lady Huang refuses because such a request would violate female propriety; she proudly endures privations and reasons that a real friend would in any case voluntarily offer assistance. As it happens, Deng does offer help without prompting from her. Li Zhi's moral high ground is sustained through the fulfillment of high expectations for friendship, the focus of Martin Huang's discussion in chapter 3.

As Li Zhi finds out about the death of his daughters, we are again presented with a spectacle of how he successfully restrains his emotions.

> "As I entered the family gate and saw my family, I was very happy. I asked about the other two daughters, and found out that they had both died a few months after I went back." At that moment Lady Huang (Huang Furen) had tears in her eyes, but seeing that the Layman's color was heightening, she greeted him with ritual propriety and asked about the burial, as well as the wellbeing of her mother. The Layman said, "That night, my wife and I grasped candles and faced each other. It was indeed like a dream! One can thus know that the emotions of women driven by exigencies are genuine. That was why I deliberately corrected my feelings [*jiaoqing*] to pacify her. Only then did I feel 'the breaking of the teeth of my clogs.'"

Instead of dwelling on his own shock and grief or the hope for consolation in sharing sorrow, Li Zhi describes how his own self-control reins in his wife's sadness. More precisely, by showing his displeasure, he intimidates his wife into submission and suppression of her own grief. The line about candles brings to mind Du Fu's (712–770) poem about seeing his wife after a long separation in the midst of political turmoil: "Night deepens, we still hold candles / As we face each other, as if waking from a dream."[36] There are also echoes of Yan Jidao's (1030–ca. 1106) lines on the reunion of lovers: "Tonight I can only hold intently the silver lamp, / Fearing it's but a dream even as we meet."[37] The image evokes Li Zhi's deep love for his wife, yet this is also a fraught moment. The urgency of her genuine emotions calls for "correction."

The clog alludes to a well-known story about the Eastern Jin statesman and commander Xie An (320–385). Throughout a momentous military confrontation between Eastern Jin and its powerful northern neighbor (Former Qin), Xie An retained his composure even as he devised a grand strategy. When news came of Jin victory, Xie An continued to play chess as if nothing had happened. Only later did he notice that the teeth of his clogs had been broken. "Such was the way he corrected emotions and showed his self-control."[38] Anecdotes about Wei-Jin (third to early fifth century) characters often describe their intense emotions, spontaneity, and wild, unrestrained behavior. At the same time equanimity and imperturbability (*yaliang*), which involve repressing the expression of emotions, continue to be upheld as ideal. This duality is evident in many examples from *A New Account of Tales of the World* (Shishuo xinyu; fifth century) and *History of Jin* (Jinshu; seventh century), popular references in the late Ming spawning many imitations and commentaries, including some by Li Zhi.[39] The pretense endemic to "correcting emotions" does not open one to the charge of bad faith if both self-expression and self-control are seen as ways of celebrating the self.[40] Li Zhi seems to accept this logic; only in his case the object of control is not only his own emotions but also his wife's. The allusion to the broken clogs reminds the reader that his calmness belies emotional turmoil, humanizing his severity and implying that the self-mastery is hard won.

The broken clog symbolizes hidden or suppressed emotions that nevertheless do have an external manifestation. It points to the desire that one will not be judged by mere appearance. Throughout "A Sketch of Zhuowu" and in his corpus more generally, there is a persistent concern with being misunderstood. Sometimes this seems to be rooted in self-doubt, ambivalence about his choices, or uncertain self-understanding. The need to forestall misunderstanding is entwined with self-contradiction in the episode in which Li Zhi prepares for and passes the examination in "A Sketch of Zhuowu":

> As he studied Zhu Xi's commentaries on the classics, he failed to grasp the meaning, not being able to commune with the deep

> intention of Master Zhu. He thus felt strange about it and wanted to give up the whole thing. But he had too much time on his hands and no wherewithal to while away his days, so he sighed and said, "This is but a game. It will suffice if I can steal from some compositions to fool the examiners' eyes. How could the examiners be all experts in the essence of Confucius the Sage!" He thus chose what was original and worthy of appreciation among examination essays and memorized a few every day, and he had committed five hundred to memory by the time of the examination. When the question came down, he just replicated the essay like a copier, and that was how he passed.

He despised Zhu Xi's commentary yet passed the examination by memorizing sample essays based on internalizing Zhu Xi's commentary. There is a mixture of self-justification and almost embarrassment. He seems eager to show that he was above the examination system even as he accepted its premises.

Episodes in "A Sketch of Zhuowu" show how self-understanding is mediated through the perspective of the actual or imagined audience. Li Zhi faces his past actions by anticipating misunderstanding. He explains how he passed the examination even as he despised its implied values and implicitly argues that neglecting his wife and children is the unavoidable consequence of following higher duties. Driven by the need to explain to the world the gap between his core and his actions, but sensing the elusiveness of that core, he ends the account with Kong Ruogu's professed confusion when Li Zhi asks him to write his biography after his death: "I [Kong Ruogu] replied, 'How can I be adequate to the task of truly knowing the Layman? In years to come, there will be a Gu Kaizhi who will truly know the Layman.' I thus set forth the brief outline of his life. Later, I wandered in various places, and have not seen the Layman for a long time. That is why I have not recorded anything after his stay in Jinling. Some said, 'The Layman died at Jinling.' Some said, 'He is still in Yunnan—he has not died yet.'" Kong Ruogu's supposed role is to probe intentions and explain Li Zhi to the world. Yet he concludes by claiming that he may not be able to rise to the occasion. He ends his record unsure even whether Li Zhi is still alive. Through Kong's deliberate evasiveness, Li Zhi implies that his true core remains opaque to others and perhaps even to himself. The famous artist Gu Kaizhi (344–406) is said to have painted a luminous portrait of the Layman Vimalakīrti in 393 on the wall of a temple in Nanjing and thereby attracted legions of almsgiving believers to the temple.[41] The narrator thus imagines a Gu-like future biographer who will "transmit the spirit and essence" (*chuan shen*) of Li Zhi.[42] But this possibility remains hypothetical.

PROBLEMATIC TRANSCENDENCE

Li Zhi wrote "An Agreement in Advance" (Yuyue) for the junior monks of Zhifoyuan Monastery in 1596 in anticipation of arrangements to be made after his death. By then he had lived in the Buddhist monastery for eight years, having invited the label of "heretic" (*yiduan*) because of his unorthodox lifestyle. "Reflections on My Life" (Gankai pingsheng), the last section of "An Agreement," departs from "Self-Summation" and "A Sketch of Zhuowu" in being told apparently without irony, donning a mask, or mediation through a fictive narrator. At the same time, the idea of a "genuine core" remains elusive, perhaps because religious transcendence that could have underscored unity and continuity of consciousness remains problematic.

Li Zhi writes about how his words and actions "could not be helped" (*budeyi*), but the context is circumstantial constraints rather than untrammeled expression. He characterizes the choice of Buddhist renunciation as the result less of conviction than of the desire for escape:

> I did not become a monk because I thought it was a good thing, nor did I do so because I believed that one must become a monk in order to cultivate the Way. Isn't staying with the family good for cultivating the Way? For my whole life I have hated being controlled by others. Once born into this world, this self is under the control of others. . . . It is only because I cannot bear the constraints of being controlled that I suffer so much and endure a life of misfortunes. Even were the whole world to turn into ink [for my brush], it would still be difficult to fully express [my misery] in writing.

In his dealings with local officials, he styles himself an "itinerant sojourner" to avoid appearing arrogant or ingratiating but claims that "shaving off [his] hair and becoming a monk" is ultimately a more effective way to manage social relations. In other words, for Li Zhi monkhood is about not being at home anywhere rather than finding a home in the Buddhist sangha.

Looking back on his official career, Li Zhi laments the contradiction of "being greedy for emolument and yet unable to bear the defilement." As an alternative to the compromised lives officials must lead, he examines the ideal of disengagement. Aside from desperate and opportunistic recluses, whom he considers unworthy of mention, there are transcendent recluses who rise above mundane cares and disdain the world, conditional recluses whose ambition to benefit the world brooks no compromise and drives them to withdraw, and circumstantial recluses who are "greedy for wealth and honor but also find poverty painful" but whose distaste for worldly constraints nevertheless drives them to choose reclusion. Li Zhi names the poet Tao Qian (365–427) as the prime example of the third category: "He found poverty painful, that was why he was ashamed of begging for food and said, 'Knocking on the door, I stumble over words'; he loved wealth and honor, that was why he sought to be the governor of Pengze. . . . But what could he do when he refused to bend low in bowing? That was why he composed 'Return' after eighty days."

In Li Zhi's scheme, transcendent recluses are legendary immortals; uncompromising recluses are moralists and philosophers. His only available model is Tao Qian, although traditional interpretation emphasizes his loftiness and Li Zhi professes himself unworthy of the comparison. "By coincidence, I share his one true concern—the inability to bear the constraints of the world." Genuineness in this case is about negotiating the art of the possible and accepting contradictions and imperfections; its corollary is an almost tragic sense of life.[43]

Li Zhi writes that a true monk is one capable of being a true filial son, a true loyal subject, and a true dutiful friend,[44] but monkhood inevitably means renouncing worldly ties. His ambivalence about Buddhist renunciation is evident in his letter to his disciple Zeng Jiquan. He is adamant that Zeng should not shave his head and become a monk. Zeng has a wife, one or more concubines, fields, estates, and no sons. For him to become a monk under such circumstances is "not only inhumane, it is also undutiful in the extreme."[45] In a similar strain, when he read the letter from Wang Shiben's mother urging her son to give up any idea of leaving home to seek Buddhist enlightenment, Li Zhi was moved to heartfelt approbation and wrote a eulogistic postscript (1596). She eloquently debates what qualifies as real detachment and equanimity ("being unmoved"; *bu dongxin*) and how mental propensity determines whether an action is "genuine" or "fake." By this logic, Wang does not have to renounce his family to become a true Buddhist. Deeply moved by Wang's mother, Li Zhi declares that filial piety is the most important virtue, and only the filial son can pray to the "real Buddha" (*zhen Fo*), not the "fake Buddha" (*jia Fo*).[46] The postscript is yet another reminder of unresolved conflicts and problematic transcendence.

Li Zhi intermittently gestures toward the possibility of transcending contradictions—the difference between adhering to social norms and dismissing them,[47] between engagement and disengagement.[48] The figure who embodies a possible resolution may be Confucius. In the numerous references to him in Li Zhi's writings, Confucius is a restless, itinerant figure tenuously attached to family and official positions, one who suffers from "having to leave everything behind,"[49] one whose persecution echoes his own,[50] an arch-individualist who "never taught others to imitate Confucius,"[51] an accidental teacher who "takes no pleasure in becoming the teacher of others but is driven by circumstances that leave him no choice."[52] At the same time Confucius seems to have resolved his own contradictions by combining his faith in the golden mean with his appreciation of defiance and by "making the whole world his home without having a home, treating worthy men rather than fields and property as his life."[53]

In Li Zhi's colophon on a portrait of Confucius in the Zhifoyuan Monastery (1588), he dramatizes the fluid line between conformity and deviation, self-definition and self-alienation.[54] He starts by declaring his own conformity: "Everyone considers Confucius a great sage, and I also consider him a great sage. Everyone considers Daoism and Buddhism heretical, and I also consider them heretical." He proceeds to undermine such opinions as uncritical adherence to inherited learning transmitted by teachers, fathers, and earlier masters and to positions misattributed to Confucius himself: "By now, even for those who have eyes that can see, there is no way to use them. Who am I that I should dare to say that I have eyes that can see? I too am following the multitude. Having followed the multitude in considering Confucius a sage, I also follow the multitude in serving him. That is why I have followed the multitude and serve Confucius at the Zhifoyuan Monastery." Honoring Confucius may be perfectly conventional, but doing so in a Buddhist monastery is not. Earnestness and self-mockery are here inextricably conjoined: even as he claims conformity, Li Zhi may yet be immodestly imitating the sage, whose decision to "follow the multitude" on certain rituals (*Analects* 9.3) is premised on judicious deliberation, not blind conformity. The gesture is self-effacing and self-aggrandizing at the same time, and Confucius continues to represent both a confirmation of Li Zhi's conflicts and their elusive solution.

Another path is to glory in persecution as a tragic hero. Li Zhi is fascinated with heroes dogged by disasters, like He Xinyin (1517–1579) and Zhang Juzheng (1525–1582).[55] He implies an affinity with He Xinyin, who "almost wanted to use death to make his name."[56] Li Zhi often reiterates the idea that calumny only makes him famous. He flaunts the negative epithets his critics impose on him to dramatize the odds he faces, fulfilling their label of "heretic" to "let those fools make their mark" so that he can despise them even more.[57] He claims in a letter to Jiao Hong (1597) that those who hate him "make" him, even as "a benign [literally, 'beautiful'] sickness [does not compare to] painful acupuncture or bitter medicine" (*meichen yaoshi*).[58] A Lu minister in *Zuozhuan* explains that the partiality of an undiscerning man is like a "benign sickness" (*meichen*), while criticism from a foe of unerring judgment is like "acupuncture or medicine stone" (*yaoshi*). Here Li Zhi is using the allusion with a twist: he obviously does not believe in his foes' judgment, whose function is to steel his spirit rather than correct his errors. "Instead of dying without friends, I could savor the sweetness of death in prison or death on the battlefield. Why must you, sir, try to save me? Even with death the fragrance of knightly bones lingers and the name of a martyr remains."[59] Martyrdom is the fulfillment of genuineness but also a paradoxical confirmation of its dependence on the sway of naming and the perception of others.

CONCLUSION

The seventeenth-century thinker Gu Yanwu (1613–1682) notes that the word *zhen* (genuine), so prevalent in late-Ming writings, does not appear in the Five Classics and contrasts its use in *Laozi* and *Zhuangzi*, where it is first used and carries implications of Daoist transcendence and immortality, with its meaning of correspondence between name and actuality (*shi*) in early historical writings.[60] Gu is one of Li Zhi's vociferous critics in the early Qing.[61] Inasmuch as Gu's critique of Li Zhi and other late-Ming writers' valorization of genuineness is based on their alleged deviance from Confucian teachings, he actually shares common ground with contemporary Chinese scholars eulogizing Li Zhi as an arch-rebel and arch-individualist. What Gu condemns is what these scholars lionize—these are but two sides of the same coin. Both Gu's critique and modern quasi-hagiography emphasize Li Zhi's consistent commitment to expressing his true "anti-Confucian" beliefs.

But for every "anti-Confucian" statement, one can easily find counter-statements in Li Zhi's vast collection. Even when he is consistent, as with his affirmation of filial piety, discussed in the following chapter, we can find examples from his actions that seem to go against such avowals (e.g., his decision to become a monk or his disregard for patrilineal claims). These all-too-human inconsistencies claim our attention precisely because Li Zhi is so insistent on reaching for and giving expression to his "true core." Autobiographical writings, perhaps more than any other kind, yield insights into the self-contradictions endemic to the quest for genuineness in his writings. The very notion of such a quest implies self-division, inasmuch as it seems to presume obstacles posed by language, conventions, and familial and social expectations.

The common thread in all the examples discussed in this chapter is Li Zhi's self-awareness of performance and his vigilant anticipation of his audience's reaction. This is perhaps most dramatic in "Self-Summation" but is also easily traceable in the device of the fictive narrator in "A Sketch of Zhuowu" and persists even through the pathos of final testament in "Reflections on My Life." He seems to be caught in involutions of self-questioning and self-exoneration as he explains life choices (such as monkhood, financial dependence on his friends, leaving his wife and children to fend for themselves) that can be perceived as morally problematic or compromising. In the process he dwells on self-division and self-observation (most obviously in "Self-Summation"), the notion of multiple possibilities for his development (perhaps answering to multiple names, as in "A Sketch of Zhuowu"), the promise of religious transcendence and moral certainty that may be clouded by inevitable compromises ("Reflections on My Life"). Ultimately, the quest for genuineness in Li Zhi becomes more compelling precisely because it is steeped in contradictions even as it beckons as an ideal.

NOTES

1 Yu, *Journey*, 1:86. As Yu explains, this process of nourishing the "inner embryo" is syncretist during the late Ming, combining Buddhist, Daoist, and Confucian elements. See also Baldrian-Hussein, "Neidan."

2 Li Zhi, "Yu Lu Tianpu," in *LZ* 3:16. All translations in this chapter are mine.

3 Cited in n. 16 of "Yu Lu Tianpu," in *LZ* 3:16.

4 Huang Zongxi, *Ming Ru xue'an*, in *Huang Zongxi quanji*, 7:280.

5 Wang Ji, *Nanqiao bieyan*, in *Wang Ji ji*, 685–86.

6 For translations of this essay, see de Bary, "The Childlike Mind-and-Heart," in *Sources*, ed. de Bary, 867–68; Li Zhi, *A Book to Burn*, 106–13.

7 "By the time of the burial, he had changed his hempen mourning clothes three times, but the hempen lapels still looked soiled." See Yang Bojun, *Chunqiu Zuozhuan zhu*, Xiang 31.4, 3:1186; Durrant, Li, and Schaberg, *Zuo Tradition*, 2:1275.

8 Li Zhi wrote about Wang Ji and Luo Rufang with deep admiration (*LZ* 1:327–29, 335–46). He referred to Wang Gen's son Wang Bi (1511–1587) as his teacher (*LZ* 3:276).

9 Li Zhi, "Da Deng Mingfu [Deng Yingqi]," in *LZ* 1:94–101.

10 Li Zhi, "Deye Ruchen houlun," in *LZ* 6:526; Li Zhi, *Dao gu lu*, ch. 10, in *LZ* 14:255.

11 *Zhuangzi jishi*, 26.944.
12 Li Zhi, "Ba wu," in *LZ* 2:59.
13 See Li Zhi, "Za shuo," in *LZ* 1:272–73.
14 See, e.g., Li Zhi's letter to Yuan Zongdao (1592), "Ji jing you shu," in *LZ* 1:171.
15 According to Sima Qian (ca. 145–ca. 86 BCE), Boyi and Shuqi, princes of the Guzhu kingdom, protest the Zhou conquest of Shang, which they see as "replacing violence with violence," by refusing to eat "the grains of Zhou" and die of starvation on Shouyang Mountain (*Shiji* 61).
16 "The man from Qi" is a liar and a braggart in an anecdote from *Mengzi*; see later.
17 Yi Yin would not compromise his moral principles even if what was at stake was no more than a blade of grass (*Mengzi* 5A.7).
18 According to Yang Zhu's philosophy of acting only on his own behalf, he would not pull out a hair even if it would benefit the whole world (*Mengzi* 7A.26).
19 The complex relationship between and Li and Geng unfolds in their correspondence, as Timothy Brook shows in chapter 4.
20 Zhang Jianye et al., *LZ* 1:357n1.
21 Being unforgiving of others can imply similarly stringent standards applied to oneself; see "A Sketch of Zhuowu," discussed later.
22 Li Zhi, "Da Geng Sikou," in *LZ* 1:76.
23 See, for example, Li Zhi's letter (dated 1594) to Zhou Sijing (d. 1597), where he asked Zhou to give up a year's salary as a third-rank official to build a study in which Li Zhi could chant poetry, write, and have the blocks for his books stored. "Yu Zhou Youshan," in *LZ* 3:35–36.
24 Li Zhi, "Fu Deng Shiyang," in *LZ* 1:25–26.
25 Li Zhi, "Yu Jiao Ruohou," in *LZ* 1:5–6.
26 Li Zhi, "Zhuowu lunlüe," in *LZ* 1:233–42. For a translation of this text, see Li Zhi, *A Book to Burn*, 75–84.
27 Wu Pei-yi, *The Confucian's Progress*, 21. See also Martin Huang, *Literati and Self-Re/presentation*, 46; Pauline Lee, *Li Zhi*, 18.
28 Li Zhi includes Li Zhicai and Shao Yong in the category of "Confucian officials with virtuous achievements" (De ye Ruchen) in *Cangshu*, in *LZ* 6:492–94.
29 Li Zhi, "Gankai pingsheng," in *LZ* 2:110.
30 See Xu Jianping, *Li Zhuowu zhuan*, 9–15.
31 See *Analects* 9.11.
32 Shen Fu, "Li Zhuowu zhuan," in *LZ* 26:76.
33 For example, in "Li Wenling zhuan," Yuan Zhongdao describes Li Zhi's encounter with "a man of moral learning" (*daoxue xiansheng*) who captures his attention with the proposition that "learning the Way is the wherewithal to be freed from the fear of death." See Yuan Zhongdao, *Kexuezhai ji*, 2:720.
34 Li Zhi, "*Dao gu lu* yin," in *LZ* 14:227–31.

35 For a woman writer's perspective on this issue, see the prosimetric narrative (*tanci*) *Tian yu hua* (Heaven Rains Down Flowers, ca. eighteenth century). Cf. Wai-yee Li, *Women and National Trauma*, 217–18.

36 "Jiangcun," second of two poems, in Du Fu, *Dushi xiangzhu*, 5.391.

37 Yan Jidao, to the tune "Zhegu tian," in Tang Guizhang, *Quan Song ci jianbian*, 131. Yan Jidao's lines are also quoted in *Pipa ji*, which Li Zhi refers to in "Za shuo" (*LZ* 1:272–75).

38 Fang Xuanling et al., *Jinshu*, 79.2074–75.

39 See Nanxiu Qian, *Spirit and Self*, 247–82.

40 This is one way that *jiaoqing* can be justified in late-Ming writings. See, for example, the essay by Li Zhi's friend Yuan Zongdao, "Lun Xie An jiaoqing," in *Yuan Boxiu xiaopin*, 244–46.

41 Zhang Dai and Zhang Jianye (*LZ* 1:241) suggest that "Gu Kaizhi" here refers to Li Zhi's friend Gu Yangqian (1537–1604), with whom Li Zhi exchanged letters and poetry (*LZ* 1:185–89, 3:415–16). Gu praised Li Zhi's achievements as the magistrate of Yao'an (*LZ* 1:189–92).

42 Gu painted the eyes as the final "enlivening" touch in his portraits because they "transmit the spirit and essence" (*Shishuo xinyu jianshu*, 21.13).

43 For similar views on Tao Qian, see Yuan Zongdao, "Du Yuanming zhuan," in *Yuan Boxiu xiaopin*, 247–50.

44 Quoted by Zhou Sijing in "Zhou Youshan wei seng Mingyu shu fayu," in *LZ* 2:26–27.

45 Li Zhi, "Yu Zeng Jiquan," in *LZ* 1:129.

46 Li Zhi, "Du Ruowu mu jishu," in *LZ* 2:19–20. This letter is also discussed in chapters 2 and 3, this volume.

47 Li Zhi, "You da Shiyang Taishou," in *LZ* 1:10–11.

48 Li Zhi, "You da Geng Zhongcheng," in *LZ* 1:46.

49 Li Zhi, "Fu Deng Shiyang," in *LZ* 1:24–27. Elsewhere Li Zhi refers to Confucius as one who "leaves home [i.e., becomes fully detached like a monk] by staying at home" (*LZ* 1:362–63). Martin Huang also discusses the meanings of Confucius "leaving home" (chapter 3).

50 Li Zhi, "Yu Zhou Youshan shu," in *LZ* 1:133–34.

51 Li Zhi, "Da Geng Zhongcheng," in *LZ* 1:40–41.

52 Li Zhi, "Da Liu Xianzhang," in *LZ* 1:61. As Handler-Spitz points out in chapter 5, Li Zhi is deeply concerned with the teacher-student relationship. Li implies a parallel between himself and Confucius the inadvertent teacher.

53 Li Zhi, "Yu youren shu [Yuan Zongdao]," in *LZ* 1:181–82; Li Zhi, "He Xinyin lun," in *LZ* 1:245–51. Elsewhere Li Zhi talks about the "unrestrained and impatient" (*kuangjuan*; *LZ* 1:66–68) and "men with a heroic spirit" (*yingling hanzi*; *LZ* 1:194–95) as being best able to understand the Way.

54 Li Zhi, "Ti Kongzi xiang yu Zhifoyuan," in *LZ* 3:309–10.

55 "He Xinyin was a hero among commoners, that is why he got killed; Zhang Juzheng was a hero among prime ministers, that is why he suffered infamy after death" ("Da Deng Mingfu," in *LZ* 1:37–38).

56 Li Zhi, "He Xinyin lun," in *LZ* 1:245–47.

57 On the moral and epistemological implications of the label "heretic," see Handler-Spitz, *Symptoms*.

58 See Yang Bojun, *Chunqiu Zuozhuan zhu*, Xiang 23.5, 3:1081; Durrant, Li, and Schaberg, *Zuo Tradition*, 2:1116–17.

59 Li Zhi, "Yu Jiao Ruohou," in *LZ* 1:152–53.

60 Gu Yanwu, *Rizhi lu jishi*, 18.433–34.

61 Gu Yanwu, *Rizhi lu jishi*, 18.439–40.

CHAPTER 2

LI ZHI'S STRATEGIC SELF-FASHIONING

Sketch of a Filial Self

MARAM EPSTEIN

THERE HAS BEEN A TENDENCY TO ASSUME THAT LI ZHI'S PHILOSOPHICAL vision meant that he rejected, or at the very least was impatient with, the conventions of *Ru*ist (Confucian) ritual as social artifice. Yet in his autobiographical essay "A Sketch of Zhuowu" (Zhuowu lunlüe), Li Zhi depicts himself as an exemplary filial son whose life choices are given integrity and coherence through his embrace of a filial identity. Despite his penchant for attacking and exposing "false" behaviors in himself and others, at no point in "A Sketch of Zhuowu" does he question or undermine the sincerity of what, on the surface, is a series of highly conventional filial gestures. On the contrary, he exposes what was likely one of the most painful moments of his life: when he learns that his actions, which were against the wishes of his wife, have resulted in the death of two of his daughters. Li Zhi justifies the choices that led to their deaths on the grounds of his desire to be filial toward his patrilineal ancestors. None of the characters in "A Sketch of Zhuowu" questions the moral or social value of Li Zhi's many sacrifices made for the sake of fulfilling his obligations to his patriline. His positive depiction of himself as a filial son raises important questions about his attitudes toward filial piety and how it fits into his construction of the "genuine."

Even as this chapter focuses on Li Zhi's construction of himself as a filial son, my broader goal is to use his life story to call into question the accuracy of the twentieth-century view of filiality as an imposed and despotic ritual structure that deprived adult men of autonomy and to reconsider the accuracy of the modern view of Li Zhi as someone who rejected ritualized behaviors as false and hypocritical. Modern views of filial piety have been largely negative and cynical, despite the recent campaign in the People's Republic of China to revive filial piety as an important and distinctive Chinese value.[1] Beginning with the May Fourth reformers, for most of the twentieth century filial piety has been attacked as the most pernicious aspect of the despotic structure of traditional feudal culture. Following the influential essays published by Wu Yu (1872–1949) on the relationship between filial piety and despotic government, the rejection of filial piety as the basis of all that was wrong with feudal Confucian virtues quickly became a mainstream attitude; being filial was placed in opposition to the development of the autonomous, individual self.[2] In 1919, Fu Sinian (1896–1950), one of the leaders of the May Fourth student protests, published an article in the inaugural issue of *Renaissance* attacking the traditional family as the "root of all evils" for the way it crushed the individual spirit and forced people to sacrifice their independence in order to support the collective family.[3] Filial piety made it impossible for people to develop themselves as autonomous individuals. Fu Sinian cited Hu Shi (1891–1962) as having said, "I am not my own person, I am my dad's son."[4] As Fu Sinian argued, by teaching children to be someone's son, the traditional family made it impossible for people to become "their own self."[5]

Among the May Fourth writers who attacked the traditional family, the scholar Wu Yu stands out for his focus on filial piety as the feudal evil that held China back from progress. In his essay "On Filial Piety," Wu writes, "[Filial piety is] just another way of teaching people to submit respectfully to being duped by those above them and to be unwilling to rebel; it has made China into a 'factory for producing a docile people.' This is the purpose of 'filial piety.'"[6] Not coincidentally, Wu Yu admired Li Zhi as an early iconoclast and launched the modern study of him in 1916 when he published a lengthy biographical essay in *Progress Journal* (Jinbu zazhi).[7]

Li Zhi has been a central focus of discussion in the twentieth-century culture wars. To give several examples, shortly after Wu Yu published his biography of Li Zhi, the famous, and famously conservative, translator of Western fiction, Lin Shu (1852–1924), lumped Yuan Mei (1716–1797) and Li Zhi together with the May Fourth radicals: "Recently, those who are proponents of the new morality denounce their parents in order to feel sexual passion; focusing on themselves, they have no bond with their parents; I once saw something to this effect in [Yuan Mei's] *Suiyuan* collection.... Zhuowu [Li Zhi] behaved like the birds and beasts."[8] In 1949, Wu Ze published an influential monograph titled *Rebel against the Ru, Li Zhuowu.*[9] During the late years of the Cultural Revolution, at the peak of Mao's anti-Confucian pro-Legalism campaign, a flurry of attention was projected onto Li Zhi as a revolutionary hero who was willing to attack the dominant neo-Confucian ideology.[10] Although post-Maoist scholarship has retreated from these political appropriations of Li Zhi by focusing on his aesthetic views and defining his place within the larger history of philosophic thought, the image of Li Zhi as critic of Confucian ritualism lives on.

It is time to reevaluate this view of Li Zhi, and with it the received understanding of filial piety as a negative social value that kept adult children, especially sons, infantilized and deprived of an autonomous self.[11] Parallel to the revisionist scholarship in gender studies that has exposed the extent to which May Fourth polemical judgments distorted the historical view of elite women as nothing but powerless victims of late-imperial culture, it is time to reconsider modern attitudes toward filial piety.[12] Because of Li Zhi's reputation as an enfant terrible willing and frequently eager to question and expose all aspects of social intercourse that smacked of hypocrisy, what better place to start a reevaluation of the role of filial piety in the late-imperial construction of the affective and ethical self than his autobiographical writings?

Li Zhi wrote his autobiographical essay "A Sketch of Zhuowu" at some point during the three years he served as a prefect in Yao'an, Yunnan.[13] This complex self-exposition marks a turning point in Li's life; after leaving Yunnan, he quit government service, left his family, and began his period of wandering, living off the patronage of friends and never returning to his ancestral home in Quanzhou, Fujian. Much of the basic biographical information about his early life is culled from this brief text that hides as much as it reveals.[14] Despite its unconventional and puzzling opening, in which the "biographer" Kong Ruogu, true to the Daoist genealogy of his name, demonstrates that Li Zhi's self is irreducible to written text, the essay has frequently been taken at face value as a transparent source for information about Li's life.[15] "A Sketch of Zhuowu" provides basic chronological details, a glimpse of Li Zhi's family life and values, and an exposition of certain events and episodes that he thought significant enough to foreground. Although I do not question the veracity of the events he weaves into this autobiographical narrative, my reading of "A Sketch of Zhuwuo" argues that his composition of the text was strategic and that he views being filial as a positive characteristic.

Given Li Zhi's reputation for impatience with social posturing, modern readers might be forgiven for expecting that his autobiographical essay would present a self that is "genuine," a self that is not hiding behind social masks and conventions.[16] As Martin Huang argues in chapter 3, Li Zhi in other of his writings eagerly presents himself as wanting to be defined through friendship, not familial bonds. Yet the identity he creates through the life events highlighted in the autobiography is remarkably conventional in the way it conforms to orthodox expectations for how a man should perform his filial obligations and affections. Throughout the essay, an iterative act of self-fashioning, Li Zhi presents himself as a filial son—an identity that is imbued with both affective and ethical integrity.[17] Having justified his actions and choices as moral, he may have convinced himself that he was justified in turning his back on official service in 1580 and finally abandoning his wife in 1587. His embrace of a filial identity suggests how well Li Zhi understood the affective, ethical, and rhetorical power of constructing himself as motivated by filial piety.

DRAMATIC SELF-FASHIONINGS: KONG RUOGU, ZHUOWU, AND THE LAYMAN WHO YEARNS FOR HIS FATHER

Central to this autobiographical essay is the narrative tension between Li Zhi's contradictory impulses to lend coherence to his own life while refusing to slot himself into the established biographical categories that might help us feel that we have some stable knowledge of our biographical subject. Even as the self that Li Zhi presents in "A Sketch of Zhuowu" is highly fragmented, the theme of filial piety lends a sense of thematic coherence to the episodes that are strung together into this biography. Li Zhi creates a split authorial self through the invention of the fictional biographer Kong Ruogu; the felicitously surnamed Kong (empty), cast in the role of historian/narrator, is made responsible for creating the biographical persona of Li Zhuowu, who rejects any authority to ascribe meaning to, or even to name, his own life. As Wai-yee Li points out in chapter 1, the invention of Kong Ruogu splits Li Zhi into two aspects: the writing self and the objectified self. (I distinguish here the fictionalized Zhuowu, the subject of the "Sketch," from the historical Li Zhi, the actual author of the account.) Ultimately, who is the Li Zhuowu presented in this essay? He is someone marked by ambivalence in most spheres of life save for his filial bond to his patriline.

In place of the more usual genealogical format used in autobiographical writing to give the subject a fixed and specific identity, Li Zhi uses a variety of techniques to hide himself from the reader. The introductory section of his biography throws up a smokescreen with its proliferation of names: Kong Ruogu, Zhuowu, the Layman, and Duwu. As Wai-yee Li argues, this resistance to creating a unified knowable self is continued in the closing paragraphs of "A Sketch of Zhuowu," in which Zhuowu takes on two more names, Hongfu and Sizhai. The one name that remains constant throughout the biography, the self with whom Kong Ruogu is in dialogue, is "the Layman," Jushi, an impersonal and objective descriptor of social identity that represents a stripping away of the individual and subjectively defined self. Even though Li Zhi wrote this text while he was still serving in office, projecting his speaking voice onto the persona of the Layman anticipates his retreat from the social by dropping those names that situate him in his former relational identities.

Only after this opening feint in which Zhuowu's chosen biographer lays out a claim that Zhuowu's name is unfixed and unknowable even to himself does Kong Ruogu begin a more conventional biography by providing his subject a date of birth. Kong then inserts another detail that mystifies more than it reveals: "He was born, and his mother née Xu passed away, leaving him orphaned. No one knows how he grew up." Typically, it is only when a child's father dies that the child is described as "orphaned" (*gu*); since men often remarried after the death of a wife, as did Li Zhi's father, this new wife would be recognized as mother to any of her husband's children. Because the biography provides no details about Zhuowu's birth mother, her death creates a mysterious void in the line "no one knows how he grew up" (*mo zhi suo zhang*). Elsewhere, Li wrote that his mother died when he was "six or seven *sui*," about the time Zhuowu began to study with his father.[18] Curiously, only after Zhuowu is described as "orphaned" is his father introduced and given a meaningful presence in the boy's life. At seven *sui*, Zhuowu begins to study with his father, learning to read, to chant odes, and to practice ritual ceremonies. The essay portrays Zhuowu's father, Master Baizhai, respectfully, as a man who models Zhuowu's own disregard for wealth and status, as someone who maintains careful self-control ("his eyes did not wander carelessly about") and shows selfless generosity to friends.

Master Baizhai is an important presence in "A Sketch of Zhuowu"; he is invoked at regular intervals in the narrative. Indeed, Zhuowu's father is a necessary character for the creation of Zhuowu as a filial son who puts the interests of his father and patriline above his individual desires. Kong Ruogu writes that by twelve *sui*, Zhuowu was able to show the fruits of his father's efforts and wrote an essay that garnered widespread praise. Whereas others pointed to Zhuowu's literary talents as a skill that could be exploited to bring his family wealth, the Layman comments that these people did not understand his father: "What sort of person was my father? He was seven feet tall and did not move his eyes carelessly. Although he was extremely poor, he would occasionally take jewelry from my mother, Lady Dong, in order to expedite the marriage of a friend. My mother Dong never stopped him. My father being like this, how could anyone compliment him on the basis of that which is commonly valued?"[19]

In "A Sketch of Zhuowu" Li Zhi deprecatingly refers to his own efforts as a pastiche of memorized essays. However, Zhuowu is able to take pride in his success at the provincial examination, showing how it enables him to fulfill his filial obligations. Rather than continue to study in the hope of passing the highest level of examination, Zhuowu cuts short his own aspirations to provide for his natal family: "The Layman says: 'My luck could not have been better. For my father was old and each of my younger siblings had reached the age of marriage.' He then took his official salary and took in his father and provided for him and concluded the marriage arrangements for each of his younger siblings."[20]

Multiple details about Zhuowu's commitment to fulfilling his obligations to his patrilineal family are woven into the narrative of his official career. Positive or even neutral details about his conjugal family, such as his marriage and the births of his children, however, are absent. What are presented are those details that show Zhuowu prioritizing his obligations to his patriline over his own desires and affective bonds, including those to his conjugal family. Historically, the two family structures of patriline and conjugal family were paired as a *gong* and *si* binary. Although commonly translated as "public" and "private or personal," in much of traditional usage *gong* and *si* should be thought of as contrastive and fluid terms that connote "appropriate, ritually sanctioned" (*gong*) and "improper, selfish, biased" (*si*). While a son's selfless love for his mother is socially appropriate and validated, if his birth mother happens to be a concubine, his love for her would be *si*, in contrast to the *gong* love he owes his formal mother; the same is true for a parent who favors a younger child or a son born to a concubine over the wife's firstborn son. A married couple's affections for each other were *si* and to be subordinated to the *gong* affections they owed the husband's parents; likewise a married woman's attachment to her natal or uterine families was *si*, in contrast to the *gong* attachment to her conjugal family. There was nothing intrinsically wrong with intimate expressions of *si* love, but ritual propriety demanded that the ritually approved *gong* relationships be given priority if a choice needed to be made.

"A Sketch of Zhuowu" repeatedly shows how Zhuowu sacrifices his personal *si* interests and ambitions for the sake of his patriline. The section following the mention of Li Zhi's examination success introduces Zhuowu's ambivalence about official service. The Layman comments that he had hoped to serve somewhere close to his natal home, but in 1557, at age thirty-one, Zhuowu is posted to Gongcheng in Henan and has the worry of leaving behind his father. There is no mention at this point of his wife, Lady Huang, whom he had married ten years earlier, or of his children, one of whom had died two years previously. Even though Zhuowu is separated from his father and son by "ten thousand *li*," the Layman wishes that his stay in Gongcheng, following the examples of the Song figures Li Zhicai (980–1045) and his disciple the neo-Confucian thinker Shao Yong (1011–1077), had enabled him to study the Way so that he could transmit it to both his father and his son.

During this period, Zhuowu takes the aspirational names Layman of Wenling (Wenling Jushi) and Man of the Hundred Springs (Baiquan Ren) or Layman of the Hundred Springs (Baiquan Jushi).[21] The embrace of Buddhist identities by examination elites during the late Ming, especially those inspired by Wang Yangming's concept of "pristine moral consciousness" (*liangzhi*), was both an act of symbolic resistance to the state's instrumental view of classical studies being geared toward examination success and an acknowledgment of the spiritual and intellectual strength of Buddhist approaches to the learning of the heart and mind (*xinxue*).[22] By taking on the identity of a lay Buddhist at this point in his career, Li Zhi expresses his regret that he is unable to make his own self-cultivation a priority.

The next recorded life event, several months into his posting in Nanjing in 1560, narrates Zhuowu's response to the news of the death of his father. His personal mourning is repeatedly disrupted by public events and responsibilities. As discussed in chapter 1, soon after he returns to Nanjing, Zhuowu gets more bad news, this time concerning the death of his paternal grandfather, a character who had not been introduced into the autobiography before this point. Zhuowu's mourning for his grandfather is the dramatic and emotional climax of the autobiography and takes up over a third of the text. This lengthy section narrates the disastrous chain of events that unfolds when Zhuowu insists on leaving his wife and children behind while he returns to Quanzhou to bury three generations of patrilineal ancestors. The pathos of his dilemma is amplified through multiple recorded conversations between Zhuowu, Kong Ruogu, and Li's wife. Consistently in this narrative segment, the emotions that Zhuowu is likely feeling are projected onto his wife and Kong, while Zhuowu now displays a remarkable degree of emotional self-discipline. Rather than emote, Zhuowu asks for his friend's help in persuading his wife to stay behind while he returns home to mourn his grandfather and arrange the burial of three generations of ancestors. Although the widespread famines make this a terrible time to leave his wife and children, Zhuowu's single focus is on settling the ritual affairs of his patriline. His family's failure to bury his great-grandparents, which he claims as his own responsibility despite the fact that they had died well before he was born, leaves Zhuowu feeling as though he has failed in his filial obligations—obligations that he treats as his highest priority. Throughout this episode, the Zhuowu character resolutely controls his emotions while his wife and friend express the emotions he represses.

Why is this particular life event given so much weight in "A Sketch of Zhuowu"? Although Li Zhi must feel some guilt over the death of his daughters, the symbolic capital he draws on to exorcize his personal failures to his wife and daughters is the extended dramatic retelling of how both he and his wife conform to ritual propriety each and every step along this tragic journey. Just as the authorial Li had earlier split off his feelings of grief over the death of his grandfather and second son onto the interlocutor Kong Ruogu, in this section he allows his wife to express, through her tears, the emotions he too must be feeling when he hears that his actions have resulted in the death of his two daughters. All the details in this extended narrative speak to the very conventional ritual value of prioritizing the *gong*, the larger, communally defined good, over the *si*, the personal interests of self, one's own children, and a married woman's natal family. In this section, Zhuowu repeatedly makes reference to his desire to be seen as filial. The episode directly highlights his unbending correctness in choosing to rank his obligations to his *gong* patriline over his *si* conjugal family. The text clearly dramatizes his painful decision to provide a proper burial for his patrilineal ancestors despite his wife's emotional plea that she be allowed to see her own mother. It then narrates his refusal to allow his family to receive special treatment while everyone else in the district suffers from a severe drought. Both of these events show Zhuowu making the ritually appropriate choice to support the communal good, identified as *gong* in ethical discourse, over the personal *si*. This episode, translated in the preceding chapter, highlights the ability of both Lady Huang and Zhuowu to subordinate their personal interests for the sake of a difficult moral choice.

Li Zhi's portrait of his wife, Lady Huang, is extremely sympathetic and positive: she first expresses her deep affective filial bond to her mother before realizing that she must repress her *si* feelings in order to support her husband's decisions. She is never depicted as questioning her husband. Moreover, despite her direct experience of the famine, she follows Zhuowu's model of rectitude; she too puts aside the personal interests of her uterine family and refuses to ask the official Deng Lincai for any special favors, despite the urging of an old woman. Lady Huang responds, "Women cannot meddle in affairs outside the household; I cannot do this." After Deng initiates the much-hoped-for act of generosity, Lady Huang demonstrates her proficiency as a manager of household resources under very trying circumstances and supports the family by weaving cloth.

After the extended and highly sympathetic portrait of Lady Huang, the narrative voice returns to the Layman. He expresses his satisfaction that he had fulfilled his ritual obligations to his patriline; the text suggests that Li Zhi believed in the religious power of his filial behaviors to bring good karma to his family. And, for the first time, he allows himself to express his affection for his conjugal family:

> The Layman said: "After I completed my mourning period and had accomplished the burial of my family members and brought good karma for three generations [*xingle sanshi yeyuan*], I gave no thought to serving as an official. I turned to face the horizon and thought of nothing but my wife and children from whom I was separated by ten thousand *li*, and so I traveled back to Gongcheng. When I entered the gates and saw my conjugal family, I was extremely happy. I asked about my two daughters and learned that they had died not several months after I had left for home."[23]

The narrative returns to Kong Ruogu's third-person description of the scene: "At that time tears welled up in Lady Huang's eyes, but seeing that the Layman's expression was changing, she bowed and asked about the burial arrangements and her mother's well-being."[24] The narrative focalization is then returned to the image of the Layman restraining his feelings of heartbreak. As Wai-yee Li observes, Zhuowu's ability to repress his emotions in this scene should not be read as a sign of hypocritical bad faith. Rather, his ability to focus on his filial obligations to his patriline over his *si* attachment to his own children is a powerful expression of his ethical self.

Life writings of other elite men also foreground the theme of how their subjects handled the mourning of status inferiors. Within a Confucian framework, the process of mourning is designed to channel emotions so that they are neither excessive nor insufficient given the status of the deceased. Since children younger than eight have no ritual status within ancestor worship, the Rites provide no guidance on how to, or indeed whether to, mourn them.[25] Although no age is given for his two girls, their status as daughters places them in a minor ritual relationship to Li Zhi; the only child for whom Zhuowu is described as mourning is his eldest son, who held an important role in the patriline as the ritual heir. The writings of the early Qing ritualist Yan Yuan (1635–1704) reveal the emotional pain of a father who was forbidden by the Rites to indulge in mourning for a beloved child.[26] Yan Yuan was acutely aware of the ritual expectation that men not indulge in inappropriate displays of emotion for status inferiors, no matter what they felt; several years after the death of his only son, Yan wrote about the need for men to control their emotions when their wives were approaching death in order "to avoid suspicion of impropriety [*bixian*]."[27] Yan's biography describes his outpouring of emotion when his grandmother was buried: he knocked his head against her coffin and howled and wailed to such an extent that a friend admonished him for his excessive display of grief.[28] However, when his son died at five *sui*, the ritually precise Yan could not express his grief directly; although deeply distressed, he first threw himself into comforting his grandmother and wife.[29] He then channeled his own feelings by creating mourning rites based on the contemporary practice of mourning adult sons for one year.[30] Substituting days for months and wearing hemp shoes and a mourning robe and cap, he observed a twelve-day period of mourning during which he withdrew from all regular activities except serving his grandparents.[31]

An event in the life of Li Gong (1651–1733), Yan Yuan's disciple, who was equally committed to ritual self-cultivation, may provide a more direct analogy to help us contextualize Zhuowu's self-control when he first heard of his daughters' death after he returned home. Li Gong rushed home when he heard that his beloved concubine, the mother of his sons, was dying. Even so, he managed to observe proper etiquette in greeting his birth mother first when he arrived at the house: "[Li Gong] returned on the twenty-third day of the second lunar month and reached home between 2 and 4 p.m. Concubine Lü had already passed away between 7 and 9 a.m. He entered the gates and first paid his respects to his mother, only then did he go to the side of her corpse to wail for her."[32] Although Li Zhi did not care about ritual form to the extent that Yan Yuan and Li Gong did, the parallels among these three acts of mourning status inferiors suggest that Li Zhi wanted to demonstrate even in this emotionally fraught moment that his behavior was appropriate. Delivering the news concerning the burials of three generations of his patriline and of his wife's mother took precedence over any expression of grief for his children.

After this lengthy anecdote that highlights Zhuowu's commitment to filial propriety and his prodigious emotional control, Kong Ruogu, the narrator of "A Sketch of Zhuowu," returns us to the chronology of Zhuowu's increasing disenchantment with his official career. This final section of the text mirrors the introductory section in destabilizing the reader's confidence that Zhuowu is a coherent and knowable subject. He is both someone who prides himself on fulfilling his filial obligations to his patriline and someone who chafes under his obligations to provide financial support to his family. He returns to Beijing and notes his growing disenchantment with official life. While his peers worry only about their financial poverty, Zhuowu feels the impoverishment of one who has not heard the Way. As the Layman comments, what stands between him and the freedom to pursue his philosophical ideals are his obligations to his family: "Rushing north and south for over ten years on behalf of the affairs of my family, I had completely forgotten those thoughts about Wenling and the Abode of Bliss at Baiquan."[33]

"Sketch" concludes with Zhuowu taking on two contradictory names. One, "Broad-Minded Elder" (Hongfu), connotes his desire to be free of obligations; the other, Sizhai, denotes his yearning for his dead father: "During the five years the Layman served on the Board of Rites, his mind was immersed in the mysteries of the Way, and he regretted that he was unable to raise [his father] Master Baizhai from the underworld, and so he yearned for Master Baizhai even more intensely. He then called himself 'The Layman of Yearning for [My Father Master Bai] Zhai' [Sizhai Jushi]."[34]

The careful structuring of the autobiographical sketch suggests Li Zhi's ambivalence about his identity and official role at the point in his life when he wrote it. Bookending the narrative of Zhuowu's life are the two significant absences of his mother and father. "A Sketch of Zhuowu" begins by undermining the certainty of Li Zhi's name, Zhuowu/Duwu, and concludes by calling into question the certainty of his own existence: Kong Ruogu admits he does not know whether Zhuowu is dead or alive.[35] The chain of names—Zhuo, Du, the Layman, the Layman of Wenling, Broad-Minded Elder Layman, Yearning for My Father Master Baizhai—presents a fractured identity that seems endlessly mutable. The two qualities that are consistent in this portrait of Zhuowu are his filial piety and his commitment to moral learning. The introduction of the less commonly used name Baixia for Nanjing in the concluding sentence echoes, consciously or not, the style used for Zhuowu's father throughout the text, Master Baizhai.[36] As a final touch, Li Zhi frames his existence in explicitly filial terms, as someone "not-yet-dead"; the expression "not yet dead" (*weisi*) parallels a term used for widows as "people not yet dead" (*weiwangren*).

For a figure reputed to be as iconoclastic as Li Zhi, "Sketch" is remarkably conventional in its construction of Zhuowu's identity as embedded in filial relationships and obligations. Li's writing of "A Sketch of Zhuowu" shortly before he left office in 1581 was no doubt strategic in that it presents him as a man who consistently made difficult choices that aligned him with established ritual values that prioritize the needs of his patriline over his conjugal family or his own desires. In this essay, Li Zhi seems to take pains to let others know that he is no scoundrel and has never acted out of selfishness. If the writing of this essay was motivated by his desire to construct himself positively, as a man who placed virtuous action above the pursuit of personal desires, it does call into question the representative value of the incidents he chose to highlight. There is clearly more to Li Zhi than he allows us to see in this work of self-representation.

What are we to make of the comparative importance of filial piety as a lived virtue in this influential essay? On some level, it was important to Li Zhi to leave an image of himself as a filial son. Unlike other late-Ming philosophers who identified Wang Yangming's concept of the individual and morally perfect "pure knowing" (*liangzhi*) with filial piety, Li Zhi did not construct a moral or metaphysical philosophy based on filial piety.[37] Indeed, of the five canonical relationships, Li Zhi is best known for his promotion of the conjugal bond and friendship. Never a systematic or consistent writer, Li Zhi's thirty-*juan* collection of anecdotes that illustrate "*Ru*ist virtue in action," *Upon Arrival at the Lake*, is organized in order of (1) the husband-wife relationship (four *juan*); (2) the father-son relationship (four *juan*); (3) fraternal relations (two *juan*); (4) relations between masters and disciples and friends (ten *juan*); and (5) the relationship between lord and subject (ten *juan*), although the collection is thematically dominated by anecdotes illustrating the ways, positive and negative, to be a friend and an official.[38]

Although he did not privilege filial piety in his philosophical discussions of virtue, in a 1596 letter to Wang Shiben (Ruowu), Li Zhi shows the depth of his feelings in response to a mother's appeal that her son wait until her death to travel in order to pursue Buddhist enlightenment. Li Zhi found the mother's letter so moving that he chastises Shiben and reminds him of the cliché that "filial piety is the first of the hundred virtues."[39] In the letter, Li Zhi argues that enlightenment must be sought in the heart and mind and that no matter how far Shiben were to travel, it would not help his pursuit of interior calm. As Li Zhi notes, intoning Amitābha's name is a false form of worship because true Buddhism must be based on a spiritual practice: "Those who pursue Buddhism must follow Buddhist practices, and filial piety is the first of these hundred practices. If you chant the Buddha's names but lack filial piety, how could Amitābha be a Buddha who is without filial piety? This logic is impossible." Li Zhi ends his letter on an affective note: "If words arise from true feelings, they naturally pierce the heart, they naturally move people, they naturally cause people to suffer. I think you must be like me, there has never been a person who can hear a mother's words like these and not suffer."[40] The primacy of filial piety as an affective bond clearly held deep meaning for Li Zhi; just as he had for himself, he treated Shiben's desire for autonomous self-cultivation as subordinate to his filial obligations and bonds to his parents.[41]

How does the portrait of Zhuowu as a filial son in "A Sketch of Zhuowu" fit with Li Zhi's established reputation as an ideological radical willing to attack all forms of rote (or ritualized) behaviors as false? As seen in both "A Sketch of Zhuowu" and his letter to Wang Shiben, Li Zhi understood filial piety not as an empty obligation imposed upon individuals by ritual convention but as a deeply held and sincere expression of a person's core ethical and affective values. As Li Zhi states in "A Sketch of Zhuowu," his wife's tears for her aging mother were an expression of "genuine emotions." So too were Zhuowu's yearning for his father and the pain he felt in his heart when reading the letter from Wang Shiben's mother requesting that her son not abandon her. Even though Li Zhi was lionized during the May Fourth and Maoist periods for his willingness to reject the empty values and gestures of Confucian society, his identification of filial piety as the core bond that informed his life choices should give us pause before we project the May Fourth rejection of filial piety as an artificial and repressive value back into the late-imperial period. As depicted by Li Zhi, Zhuowu is a filial son who repeatedly prioritizes his filial bonds over his ties to his wife and children and over his aspirations for himself. The affective tone of the autobiography is dominated by Zhuowu's yearning for his dead parents, emotions that bookend the narrative. In essence, his filial emotions are as genuine an expression of himself as his desire for the autonomous freedom to pursue the Dao.

NOTES

This chapter began as comments on Wai-yee Li's paper presented at the Li Zhi Conference at the University of Chicago (2013) on the genuine in Li Zhi; I am indebted to her and the other conference participants for this opportunity to reconsider the relationship between filial piety and "genuine emotions" in Li Zhi's writings. Portions of this chapter draw from material published in my monograph *Orthodox Passions: Narrating Filial Love during the High Qing.* Harvard University Asia Center, 2019.

1 Shortly before the 2013 passage of laws known as "Protection of Rights and Interests of Elderly People" requiring that adult children visit their parents "often," PRC governmental bureaus concerned with women and aging began to circulate a modernized version of the traditional *Twenty-Four Exemplars of Filial Piety* called the "New Twenty-Four Ways of Filial Piety" (Xin ershisi xiao).

2 See Wu Yu, "Jiazu zhidu wei zhuanzhizhuyi zhi genju lun," "Shuo xiao," and "Chiren yu lijao" in *Wu Yu wenlu,* 1–13, 14–23, 63–72.

3 Fu Sinian (published under his courtesy name, Meng Zhen), "Wan'e zhi yuan."

4 Meng Zhen, "Wan'e zhi yuan," 125.

5 Meng Zhen, "Wan'e zhi yuan," 127.

6 Wu Yu, "Shuo xiao," in *Wu Yu wenlu,* 15. Quotation marks follow the Chinese text.

7 *Jinbu zazhi* published only the first installment of this essay. Wu Yu, "Ming Li Zhuowu biezhuan," *Jinbu zazhi* 9, no. 3 (1916): 19–24; Wu Yu's complete essay can be found in *Wu Yu wenlu,* 2:20–51. This essay is also reprinted in *LZ* 26:313–23.

8 Lin Shu, "Zhi Cai Heqing shu," cited in *LZ* 26:325.

9 Wu Ze, *Rujiao pantu Li Zhuowu.*

10 After one article on Li Zhi was published in 1973, over 105 were published in 1974 and 1975. See *LZ* 26:362–66.

11 For recent discussions on the negative impact of the culture of filial piety on individual psychological development, see Sun Longji, *Weiduannai de minzu* and *Zhongguo de shenceng jiegou.*

12 Two important examples are Ko, *Teachers of the Inner Chambers,* and Lu, *True to Her Word.*

13 The text can be found in *LZ* 1:233–42. For an English translation, see Li Zhi, *A Book to Burn,* 75–83. Translations are my own. Zhang Jianye dates the composition of this essay to 1578, but Lee places it closer to 1580; see Pauline Lee, *Li Zhi,* 154n1.

14 See, for example, Rong Zhaozu's (1897–1994) annalistic biography of Li Zhi's life that draws heavily from this essay, *Ming Li Zhuowu.*

15 Pei-yi Wu discusses how the format of the account is based on the generic conventions of the "commentary" (*lun*), brief judgments by the historian appended to the biography (*zhuan*) in dynastic histories (*The Confucian's Progress,* 20). Also see Pauline Lee, *Li Zhi,* 17–18.

16 For a critical reading of Li Zhi's use of the term "genuine," see chapter 1.

17 On autobiographical writings as iterative, see Marjorie Dryburgh, "Introduction: Writing and Reading Chinese Lives," in Dryburgh and Dauncey, *Writing Lives in China*, 11.

18 Li Zhi, "Yu Geng Kenian," in *LZ* 3:65.

19 Li Zhi, "Zhuowu lunlüe," in *LZ* 1:233.

20 Li Zhi, "Zhuowu lunlüe," in *LZ* 1:233.

21 For more on the significance of these names and Li's relationship to Shao Yong, see chapter 1.

22 Brook, *Praying for Power*, 90; Eichman, *Late Sixteenth-Century Chinese Buddhist Fellowship*, 48.

23 Li Zhi, "Zhuowu lunlüe," in *LZ* 1:235.

24 Li Zhi, "Zhuowu lunlüe," in *LZ* 1:235.

25 For the rules on mourning children, see Ebrey, *Chu Hsi's Family Rituals*, 95–96.

26 Epstein, "Writing Emotions."

27 Yan Yuan, "Juyou yujian," 164.

28 Li Gong, *Yan Yuan nianpu*, 22.

29 Li Gong, *Yan Yuan nianpu*, 15.

30 See Ebrey, *Chu Hsi's Family Rituals*, 89n70.

31 Li Gong, *Yan Yuan nianpu*, 15.

32 Feng Chen, *Li Gong nianpu*, 115.

33 Li Zhi, "Zhuowu lunlüe," in *LZ* 1:235.

34 Li Zhi, "Zhuowu lunlüe," in *LZ* 1:235.

35 For discussion of Kong Ruogu's uncertainty and translation of relevant passages, see chapter 1.

36 The essay concludes, "Some say the Layman died in Baixia; others say that he is still in Yunnan and is not yet dead."

37 Miaw-fen Lu has written extensively about a group of mainstream Zhejiang scholars who promoted filial piety as both the foundation of ethics and generative materialism; see Lu, "Wan Ming *Xiaojing*," published in English as "Religious Dimensions of Filial Piety." Also see her *Xiao zhi tianxia*, especially 120–21, 133–68.

38 Li Zhi, *Chutanji*. It is important to note that Li Zhi's famous essay on the primacy of the conjugal bond, "Fufu lun," actually promotes the cosmological importance of husbands and wives as the material embodiment of *yin* and *yang* energies. Li Zhi, "Fufu pian zonglun," in *LZ* 12:1.

39 Li Zhi, "Du Ruowu mu jishu," in *LZ* 2:19.

40 Li Zhi, "Du Ruowu mu jishu," in *LZ* 2:19–20.

41 The prioritizing of filial obligations to parents and unmarried children was a common pattern among late-Ming literati who were drawn to Buddhism; see Eichman, *A Late Sixteenth-Century Chinese Buddhist Fellowship*, 62–65.

PART TWO

FRIENDS AND TEACHERS

CHAPTER 3

THE PERILS OF FRIENDSHIP

Li Zhi's Predicament

MARTIN W. HUANG

VERY FEW CHERISH FRIENDSHIP AS MUCH AS LI ZHI DID. IN THE eyes of his conservative detractors, his moral deficiency was directly related to his pursuit of friendship at the expense of many of his more sacred Confucian duties. Despite Li Zhi's efforts to portray himself as a filial son, analyzed in the previous chapter, his critics focused on his neglect of his family and his failure to fulfill his filial obligation as a Confucian man to have a male heir to carry on his family line.[1]

Li Zhi was one of those rare historical figures who, while actively pursuing friendship most of their lives, also seriously pondered the meanings of friendship. As far as friendship is concerned, he was a giant of both theory and practice. He personified many of the complexities and ambiguities associated with friendship as it was celebrated and theorized with unprecedented enthusiasm during the late Ming.[2] What did it mean for an educated man in late imperial China to have placed so much importance on his friendships with other men? How did he conceive of himself as a friend in relation to his other social roles, such as that of a son or a husband? How was his self-image as a man related to his friendships with other men?

Li Zhi was a man of apparent contradictions: for the last two decades of his life, he deliberately chose to live among his friends and far away from his hometown and family, and yet he complained bitterly about his loneliness and lamented that he could not find a true friend, whom he considered someone worth dying for; however, he characterized such a friend as a "buyer" (*maizhe*) and deemed friendship of the highest order as an exchange relationship in terms of "a big deal" (*da maimai*) between a seller and a buyer.[3] In Li Zhi we seem to have found the interesting coexistence of a deep yearning for spiritual companionship and a surprisingly utilitarian understanding of friendship; he believed that a true man should travel far away from home and must not spend too much time with his wife. He sent his wife back to his hometown while he himself stayed with his friends until he was arrested; he insisted that he would rather die in the company of his friends than face the feminizing prospect of dying in the arms of his wife, and yet, at the same time, he argued eloquently for the importance of relationships between husbands and wives; he seemed obsessed with his own image as a masculine man and detested feminized men,[4] and yet he was one of the very few male literati at that time who openly accepted female students and valued their friendships, scandalizing many of his straitlaced Confucian peers.

FRIENDSHIP AND ITS CONFLICTS WITH OTHER HUMAN RELATIONSHIPS

The writer Yuan Zhongdao (1570–1623) once characterized Li Zhi this way:

> He had an obsession with making friends ever since he was very young. . . . Throughout his life, he never considered the home of his wife and children to be his own; instead, he considered his friends' homes to be his own; he never regarded his hometown as his own; instead he regarded the hometowns of his friends as his own; he never treated his life as his own; instead, he treated the lives of his friends as his own. When poor he forgot his own poverty once he saw his friends; when old he forgot his old age when he met his friends.[5]

Indeed, friends occupied an almost sacred place in Li Zhi's heart, as he once said:

> For those who have yet to firmly set their feet in their pursuit of the Way, the company of friends is indispensable. For those who already have their feet firmly set, the company of friends is even more indispensable. Why? "Friend" [*you* 友] means "enabling one to have" [*you* 有]. This is why people often say that one's friends and teachers enable one to have virtue. This certainly testifies to the indispensability of friends. In this world, however, it is hard to have a genuine friend but even more difficult to have a genuine

> friend who is also a comrade. For ancient people, having a comrade was more important than having a brother; one's brother shares with one many physical similarities, whereas one's comrade enables one to wholly fulfill one's inborn virtue in that body. Confucius and Mencius traveled everywhere under Heaven. Why did they do this? They were only in search of comrades.[6]

Here Li Zhi is making a fine distinction between the general term "friend" and the narrower concept of "comrade" (*tongzhi*), a term becoming increasingly popular among the members of the School of the Mind (Xinxue) branch of neo-Confucianism in the late Ming).[7] Elsewhere, Li Zhi differentiated between *xiang'ai* (someone to whom he was attached) and *xiangzhi* (someone he really understood and appreciated); the former was a friend who was emotionally close, whereas the latter was a comrade or an intellectual soulmate. He considered some of his friends to be his *xiang'ai* but not yet his *xiangzhi*.[8] Obviously, for him, the latter was a level higher than the former. However, an ideal friend must be more than a mere comrade. More significantly, he was suggesting that having such a genuine friend or comrade was more important than having a brother (a family member) and that men usually needed to travel far away from their family and hometown to search for friends and comrades just as the sages in the past had done.

Given the importance of *jia* (home/family) and native place in a Chinese man's life at that time, Li Zhi's devotion to friends was indeed remarkable as well as disturbing to some of his contemporaries, although he did not lack admirers in this regard. His seemingly unconditional championing of friendship directly challenged the core values of the Confucian concept of *wulun* (the five cardinal human relationships), in which family was sanctioned as the most sacred. In this chapter I explore the implications of the conflicts within Li Zhi himself as well as between him and others as a result of his relentless pursuit of friendship.

Among Li Zhi's friends, the Geng brothers, Geng Dingxiang and Geng Dingli, were probably two of the most important in that they might have helped change the course of Li Zhi's life after he quitted officialdom in 1580. The deterioration of the relationship between Geng Dingxiang and Li Zhi was largely a result of their ideological differences and Li's supposedly unconventional behavior, something Geng Dingxiang found increasingly difficult to tolerate after the death of his younger brother, who was apparently much closer to Li. Such differences between Li Zhi and Geng

Dingxiang were clearly manifested in their divergent attitudes toward two controversial figures at that time, He Xinyin and Deng Huoqu, both of whom were accused by conservatives of going to extremes in pursuing friendship while totally disregarding the other four human relationships (see also chapter 4). Both He Xinyin and Deng Huoqu, two radical activists and members of the neo-Confucian School of the Mind, were once guests at the residence of the Gengs. Geng Dingxiang offered detailed accounts of these two in a collective biography titled "The Biographies of Three Eccentric Visitors to the Village." According to Geng Dingxiang, one particularly disturbing moral failure shared by these two eccentrics was their total disregard for their familial obligations. He Xinyin was said to have "ruined his own family and destroyed himself," and Geng accused Deng Huoqu of having committed the egregious sin of unfiliality for neglecting his aged father when the man was alive and failing to mourn him after he died.[9] Contrary to Geng Dingxiang, Li Zhi praised He Xinyin as an outstanding man and expressed deep admiration for Deng's determination to seek friends/comrades at the expense of his own career success and the interests of his family.[10] One important reason Li Zhi spared no effort in defending the two, neither of whom he had ever met in person, was, at least in part, because he saw himself as the target of similar accusations, as he mentioned that He Xinyin had been accused of "disregarding four of the five cardinal human relationships."[11]

These controversial proponents of friendship, especially He Xinyin and Li Zhi, shared many similarities: like He and Deng, Li Zhi lived away from his family and hometown for long periods; also like both of them, Li Zhi considered the company of friends and comrades more important than that of his own family members. All three alarmed their conservative contemporaries and some officials in power with their unconventional deeds as well as views, and all were accused of being heterodox. Like He Xinyin, Li Zhi was arrested, although he eventually committed suicide in jail, while He Xinyin was executed by a local official.

What Geng Dingxiang dreaded in He Xinyin and Deng Huoqu was precisely what Li Zhi admired in them. The profound differences between Li Zhi and Geng Dingxiang were captured by Zhou Sijiu (1527–1592), who was friends with both, when he characterized Geng as someone who emphasized *mingjiao*, or the Confucian teachings of social order, but described Li Zhi as someone who excelled at capturing the truth through subtle intuition. Geng himself, however, strongly disagreed with these characterizations.[12]

In 1593, after almost a decade of tension between Li Zhi and Geng Dingxiang, the two, at the urging of several mutual friends, finally reconciled, although that did not necessarily mean that either had substantially revised his position on a variety of issues. However, it is probably worthwhile to examine a related incident that seems to have drawn them closer to each other. A brief look at this incident can serve as a good point of departure for our discussion of how Li Zhi tried to come to terms with the conflicts between his familial obligations and his passionate pursuit of friendship.

A few years after their reconciliation, Geng Dingxiang mentioned the delight he experienced when he read Li Zhi's essay "Reading a Letter from Ruowu's Mother" (Du Ruowu mu jishu; see also chapter 2).[13] The essay recounts Li Zhi's emotional reaction to reading a letter written by the mother of the monk Ruowu (Wang Shiben) to her son. In this letter, the mother begs her son not to leave her to pursue Buddhist enlightenment.[14] Reading this letter made Li Zhi regret his own previous remarks congratulating Ruowu on taking the tonsure because he now realized that if one genuinely believed in Buddha one should start with the practice of filiality.[15]

One of the disputes between Geng Dingxiang and Li Zhi, according to the former, was that Li disregarded basic human relationships in his pursuit of comradeship and personal enlightenment. Apparently, Geng Dingxiang regarded Li Zhi's expression of regrets and acknowledgment of his past mistakes as evidence that Li had now renounced his previous position on a man's right to seek personal enlightenment and to take the Buddhist tonsure. However, despite his apparent regrets and acknowledgment of mistakes, Li Zhi's views on the tension between one's filial obligations and one's right to seek the company of friends and personal enlightenment probably had not changed as much as Geng wanted to believe. First of all, what moved Li Zhi about the mother's letter must have been the old woman's almost Chan-like rhetoric, as she argued that the heart and mind must be "quiet." To her, this took precedence over finding a tranquil environment in which to study the Dao, which her son gave as his reason for leaving her. She contended that if her son's mind was quiet, then whether he sought his enlightenment at home or in a faraway temple should not matter. What further moved Li Zhi must have been the simple and genuine feelings of an aging mother. Elsewhere he condemned as hypocritical anyone who claimed to be a filial son yet neglected his parents' health in order to seek career success far from home.[16] As Wai-yee Li argues in chapter 1, what mattered to Li Zhi was being genuine in one's feelings or beliefs: "When you want to pray to Buddha, pray to Buddha; when you want to visit your mother, visit your mother. One does not need to be affected; one does not need to go against one's own nature; one does not need to go against one's conscience; one does not need to suppress one's own intention; following one's own heart is true Buddha nature."[17] Li Zhi never questioned the validity of one's filial love, but he did see much hypocrisy in the manipulation of the concept of filial piety by his many contemporaries.[18]

In his earlier defense of Ruowu's taking the Buddhist tonsure, Li Zhi contended that even Confucius, though he never formally renounced his family (*chujia*), as Buddha Sakyamuni did, traveled throughout his life to seek soulmates for saving. Here Li Zhi employed the word *chujia* as a double entendre (switching between its literal meaning, "leaving family or home," and its special meaning of "taking the Buddhist tonsure"; the latter was used anachronistically in the case of Confucius since Buddhism did not begin to influence China until long after the death of the Master). According to Li Zhi, Confucius was away from home all the time even though technically he "had remained home" and never undergone the ritual of renouncing family to take the tonsure. More significantly, Li Zhi confessed that he felt fortunate that he had no familial obligations to constrain him, since by that time his parents and wife had passed away.[19] In other words, he believed that the conflicts between familial obligations and the right to seek soulmates for personal salvation had been resolved, since he had already fulfilled all his familial obligations. In fact, Li Zhi must have felt that a large part of his life was already devoted to the welfare of others in his family (taking care of his father and other family members): after passing the provincial examinations, he gave up the chance to continue to study for the prestigious *jinshi* degree because he had to find employment immediately to support his family. After the deaths of both parents and later his wife, and with his sisters and brothers having already started their own families, he finally felt that he was entitled to live for his own self.[20] However, some still deemed him unfilial since, although he had no heir, he refused to take a concubine.[21] Once again he was forced to appeal to the example of Confucius for self-defense; according to Li, not only did Confucius travel extensively and seldom stay at home long, but after the death of his wife, Confucius also did not remarry. Apparently, Confucius was not that attached to the idea of family after all.[22]

Of course, there were different kinds of family obligations. Like many of his contemporaries, Li Zhi apparently took far more seriously his duties toward his elders than his duties as a husband.[23] He could sometimes be quite indifferent toward his wife. When he was appointed prefect of Yao'an in Yunnan, he reluctantly agreed to take his wife along only after she repeatedly pleaded with him. She insisted on going to Yao'an with him because he had often failed to return home for long periods of time whenever he traveled elsewhere.[24] A few years later, when he decided to quit officialdom, he simply sent his wife back to his hometown so that he could embark on a journey seeking soulmates and personal enlightenment. He deplored that his wife was not an intellectual "comrade" for him,[25] yet he nevertheless regarded her with affection, as evidenced in some of the poems and letters he wrote after he learned that she had passed away.[26] Li Zhi's complaint that his wife was never his spiritual companion and his apparent neglect of her may come as a surprise at first, given the views he expressed in his essay "On Husband and Wife" (Fufu lun). There, he argued eloquently for the importance of the husband-wife relationship.[27] The apparent discrepancy between the rather abstract views he put forth in that essay and his own behavior toward his wife points to gaps between his theory and practice. Viewed from a different angle, however, this may not necessarily be a case of inconsistency on Li Zhi's part: precisely because he valued the husband-wife relationship so highly, his wife's failure to be his spiritual companion must have greatly disappointed him.[28]

On the other hand, several of Li Zhi's friends believed that he simply lacked interest in women altogether or even loathed being intimate with women.[29] Whereas being able to have many friends was usually considered an important sign of manliness,[30] spending too much time with one's wife and family was often considered detrimental to one's image as a true man. Li Zhi considered confining oneself to the company of one's wife and children something only a vulgar person would do.[31] Jiao Hong observed in his eulogy for Li Zhi, "His willingness to die for his friends should put to shame those who only worry about how to preserve their own lives and protect their wives and children."[32] Here again, wife and family are cast as potentially compromising one's manhood.

Yuan Zhongdao also observed that Li Zhi once praised the famous Tang poet Du Fu (712–770) for helping his friend Cen Cen (ca. 715–770) before attempting to rescue his own wife during the chaos caused by the An Lushan rebellion.[33] Another friend of Li Zhi's, Li Cai (1520–ca. 1606), was once deeply moved by Li Zhi's demonstration of friendship and wondered how he could have shed so many tears upon learning of the sufferings of a friend such as himself and yet remain utterly unmoved when he sent his own wife and daughter back to his hometown.[34] Apparently Li Zhi wanted his manhood to be defined by his willingness to place the interests of his friends above those of his own wife and family.[35]

However, there were more pressing reasons for Li Zhi to leave behind his family. More than once he expressed the sentiment that his wife and family had become impediments to his pursuit of friendships and personal enlightenment, whereas having friends/comrades and achieving personal enlightenment were virtually inseparable. One of the main purposes of his *chujia* (taking the tonsure) was to make it easier to seek friendship and inquire about the Way throughout the four corners of the earth (*sifang qiuyou wendao*).[36]

Whereas friends occupied a very important place in the lives of many enthusiastic proponents of philosophical debates (*jiangxue*), such as Wang Ji (1498–1583), Luo Hongxian (1504–1564), and Luo Rufang (1515–1588),[37] probably no one pursued friendship with such desperate passion as Li Zhi and no one gave up for the sake of friendship as much as Li Zhi did. As an enthusiastic participant in the *jiangxue* movement himself, Li Zhi was deeply influenced by Wang Ji and Luo Rufang, and he shared their view that without the help of friends and comrades it was difficult to master any true learning.[38] In his mind, regular participation in assemblies for philosophical debate (*jianghui*) was closely associated with opportunities to cherish the company of friends (*zhongyou*) and to realize the importance of the Way (*zhongdao*).[39]

In Li Zhi's case, friendship could also be much more personal. In a recent study, Xu Jianping mentions two possible reasons for Li Zhi's obsession with friendship. First, the adult Li Zhi was probably seeking compensation in the company of his friends for his lost maternal love (his mother died when he was only a young child). He once admitted that as a child, he had very few friends. Later, the deaths of many of his family members also contributed to his loneliness; thus he conceived a more desperate need for friends. Second, he came to a fuller realization of the importance of friends when his friend Deng Lincai offered crucial help to his wife and children during the drought while he was away arranging the burial of his great-grandfather, grandfather, and father.[40] However, neither of these reasons explains why Li Zhi turned away from his family in his pursuit of friendship; for example, one may wonder why the loss of his mother early in life failed to make him cherish his relationship with his wife.

One thing that Li Zhi emphasized repeatedly about himself was his spirit of independence: "Ever since I lost Mother at six or seven, I have become quite capable of depending on myself. Now at seventy, I live by myself and am quite independent."[41] In explaining why he joined the Buddhist order instead of taking the less radical step of becoming a lay Buddhist, he said that joining the Buddhist order enabled him to achieve true independence, for if he merely became a lay Buddhist he would still have to take orders from local officials.[42] It is this profound dread of having to take orders from others and his cherishing of independence that led Li Zhi to make the decision to quit his post as prefect of Yao'an and to take the Buddhist tonsure instead of returning home. Homeless and without income, he turned to his friends, believing these more egalitarian relationships would allow him to regain or even enhance his independence. He was only partly right.

TENSIONS WITHIN FRIENDSHIP(S) AND THE ISSUE OF LIFE AND DEATH

After leaving his family, did Li Zhi achieve the kind of independence he aspired to? One of the immediate consequences of his feud with Geng Dingxiang was the painful realization that he was never as independent as he believed himself to be. With virtually no regular income, economically he was totally dependent on his friends, a not so pleasant fact he probably did not fully appreciate until he had to leave the villa of the Geng brothers in Huang'an to find another place to live after the death of Geng Dingli and the deterioration of his relationship with Geng Dingxiang. In late 1584 Li Zhi had already tried to leave Huang'an, where he had lived for the past five years, to move to Macheng, but he had to postpone the move because he could not find accommodation there. (Probably he could not afford what he found.) Not until the third month of the following year was he able to make the move, after Zeng Zhongye, the son-in-law of his friend Zhou Sijiu, provided temporary housing for him in Macheng. Later Zhou Sijing (*jinshi*, 1568; Zhou Sijiu's younger brother) had a house converted into a temple for Li Zhi to live in, a place Li Zhi would call home for the next three years.[43] Li Zhi once mentioned with deep gratitude the specific amount of money (seventy-two taels of silver) Zhou Sijing contributed to cover part of the cost of getting the temple ready for him. In a letter to Jiao Hong, Li Zhi expressed his gratitude to Yang Qiyuan (1547–1599) for asking Li's disciple, the monk Wunian, to bring money to him from Nanjing.[44] Another time, Li Zhi had to ask for funds from his friend to build a Chan studio for himself.[45] In addition to his livelihood, Li Zhi's scholarship depended on the goodwill of his friends, since he had to obtain financial support from others in order to have his works published.[46]

Obviously, Li Zhi was keenly aware of his economic dependence on his friends. Once he had to cancel his plan to visit Jiao Hong in Nanjing for fear that he could become a financial burden on his friend, whose financial situation then was precarious.[47] In another letter, Li Zhi asked Jiao Hong not to worry about him because as a mendicant he could look for food wherever he went since there would likely be almsgivers everywhere.[48] Ironically, the image of a mendicant captured Li Zhi's homelessness as well as his economic dependency.

Living on the goodwill of others (even one's friends) was probably never as "liberating" as Li Zhi had thought it would be, and later in life he often complained about loneliness. At the death of Geng Dingli and the break with Geng Dingxiang, his loneliness only deepened.[49] When the feud with Geng Dingxiang escalated, many of Li Zhi's best friends who were also good friends or students of Geng Dingxiang's had to choose between them. During the heated moments of their feud, Li Zhi must have felt very disappointed that few of these friends came to his defense while several of them openly sided with Geng. Such disappointment became even more bitter precisely because these friends were often those he cherished most and because he was a person who lived for his friends. For example, after Li Zhi's rupture with Geng, Guan Zhidao (1537–1608), one of Geng's disciples, wrote Li Zhi to ridicule him, and Zhou Sijing, one of Li Zhi's best friends, deliberately distanced himself.[50] At the same time Li Zhi was also aware of the quandary his feud with Geng must have caused for many of their common friends. A dozen years later, after he and Geng had reconciled, Li Zhi became even more appreciative of the sacrifices made for him by friends caught in between, such as Zhou Sijing, who was Geng's student and relative but who nevertheless did his best to help Li.[51]

Another of Li Zhi's close friends caught in the feud was Jiao Hong, who also happened to be a student of Geng Dingxiang's. Historians have noted many signs of awkwardness in their relationship after the hostilities became public.[52] People could well imagine the frustrations Li Zhi must have felt given the importance of his friendship with Jiao Hong. Indeed, even before the strain on his relationship with Geng Dingxiang became publicized, Li Zhi expressed his frustrations in an essay titled "On Mr. Li's Ten Kinds of Friends." He complains that he has yet to find a friend to whom he can entrust "life and death."[53] In this essay he divides his friends into ten categories, the highest being what he terms "friends of life and death" (*shengsi zhi jiao*) and the second highest being "friends of the heart" (*xindan zhi jiao*). He regarded Zhou Sijing as a friend who really understood him, whereas elsewhere in his writings he characterized others, such as Yang Dingjian, as friends who were merely emotionally close to him: "Although I could not consider them friends who really understand me [*xiangzhi*], I have to deem them friends who really love me [*xiang'ai*]."[54] In other words, although Li Zhi felt emotionally attached to people such as Yang Dingjian who provided for his material needs, he did not consider them close intellectual companions. And yet he did not shy away from the fact that the friends he socialized with most frequently, and probably needed most on a daily basis, were friends who could share wine and food with him. He relegated them to the end of his list of categories of friendship, despite the fact that he relied heavily on their generosity for his daily survival.[55] However, such reliance did not stop him from pursuing his ideal friends. Furthermore, what Li Zhi cherished most in a friendship was intellectual companionship rather than emotional closeness, although the latter was also important. He insisted that common people's understanding that a friend was merely someone emotionally close or intimate was inadequate ("tuyi jiejiao qinmi zhe wei zhi you").[56] For him, a true friend also had to be someone who was intellectually worthy of the title of a teacher, someone he could learn from. However, what is particularly surprising is that he even regarded Zhou Sijing as belonging to only the second tier, "friends of the heart," rather than the top tier, "friends in life and death."[57] Consequently, his best friends, such as Zhou Sijing and Jiao Hong, still fell short of his highest ideal of friendship.

One of the important criteria by which Li Zhi judged whether someone fit his ideal of friendship appears to be whether that friend was intellectually curious enough to be interested in the fundamental issue of life and death, a question he himself had become obsessed with in the second half of his life.[58] He felt that some of his best friends, such as Jiao Hong, were too worldly to be fully interested in the issue of life and death, and he was disappointed that in Nanjing, where he was staying at that time, he could not find anyone seriously interested in this issue.[59] He expressed similar disappointment in another friend and colleague, Gu Yangqian (1537–1604): "Although Gu Tongzhou [Gu Yangqian] loves [*ai*] me and his moral character is also worth my emulation, he does not pay too much attention to the question of 'life and death.'"[60]

That Li Zhi's pursuit of friendship was inevitably tragic is a view shared by some of his contemporaries who were convinced that he had such a high standard that people were bound to disappoint him.[61] Since his standards were too high and he was probably too frank and straightforward in his dealings with others, he tended to alienate many of his friends. In one of his letters to Zhou Sijiu's son after Zhou's death, Li Zhi sought understanding by acknowledging that his own quick temper might have contributed to generating the dispute between himself and Zhou.[62] Indeed, striking the right balance between criticizing a friend whom he believed to be at fault and maintaining harmony was a delicate issue that anyone serious about friendship has to face, and Li Zhi was not very successful in this regard.

That was probably why he bitterly complained that it was much harder to be a genuine friend who was willing to point out the mistakes of his friend than to be a minister who openly criticized the emperor with the expectation that he might be put to death for upsetting the sovereign. This was because a man would get nothing from criticizing his friend (except that the two might become enemies), whereas the minister who dared to criticize the emperor was guaranteed to win a reputation for "remonstrating at the risk of death," even if the emperor did not actually execute him.[63]

In the last few years of his life, Li Zhi complained even more frequently about the hardships and loneliness associated with his life as a self-styled mendicant. He once asked, "I have wandered around throughout my life. When will I be able to settle down?"[64] As the aging Li Zhi sensed death approaching, his search for a friend in whose company he could die peacefully intensified. When Jiao Hong tried to persuade him to return to Dragon Lake, the site of his temple-residence, because he suspected that some of Li's enemies might try to have him killed, Li Zhi replied:

> I learned that you were able to stop someone from trying to have me killed. I am very grateful to you for that. However, I would rather travel beyond the Great Wall and die in a foreign land, since in the Middle Kingdom I have not been able to find anyone who truly understands me, even though I was born in this country. Why should you urge me to return to Dragon Lake? Dragon Lake is not a resting place for me because I will only die in a place where I have real friends and someone who can truly understand me. . . . Given no chance to die among friends, I would much prefer to die in prison or on the battlefield. . . . Generally speaking, a man who does not want to die for the sake of his wife and children is determined to die for the sake of his friends. The reason for this should be quite obvious.[65]

Ironically, "to die in prison" became his self-fulfilling prophecy. (Also note his negative reference to "dying for the sake of one's wife and children.")

Elsewhere Li Zhi repeatedly expressed his disappointment that he could not find any real friend for whom he would die or in whose company he could die. To find a friend or friends in whose company he could die became a mission that constantly occupied his mind as he was getting old: "Now I have grown old and have few friends [close by]. Reading books all day is not what an old man should do. At the moment I am only waiting to die. If I don't want to die in the company of my wife and other family members or among those pseudo neo-Confucians, in whose company should I die?"[66] He sometimes even became impatient that death was approaching too slowly: "Death did not come to me this year and it will not come to me next year. Each year I expect to die. Disaster came, but death did not."[67] Not long before his arrest and eventual suicide, he wrote in his will, "Since spring I have often been ill and I am anxious to bid farewell to this world. Fortunately, I am going to die in the company of my good friends if I die now. Such a happy arrangement is difficult to accomplish and I feel very lucky. You should not fail to know the importance of this matter."[68] Now staying with his new friend Ma Jinglun, who admired him tremendously, Li Zhi appears to have finally found a friend in whose company he could die content, although he probably would not regard the much younger Ma Jinglun as a friend belonging to the top category of his "ten kinds of friends." Unfortunately, he would soon be arrested and deprived of the company of even this friend.

In many ways, for Li Zhi the values of true friendship could be fully understood and appreciated only in the context of death. Interestingly, he closely associated friendship with death in that he always considered a good friend someone worth dying for or somebody in whose company one would be happy to die. Such close association of friendship with death probably had its origin in Li Zhi's own life-long obsession with the issue of death (discussed in chapter 11). This obsession might have a lot to do with his trying to come to grips with the sudden deaths of many of his family members. (All his four sons and two of his three daughters died very young.) As he reached old age himself, the issue of how to come to terms with death became even more urgent and personal.[69] His seeking a true friend was tied to his attempts to confront the approach of his own death. In his essay "On Five Ways of Dying," Li Zhi lists what he considered five honorable ways of dying, using historical figures as illustrations. Almost all of them had died either for someone who had demonstrated real appreciation of their talent or for a great cause (benefiting the society or country). At the end of the essay, Li Zhi turns to discuss the limited options for death available to himself:

> There must be a reason for the birth of a true man. If so, how could this man die without a proper reason? If there is a cause of his birth, there must be good reason for his death. . . . Now I have grown old and won't be able to die in any of the five ways that I have mentioned above. If I cannot die in one of these ways, to die otherwise would certainly not be how a heroic man should

> behave. Then how should I choose the way I die? The only option left is to make a few small deals. I left my hometown long ago and gave up my servants. I have come all the way here in search of a buyer [someone who really understands my worth]. However, I have yet to find any soulmates. How could I die without any soulmates? I understand striking a great deal is already something beyond my reach. Being a heroic man and lacking both any outlet for my frustrations and any soulmates worth dying for, I would die among those who have failed to understand me just in order to give vent to my pent-up frustrations. I wrote this to inform those who claim to understand me: when you come to see me after learning of my death, do not collect my body![70]

Li Zhi's reference to that elusive "true friend" as a "buyer," who, however, refuses to show up, had much to do with the traditional emphasis on the centrality of "recognition" in a relationship between two men, whether or not they were social equals.[71] However, such blunt insistence on the parallel between "finding and dying for a true friend" and a business transaction did have its intended shock value. It was as if Li Zhi wanted to remind people of the ambiguities associated with friendship, something he had already tried to come to terms with when he was classifying his friends and acquaintances. At the same time, we can also feel his tremendous frustration at being unable to die the way he wanted because he could not find a true friend (a buyer, to use his word) to die for. For him, a true friend was someone to whom he could entrust his "life and death" and who was as deeply concerned with the fundamental question of life and death as he was. Given his almost overwhelming concern with how he should meet his death and the important role he assigned to a friend in helping him to transcend death, friendship acquired an importance for him that was almost religious. By insisting on dying for a true friend or dying in the company of a true friend, Li Zhi seems to have proposed a new concept of *wulun*, in which friendship was elevated to the most sacred position. Friendship became almost "transcendental," for he believed it would be able to help him overcome the boundary between life and death. The fervor with which he pursued friendship and his obsession with the issue of life and death were certainly related to the *jiangxue* movement and some of its members' zealous pursuit of transcendence, which was also quite religious.[72]

Li Zhi's tragic pursuit of friendship highlighted and dramatized the tension between family and friends in the life of a man completely devoted to studying the Way. Being unable to die in the company of a true friend, he chose to die in jail rather than be forced to go back to his hometown to die. Such adamant rejection of family, home, and native place must have appeared quite shocking to many of his more conservative contemporaries.[73] The case of Li Zhi was probably unique at that time, but it points to the potential and yet serious threats friendship could pose to the sanctity of the most sacred Confucian institution: family. Thanks to the unprecedentedly radical nature of his approach to friendship, Li Zhi personified the pluralistic intellectual atmosphere of the late sixteenth-century China, when friendship enjoyed a degree of legitimacy it never had before. At the same time, his tragedy highlighted the potential conflicts between friendship and family that orthodox Confucians were often reluctant to confront.[74] In a way, contrary to the arguments made by more conservative late-Ming promoters of friendship—namely, that friendship was beneficial to the other four human relationships—Li Zhi's case painfully demonstrated to people then and later that friendship, when pursued as passionately as he pursued it, could fundamentally challenge the ethical underpinning of the orthodox Confucian understandings of the most important human relationships. Moreover, it could call into question the carefully constructed hierarchical order envisioned among these relationships. Indeed, no one had challenged the Confucian limits of friendship as rigorously as Li Zhi did, both in theory and in practice. Although the perceived radicality of his approach to friendship almost predetermined its tragic outcome, his influence on his contemporaries and the people of later generations in terms of how friendship was theorized and practiced cannot be underestimated.

NOTES

1 "Deng Lincai zhuan," in *Neijiang xianzhi*, *j.* 1, quoted in Lin Haiquan, *Li Zhi nianpu kaolüe*, 151.

2 See Martin Huang, "Male Friendship in Ming China"; Timothy Billings, introduction to Ricci, *On Friendship.*

3 Li Zhi, "Wusi pian," in *LZ* 2:69.

4 On Li Zhi's image, see chapter 6.

5 Yuan Zhongdao, "Dai Hushang shu," in *Kexuezhai ji*, 807. Elsewhere Yuan Zhongdao quotes Li Zhi as saying that as long as he could enjoy the company of a few good friends, there was no need for him to return to his hometown ("Li Wenling zhuan," in *Kexuezhai ji*, 720).

6 Li Zhi, "Yu Wu Dechang," in *LZ* 3:55.

7 Martin Huang, "Male Friendship and *Jiangxue*."

8 Li Zhi, "Qiongtu shuo," in *LZ* 3:210; more on this later.

9 Geng Dingxiang, "Lizhong san yi zhuan," in *Geng Tiantai xiansheng wenji*, in *Mingren wenji congkan*, 6.30a (1633).

10 Li Zhi, "Yu Jiao Yiyuan Taishi" and "*Nanxun lu* xu," in *LZ* 3:86 and 3:191.

11 Li Zhi, "He Xinyin lun," in *LZ* 1:246. Li Zhi faced the similar accusation that he "had disregarded the basic principles of human relationships" (*qi renlun*); Li Zhi, "Fu Deng Shiyang," in *LZ* 1:25.

12 Geng Dingxiang, letter 18 in the twenty-one letters under the title "Yu Zhou Liutang," in *Geng Tiantai xiansheng wenji*, in *Mingren wenji congkan*, 3.54a (352).

13 Geng Dingxiang, "Du Li Zhuowu yu Wang seng Ruowu shu," in *Geng Tiantai xiansheng wenji*, in *Mingren wenji congkan*, 19a–23b (1861–68). While in her chapter Epstein demonstrates the importance Li Zhi attached to the Confucian notion of filiality, in this chapter I draw attention to his differences from those more conservative in terms of his view of specific filial obligations. For example, as I discuss later, he refused to remarry or take a concubine even though he did not have a male heir. Apparently, he carefully distinguished between his obligations to his elders and responsibilities to his wife and children. For him, family could have different meanings, depending on whether it included parents.

14 Li Zhi, "Du Ruowu mu jishu," in *LZ* 2:19.

15 Li Zhi, "Du Ruowu mu jishu," in *LZ* 2:19.

16 Li Zhi, "Fu Deng Shiyang," in *LZ* 1:25. Elsewhere, Li Zhi argues that filiality cannot be taught, implying it is innate ("Yu Jiao Ruohou Taishi," in *LZ* 3:50).

17 Li Zhi, "Shiyan sanshou," in *LZ* 1:199.

18 In fact Li Zhi repeatedly advised others not to take the tonsure (*chujia*) if they could be lay Buddhists (*zaijia xiuxing*) while citing himself as an exceptional case ("Yu Zeng Jiquan," in *LZ* 1:129). See also chapter 6.

19 Li Zhi, "Shu Huang'an er Shangren shouce," in *LZ* 1:363. Elsewhere, Li Zhi defended Ruowu's taking the tonsure as an act of great filiality because it was aimed to save all under Heaven as a way to repay the kindness of his mother ("Daxiao yishou," in *LZ* 1:194). This is a conventional defensive tactic against the accusation that taking the tonsure and leaving one's family were unfilial acts.

20 Li Zhi, "Fu Deng Shiyang," in *LZ* 1:25.

21 Li Zhi, "Da Geng Sikou," in *LZ* 1:76–77. According to Li Zhi, Geng Dingxiang complained that Li's otherworldly (*chaotuo*) lifestyle and his neglect of the important matter of his own male heir in particular might have a bad influence on Geng's own son.

22 Li Zhi, "Fu Deng Shiyang," in *LZ* 1:25. (Here Li Zhi is defending the controversial monk Deng Houqu rather than himself, but self-defense was certainly part of his agenda.) On Li Zhi's refusal to take a concubine, see also chapter 6.

23 Li Zhi, "Zhuowu lunlüe," in *LZ* 1:233–35. For a discussion of this autobiography, see chapters 1 and 2. See also Wu, *The Confucian's Progress*, 19–24. To a modern reader, in this account of the dispute with his wife, the image of Li Zhi is that of a very unsympathetic or even callous husband. However, this might well be the kind of masculine image Li Zhi was seeking, which might not have been problematic to many of his contemporary male readers.

24 Li Zhi, "Zeng Yao'an shou Wenling Li xiansheng zhishi qu Dian xu," in *LZ* 1:189.

25 Li Zhi, "Da Liu Jinchuan shu," in *LZ* 1:140. For Li Zhi's complaint that his wife could not understand him, see "Ji Jiao Ruohou," in *LZ* 3:30.

26 See his letter to his son-in-law, "Yu Zhuang Chunfu," in *LZ* 1:108, and the six poems titled "Ku Huang yiren," in *LZ* 2:262–63. Living far from his hometown, Li Zhi apparently never attended his wife's funeral.

27 Li Zhi, "Fufu lun," in *LZ* 1:251–52.

28 Another factor to be considered is that this essay was probably written by Li Zhi shortly after he learned of his wife's death (see Lin Haiquan, *Li Zhi nianpu kaolüe*, 202–3). It might have been related to his guilt about neglecting his wife (a feeling he had expressed in some of his compositions mourning his wife, such as the poems "Ku Huang yiren liu shou," in *LZ* 2:262–65.). Li Zhi's ideal would have been to find a best friend among his own family members. He once told Geng Dingxiang that Geng was extremely fortunate to have been able to find his best friend within his own family (namely, in his younger brother Geng Dingli); see Li Zhi, "Fu Geng Zhongcheng," in *LZ* 1:212.

29 Yuan Zhongdao, "Li Wenling zhuan," in *Kexuezhai ji*, 720. See also the testimony of Ma Jinglun, one of Li Zhi's admirers and friends, who tried to help him when he was arrested in 1602: "Yu Zhangke Li Linye zhuan shang Xiao Sikou" and "Li Zhi shengping zhuanji ziliao huibian," in *Li Zhi yanjiu cankao ziliao* 2:54–55. Ma equates a man's tendency to study hard with his disinterest in women, implying that a manly man like Li Zhi, who studied so hard, would take little interest in women (thus refuting the accusation that Li Zhi was a womanizer). For discussion of Li Zhi's manliness and his relations with women, see chapter 6.

30 Li Zhi certainly shared this view; see the second letter in "Fu Gu Chong'an weng shu, you shu," in *LZ* 1:186.

31 Li Zhi, "Wusi pian," in *LZ* 2:69.

32 "Zuijian shu," in *Li Wenling waiji*, reprinted in "Li Zhi shengping zhuanji ziliao huibian" in *Li Zhi yanjiu cankao ziliao* 2:67. This is a common phrase used to ridicule the unmanliness of officials who were disloyal to the throne due to their fear of losing their own lives in critical situations. See Sima Qian, "Bao Ren'an shu," in Yan Kejun, *Quan Shanggu Sandai Qin Han Sanguo Liuchao wen*, 501.

33 Yuan Zhongdao, *Zuolin jitan* in *LZ* 18:309.

34 Li Jianluo (Li Cai), "Wei Zhongxian chanke shujuan," in *Zhengxue tang gao*, vol. 34, reprinted in *Li Zhi yanjiu cankao ziliao* 2:31.

35 Li Zhi appears to have had quite a strong sense of how a masculine man should behave and how such a man should die. See "Wusi pian," in *LZ* 2:69. His obsession with his masculine image can also be confirmed by the high frequency with which the term *zhangfu* (true man) appears in his writings: twenty-four times in *Fenshu* and *Xu Fenshu* (based on a search of the electronic texts of these two works in the online database *Guoxue baodian*).

36 Li Zhi, "Da Li Weiqing," in *LZ* 3:73.

37 Martin Huang, "Male Friendship and *Jiangxue*."

38 Li Zhi, "Da Shen Wang," in *LZ* 3:128–29. On Li Zhi's relationships with these two masters, see chapter 5.

39 Li Zhi, "Huiqi xiaoqi," in *LZ* 1:181. In fact, one of Li Zhi's major disappointments with his wife was her lack of interest in *jiangxue* (see "Yu Zhuang Chunfu," in *LZ* 1:108).

40 Xu Jianping, *Li Zhi sixiang yanbianshi*, 141–43.

41 Li Zhi, "Yu Geng Kenian," in *LZ* 3:65.

42 Li Zhi, "Gankai pingsheng," in *LZ* 2:109.

43 Li Zhi, "Yuyue," in *LZ* 2:104–5.

44 Li Zhi, "Fu Jiao Ruohou," in *LZ* 1:110. In his letter "Yu Pan Xuesong," in *LZ* 3:123, Li Zhi told Pan not to worry about the expense of his trip to Beijing because everything was already taken care of.

45 Li Zhi, "Da Liu Jinchuan shu," in *LZ* 1:140.

46 Li Zhi, "Yu Fang Ren'an," in *LZ* 3:24. On the publication of Li Zhi's writings, see chapter 8.

47 Li Zhi, "Yu Ruohou Jiao Taishi," in *LZ* 3:69.

48 Li Zhi, "Fu Jiao Ruohou," in *LZ* 3:34. In his discussion of the financial assistance Li Zhi received from his gentry-official friends, Ray Huang emphasizes how their help enabled Li Zhi to lead a relatively comfortable life. Huang's analysis aims to refute some mainland Chinese scholars' attempts to characterize Li as the "spokesman for the peasantry against the exploiting classes" (*1587*, 189, 194–95).

49 See Li Zhi, "Shu Changshun shoujuan cheng Gu Chong'an," in *LZ* 1:230. It was probably written in 1589 (see Lin Haiquan, *Li Zhi nianpu kaolüe*, 216). See also Li Zhi, "Gaojie shuo," in *LZ* 1:294–95 (probably written in the same year), where he defends himself against the accusation that he is too arrogant to have many friends.

50 Cf. Li Zhi, "Yu Zeng Zhongye," in *LZ* 1:128. In this same letter (probably written in 1590) Li Zhi also mentions that he is quite relieved that with the help of Zeng, he has reconciled with Zhou Sijiu. The strained relationship with Zhou was apparently related to Li Zhi's dispute with Geng Dingxiang. It was said that some years later, when Zhou Sijing (Sijiu's younger brother) learned of the reconciliation between Li Zhi and Geng Dingxiang, he shed

tears of joy. See Zhou's postscript to Li Zhi's "Geng Chukong xiansheng zhuan," in *LZ* 2:22–23.

51 Li Zhi, "Da Mei Qiongyu," in *LZ* 3:74.

52 Zuo, *Li Zhi yu wan Ming wenxue sixiang*, 114.

53 Li Zhi, "Li sheng shijiao wen," in *LZ* 1:354 (most likely written in 1583; see Lin Haiquan, *Li Zhi nianpu kaolüe*, 139).

54 Li Zhi, "Qiongtu shuo," in *LZ*, vol. 3.

55 Li Zhi, "Li sheng shijiao wen," in *LZ* 1:354.

56 Li Zhi, "Zhenshi," in *LZ* 1:197. Obviously, Li Zhi was following Confucius's admonishment "Do not accept as friend anyone who is not as good as you" ("Xue'er," in Yang Bojun, *Lunyu yizhu*, 8; Lau, *The Analects*, 1.8, 60). In his writings, Li Zhi frequently used the term *shengji* (someone morally or intellectually superior to oneself) as an alternative term for "good friend" (see, for example, "Yu Jiao Ruohou," in *LZ* 3:19). Although teacher/friend (*shiyou*) was quite a common concept in late-imperial Chinese culture, as Rivi Handler-Spitz mentions in chapter 5, Li Zhi's observation on the tendency of many of his contemporaries to consider "emotional closeness" or "intimacy" the defining element in friendship is very interesting, pointing to the emotional aspect of the late-imperial conceptualization of friendship, which, however, was not a prominent topic in more formal contemporary discourses on friendship. On the other hand, Li Zhi also argued that one must not take as a teacher anyone in whom one did not feel comfortable confiding ("Zhenshi," in *LZ* 1:197–98).

57 Li Zhi, "Li Sheng shijiao wen," in *LZ* 1:354.

58 For a discussion of Li Zhi and the issue of life and death, see chapter 11.

59 Li Zhi, "Yu Ruohou Jiao Taishi," in *LZ* 3:69.

60 Li Zhi, "Da Liu Jinchuan shu," in *LZ* 1:140.

61 "Xiling tongzhi" in "Baichan gongde shu," *Li Wenlin waiji*, *j*. 1, reprinted in "Li Zhi shengping zhuanji ziliao huibian" in *Li Zhi yanjiu cankao ziliao* 2:68.

62 Li Zhi, "Yu Zhou Guiqing," in *LZ* 3:99.

63 Li Zhi, "Da Geng Sikou," in *LZ* 1:71.

64 Li Zhi, "Yu Fengli," in *LZ* 3:115.

65 Li Zhi, "Yu Jiao Ruohou," in *LZ* 1:153.

66 Li Zhi, "Shu Changshun shoujuan cheng Gu Chong'an," in *LZ* 1:231.

67 Li Zhi, "Yu Zhou Youshan," in *LZ* 3:35.

68 Li Zhi, "Li Zhuowu xiansheng yiyan," in *LZ* 3:314.

69 Cf. Xu Jianping, *Li Zhi sixiang yanbianshi*, 351–66.

70 Li Zhi, "Wusi pian," in *LZ* 2:69.

71 For a discussion of this "recognition" motif in writings from early China, see Henry, "The Motif of Recognition." Many cases Henry examines are related to the relationships between powerful lords and their retainers.

72 See Martin Huang, "Male Friendship and *Jiangxue*."

73 Li Zhi might have believed that what he did was not that radical. As I mentioned earlier, he must have felt that he had decided to pursue friendship and personal enlightenment away from his family and hometown only after he had already fulfilled all his familial obligations. At least, it seems that he was not intentionally trying to be radical in this regard.

74 Orthodox Confucian discourse emphasizes the commonality among all the five relationships, namely, a good minister/subject makes a good friend; a good friend in turn makes a good son. See, for example, *Zhongyong* (The Doctrine of the Mean), in Legge, *The Chinese Classics*, 1:412.

CHAPTER 4

A PUBLIC OF LETTERS

The Correspondence of Li Zhi and Geng Dingxiang

TIMOTHY BROOK

LI ZHI'S RADICAL APPROACH TO FRIENDSHIP—AS A PHILOSOPHICAL value and as an opening for the production of new moral meaning—is the subject of the preceding chapter. There Martin Huang examines the place that friendship came to assume in Li's life, a development driven in part by the break with a close friend, Geng Dingxiang, in the summer of 1584. Li had spent the previous three years as the guest of Geng and his two younger brothers in Huang'an County in northeastern Huguang, where the brothers had gone home to observe mourning.[1] Geng Dingxiang's decision to return to service that spring, followed by the sudden death of his middle brother and Li Zhi's particular friend, Dingli, that summer, drove a wedge between the two. The break is noteworthy, and knowable, because it left a train of recriminatory letters that managed to survive. This chapter attends less to the message of the letters than to the medium through which Ming writers most often expressed not just their friendships but their ideas about friendship.

Friendship is usually initiated as a face-to-face relationship, but it often survives, now as then, by being sustained through writing. As time and distance attenuate contact, writing becomes the relationship, a way of maintaining contact with a friend now absent, whether across town, across the country, or across time. As friendship is the condition for writing letters, so letter-writing becomes testimony to that condition, and often a reflection of it. But a letter is also a form of text, and like any literary text, cleaves to genre conventions and operates within shared expectations. The conventions and expectations organize what is put on paper and, in so doing, act to guide and restrain the readership. We shall see this process at work in the course of examining the correspondence of Li and Geng.

Interpreting letters from the late Ming is necessarily a mediated exercise, as few originals from the period survive, and none by Li Zhi.[2] We can read their correspondence only through the two filters between us and them. Copying supplies the first filter. Writers often made copies of their letters to others, which then might be recopied so that the author and addressee could share them with friends and relatives. They might even be recopied in order to circulate to a larger, informal readership. But just as we have none of the originals, so none of the handwritten copies survives either. We read them only as they have been printed in the collected works of the two men. The second filter is publication. As I have tried to sequence their letters into a single stream of correspondence, as they were first written, I have become persuaded that their letters were heavily redacted on both sides before going into publication. It is evident that Li reworked his letters before publishing them in *A Book to Burn*, for he chose to combine some of the letters into a single extended text, turning what was a sequence of discrete texts into an extended essay designed to produce a more general argument. Similarly, Geng's letters evince heavy redaction in *The Collected Writings of Master Geng of Tiantai* (Geng Tiantai xiansheng wenji), which appeared only in 1598, two years after his death. His letters there read more like extracts.[3]

The result of these two filters is that we are unable to read the actual letters that Li and Geng sent to each other. What we are reading, instead, is what they wanted us to read after the fact, prepared and staged to make their appeals persuasive to readers. The original letters may have been milder or fiercer, depending on the moments at which they were written in the larger emotional arc that their letters created. Casual barbs tossed off in the heat of writing may have intensified the gap between the two to a degree that face-to-face communication might have moderated—as appears to have happened when Li called on Geng to patch things up shortly before his old friend died. To recognize the difference between letter and print is not to nullify the interpretive work in this or the preceding chapter, but it is a condition to bear in mind as we reflect on how letter-writing shaped, and even made possible, their debate over friendship.

That noted, putting their letters into print is an important fact for assessing the terms of their debate. While publication suggests that the letters have been altered, it also signals that each man made a decision to go public. This implies a certain agreement that their exchange of views over how to weight the Confucian value of friendship was worth involving anonymous readers. Making their letters public attested to a state of mutual trust that neither man rejected. However strained their friendship became, they remained friends. So too they remained colleagues in the same tradition, differing only in how each sought to shape the content of that tradition. Their letters—as also the letters of the other late-Ming intellectuals who printed their correspondence—helped create a public that, by reading, could participate in this phase of the unfolding of neo-Confucianism.

These remarks bring us to the end of the process in which Li and Geng were involved. Let us begin instead by considering the material conditions that allowed someone in the late Ming to expect that a letter written would be a letter received, which is to say, mail.

LETTERS AS MAIL

Letter-writing was hardly a late-Ming invention, yet the rate of survival of letters from the period suggests that more people were writing, circulating, and reading them than at any earlier time.[4] Letters were socially inclusive, as full literacy was not required to send them, given the inclusion of the sample letters in letter guides and household encyclopedias.[5] They also marked out socially inclusive space by extending social interaction beyond face-to-face meetings. Acts of expression, they were also acts of connection between family members, peers, and friends. By defying physical separation, letters strengthened the ties between those who wrote them and those who received them, confirming familiarity, identity, and common purpose.

If the exchange of letters grew in the late Ming, it was assisted by the emergence of institutions to handle mail, for which there is evidence as early as the fifteenth century. The state operated its own mail service through the Ministry of War, its couriers traveling the thoroughfares linking every county seat with the capital administrations in Beijing and Nanjing, but that system was for handling official correspondence (*gongwen*) and not "private articles" (*siwu*), in the language of the Ming Code.[6] Couriers were undoubtedly asked to carry personal letters under official cover, but that was not why the service existed, nor was it available to those not authorized to send documents through the system. The great majority of people who could not access the system could dispatch letters only by sending them with travelers. This practice is attested in the letters that Xu Guangqi sent home from Beijing, where he was posted, to his family back in Shanghai in the early decades of the seventeenth century. In the letters themselves he refers to sending and receiving letters via friends, servants, and acquaintances traveling to Shanghai. In one, for example, he instructs his son, "Watch for anytime to find a convenient messenger to send a letter to us." He made a point of numbering his letters and asking his son to confirm in his replies which letters he had received and which he hadn't in an attempt to verify which deliveries had been made and which had failed. Xu also used letters home as a chance to enclose letters to other recipients, which he asked his family to forward.[7]

Xu's letters give no indication that he used a commercial service to handle his mail. Such services emerged slowly in the Ming, probably evolving from the services that commercial guilds made available to members and therefore limited to the routes along which their members regularly circulated. The late fifteenth-century edition of the standard Chinese-language textbook for Koreans, *My Khitan Buddy* (Lao Qida), sets one of its lessons at the livestock market outside the southwest gate of Beijing, where a certain shop run by a Korean proprietor held and forwarded letters going back and forth between Beijing and Korea.[8] Gradually, agencies specializing in this sort of service and open to broader use emerged. Similarly, there is evidence from the same century that Ningbo merchants were able to take advantage of Ningbo guilds scattered across the realm to send and receive mail. As Macheng, the county out of which the Gengs' county of Huang'an was carved in the mid-sixteenth century, was closely linked to a Ningbo commercial network extending up the Yangzi Valley into Sichuan, this was a service that could have been available to Geng and Li.[9] There is evidence of commercial agencies eventually emerging outside such associational networks to take on the task of forwarding letters. "News bureaus" (*baofang*), which appeared in the late Ming to reproduce and sell the official *Beijing Gazette* in provincial capitals, began sending and receiving letters in the seventeenth century. So too, though the evidence for them does not come into view until the early Qing, "stamp agencies" (*piaohao*) were operating in larger towns specifically to handle private mail.[10]

The emergence of postal agencies independent of state institutions could have come about only in response to a strong demand for such services. We cannot yet recover the structure of that demand. It would seem reasonable that the new services emerged in response to the need for regular business communication as the commercial economy expanded rather than for handling personal correspondence. Business communication would have flowed along well-established, predictable routes between markets, whereas private letters moved in the more random patterns linking writers and recipients. Accordingly, even after mail-handling services emerged, families such as Xu Guangqi's relied on their own networks of personal connections to forward their letters. It helped, of course, that Xu was in Beijing, the highest central place in the political system, which Huang'an was not. But as agencies formed and the scheduled relay of documents became a feature of urban life, the circulation of private letters outside family networks became a more regular feature of Ming life. Letter-writers could anticipate that a letter sent would be a letter received, and that a letter received created the possibility of a letter in reply. Letters were no longer confined to family circles but were connecting otherwise unconnected people on a regular basis, thereby shaping a larger social zone of interaction.

One sign of the increase in the use of mail was the publication of letters in authors' collected works. As letters more regularly entered communication circuits, so they carried enough weight to feature in an author's literary oeuvre. Addressed initially to a single recipient, letters came to be written for the world to read. The exchange of ideas about matters of concern to the writer and recipient could be uploaded to a broad reading public and, indeed, could assume that such a public existed to read these letters. In other contexts, in Europe, for example, the emergence of mail services heightened concerns about the privacy of communication, to the point of elevating privacy to a new value. But not in Ming China. The political constitution of the dynasty energetically denied the legitimacy of the private, but lest we resort to a "Chinese" ideology of the illegitimacy of the private, take note of media historian and theorist Bernhard Siegert's proposition that the idea of the private emerged in Europe only *after* the installation of the postal system. He argues, "The private did not precede the private letter in the process of this transformation—in either a chronological or a causal sense."[11] For Siegert, private life emerged as "an epoch of the postal system," not as its prior condition. Arguably, the same logic could be applied to the emergence of privacy in China, but that is a proposition for an essay other than this one.

What I find striking in the late-Ming context is the insistence of Li Zhi and others that it was legitimate to express private views on public matters outside the embargoed space of officeholding authority and that the publicly circulated letter was a vehicle for that expression. To bend the language of the Ming Code, views expressed in letters may have been counted as "private things"—*siwu* in the language of Ming regulations for couriers—but they were not thereby barred from entering the sphere of public texts, *gongwen*. Rather than administrative documents, these were understood as discourses on matters of public import. At the same time, among the more radical wing of late-Ming intellectuals, going public should not be taken as an offense against official doctrine. There should be public space for private views.

The tension between public and private is central to the exchange of letters between Li Zhi and Geng Dingxiang, as the powerful current running beneath the surface of their extended dispute was the issue of whether a person with less than a sage's wisdom should seek office in the belief—false for Li, true for Geng—that he could act benevolently on the world. This issue was Li's stated reason for withdrawing from state service, just as it was Geng's reason for rejecting eremitism as a morally sufficient position. They agreed that the highest moral task of the Confucian was to shoulder the burden of serving the public interest, but they were divided over whether taking a post in the bureaucracy was the way to acquit that duty. To argue this issue, Li took their disagreement to a public readership in 1590—Geng's heirs would follow in 1598—by printing the letters that passed between them.

To argue that social conditions created by the commercialization of the late-Ming economy enabled individuals to appeal to a public of letters to elevate *si* as a vehicle for attaining what is *gong*—and thereby incubate that public as a zone in which to express an ethical claim of moral independence from state ideology—may strike some readers as excessively materialist. Rather than make that claim, I intend more modestly to suggest that commercial postal relay played a role in enhancing social capacity to communicate ideas on a regular schedule and that, consequent to that regularity of exchange, this condition stimulated the production of ideas as a range of alternative possibilities rather than as a rehearsal of a single unified view. The possibility of publishing letters, which, as it happens, was also a consequence of the commercialization of the economy, in turn encouraged the crafting of letters that, as originals, were addressed to a unique recipient but that, as printed copies, became available for "public consumption" by a general third-party readership in a public of letters.[12] This was something new.

Nonetheless, it is worth bearing in mind that letters were a genre choice that entailed personal connection. Essays were formally addressed to anyone who could read them. A letter was addressed to one person alone. It claimed not just acquaintance but a right of acquaintance, whether on the grounds of kinship or of friendship. This right in turn implied a bond of intellectual connection, even community, within which it was permissible not just to exchange ideas but to disagree, and to agree to disagree. Publishing letters extended that bond of community between two people outward to a community of readers by inviting them to participate vicariously in the exchange. Private letters enabled a public exchange, and to that public, Li Zhi made his appeal.

The earliest surviving letter between Li Zhi and Geng Dingxiang is Li's letter of condolence on the death of Geng Dingli (#1).[13] For Li, his attachment to Dingli expressed the ideal of friendship that he placed at the heart of the Confucian program. Friendship, not social hierarchy, was the essential condition for higher learning.[14] He closes his letter by suggesting that Geng's decision to reengage in government service signals his prioritizing of career over friendship and his abandonment of the task of learning, which is possible only when one withdraws from politics. A hasty return to service, even by someone of great dedication, can lead only to bad outcomes.

Geng's collected works do not include his response to this letter. His first letter in that collection (#2) is a reply to another, later letter, now lost. In that letter, Li had asked whether Geng felt he was "really able to avoid sticking to the model of the ancients, and really able to avoid relying on principles derived from what [he has] seen and heard from others." In his reply, Geng writes that he does not claim that the ancients had unalterable answers to everything. He has sorted their models into two types: those that have changed over time—models based on experience and that therefore are mutable—and those that have persisted without alteration for thousands of years because their minds perceived rules laid down by heaven, not by people. Geng concedes that times change and that particular policy recommendations that a wise person might make must change with them, yet this does not alter the fundamental truths from which the moral life arises: "That it is painful to be struck or hurt, or miserable to be starved or drowned, is a pattern that has existed for thousands of years. That it is calamitous to be orphaned or rulerless, or sinful to be an unruly subject or an unprincipled son, is also a pattern that has existed for thousands of years. The ancients expended great effort and thought to create a model so that you and I might have adequate shelter and be sufficient in food and clothing, and they instructed us in ethics so that we might avoid being like wild animals."

The task of a statecraft activist is to conjoin the physical and moral realms on the basis of a unity of knowledge and action of the sort he believes Wang Yangming would have appreciated. The sage adapts to the time and does what is necessary, but what is necessary is already predetermined in the cosmic order and not up to the individual. Geng's analogy is a silkworm cocoon: "When a spring silkworm spins its cocoon, it takes its shape from the thing to which it attaches itself." The worm's spinning is unalterable, but the shape conforms to what is at hand. That inalterability Geng calls "being unable to stop" or "not allowing oneself to stop" (*budeyi, burong ziyi*), which I translate here as "the compulsion to act." Not unlike Wang Yangming's concept of the production of action from "pristine moral consciousness" (*liangzhi*), the compulsion to act is almost autonomic, something embedded in nature rather than requiring self-reflection. Worried by Li's attraction to the Buddhist doctrine of karma, Geng insists that the principles of right action are pre-inscribed, not imposed by past moral acts. He who renounces secular activism by "leaving the world," as the pursuit of Buddhist cultivation was termed, abandons his compulsion to act and abdicates his responsibility to improve the world.

In his response to this letter (#3) Li takes issue with the authority of the ancients, conspicuously Confucius. He is offended that Geng should put forward Mencius's self-declared failure on this point as an example for himself. He dismisses Geng's reverence for Confucius as his "family teaching"—a pejorative term among Ming intellectuals, but a sensitive one given Li's former position as tutor to Geng's family—and scoffs at the idea of learning anything from Confucius. "Confucius never told anyone to learn from Confucius," he writes. In support of this judgment he quotes Confucius's advice to his disciple Yan Yuan that "the practice of benevolence comes from oneself." Li goes further by insisting that "Confucius had no method to pass on to his disciples," then makes a Buddhist feint by declaring that "his method was learning that depends on there being neither self nor other." His point is that the teacher must adapt to the student, not the other way round.[15] This is not current practice, which is why the self-appointed guardians of moral truth tend to instruct people by upholding the wooden models of applying "virtuous conduct and ritual to restrain their minds, and administration and punishments to constrain their bodies." The task of education—and by extension, the task of ruling—is not to force people into regimens but to shape their natural impulses. Only by recognizing and shaping selfishness can the sage hope to bring peace to the world. "If everyone goes after what he likes and devotes himself to what he is good at, there will not be a single person who is without his function. How easy to rule in this way!"

Toward the end of the letter, Li praises Geng for being earnest in his practice of moral cultivation but reminds him, "Not everyone is like you." Geng should not expect everyone to do as he does just because he thinks he is right, nor should he impose uniformity on the natural variety of individual responses. "I respect you," Li concludes, "but I don't have to be just like you." Li is not arguing for moral relativism. He wants space for an ecumenism of method, with final moral decisions left to the individual. Only by mobilizing individuals can Geng hope to bring "the ignorant and unrighteous" to morality. Haranguing them with quotations from Confucius will never work. Li and Geng both were devoted to achieving the unity of knowledge and action that Wang Yangming called for, but they differed on how that was to be done. That difference would split the Wanli intellectual world down the middle.

There is a short fragment of a letter in Geng's collected works, which I have placed next in the sequence (#4), that seems to challenge Li's interpretation of Geng's concept of the compulsion to act. Li raised the legitimacy of desire as a moral wellspring, but desire, Geng writes, has nothing to do with moral action. In his psychology, acting morally is a natural compulsion that overrides mere desire. The mechanism for ensuring this is the mind, for it is the mind that controls desire and thus opens the path for right action. Li's reply in turn is that desire and moral action work in tandem, not against each other (#5). Desire becomes a problem when officials let the desire of their ambition overwhelm their judgments. If an official's desire is to effect positive change in the world, he should retire from the fray as soon as his work is accomplished, not seek advancement and the corruption that entails. Li then switches—perhaps because he has stitched two letters together into a single text—to an extended complaint about Geng's criticism of a mutual acquaintance, Deng Huoqu, who chose to abstain from public service. He chides Geng for not conceding the value of detachment to those who choose to practice it and, by implication, for mistaking what Geng feels is his disinterestedness with an interestedness on his own part, which is exactly what prevents him from achieving the detachment necessary to be truly useful to the world.

The next letter in the sequence, also from Li, struggles with the problem of the contradiction between the interests of self and of others (#6). The self/other dichotomy, which is central to Buddhist ontology, Li argues, is ignored by Confucians, to their peril. It arises in Mencius's famous conversation with King Hui of Liang in which he deplores the king's self-interest but offers no alternative other than banishing it. Li accepts that Geng regards his public service as disinterested, yet his failure to take account of interests—his own and those of the people—will doom his efforts at statecraft. His program of moral renovation makes impossible demands on people and is therefore impractical. Rather than force people to set aside their interests, Geng should let them pursue those interests to bring about change. Li's next three letters (#7, 8, 9) enlarge on the danger of serving without a more profound knowledge of how to guide people, the danger being that malevolence will overwhelm benevolence.[16]

The next letter from Li is by far the longest on either side. As four of Geng's letters respond to different parts of this letter, I treat this as a composite later edited for publication into a single continuous text. To catch the flow of their conversation, I have broken the first part of this long letter into what seem to me to be its original constituent parts (#10, 12, 14, 16), interspersed with Geng's replies (#11, 13, 15, 17).[17]

Li opens his letter by thanking Geng for an earlier letter, now lost (#10). He gives Geng the strongest possible compliment by saying that Geng's desire to instruct him, and his own willingness to receive that instruction, are positive testimony to Geng's concept of the compulsion to act, though Li reminds him that the corollary must be recognition that the views offered on both sides are equally genuine. Li then goes on to deplore the fraying of their friendship. He blames Geng's commitment to serve a troubled regime as the context of that fraying. To prove the danger of serving, he goes back to an event that set them at odds eight years earlier, the death of their mutual friend, He Xinyin. He Xinyin had been living in Huguang, possibly as a guest of the Gengs in Huang'an, in 1576, when his social activism led the provincial governor to order his arrest. He went into hiding but was apprehended three years later and died of torture in prison in Wuchang.[18] At the time Geng had been in a position to influence the outcome of the case, yet he had not acted to defend He. (He Xinyin's biography uncannily anticipates Li's own, for Li too would be driven out of Huguang by a censorial official a dozen years after he wrote this letter and end up dying in prison for want of intervention from higher officials.) "Your 'compulsion to act' consists of indiscriminately loving people without addressing them individually," Li chides. "My compulsion to act involves finding people in the course of practicing my Way and not treating them lightly. I suspect that these are different."[19] Li then goes on to compare Geng's moral standards to the sort of rote moralism dunned into schoolboys, and his own to the moral wisdom that resides in the Confucian classic *The Great Learning* (Da xue). Geng's problem, according to Li, is that he cannot discriminate: he soaks everything in the same moral downpour, whereas Li's compulsion to act is like frozen snow that stores moisture until it is needed to ease drought. Geng is no better than a village schoolmaster who drills his pupils without getting results, whereas Li is like a general who sends out crack troops to capture the opponent's king, achieving great effect with little effort. "Your compulsion to act is a case of knowing that you are not permitted to halt, but the true compulsion to act depends on really desiring not to halt. My compulsion to act is a case of not knowing that I am obliged to act." This might not be how Confucius would do it, but it is the best course for him.

In his reply, Geng is clearly offended by Li's belittling comment that his teaching is nothing better than drilling schoolboys in filial piety and deference (#11). He turns the tables and argues that training the young in deference is precisely the foundation on which virtue can arise and which Li's Buddhistic borrowings cannot account for. "Take away filiality and deference, and what virtue is left to illuminate? I suspect that what you call 'illuminating virtue' is watching for the evanescent principle of nonbirth from the vantage of perfect silent self-annihilation, and then saying that it is bright." It is not possible to transcend the elementary building blocks of moral life by wishing them away with a wave of Buddhistic nonaction. Geng ends his letter as personally as Li started his, invoking an unpleasant incident from even earlier, when Li, obliged to return to Fujian to observe mourning for his grandfather, left his family in Gongcheng, Henan, the site of his first official post, returning in 1566 to learn that in his absence two of his daughters had starved to death during a famine.[20] Geng implies Li's responsibility for their deaths.

The breach between Geng and Li had now widened, and in his reply Li chastises Geng for "holding to [his] course without doubting" and failing to see the narrowness of his perspective (#12). More damning, what Geng thinks differentiates him from everyone else is precisely what makes him the same as everyone else, the selfish desire to survive and get ahead:

> Morning to night, they plow in order to get food, buy land in order to plant, build houses in order to find shelter, study in order to pass the examinations, hold office in order to win honor and fame, and search for propitious sites in order to provide good fortune for sons and grandsons. The daily round of tasks is done for the benefit of oneself and one's family, and not a bit for others. Yet whenever you start talking about learning, you say: "You are for yourself alone, whereas I am for others; you are out for your own advantage, whereas I wish to benefit others."

In the background lurks Mencius's observation, to which Li alludes, that goodness and self-advantage are polar opposites, with Sage-Emperor Shun standing for the one and the infamous Robber Zhi for the other. Li Zhi sides with the bandits against the sages, doubting that the sages had a perfect understanding of all matters for all time. All are "slaves to self-advantage," he argues. To pretend otherwise is to put words and deeds at odds. Even Confucius and Mencius went about their business just like everyone else, no different from traders and farmers: "You are not the equal of peasants in the marketplace talking about what they do. Those who do business say it is business; those who do farm work say it is farm work." Geng's inability to own up to his own self-interest makes him their moral inferior.[21] Li closes by reminding Geng of Wang Yangming's famous remark, "The streets are full of sages," and the Buddhist adage, "Everyone is a Buddha." Even Confucius made no distinctions when it came to accepting students.

Geng rejects Li's charge that he is holding to the old course without doubting himself (#13). He agrees that doubt is necessary for the exercise of moral thinking and insists that the Confucian concept of benevolence requires doubt if it is to attain any depth. But this is precisely where the Buddhist approach to moral action goes wrong as a philosophy of education. Reducing reality to mere appearance drains the student's capacity to delve below the surface of things and find the deeper foundation of moral being. Li responds by accusing Geng of condemning others while regarding himself as immune to moral failure (#15). Geng in his turn goes back to his starting point by insisting that Confucius and Mencius are worth emulating because their "tradition of benevolence . . . compelled them to act." Weary of metaphysical sparring, Geng wants to bring the issue back into the realm of action, which is where he feels he can make his contribution and the withdrawn Li cannot. Li responds with a reminder about the emptiness of words—here he too seems to have tired of metaphysics—and asks Geng once again to allow other methods than his own to bring people to goodness (#16). After all, he and Geng are on the same path of illuminating virtue and, as such, equals: "[Accept this,] and then you can forget everything you have ever said about my discarding ethics, leaving my wife and family, shaving my head, and wearing Buddhist robes. What do you think? There has never been anything in which I have not been the same as you, except for your being a high official. How can your learning be superior to mine because of your high office? If it is, then Confucius and Mencius would not have dared open their mouths!" It is an artful dodge, and Geng responds by telling Li so (#17). Yes, the great teachers of the Confucian, Buddhist, and Daoist traditions understood that they were "setting up names and appearances to change those who came after them," quoting directly from Li's letter, but the lesson is not that their formulas are equally valid versions of reality, or that the distinctions among them do not matter. The challenge is to decide which of the sages offers the best program.

The most important letter on Li's side is his "Farewell to Justice Minister Geng" of 1588, when Li left Huang'an for neighboring Macheng County, where the local gentry were more tolerant of his Buddhist inclinations (#18).[22] He writes that he went to the Geng family compound to take his leave but found only two or three youths to whom he could not utter what was in his heart. That situation led him to reflect on Confucius's saying, "Not to talk to one who could be talked to is to lose a person; to talk to those who cannot be talked to is to waste one's words."[23] Discouraged, he presses ahead with his complaint that Geng has behaved like one who "follows old paths" and "treads in old footsteps"—one of the "sanctimoniously orthodox" (*xiangyuan*) whom Confucius singled out as conventionally minded—whereas he himself is an impetuous soul, "like the phoenix flying at a great height," ambitious and uncompromising (*kuang*), who aspires to "hear the Way."[24] "There exist impetuous and uncompromising people who have not heard the Way, but never has there existed anyone who could hear the Way who was not impetuous and uncompromising." How could Geng hope to "hear the Way" if he continued to cleave so closely to proper behavior?

In his reply, Geng chides Li for his condescension. People in the category of "the sanctimoniously orthodox" are not stupid; they just feel that they do not have the capacity "to enter the Way of Yao and Shun" [#19]. With proper instruction, though, they could. After all, that Way "is simply the tradition of benevolence by which these men felt a compulsion to act." The problem is not the slow, patient learning that Confucianism offers, but the refusal of "the Chan fanatics of this era" to compromise. Buddhism has simply given people a deceptively easy alternative that produces no results. "The Way of Sakyamuni is certainly difficult to penetrate," Geng accepts, but that does not mean it is on a par with "the Way of Yao, Shun, Confucius, and Mencius." Despite Li's departure from Huang'an, Geng asks Li to think over what he has said in hopes that their conversation might continue. And there the stream of letters ends.

LETTERS AND FRIENDS

The charges of personal moral failure that Li and Geng laid against each other in these letters must have been difficult for one friend to hear from another. Still, it behooves us to remember the genre: these were letters between friends, no matter how estranged. The bonds between them were deep. As Li reveals in a later letter to another friend, his early years in Huang'an were the happiest of his life. "All three Geng brothers treated me so warmly," he recalls. "Dingxiang was my strict master, Dingli was my understanding friend, and it goes without saying that Dinglih was also very close. In affection they were generous; in protective influence, even more so."[25] Despite everything, he remembered all three with great fondness.

It was the strength of their friendship that made their disagreement so heated. Each was disappointed in the other. As friendship was central to Li's philosophy of the conduct of ethical life, the pain of Geng's withdrawal of friendship was all the more sharp. As Li writes in his first letter, "Though the space within the four seas is great, finding a friend is difficult"; once found, that friend should not be abandoned. After enlarging on this theme, Li writes with sadness, "[I] had hoped to live and die in the hands of my friends, but now cannot." He concludes by admitting to Geng, "How troubled I feel."

The ideal of friendship runs through Li's letters. In the tenth letter in the sequence, he praises Geng for a now lost letter in which, he writes, Geng took the trouble to correct him. Correction, Li declares, is a sign of "true friendship." Even at the height of their disagreement, at least from Li's side, the two recognized each other as friends. And yet Li wouldn't leave the issue there. In his letter chastising Geng for how he failed to handle the He Xinyin affair, he uses the word "friend" nine times to underscore the emotional devastation he feels. Geng owed He the duty of friendship but retreated to the obligations that serving the state imposed on him. In reply, Geng invokes a statement in the *Doctrine of the Mean* (Zhong yong) and explains, "What I call obligation to action is when the minds of sons, subjects, younger brothers, and friends grasp the constant way of living." This is an important declaration on Geng's part. It declares that friendship is only the fifth of the five cardinal relationships, posterior to all the other relationships based on the hierarchies of kinship (parent-child, elder brother–younger brother, husband-wife) and the political order (ruler-subject). As several scholars, including Timothy Billings and Martin Huang, have noted, some late-Ming philosophers desired to elevate the fifth relationship, of friend-friend, above the other four.[26] In his ordering, Geng has declined to move friendship up ahead of the others. The first four bonds have to be fulfilled before friendship can be permitted to direct action.

In his response, Li subtly corrects Geng's citation from the *Doctrine of the Mean*, reminding him that Confucius names the four prior bonds in the context of declaring that he himself failed to live up to any of them. The point of the passage was not to establish a hierarchy among these bonds; rather, Li maintains, it was to express how difficult they are to uphold. Geng quietly accepts the correction in his reply, suggesting that the key message of the passage is humility. But Confucius admits his errors, and Li doesn't. Geng does not deny the bond of friendship but insists that it must coexist with the other bonds. By implication, society is best organized by hierarchy; equality can only ever supplement what hierarchy provides. In his farewell letter, though, Li acknowledges that the blame for "losing a friend" is entirely his. He does not insist that friendship is a higher bond than the others, but he does call Confucius to his side by instancing his sadness at the death of his most favored disciple, Yan Yuan, in unspoken parallel to his own loss of Geng Dingli. "Confucius in his time certainly realized how hard it is to find a friend. How much harder it is today!"[27]

When Li Zhi found himself caught in the crossfire of the politics swirling around the conduct of Chief Grand Secretary Shen Yiguan, whose denunciation he was falsely rumored to have been composing, he had only his friends to turn to, and some of them came to his defense.[28] Ma Jinglun, with whom he was lodging at the time, wrote to officials in charge of his case and defended him on the grounds that it was unreasonable to require a uniformity of views. "Since everyone has his own view," Ma pointed out, "how can everyone be the same? Why should it be necessary that their views all be the same?" He suggested that they recall the great founding figures of neo-Confucianism in the Song dynasty: "If all philosophers who agreed completely were judged acceptable, and all who disagreed unacceptable, then Zhu Xi and Lu Jiuyuan would not have had their debate."[29] Rather than mount a general argument about a right to privacy in the expression of personal views, Ma preferred to situate Li's outspoken disagreements with Geng and others squarely within the Confucian tradition. To do so was to assume that Confucianism was still a living body of thought, subject to public scrutiny and evaluation, not a doctrine that had achieved its final form. It was more than most sitting officials were willing to endorse.

Arguing for the diversity of views rather than uniformity may have been behind the decision to include a fragment of one of Li's letters to Geng in the posthumous collection of his writings, *Another Book to Burn*, in 1618. The scholar in charge of the edition was the moderate Wang Yangming adherent Jiao Hong, then the senior neo-Confucian in Nanjing. Inclusion of the letter could be seen as a provocation to reopen the Li-Geng dispute, or it could indicate that Jiao did not think the discussion should be buried; perhaps he wanted to invite the reading public to think again about what the two men had written. The altercation had not been a petty personal squabble but a principled debate between friends who cared deeply enough about issues of common concern to want to bring each other over to the other side. Indeed, this is more or less how Li represents their difference in every letter he wrote to Geng, assuring him of his friendship and asking Geng to recognize this bond.

Despite their falling out over the compulsion to act, friendship prevailed in the end. Li returned to Huang'an shortly before Geng died in 1596 to effect a reconciliation. Once Geng was gone, however, the protection that Li had enjoyed in the area dissolved and he departed. He returned to the area three years later, but after only one season he was driven out by Administration Commissioner Feng Yingjing. Ironically, or cruelly, Feng moved to Beijing shortly after Li fled there, developed a friendship with Matteo Ricci, and contributed a preface to the third (1601) edition of his book on friendship. Li died in custody the following year, neither condemned nor vindicated and without having resolved the tensions—between hierarchy and friendship, service and withdrawal, moral inadequacy and moral perfection, action and thought—that animated his philosophy and that have continued to echo in the public of letters down to the present.[30]

NOTES

1 Geng Dingxiang's mourning status is noted in one of the prefaces to the first draft gazetteer of Huang'an County (completed 1588). Geng is celebrated there because he was instrumental in founding the county by separating it from Macheng County. See *Huang'an xianzhi* (1822), yuanxu, 6a–b.

2 For a selection of original letters from the late Ming, see Shi and Yang, *Mingdai mingxian chidu ji*; neither Li nor Geng is represented in this collection. The collector of these letters, Gary Ho, says that Geng's letters are difficult to find, and Li's impossible. On the interest of the genre for the history of calligraphy, see Bai, "Chinese Letters."

3 A selection of these letters has been translated in Brook, "Li Zhi and Geng Dingxiang Correspondence" in *A Book to Burn*, 34–62; quotations from the letters have been taken from this text. For a summary of the exchange between Li and Geng, see Brook, *The Troubled Empire*, 179–81.

4 Most surviving letters reside in the collected works of their authors, though some have been reproduced for their calligraphic interest, for example, Shi and Yang, *Mingdai mingxian chidu ji*.

5 Popular household manuals of the late Ming included letter-writing guides, e.g., Yu Xiangdou, *Wanyong zhengzong*.

6 Lei, *Dulü suoyan*, 293 (prohibition on carrying "private goods"), 289 (prohibition on carrying "luggage" for other people); translated in Jiang Yonglin, *The Great Ming Code*, 151–52.

7 King, "The Family Letters of Xu Guangqi," 9, 10, 23, 24, 26, 27.

8 Dyer, *Grammatical Analysis*, 397–403. For more on this book, see Brook, *Great State*, 131–35.

9 Shi Shi, "Cong Mingdai kaishi de minyou," 10–11, 21; Lou, *Zhongguo youyi shiliao*, 53–54.
10 Brook, *The Confusions of Pleasure*, 186–89.
11 Siegert, *Relays*, 13.
12 The term "public consumption" is taken from Bai, "Chinese Letters," 386.
13 Numbers in parentheses correspond to the sequence of numbers of the letters of Li Zhi and Geng Dingxiang published in Li Zhi, *A Book to Burn*.
14 On Li Zhi's attitudes toward friendship, see chapter 3.
15 On Li Zhi's relationships with and attitudes toward his teachers and students, see chapter 5.
16 The eighth letter is a short extract from the seventh, which Jiao Hong chose to include in *Another Book to Burn*, rather than a separate letter.
17 The four fragments on Li's side make up only the first third of the composite letter.
18 Wu Pei-yi and Julia Ching, He Xinyin biography in *Dictionary of Ming Biography*, 513–15.
19 Li Zhi was not alone in blaming Geng. Huang Zongxi also held Geng responsible for He's death, observing, "If Master Geng took as his ruling principle the compulsion to act, how then could he not have acted in this case?" (*Ming Ru xue'an*, 815).
20 For interpretations of Li Zhi's accounts of these events, see chapters 1 and 2.
21 For additional interpretation of this passage and the conflict between Li and Geng, see chapter 8.
22 On the Macheng gentry's tolerance of Buddhism, see *Macheng xianzhi* (1882), 10.10b.
23 *Analects* 15:10, adapted from Waley, *The Analects of Confucius*, 194–95.
24 *Analects* 17:13, in Legge, *The Confucian Classics*, 1:324. I take "the sanctimoniously orthodox" from McMorran, "Wang Fu-chih," 426.
25 Li Zhi, "Da Mei Qiongyu," in *LZ* 3:73–74.
26 Billings, introduction, 37; Martin Huang, "Male Friendship and *Jiangxue*," 168; see also chapter 3.
27 Eleven years after the correspondence ended, Li Zhi met Matteo Ricci in Nanjing. The second edition of Ricci's collection of one hundred European maxims on friendship had just been published. Li was so pleased with the book that he had several copies made to distribute among his students. See Billings, introduction, 23.
28 Shen Defu, *Wanli yehuo bian*, 691.
29 Ma Jinglun, "Yu Zhangke Li Linye zhuan shang Xiao Sikou" and "Li Zhi shengping zhuanji ziliao huibian," in *Li Zhi yanjiu cankao ziliao* 2:54–55.
30 On the continuing state pressure to discourage a public of letters today, see Howard Choy, review of Fang Fang, *Wuhan Diary: Dispatches from a Quarantined City*, Modern Chinese Literature and Culture, The Ohio State University: https://u.osu.edu/mclc/2020/08/19/wuhan-diary-review-2/

CHAPTER 5

AFFILIATION AND DIFFERENTIATION

Li Zhi as Teacher and Student

RIVI HANDLER-SPITZ

IN LI ZHI'S MIND, NO WORD WAS MORE STRONGLY ASSOCIATED with "friend" (*you*) than "teacher" (*shi*). In an essay titled "True Teachers" (Zhen shi), he asserted, "Teachers and friends are essentially the same."[1] Since he equated pedagogical relationships with friendship, it should come as no surprise that he nurtured with his teachers and students relationships no less complicated or emotionally fraught than those he cultivated with friends. Part of the difficulty of analyzing these relationships, however, lies in Li Zhi's explicit disavowal of them. Although he wrote prolifically on the subject of friendship, he proclaimed, "I have never bowed four times and accepted assignments from a single teacher, nor have I ever received four bows and officially taken on a friend."[2] Elsewhere he avers, "I will not take on one single disciple."[3] Yet despite these denials, the historical record demonstrates beyond any doubt that Li Zhi did indeed study under leading scholars and take on a wide array of disciples. This chapter analyzes Li Zhi's attitudes toward teacher-student relationships from three perspectives: his theoretical discussions of pedagogy, his conversations with some of his own pupils, and his relationships with two of his most renowned mentors, Wang Ji and Luo Rufang. As prominent members of Wang Yangming's School of the Mind, these teachers promoted an eclectic, syncretic philosophy, central to which was the cultivation of students' individual nature. Their teachings raise the question of how, or even whether, a student educated in this tradition can pay homage to his mentors. Should the student strike off on his own, thus demonstrating his independence of thought? Would acknowledging a debt to his masters signal the teacher's failure to nourish the student's originality? Li Zhi and his pupil Yuan Zhongdao grappled mightily with these problems and arrived at slightly different conclusions. Whereas Li emphasized his affiliation with his teachers and deployed the powerful discourse of friendship to cast himself as "one who understood" them, Yuan opted to accentuate his radical autonomy from Li.[4] Each man in his own way struggled with the challenges of affiliation and differentiation within a distinguished intellectual legacy.

Examining his relationships with his teachers and students requires consulting sources both by and about Li Zhi. *A Book to Burn* contains funerary tributes Li Zhi composed for Wang Ji and Luo Rufang. These texts provide windows onto his attitudes toward each master. Biographies of both teachers also appear in *Another Book to Keep (Hidden)*, a work of history attributed to Li Zhi. However, these biographies provide only ancillary evidence, since according to a preface by Li Weizhen, Li Zhi compiled *Another Book to Keep (Hidden)* by excerpting and recombining passages from existing histories.[5] The authenticity of this book has also been doubted because of its posthumous publication.[6] Nonetheless, the biographies it contains supplement and complement more dependable sources. For Li Zhi's theory of education, I have relied on a substantial afterword published in *A Book to Burn*. Evidence concerning his interactions with his students was recorded in four collections of recorded sayings (*yulu*), all compiled by his students: *Conversations by the Lake* (Hushang yulu), *Illuminating Discussions of Antiquity* (Mingdeng dao gu lu, also known as *Discussions of Antiquity*, Dao gu lu), *Answers to Questions at Yongqing Temple* (Yongqing dawen), and *Conversations in the Oak Grove* (Zuolin jitan).[7]

Conversations in the Oak Grove was the liveliest of these accounts. It was composed by Li Zhi's distinguished protégé Yuan Zhongdao probably in the late 1590s and likely not published until two decades later. Although a preface to this collection claims that the text, which presents anecdotes and brief dialogues between Li Zhi and his pupils, "depicts Li Zhi just as he really was," many of its vignettes are historically unverifiable.[8] Moreover, compiling collections of "recorded sayings" necessarily involved translating fleeting oral discourse into static written documents and, as Jiang Wu argues in chapter 9, the production of such compilations, at least in Buddhist circles, also necessitated adapting source material to conform to established generic conventions. Thus, it would be unwise to regard Yuan's text as an accurate rendering of actual conversations between Li Zhi and his students. Rather, I propose that this text be interpreted as providing vivid images of Li Zhi's pedagogical style as remembered, creatively reimagined, or strategically constructed by one of his more accomplished and original students. Just as Li Zhi crafted images of his teachers in the essays he wrote to commemorate their deaths, so too did Yuan Zhongdao fashion a literary portrait of Li Zhi in *Conversations*.

IN THE FOOTSTEPS OF THE MASTERS

Writings by and about Li Zhi closely affiliate him with distinguished teachers, including the founder of the Taizhou branch of the School of the Mind, Wang Gen, as well as Wang Ji, Luo Rufang, and many others.[9] Wang Gen and Wang Ji were among the most prominent disciples of Wang Yangming, while Luo Rufang was a generation younger and studied under Wang Gen's protégé Yan Jun (1504–1596). Upon meeting Wang Ji and Luo Rufang in Nanjing in the early 1570s, when he participated in "lecture meetings" (*jianghui*), Li Zhi swiftly developed a deep respect for both men.[10] Despite their relatively brief in-person encounters, these two masters profoundly influenced Li Zhi. Eager to showcase his debt to them, he quotes one of his own students' description of the sway they held over Li: "The name Master Wang [Ji] was always on [Li Zhi's] lips, followed by that of Master Luo Rufang." In Li Zhi's account, the student adds, "not a year passed when [Li Zhi] did not read books by these two masters, [nor did he ever] open his mouth without speaking of their teachings."[11] Li Zhi's decision to place these comments in the mouth of his student lends them an air of objectivity that enhances their credibility.

In his funerary tributes to Wang Ji and Luo Rufang, Li Zhi also uses his own voice to highlight his deep affective bond with these teachers. The latter text begins by lamenting that Luo died without being able to pass on his teachings to a worthy student. Here, Li Zhi empathetically imagines how the master may have felt when, "on the verge of death, just as he wanted to cry out but dared not, [Luo] conceived the desire to persevere one more day in the hope of finding [someone who truly understood him]. But in the end, he was unable to find such a person." Having himself suffered anguish over the possibility of dying friendless and alone, Li Zhi poignantly comments, "A thousand years hence, when people hear this story [about Luo Rufang's dying without a worthy disciple or friend], they will still shed tears over the unendurable pain the master suffered."[12] The pathos with which he recounts Luo's death rhetorically strengthens Li Zhi's emotional connection to his master.

This bond may explain why, even though in this essay Li Zhi emphatically repeats that he "never formally studied with the master," he nonetheless takes upon himself the weighty ethical responsibility of ensuring that

Luo's teachings be carried on.[13] Li writes, "For the master's sake, I must not hesitate to trek high and low searching among his disciples for a truly understanding and accomplished person. When I find this person, I will commemorate the master and utter . . . words intended to reassure his soul. . . . Those who leave behind no descendants have nothing more to hope for; but the master was not one of these."[14] Devoted as he was to Luo Rufang, Li Zhi evidently could not bear the possibility of his master's dying without an heir. But it is difficult to account for the discrepancy between his previous claim that Luo Rufang died without a successor and his confident tone here—in the same essay—that the master did indeed have an heir. The contradiction could perhaps be resolved by reference to Luo Rufang's recorded conversations, a text to which Li Zhi alludes.[15] Did Li Zhi believe that at the time of Luo Rufang's death none of his disciples fully grasped his teachings, but later, by studying Luo's recorded sayings, someone gained insight into them? Li Zhi appears to have been in quest of such a person. Yet, unless and until such an outstanding student were actually found, his confident tone scarcely seems warranted. On what grounds could he so confidently affirm that the master left behind a worthy disciple? The text hints at one possibility but shies away from affirming it: perhaps Li Zhi considered himself Luo Rufang's special student.

The text's focus on Li Zhi's acute grief upon learning of the master's death lends credence to this interpretation and suggests that he may have viewed himself not merely as Luo's disciple but also as his trusted friend. This interpretation is further bolstered by his use of the term "understand" (*zhi*) in the following passage. In the late Ming, this word was redolent of associations to friendship, construed as one man's heartfelt appreciation for another. In this text, Li Zhi remorsefully confesses that he did not begin writing the memorial testimony for Luo until goaded to action by one of his own disciples. The hyperbolic assertions and dramatically repeated rhetorical questions that follow ostensibly aim to lessen his sense of guilt for not having acted sooner, but they also serve the rhetorical purpose of strengthening Li Zhi's connection to his master. By rationalizing his initial silence as sorrow so overwhelming it could not be expressed in words, he positions himself as the master's most emotionally receptive and therefore most authentic disciple—and his bosom friend.[16]

> Ever since I heard the news of the master's death, I have felt as if I've been passing my days in a dream. Only now do I understand that the phrase "True grieving expresses no grief; true weeping sheds no tears" is not just empty words. I now struggle to calm

> my anguished thoughts. Looking back on the past, how ridiculous it seems! Could anyone say I did not think about the master? Indeed I did think about him. Could anyone say I did not understand him? Indeed I did understand him, deeply. Could anyone say I was incapable of speaking about the master? Indeed no one was more capable of speaking about him than I! And yet my lips were sealed, my mind a blank; I was paralyzed, unable to lift my brush. Even I do not understand the reason why.[17]

Casting himself as the one person who "deeply understood" his master, Li Zhi arrogates to himself the authority to pass on the master's teachings, a right he exercises by composing the commemorative essay itself. This text ensured that at least the aspects of Luo Rufang's teachings he found most compelling would indeed be conveyed to future generations, and made himself the conduit of this transmission. In this context, Li Zhi's confident assertion makes sense: the master did have a successor: Li Zhi himself. More difficult to explain, however, is Li Zhi's earlier claim that the master died without such an intellectual heir. One may speculate that perhaps Li Zhi considered it self-aggrandizing or unseemly to assert this privilege openly. Yet in light of his well-documented arrogance, this conclusion scarcely seems warranted. As is so frequently the case in Li Zhi's writings, the tension stands unresolved. But what is clear is that he strove to present himself publicly as the legitimate inheritor of an illustrious intellectual lineage, and he expressed this connection through the vocabulary of friendship.

If Li Zhi's writings convey ambivalence about his role vis-à-vis Luo Rufang, his funerary tribute to Wang Ji provides greater clarity. Here Li Zhi presents himself as unequivocally qualified to carry on Wang Ji's legacy and interpret his teachings. He dismisses all contemporary scholars except himself for failing to appreciate the profundity of Wang's precepts—lessons he compares favorably to those of Confucius himself—and recounts that on first encountering Wang Ji, he "immediately acknowledged [the master] as an extraordinary person."[18] This detail bolsters the image of Li Zhi as a man of discernment. Having thoroughly disparaged his contemporaries, he concludes with a resoundingly self-congratulatory flourish: "[Wang Ji] surely would consider me someone 'skilled in interpretation'! He surely would regard me as someone who understood him!"[19] Here again Li Zhi invokes the discourse on friendship, casting himself as a uniquely insightful student. Indeed, more than a decade later, in 1599, he would publish an annotated volume of Wang Ji's recorded conversations, thus ensuring that his master's words—along with his own interpretation and commentary—would be transmitted.[20]

Li Zhi was particularly inspired by Wang Ji's and Luo Rufang's flexible, antihierarchical teaching styles, which, drawing on the tradition of Wang Yangming before them, encouraged students to seek understanding for themselves.[21] He also admired these teachers' ability to inspire and transform students of diverse backgrounds. For example, in his funerary essay on Luo Rufang, he provides a lengthy description of the many types of students the master taught:

> [The master] took his students from shepherd boys and woodcutters, old fishermen, street urchins from the marketplace, officials from the yamen, peddlers and retailers, weaver women, and plowmen, reputable Confucians who might "steal straw sandals" and great bandits wearing caps and robes.[22] If only they "had the right mindset," the master did not . . . care at all whether his followers were poor scholars wearing threadbare clothes, hermits who lodged by streams and cliffs, pale-skinned young students, provincial degree holders wearing green-collared robes, Daoists wearing yellow robes and feathery accoutrements, Buddhist clergy wearing black garments, or Confucian officials.[23]

Impressed by Luo's ability to communicate his down-to-earth philosophy to students of both sexes, diverse religious commitments, and all strata of society, Li Zhi surmised that he "never interacted with anyone in vain" and added, "I doubt that any student who came to his door could have left without receiving his teachings."[24] He described Wang Ji as possessing an equally agreeable temperament and likewise making no social distinctions among his students.[25]

To match Wang Ji's welcoming stance toward all students, this master's biography in *Another Book to Keep (Hidden)* attributes to him a remarkably egalitarian pedagogical method. It portrays him rejecting the traditional hierarchy of masters over disciples and instead promoting collaborative learning among equals. The biography quotes Wang as stating, "[My disciples and I] cannot refrain from honing our understanding together with people of similar aspirations. If in the process someone is stimulated to share his understanding of spirit-and-nature [*xingming*], then naturally everyone benefits. It is not the case that I have a method that can be transmitted."[26] Li Zhi's funerary tribute to Wang Ji likewise compares this master's influence on his students to healing rain that nourishes and prompts new growth.[27]

Eventually, when Li Zhi himself became a teacher, he developed methods inspired by his masters' examples. Like Wang and Luo, he attracted a motley array of students, including Buddhist clergy, laymen, and even gentry women, and engaged in what Jiang Wu describes as a community of Dao learners (*xuedaoren*).[28] He fully embraced his teachers' antihierarchical philosophy, instructing pupils not to place undue credence in authority figures since "sages are no different from ordinary people."[29] And, praising Confucius's ability to "depart from the ordinary," he implied that one need not be hemmed in by rigid social conventions.[30] Perhaps paradoxically, the proof of his own mastery of these teachings lay in his ability to abandon his teachers' precedents and strike out on his own. Thus Li Zhi pioneered a theory of pedagogy that even more radically minimized the role of teachers and insisted instead on students' attaining self-sufficiency.

FINDING ONE'S OWN VOICE: LI ZHI'S THEORY OF EDUCATION

In "Afterword to *Journeying with Companions*," a short essay published in *A Book to Burn*, Li Zhi articulates a theory of pedagogy that aims to liberate pupils from the authority of their masters.[31] Although this essay deals with musical—not ethical—education, it nonetheless provides a valuable lens through which to examine Li Zhi's relationships with his students. The text pivots away from his vision of a disciple as one who "understands" (*zhi*) his master. Instead, it calls to mind the related metaphor of the *zhiyin*, "one who understands the sound."[32] Li Zhi maintains that teachers must not presume to understand their students or offer too much guidance. Each student must discover his own voice. The text alludes to a heated discussion between Li Zhi and his close friend Jiao Hong regarding interpretations of a legend from *The History of the Zither* (Qin shi). The two friends disagreed on the moral of the story: Jiao Hong considered the tale proof that teachers can effectively guide students to refine their talent; Li Zhi, on the other hand, regarded the story as evidence of the superfluity of teachers and argued that students must undertake the difficult work of self-discovery.[33]

The story concerns a student named Bo Ya, who, in ancient times, studied under a renowned zither master. Although Bo Ya attained a high degree of technical proficiency on his instrument, his teacher criticized his playing on the grounds that it did not express the full range and depth of human emotion. To remedy the problem, the teacher invited Bo Ya to accompany him on a journey to meet his own master. Together, teacher and student traveled beyond the edge of civilization to the sea, whereupon the teacher left, promising to return with his master. Bo Ya waited patiently for ten days, but his teacher did not return, nor did the teacher's master appear. Frightened and alone, Bo Ya became frantic. He craned his neck in every direction, searching for some sign of his teacher, but he heard nothing but the crashing of waves on the seashore and the sad cries of birds overhead. Gazing up at the sky, he cried, "My teacher *has* no master! He left me here in order to excite my emotions!" With that, he picked up his zither and composed his most harrowing song, "The Melody of Water Immortals."[34]

Jiao Hong maintained that the chief lesson to be learned from this story was that great art depends on both raw talent and formal instruction from a teacher. Were it not for the technical foundation Bo Ya acquired from his teacher first, his wilderness adventure would have produced nothing deserving the name of art. Li Zhi disagreed. He claimed that Bo Ya's training was irrelevant, perhaps even detrimental to his musical accomplishment. Only by going out into nature and forgetting the skills he had previously been taught was Bo Ya able to produce such powerful music. Li Zhi wrote, "It was only because Bo Ya went to a remote seashore, a wilderness of hollow caves, a place distant from any human trace, that the ancient scores *ceased to exist for him* and there was no longer anything to be passed on *nor any teacher to be found*; in short, when none of the things he had formerly studied were available to him, he attained understanding *by himself*." This passage evinces Li Zhi's deep suspicion of a teacher's ability to transmit knowledge or skills.[35] His opinion resonates with Wang Ji's denial, mentioned earlier, of his ability to communicate any method to his students. Expanding on this idea, Li Zhi argues in this text that students must seek understanding for themselves. By making Bo Ya the agent of the story, Li Zhi credits the student with the entire educational experience: traveling to the remote location, forgetting everything he had previously learned, and attaining understanding *by himself*.

However, Li Zhi's interpretation overlooks the fact that Bo Ya did not undertake this journey of his own accord. It was the teacher's idea to embark on this perilous field trip; the teacher engineered this transformative experience and then removed himself strategically so that Bo Ya could taste autonomy. And yet, although Li Zhi omits these details from his interpretation, the pedagogical strategies Yuan Zhongdao attributes to him in *Conversations* suggest that on some deep level Li Zhi understood—and even practiced—methods similar to those of Bo Ya's zither teacher. Li Zhi implemented pedagogical methods designed to stimulate his students' own processes of self-discovery. The text portrays him goading them repeatedly to reduce their reliance on formal instruction and urging them instead to arrive at their own conclusions. It even suggests that these methods proved as efficacious for at least one student as they did for Bo Ya.

LI ZHI, PEDAGOGUE

Throughout the 1590s, a stream of students made the long trek to study with Li Zhi in his remote monastery by the edge of Dragon Lake.[36] Yuan Zhongdao's *Conversations* depicts Dragon Lake as a friendly, convivial pedagogical environment: students and teacher not only discoursed on serious matters; they also joked and teased one another outdoors, enjoying the moonlight and sometimes indulging in alcohol until the wee hours of the night.[37] Li Zhi is shown elaborating on and creatively adapting Wang Ji's and Luo Rufang's traditions of avoiding rigid doctrines and instead fostering students' self-discovery through open-ended discussion. Central to his project is weaning his students from their dependence on his own authority as teacher.

Again and again the text shows Li Zhi resisting providing direct answers to students' questions. For instance, when one student asks how to tell the difference between a sage and an ordinary person, Li Zhi behaves as a Chan master, turning the question back on the student: "Whom would *you* regard as a sage? Whom would *you* regard as an ordinary person?"[38] Elsewhere, the text portrays Li Zhi inviting his students to ponder what a certain Song dynasty Chan master failed to understand. Stumped, his students mull over the question in silence until Yuan Zhongdao, assuming the question is a test, blurts out, "What was it? What *did* he fail to understand?" Li Zhi enigmatically replies, "I don't know any more than you do!"[39] Here Li Zhi is shown deliberately frustrating his students' desire to rely on their teacher for guidance. In fact, his question prompts students to seek answers beyond what he himself knows. In one instance, he even explicitly calls upon them to teach *him*: "Since you've come all the way here, what do *you* have to teach *me*?"[40] Perhaps more striking, in another passage a student's diffident answer to a question elicits a harsh rebuke. When Li Zhi compliments a student on his spiritual attainment, the student bashfully replies, "And yet, I need a teacher to show me the path." Li Zhi responds with anger. Making a face, he blurts out, "That kind of remark is just despicable!"[41] These several incidents demonstrate Yuan Zhongdao's perception that Li Zhi placed a premium on students' releasing themselves from reliance upon their master's authoritative judgments.

Yuan Zhongdao's observations find corroboration in works authored by Li Zhi. In letters and essays, including his most influential piece, "On the Childlike Mind" (Tongxin shuo), Li Zhi repeatedly warns of the dangers of merely transmitting the teachings of others, and elsewhere he analogizes this behavior to "lapping up [other people's] snot and spit."[42] To avoid this error, he exhorts readers to develop their own moral and aesthetic compass and states, "Whether people are virtuous or not depends on their standing on their own two feet; it has nothing to do with teachers or friends."[43] To further emphasize this point, in his epistolary correspondence he even went so far as to address some of his students by the respectful title "Teacher" (*shi*).[44] This highly unusual practice underscores Li Zhi's commitment to encouraging students to question rather than accept his authority as master.

Yet despite Li Zhi's explicit statements on the importance of fostering students' independent thinking, conversations recorded by students other than Yuan Zhongdao do not especially stress this aspect of Li Zhi's pedagogy. One could surmise that, following the example of his own teachers—and of Confucius before them—Li Zhi adapted his pedagogical strategies to meet his students' individual temperaments and abilities: having identified in Yuan a student who thrived on intellectual sparring, Li Zhi engaged him especially frequently in such repartee. More likely, because Li Zhi had a nationwide reputation for gruffness and irascibility, he provoked all students equally.[45] Why, then, did other pupils omit this aspect of his pedagogy or minimize its significance? One possible answer concerns the students' purpose in seeking instruction. The students who compiled *Illuminating Discussions of Antiquity* studied Confucian classics with Li Zhi. Because this subject related directly to the imperial examinations, they may have privileged content over form in compiling their record.[46] Yuan Zhongdao, on the other hand, not motivated by such utilitarian concerns, paid closer attention to Li Zhi's pedagogical methods. Li's emphasis on fostering students' individuality resonated powerfully with Yuan's own nascent aesthetic sensibilities and his budding understanding of the individual as the source of creativity. Years later, Yuan Zhongdao, along with his brothers Yuan Hongdao and Yuan Zongdao, would found an artistic movement, the Gong'an School, that championed a "romantic vision" of poetry as untutored outpourings of the soul, not laboriously crafted homages to past masters.[47] Yuan's abhorrence of anything smacking of imitation made him leery of overt displays of filiation and especially receptive to Li's provocative pedagogical methods, which he enshrined in *Conversations*.

A PARTICULARLY INDEPENDENT STUDENT?

Conversations presents itself as testimony to Yuan Zhongdao's independence of mind, fostered through his interactions with Li Zhi but not limited to what Li taught him. Perhaps the most salient indication of Yuan Zhongdao's self-portrayal as independent from his teacher lies in his complete omission of Li Zhi's name from the text. Instead, the text consistently refers to him as "the old man" (*sou*). Yuan even disingenuously states, "I'm not sure of the identity of the Old Man of the Oak Forest. . . . He was an exceedingly peculiar person." The text relates that after having studied with "the old man" for some time, Yuan and his brothers left Macheng to continue their travels. When they later returned to seek further instruction, "the old man" had disappeared.[48] By deliberately omitting Li's name, Yuan renounces any possibility of filiation or indebtedness to his teacher. He presents himself squarely as his own man, unencumbered by any scholastic tradition. Additionally, the details about Li Zhi's disappearance and the emphasis on his residence in an oak forest resonate with the pedagogy of Bo Ya's teacher: in each case, an eccentric master renders himself physically inaccessible so as to compel the student to develop greater powers of self-reliance. Significantly, this transformative experience occurs far from society, in nature, where the authentic self can thrive unencumbered by social conventions.[49]

Additionally, unlike Li Zhi, who fashioned for himself the public image of a student steeped in his masters' teachings, Yuan Zhongdao cast himself as extraordinarily willing to differentiate himself from his teacher and assess him from a critical perspective. Although in the text Yuan Zhongdao occasionally presents himself as a favored pupil, he also unflinchingly paints himself as the butt of Li Zhi's derision. More than once, the text portrays Li Zhi dismissing Yuan Zhongdao's questions and comments as "irrelevant" (*bu xianggan*) or "illogical" (*bushi daoli*).[50] These ostentatious, tongue-in-cheek performances of humility showcase the student's disregard for his master's opinions and his far greater interest in conveying his own ideas. Had he truly been ashamed of his teacher's disapproval, Yuan could simply have omitted unflattering remarks. His decision to include them exhibits his rejection of the idea that his teacher's judgments must be authoritative. This point is strongly corroborated in Yuan's biography of Li, in which he emphatically affirms that although he admired Li, he absolutely did not consider himself Li's "follower."[51] This example further underscores

Yuan's eagerness to present himself as standing on his own two feet rather than bending to his teacher's influence or authority. Thus, *Conversations* presents Yuan as a Bo Ya–like figure, whose crowning achievement lies in his original composition. It likewise casts Li Zhi as a pedagogue whose chief objective is to get out of the way and allow his student to come fully into his own.

CONCLUSION

Yuan Zhongdao's presentation of himself as a student who has definitively broken free of his master's authority seems to clash with Li Zhi's sustained efforts to call attention to his prestigious pedigree. Yet both men's actions exhibit their struggles with the twin challenges of affiliation and differentiation. While Yuan's text pretends to minimize the role Li played in his education, the very existence of this text belies this implicit claim. Had Yuan gained total independence from his master, he would not have felt compelled to transmit his master's conversations, much less lovingly record his biography. A similar ambivalence radiates throughout Li Zhi's writings, which simultaneously celebrate and disavow the lineage of Wang Ji and Luo Rufang. Both cases provide examples of students attempting to craft their public image through the medium of print. And while one leaned toward embracing his connections with renowned teachers and the other accentuated—or perhaps even exaggerated—his autonomy from his master's influence, both men struggled to adapt and transform their teachers' precepts, making them more fully their own. In the late Ming era, a period known for its unprecedented emphasis on the individual, Yuan and Li each forged names for themselves as distinguished disciples as well as individuals remarkable in their own right.

NOTES

Many thanks to Robert Hegel, Pauline C. Lee, Haun Saussy, Ellen Handler Spitz, Robert Schine, and especially Suyoung Son for commenting on earlier drafts of this chapter. Thanks also to Ann Waltner and the members of the University of Minnesota's classical Chinese reading group.

1 Li Zhi, "Zhen shi," in *LZ* 1:197; Li Zhi, *A Book to Burn*, 25. This idea is reinforced in his prominent use of the term "teacher-friend" (*shiyou*) to classify relationships in *Upon Arrival at the Lake* (Chutanji), a text in which he reorganizes and comments upon anecdotes from the fifth-century collection *New Account of Tales of the World* (Shishuo xinyu) and the more recent work *Mr. Jiao's Grove of Categories* (Jiaoshi leilin) by Jiao Hong.

Li Zhi's comments on the relationships between teachers and friends in *Upon Arrival at the Lake* deserve serious analysis but are beyond the scope of this chapter. On the compilation and structure of *Upon Arrival at the Lake*, see Ren, *Li Zhi shixue*, 28–34.

2 Li Zhi, "Zhen shi," in *LZ* 1:198; Li Zhi, *A Book to Burn*, 26–27.

3 Li Zhi, "Yuyue," in *LZ* 2:105. For further instances of Li Zhi's disavowal of his role as a teacher, see chapter 8. See also Li Zhi, "Da Liu Jinchuan," in *LZ* 3:128.

4 On the rhetoric of the friendship in premodern China, see Shields, *One Who Knows Me*; Martin Huang, "Male Friendship in Ming China"; Billings, introduction.

5 Li Weizhen, "Li Weizhen xu," in *LZ* 11:359.

6 Even at the time of publication, the authenticity of this book was doubted. See Jiao Hong, "*Xu Cangshu* xu," in *LZ* 11:367; Sheng Yusi, *Xiu'an yingyu, Xiyouji wu*, cited in Ren, *Li Zhi shixue*, 9n1; Zhang Dai, "Li Zhi, Jiao Hong liezhuan," in *Shikui shu*, 9:205.2986. However, not all the contents of *Xu Cangshu* are considered spurious. The contemporary historian Ren Guanwen has divided the material into three categories: portions likely by Li Zhi, portions likely by others, and portions of uncertain authorship. According to his classification, the biographies of Wang Yangming, Luo Rufang, and Wang Ji all fall into the most reliable category (cited in Ren, *Li Zhi shixue*, 17–18).

7 Although Yuan Zhongdao visited Li Zhi at Dragon Lake in 1590, accompanied by his brothers Yuan Hongdao and Yuan Zongdao, it seems that *Conversations* depicts discussions that occurred on a later visit, in 1592 or 1593. Yan and Zhu, *Li Zhi zhuan*, 233n4. *Conversations by the Lake*, no longer extant, was recorded by the monk Wunian; *Illuminating Discussions of Antiquity* was assembled by Liu Yongxiang and Liu Yongjian, the son and nephew of Li Zhi's patron Liu Dongxing, and published by Li Zhi in 1597; *Answers to Questions at Yongqing Temple* was compiled by She Yongning and published in 1602. On the compilers of *Illuminating Discussions of Antiquity* and their motivations for publishing this book, see chapter 8. On the compilation of *Answers to Questions at Yongqing Temple*, as well as analysis of this text, see chapter 9.

8 Pan Zenghong, "Shu *Zuolin jitan*," in *LZ* 18:303.

9 Li Zhi provides a detailed account of his intellectual pedigree and mentions the teachers Wang Gen, Xu Yue (d. 1551), Yan Jun (1504–1596), Zhao Zhenji (1508–1576), Deng Huoqu (1498–ca. 1569), Luo Rufang, He Xinyin, Qian Tongwen (n.d.), and Cheng Xueyan (n.d.). Li Zhi, "Da xiao," in *LZ* 1:194–95; Li Zhi, *A Book to Burn*, 24–25. Several of these teachers also appear in *Conversations*, as well as in *A Book to Burn*. For Li Zhi's attitudes toward Yan Jun, see "Da Zhou Liutang," in *LZ* 1:218–26; *A Book to Burn*, 65–74. For his views on He Xinyin, see "He Xinyin lun," in *LZ* 1:245–51; *A Book to Burn*, 84–88.

10 Several years later, Li Zhi again interacted with Luo Rufang. Li Zhi, "Luo Jinxi xiansheng gaowen," in *LZ* 1:343n36. On Li Zhi's appreciation of Wang Ji's teachings, see also chapter 11.

11 Li Zhi, "Luo Jinxi xiansheng gaowen," in *LZ* 1:339. A letter Li Zhi wrote to Jiao Hong in 1589 exhibits his eagerness to read Wang Ji's complete works as soon as they are published and his conviction that the recorded sayings of Luo Rufang require a discriminating reader. Li Zhi, "Fu Jiao Ruohou," in *LZ* 1:112.

12 Li Zhi, "Luo Jinxi xiansheng gaowen," in *LZ* 1:339; Li Zhi, *A Book to Burn*, 152. On Li Zhi's unfulfilled yearning to die in the company of a cherished friend, see chapter 3. Li Zhi surmises that even Confucius died without successfully transmitting his teachings, since the sage's most promising student, Yan Hui, predeceased him. Li Zhi, "Da Liu Fangbo shu," in *LZ* 1:131; Li Zhi, *A Book to Burn*, 17. See also "Da yi nüren xue dao wei jianduan shu," in *LZ* 1:144; *A Book to Burn*, 31, analyzed in chapter 7.

13 Li Zhi, "Luo Jinxi xiansheng gaowen," in *LZ* 1:340; Li Zhi, *A Book to Burn*, 154.

14 Li Zhi, "Luo Jinxi xiansheng gaowen," in *LZ* 1:341; translation slightly modified from Li Zhi, *A Book to Burn*, 157.

15 Li Zhi, "Fu Jiao Ruohou," in *LZ* 1:112.

16 Elsewhere, Li Zhi claims that the authenticity of his writings derives from the fact that they are rooted in insuppressible emotions ("Za shuo," in *LZ* 1:272–76). For interpretations of this claim and its connection to the concept of authenticity in Li Zhi's oeuvre, see Pauline Lee, *Li Zhi*, 69–99; Handler-Spitz, *Symptoms*, 28–32.

17 Li Zhi, "Luo Jinxi xiansheng gaowen," in *LZ* 1:340; Li Zhi, *A Book to Burn*, 154.

18 Li Zhi, "Wang Longxi xiansheng gaowen," in *LZ* 1:335; Li Zhi, *A Book to Burn*, 148.

19 Li Zhi, "Wang Longxi xiansheng gaowen," in *LZ* 1:335; translation slightly altered from Li Zhi, *A Book to Burn*, 149.

20 Li Zhi, "*Longxi xiansheng wenchao lu* xu," in *LZ* 1:327–29.

21 Wang Yangming was known for encouraging students to question received traditions and is often cited as saying, "If words are examined in the mind and found to be wrong, even if they have come from the mouth of Confucius, I dare not accept them as correct." Wang Yangming, "Da Luo Zheng'an Shaozai shu," 248; Wang Yangming, "Letter in Reply to Vice-Minister Lo Cheng-an," 159. For a similar statement by Li Zhi, see *Dao gu lu*, in *LZ* 14.11.306.

22 According to an anecdote in the *Mencius*, a pair of straw sandals was missing from the hostel where Mencius and his retainers were staying. When asked whether one of his men might have stolen them, Mencius replied, "In setting myself up as a teacher, I do not go after anyone who leaves, nor do I refuse anyone who comes. So long as he comes with the right mindset, I accept him.

That is all" (*Mengzi* 7B30; translation slightly altered from Lau, *Mencius*, 200).

23 Li Zhi, "Luo Jinxi xiansheng gaowen," in *LZ* 1:340; Li Zhi, *A Book to Burn*, 154.

24 Li Zhi, "Luo Jinxi xiansheng gaowen," in *LZ* 1:341; translation slightly altered from Li Zhi, *A Book to Burn*, 157.

25 Li Zhi, "*Longxi xiansheng wenchao lu* xu," in *LZ* 1:327.

26 Li Zhi, "Langzhong Wang gong," in *LZ* 11:113. As Wai-yee Li points out in chapter 1, the notion of an accidental teacher possessing no fixed method resonates strongly with Li Zhi's interpretation of Confucius.

27 Li Zhi, "Wang Longxi xiansheng gaowen," in *LZ* 1:335; Li Zhi, *A Book to Burn*, 147.

28 See chapter 9.

29 Li Zhi, *Dao gu lu*, in *LZ* 14:11.260. Li Zhi's best-known female disciple was Mei Danran, daughter of the prominent statesman Mei Guozhen (1542–1605). Although Li Zhi disavowed his role as her formal mentor, he clearly guided her study of Buddhism. His letters to her and other women of her household are recorded in "Guanyin wen," in *LZ* 2:76–95. In chapter 6, Ying Zhang analyzes the ways in which Li Zhi's interactions with female disciples, especially Mei Danran, complicated his public image. On the influential position of the Mei family in Macheng society, see Rowe, *Crimson Rain*, 85–90.

30 Li Zhi, "He Xinyin lun," in *LZ* 1:245. In this essay Li Zhi extols He Xinyin for his bold disregard of social mores. Li Zhi's hero-worship of He Xinyin, a man he never met, contrasts with his more ambivalent feelings toward his actual teachers, especially Luo Rufang. Perhaps the absence of any real relationship with He Xinyin freed Li Zhi to give full-throated expression to his admiration of this man without fearing compromising his own independence. I am grateful to Haun Saussy for suggesting this idea.

31 Li Zhi, "*Zhengtu yugong* houyu," in *LZ* 2:11–13. *Journeying with Companions* (Zhengtu yugong), a book no longer extant, contained study notes by Li Zhi's son-in-law Zhuang Fengwen (1554–1606) and his study companion, the Ningzhou magistrate Fang Hang (1542–1608). See *LZ* 2:12n1.

32 According to legend, whenever Bo Ya played his zither for his friend Zhongzi Qi, Zhongzi Qi wordlessly understood Bo Ya's subtlest implications, so deep was the empathy of this extraordinary listener and friend. *Liezi*, "Tang wen."

33 Li Zhi's position in this debate is rooted in Wang Yangming's teachings emphasizing the value of attaining understanding for oneself (*zide*).

34 Zhu Changwen, *Qin shi*, 2:12. See also Li Zhi, *A Book to Burn*, 158–59.

35 In this way, Li Zhi's theory is reminiscent of Zhuangzi's parable of Wheelwright Bian. *Zhuangzi*, "Tian dao," *j.* 13.

36 For an English-language description of the pedagogical scene at Dragon Lake, see Rowe, *Crimson Rain*, 95–103.

37 A similarly casual pedagogical environment is described in Li Zhi's preface to *Illuminating Discussions*, "*Dao gu lu* yin," in *LZ* 14:227.

38 Yuan Zhongdao, *Zuolin jitan*, in *LZ* 18:305.1. On the Chan overtones in this text and especially *Answering Questions*, see chapter 9.

39 Yuan Zhongdao, *Zuolin jitan*, in *LZ* 18:312.14.

40 Yuan Zhongdao, *Zuolin jitan*, in *LZ* 18:319.23.

41 Yuan Zhongdao, *Zuolin jitan*, in *LZ* 18:314.17.

42 Li Zhi, "Yu Ma Lishan," in *LZ* 3:11; Li Zhi, "Tongxin shuo," in *LZ* 1:276–79; Li Zhi, *A Book to Burn*, 242, 106–13.

43 Li Zhi, "Xun Qing, Li Si, Wu Gong," in *LZ* 2:210; Li Zhi, *A Book to Burn*, 205.

44 His students, including Mei Danran and Yuan Zhongdao, reciprocated by addressing him in like fashion. See Li Zhi, "Yuyue," in *LZ* 2:105; Li Zhi, "Guanyin wen," in *LZ* 2:76–96; Yuan Zhongdao, *Zuolin jitan*, in *LZ* 18:325.32.

45 In *Answers to Questions*, Luo Rufang's student Yang Qiyuan suggests that the compiler and his friend Wu Shizheng visit Li Zhi. They express trepidation, citing rumors that Li Zhi often lashes out at guests. Li Zhi, *Yongqing dawen*, in *LZ*, 18:1.334. Li Zhi's irascibility was a central part of his public persona and was even deliberately imitated by the author of the spurious "Li Zhuowu" fiction commentaries (see chapter 10). He was also roundly excoriated by early Qing scholars on account of his arrogance (see chapter 11).

46 On Li Zhi's efforts to help students prepare for imperial examinations, see chapter 8.

47 The phrase is borrowed from Hung Mingshui, *The Romantic Vision*. On Yuan Zhongdao's involvement with the Gong'an School, see also Chou, *Yüan Hung-tao*; Zhou Qun, *Yuan Hongdao pingzhuan*, 259–309.

48 Yuan Zhongdao, *Zuolin jitan*, in *LZ* 18:305. Yuan was not unique in writing about Li Zhi in ways that disguised his identity; Li Zhi also wrote about himself anonymously. For analysis of his use of the impersonal term "layman" (*jushi*), see chapter 2.

49 The sylvan location may simply be a literary conceit, as there was an Oak Forest Lake (Zuolin Tan) near Yuan Zhongdao's home in Gong'an. Yuan Zhongdao, "Guan mujiang zhuan," in *Kexuezhai ji*, 2:703. Nonetheless, Li Zhi's preface to *Illuminating Discussions* also emphasizes the remoteness of the locale, Pingshang, where his discussions with Liu Dongxing took place. Li Zhi, "*Dao gu lu* yin," in *LZ* 14:227.

50 Yuan Zhongdao, *Zuolin jitan*, in *LZ* 18:310.10, 18:319.23.

51 Yuan Zhongdao, "Li Wenling zhuan," in *Kexuezhai ji*, 2:724-25; Li Zhi, *A Book to Burn*, 333. For a feisty exchange in which Yuan Zhongdao challenges Li Zhi, see "Shu Xiaoxiu shoujuan hou," in *LZ* 3:201–3; Li Zhi, *A Book to Burn*, 267–69.

PART THREE

MANIPULATIONS OF GENDER

CHAPTER 6

IMAGE TROUBLE, GENDER TROUBLE

Was Li Zhi An Enlightened Man?

YING ZHANG

LI ZHI'S FAME AND NOTORIETY COMBINE TO CREATE AN EXAMPLE of "image trouble": fragmented, polarized images being circulated beyond the individual's control, a reality that troubled many prominent political and cultural figures in the seventeenth century. This image trouble was deeply gendered: as the literati engaged in new intellectual, spiritual, and social explorations on intensely mediatized and mediated platforms, their reputations were often reduced to how such explorations led them to either excel or fail in performing Confucian masculine roles. Li Zhi's case sheds light on the various intersecting developments that gave rise to this historical phenomenon. Intellectual and religious debates at a time of intensified syncretism produced innovative writers and thinkers but also generated more pressure on linguistic, textual, and moral clarity. As established gender ideals were contested or negotiated in society to an unprecedented extent, print culture and social networking helped disseminate information widely but unevenly. All these can be observed in literati reactions to the ways in which Li Zhi—and his enemies and friends—employed gendered language to discuss social norms and literati self-cultivation in published works and circulated letters.[1]

Li Zhi and his audience did not have the digital platforms that saturate our lives today or the convenience of modern mass media. But the sample of texts by and about him that ended up in wide circulation among contemporary readers operated just like the news headlines we live with today. This mechanism led to sensationalism and polarization in the perceptions of and debates about Li Zhi among his contemporaries. In addition, as scholars have pointed out, print proliferation in the late Ming had paradoxical consequences. For instance, it further disseminated Confucian orthodoxy but at the same time undermined its authority by propagating deliberate misreading and creative reinterpretation of canons.[2] This cultural environment was destined to encourage both creativity and abuse. Hence, having an "image problem" was a historical condition and phenomenon that the individuals could not control, even though they could make choices and take action. A product of print culture, Li Zhi both deployed print as a weapon and also fought against its negative impact on his reputation. His image as a man remained at the center of these battles, and his published writings and public correspondence by him, his friends, and his critics reveal the complicated ways in which gender concerns shaped political communication in the late Ming.

A REAL MAN AND HIS GENDER TERMINOLOGY

Li Zhi's use of multiple names and categories for himself in published works manifests an intense desire to clarify and finesse his message about living the life of an enlightened person. Chapters 1 and 2 have shown that it is more productive for us to read his writings as self-exploration than as transparent, consistent confessions.[3] The gendered vocabularies he employed, drawing on and synthesizing different traditions, actually exhibited much intellectual coherence, even though such coherence got lost in readers' minds and in fragmenting media at a time when gender was a destabilized and destabilizing discursive field.

Li Zhi's self-references borrowed from the gendered vocabularies of Buddhism and Confucianism. In *Upon Arrival at the Lake* (Chutanji), explaining why he publishes commentaries on women, he lets his thought come out through the voices of "Li Wenling" and "Zhuo lao":[4]

> Li Wenling comments: Students of the Buddhist truth consider life as suffering; they hope to break away from samsara and reach nirvana. If people cannot break away from the living, they not only indulge themselves in the extremes of sensual pleasures, but also get mired in suffering. Even chaste wives and exemplary daughters, whom Zhuo lao praises and admires as having accomplished what only a *real man* [*zhen nanzi*] could, suffer tremendously from the living. [Zhuo lao] puts three enlightened women's stories at the end of this part of the book to show the sufferings of the living and teach people how to realize the

> ultimate happiness of nirvana. This is in line with his original intention to compile these sections titled "Husband and Wife" [Fufu].[5]

The voice of Li Wenling illuminates the significance of Zhuo lao's writings on women and expresses appreciation for his comments on Buddhist transcendence. But this Li Wenling also explains to the reader that Zhuo lao (also known as Zhuowu and Zhuowu zi) is a true Confucian man despite his shaved head: "Zhuowu had his reasons to shave his head. Although he has shaved to become a monk, he is truly a Confucian. Thus he first compiled Confucian books, and placed morality at the forefront of these books. Zhuowu, more than anyone else, knows how to read Confucian books and illuminate the meaning of morality."[6]

In this text, Li Wenling assumes the voice of the Confucian literatus who recognizes the moral qualities of Zhuo lao, an enlightened Buddhist who does not abandon Confucian morality as his fundamental belief. In the particular intellectual and religious atmosphere of the late sixteenth century, when many literati explicitly advocated the compatibility of Buddhism and Confucianism in their self-cultivation, it was possible for these two affiliations to jointly sustain and enrich the public image of exemplary men.[7] But Li Zhi went further. His texts demanded that the reader suspend the everyday usage of certain gendered terms to appreciate his particular intellectual and spiritual agenda. Take, for example, "real man" (*zhen nanzi*), a key concept in his scholarly and personal writings and a term he applied to both men and women: "Wuji's mother, Ban Zhao, Huang Chao's women followers, Sun Yi's wife, Li Xinsheng, Li Kan's wife and Mother Lü of Haiqu,[8] each of these women can indeed be considered a 'real man' [*zhen nanzi*]. Men are everywhere in the world. [But] how many of those who call themselves 'real men' actually are not 'real men'? And how many men in this world can be considered 'real men'? Unless I used the word 'real' [*zhen*] here, I'd be afraid that ordinary men would think I was just a 'man' [*nanzi*]. This is why I put 'real' in front of 'man.'"[9] Elsewhere in *Upon Arrival at the Lake,* Li Zhi refers to "twenty-five women [who] possessed extraordinary intelligence and sharp vision. If some could have been trusted with important military and political responsibilities, they would have achieved success. That among them, Zhao E, a girl who had no one to depend on, and who single-handedly exacted revenge on the person who had killed her father, is especially amazing. The venerable Li Wenling [*zhangzhe*] remarks: These are *real men* [*zhen nanzi*]! *Real men*! He then comments again: Men [*nanzi*] are inferior [to them]!"[10]

Who are the "men" in this context? Li Zhi complicates this gender category in a famous public letter on women's capacity for learning and enlightenment: "A woman may have a female body but may also have male insights; [she may] appreciate serious teachings and know the bareness of vulgar speech; [she may] delight in learning Buddhist teachings and realize that this floating world is not worth cherishing. I am afraid that before such a woman, today's men [*nanzi*] would feel ashamed and shut their mouths."[11]

But could the boundaries between abstract concepts and everyday usages be kept so neat in real-world life and politics? Li Zhi's repeated attempts to explain his usage of "men" and "real men" only foregrounded the difficulty of demanding terminological clarity. He was not the first to praise some women as better than ordinary or unenlightened men, or to apply to extraordinary women such categories as "manly man," *zhangfu*. The Chinese term *da zhangfu* had been used by Buddhist masters to refer to "honorary men" or "great men" who possessed the ideal qualities that could be attained by both men and women. But as Beata Grant argues, the application of the term *da zhangfu* to male and female Buddhists shows "a range of ambivalent, and sometimes confused ideas which point to a continued awareness of, and unease about, the misfit between a universal and non-dualistic metaphysical vision of ultimate reality and the traditional gendered binary divisions and hierarchies central to the traditional Chinese social order."[12] Meanwhile, engaging Confucian ideals through creative and deliberately vague use of categories was also a defining feature of gender discourse during this time.[13] Therefore, writing at the intersection of popular and intellectual understandings of Buddhist and Confucian gender terms, which had already made contemporary gender discourse volatile, Li Zhi's use of the locution *zhen nanzi* to illuminate the meaning of self-cultivation was apt to earn both praise and criticism.

At the risk of committing historical mind reading, let us take a step further and consider the implications of Li Zhi's experiments with gendered vocabulary. In his published works, he reserved the category "real man" mostly for historical and contemporary women who excelled in their intelligence and morality. The only male historical figure he praised as a "real man" in his massive historical work *A Book to Keep (Hidden)* is Lin Xiangru, an official and strategist during the Warring States Period (fifth century–221 BCE), whose intelligence and bravery prevailed against the mighty king of Qin. Li Zhi considered Lin a "real man" and a "true sage" and also referred to him as a "bodhisattva" and even a "Buddha."[14] Here, the "real man" as a category identifies a superior kind of masculine person; its usefulness lies in taking the question beyond conventional gender distinctions while still managing to signify a gendered superiority. When Li Zhi repeatedly called himself a "real man" while rarely applying this category to other men, he boosted its gendered value and unambiguously asserted his own accomplishments as a superior man.

Real-life consequences of manipulating gender terms can be detected in people's strong reactions to Li Zhi's use of two other terms that he liked to apply to himself: *daren* and *zhangzhe*. *Daren* is a respectful salutation used when addressing elders or men of noble character and lofty aspirations. *Zhangzhe* refers to venerable male elders and influential figures. Unambiguously masculine, these terms highlight seniority and moral and spiritual superiority, valued qualities of literati manhood. When Li Zhi used these words to refer to himself, he differentiated himself from unenlightened men and drew attention to the heights of self-cultivation he had attained. But his usage of these terms deliberately isolated the age factor and, deviating from the conventional understanding, granted older men—or more precisely, himself—the right to practice self-cultivation without engaging in Confucian ethical relations. For neo-Confucians who believed in coherent, consistent, and interconnected moral-spiritual efforts throughout one's life, the implication of this kind of terminological manipulation was ontologically and socially dangerous. This was especially clear in Li Zhi's uncomfortable position vis-à-vis the discourse of filial piety.

Arguably the most important masculine virtue for the literati, filial piety went beyond taking care of one's parents and performing filial rites diligently. By the end of the sixteenth century, Confucian thinkers had become increasingly convinced that filial piety was not only central to moral cultivation but also critical to comprehending the ultimate truth and sagehood.[15] Li Zhi did not oppose upholding this ethical ideal in everyday life; in fact, as Maram Epstein demonstrates in chapter 2, his writing represented him as the embodiment of this virtue.[16] But he also argued that because he was a *daren* who had reached an advanced age and had fully grasped the spiritual value of filial piety, he no longer needed to pursue self-cultivation by fulfilling familial roles. After all, adhering to form was superficial and inferior to living in accordance with the *essence* of Confucian ethical ideals. The idea underlying Li Zhi's self-expression as a senior, enlightened man reflected the influence of the Yangming School, which privileged individualized, authentic articulation of the true spirit of Confucian teachings rather than superficial study or display. But this way of thinking disturbed many prominent Confucian thinkers, including some within the Yangming School in the late Ming, who became increasingly vigilant about the potential fallout of downplaying everyday performance of Confucian ethics. For instance, the scholar-official Geng Dingxiang repeatedly discussed the dangerous implications of Li Zhi's claim that cultivating virtues such as filial piety was of minor concern and necessary only for youths (*dizi*), not for mature adult men (*daren*). In a letter, Geng criticizes some people's misunderstanding of a line from the *Analects*, "Young people should be filial at home, brotherly with others" (Dizi ru ze xiao, chu ze ti),"[17] partly in response to Li Zhi's argument that traditional educational material such as "duties of juniors" (*dizi zhi*)—as well as books about familial duties—was proper for boys younger than fifteen; adults should study the universal truth.[18]

Li Zhi's realignment of the age factor with the ideal of manhood was not merely terminological, nor did it appear only in his writings; he embodied this idea in his life. He sent his wife back to Quanzhou in 1587 and shaved his head in Macheng in 1588. These actions, which demonstrate his dedication to his intellectual and spiritual endeavors, immediately alarmed local critics, who described him as someone who had "cast aside human ethics and abandoned his wife" (*qi renlun li qishi*). But Li Zhi repeatedly maintained that his actions did not amount to "abandonment," citing his age as the main factor. In response to a local literatus who expressed a desire to model himself after Li Zhi, he replied that an old man like him, who had already fulfilled his familial duties, could live as a monk and did not have to be burdened with "mundane affairs" (*sushi*). He told this young friend that he should not abandon his familial responsibilities but instead pursue self-cultivation at home.[19] He used half of the letter to discuss his own life experience so as to show that, before shaving his head, he had made steady and significant progress in self-cultivation by doing his utmost to fulfill his public duties as an official and his familial roles as a son and husband.[20] According to this self-portrayal, before he shaved his head Li Zhi lived in a perfectly neo-Confucian way by pursuing a kind of "mundane transcendence" based on critical reflection on and engagement with his everyday sociopolitical responsibilities and roles.[21]

Li Zhi even employed Confucius as his model to justify his terminological maneuver around age and his choice to pursue a style of self-cultivation that increasingly appeared Buddhist. "We don't hear that Confucius remarried; neither do we hear that he took concubines. Confucius was quite uninterested in conjugal intimacy," he writes to a longtime friend.[22] To his key critic, Geng Dingxiang, Li Zhi retorted that he had had four sons but that they had all died. If even Confucius, after the death of his son, had not remarried or tried to take a concubine, on what grounds could Geng find fault with Li? Was he not pursuing the Way in the very same manner that Confucius had?[23]

In these ways, Li Zhi employed various gendered vocabularies available at the time—social, metaphysical, neo-Confucian, and Buddhist—to articulate an enlightened man's view on life and self-cultivation. His image problem partly resulted from the tensions among these vocabularies and from their complex usages. His multiple names, obsessive explanations of categories, and repetitive invocations of theories and precedents reveal his struggle to grapple with the reality that not all his readers accepted his terminological system. In addition to the difficulty of achieving linguistic clarity or terminological coherence in this volatile intellectual and religious environment, when words could travel widely and quickly in print and were received by an audience that indulged in liberal reading (as Li Zhi himself did), an author who believed he had the ultimate authority to interpret his own words and control his image was just fooling himself.

TEXTUAL AND SEXUAL SCANDALS

Li Zhi's image trouble cannot be reduced to a generalized backlash from the so-called Confucian conservatives, as is clear from the difficulties he encountered in manipulating gender terminology to express his ideas. Further complicating this challenge was the intersection of late-Ming print culture with gender discourse. While rumors, exaggeration, speculation, and facts mingled in the controversies surrounding Li Zhi, the bits and pieces most cited focused on his gender behavior. Li Zhi himself contributed to his image trouble by publicizing an "antihypocrisy" self-image using provocative gender rhetoric.[24]

The most notorious example is Li Zhi's published letter to Zhou Hongyue, a Macheng native who had served as a metropolitan official and written to express criticism of Li Zhi. In the letter Li Zhi explains the relationship between his intellectual-spiritual exploration and his "deviant" behavior, using his own experience to illustrate a path to enlightenment. He mentions that, after he had moved to Macheng, he turned himself into a free spirit and even visited brothels in his pursuit of the Way. But he realized that living as a recluse in temporary retreat did not yield true enlightenment. Nor did his experiments with alternative methods of self-cultivation—such as "visiting brothels" (*churu yu huajie liushi zhijian*)—bring him peace of mind because Confucians reviled such behavior. Therefore, he resorted to an extreme strategy: "If I shave my head and ruin my appearance, I will be loathed not only by the Confucians but by the masses as well."[25]

But Li Zhi's readers might have paid attention not to his spiritual agenda but to the public acknowledgment that he had experimented with lifestyles, from seclusion to fooling around to head shaving. The explosive image of "visiting brothels" in particular proved to be distracting. In her analysis of the controversies caused by these words, Jin Jiang has argued that this passage demonstrates how Li Zhi, inspired by the example of Vimalakīrti, at some point associated "commoners and their presumably carefree lifestyle, symbolized by wine and sex," with "nature, enlightenment, and health." She suggests that Li Zhi tried to "legitimize such 'deviation' [from] orthodox morality" and that this "action of theorization" could constitute an offense to the Confucian elite who single-mindedly stressed moral behavior.[26] William Theodore de Bary suggests that, to his "sophisticated" readers, Li Zhi might have adopted the "epicurean attitude toward sexual indulgence" preached by some Buddhist monks to show that indulgence is empty.[27] If modern historians cannot agree on how to read Li Zhi's message here, one can imagine how his contemporary audience reacted. Just which Buddhist idea inspired him and his rhetoric is not our main concern here. More important is the fact that even had he meant to use "visiting brothels" as a Buddhist rhetorical device to convey an "innocent" method of spiritual transcendence, his readers not only fixated on this small detail in a long letter but also insisted on different readings, just as they did with the gender terms he manipulated.

Hence, to understand Li Zhi's increasingly polarized public image as either exemplary or licentious, we need to take seriously the heterogeneity of the readership and the fragmenting effects of media. Those who defended the superiority of neo-Confucianism to Buddhism for literati self-cultivation and those who dismissed or even condemned Buddhist learning as misleading and altogether corrupting would definitely denounce Li Zhi's rhetoric and approach manifested in this letter. Prominent Buddhist masters condemned him, not for his alleged immoral behavior but for his egoistic performance, a misleading model for others.[28] Meanwhile, among Li Zhi enthusiasts, some truly appreciated his approach on both intellectual and spiritual levels; some did not fully comprehend but nonetheless cited him freely for their own purposes. When these readers, either opposing or supporting him, circulated excerpts of this letter, the context of the exchange got lost. What spread most quickly and most widely tended to be catchy, sensational, and provocative selections that fed opposing perceptions of him. Li Zhi's close friend and official Yuan Hongdao reported:

> Throughout his life, Li Zhi detested hypocritical teachings. When he went to the academy or lecture hall, he would put on his Confucian scholar outfit. If a student went up to him with questions about the Classics, he would wave his sleeves and say, "Oh, I would rather spend time with singing girls and dancing ladies, sipping wine and singing songs." Once he saw a student walking up with a prostitute. He smiled and said, "This is at least better than having a Confucian scholar as company." Therefore, in Macheng and Huang'an counties, the lecturers hated him to the bone. Thus appeared the malicious charge that he preached indecency and corrupted society.[29]

To further explore the centrality of the questions of perception and sensationalism, I shall now return to examine more closely the famous debate between Li Zhi and the retired official, his old friend Geng Dingxiang. Geng grew increasingly concerned about how Li Zhi *was understood* much more than what Li actually meant to preach. On the surface, Geng's opposition to Li seemed similar to his attitude toward Deng Huoqu and Fang Yilin, two prominent figures who had created an uproar in the recent history of the Huang'an-Macheng area. Deng and Fang became devoted Buddhist teachers and as a result left their familial responsibilities behind. Geng harshly denounced Deng's teachings as "encouraging sensual pursuits and abandoning self-discipline" and therefore extremely threatening to social stability.[30] Li Zhi's life decisions generated an obviously similar image: head-shaving, traveling, abandoning familial responsibilities, promoting Buddhism, and preaching the legitimacy of human desire. But Li Zhi was more dangerous than the other two because he had published so much more. Geng realized that Li's words, especially those concerning literati masculine ideals, were read in wildly different ways by readers who had varied intellectual capacities, intentions, and interests. In the aftermath of Li's head-shaving, for instance, Geng wrote off those who obsessively speculated or opined on why Li decided to shave his head, dismissing them as "pointlessly fussing over the hair" because they mistakenly framed the incident as a man choosing between Buddhism and Confucianism.[31] Geng told others that a shaved head meant different things to men who harbored different aspirations; Li was but one ambitious man trying to achieve his particular intellectual and spiritual goals through this action.[32] Intellectual differences aside, Geng was annoyed and worried that most of the audience of Li's spectacle were not equipped to critically appreciate his project; their weakness drove them to disseminate and follow what they *believed to be* his position, namely, abandoning Confucian ethical expectations. Indeed, when young men in their community had begun enlisting Li's words to justify their own pursuit of sensual pleasures or self-indulgence, Geng's worst nightmare came true.

While Geng Dingxiang focused on how Li Zhi's dramatic actions were received by a shallow audience, Li saw this controversy as an open debate between him and Geng on a public stage as representatives of two *intellectual* camps.[33] Li's spin successfully shaped how the literati of the time understood the difference between these two men: they saw Geng as an advocate of Confucian moral teaching (*mingjiao*), whereas they regarded Li as a teacher of universal truth (*zhenji*).[34] Li's letters to his friends portrayed Geng as taking an intellectual debate so personally as to organize attacks against him based on fabricated rumors of his immorality.[35]

Geng, in the meantime, was disturbed by this false dichotomy Li put forth. Earlier, Geng had indeed tried to debate metaphysical and epistemological issues with Li, but soon he seemed to shift his attention to the reading public's perceptions of Li. He concentrated his efforts on explaining how Li should *not* be interpreted, hoping that this might help limit his influence on local youths. Geng's comment on Li's head-shaving is a good example. Another example can be found in Geng's letter to Zhou Sijiu, an old friend of Li Zhi's, on the news that Li had bragged about hanging out with prostitutes and encouraged local youths to follow suit. In this letter, Geng clearly laid out what he considered to be the real stakes:

> As to the question of hanging out with prostitutes [*xiaji zhi shi*], that might be fine in Zhuowu's [Li Zhi's] case, but it is not proper for you. *I insist on [making] this distinction. The distinction has large and small implications that are difficult to explain in a letter. But let me try to explain briefly. Zhuowu's intellectual endeavors only need to solve his own problems; they are not meant to help others. We should simply let him be.* But can you, a widely influential figure in our hometown, set an example like this for young men? That would destroy them! I can imagine when Zhuowu hears what I am saying here, he will probably mock me again. That doesn't matter. But you have only one son. His physical energies are not fully controlled yet. Where do you want to direct him with this kind of teaching?[36]

Since the late Ming, much has been written about the debate—especially its intellectual aspects—between Geng Dingxiang and Li Zhi, some of which took place in their correspondence with shared friends. We should also consider how Geng's approach to Confucian learning shaped his reaction to Li as a media phenomenon. Fundamentally, Geng was a practical man.[37] In the local community, he advocated education and scholarship that emphasized filial piety and fraternal respect so that youths would not consider their families a burden or detest Confucianism as if it were nothing but a set of rigid rules.[38] In the government, he worried about corruption, irresponsibility, and bad politics. Interestingly, he had voiced opposition to a recent trend in political communication among officials: lodging personal attacks based on rumors of sexual immorality, to which Li Zhi himself fell victim.[39] Geng's emphasis on the practical naturally led him to pay more attention to the literati's *perception* of Li than to what Li actually intended to do.

None of this seemed to have mattered. Neither Li Zhi nor Geng Dingxiang could control the direction of the debate. As Timothy Brook points out, Li Zhi's notoriety "derived in part from his skill in getting his books into circulation and read. Even his letters with prominent debating partners he got into print as soon as he was able to collect enough for publication."[40] Overexposure in print operated as a double-edged sword. Li Zhi's letters responding to Geng Dingxiang, published in the best-seller *A Book to Burn*, for instance, popularized his image as a truly enlightened person and victim of hypocritical Confucians, a framing that Geng had resisted. In the meantime, Li began to face more aggressive threats from Geng's self-proclaimed supporters, who portrayed him as a heretic and an immoral man.[41] In 1591, the hostility toward Li Zhi in Macheng ran so high that, during a trip he took to nearby Wuchang with Yuan Hongdao, he was physically assaulted and chased out of town. It took the efforts of many patron-friends to secure his return to the area.

Still, Li Zhi was reluctant to surrender to the reality that authors lacked the power to control the reception of their printed words, even if the subject matter involved women or sexual morality. Earlier we examined how the multiple gender vocabularies employed by the literati in the late Ming created new opportunities for self-expression but also created problems based on competing interpretations. In Li Zhi's alleged "sexual scandal" in Macheng, publicizing his writings to openly celebrate cavorting with women in the name of Buddhist learning simply did not convey an image of enlightenment or moral superiority. Instead it invited image trouble.

Mei Danran, one of the Macheng gentry women who discussed Buddhist learning with Li Zhi, was the second daughter of Mei Guozhen, Li Zhi's friend and a scholar-official who became famous across the empire for supervising a successful military campaign on the northern frontier in 1592. Mei Danran devoted herself to Buddhist studies after she was widowed at a young age. Mei Guozhen supported his daughter's spiritual pursuits. According to the local history, "[Mei Guozhen] was familiar with Buddhist teachings in his late years. His daughter Mei Danran became a stay-at-home nun during her widowhood. Mei Guozhen made no attempt to prohibit her from doing so. Mei Danran strictly observed the moral rules and reached a notable level of accomplishment in her Buddhist pursuits. *Father and daughter also discussed Buddhist teachings in their correspondence.*"[42] In the late Ming, a young widow from a prestigious gentry family could earn respect for her piety and chastity by devoutly pursuing Buddhism as long as she did not violate Confucian behavioral norms.[43]

If women practicing Buddhism was commonplace in late-Ming Macheng, why did Mei Danran and other women of the Mei family attract gossip and criticism for corresponding with Li Zhi to discuss Buddhist teachings? Obviously, these criticisms targeted Li Zhi, who touted his presence in these women's self-cultivation, even though it was only "textual." Some locals threatened to tear down the monastery that Li Zhi's rich friend had renovated and let him inhabit.[44] Li Zhi insisted in letters to friends that he was a victim of attacks launched by men who disapproved of women's learning. To those who suggested forcing him to return to his hometown to "restore morality" (*zheng fenghua*) in Macheng, he insisted, again citing his advanced age, that he was but an old monk who posed no threat to the moral order.[45]

Then he resorted to print. In 1596, responding to rumors about his motives for interacting with the Mei women, Li Zhi published *Questions of Guanyin*, a compilation of his letters to the women over several years, in which he discussed Buddhist learning and praised the moral and spiritual accomplishments of his female correspondents. He also wrote a series of letters and essays arguing that women were fully capable of seriously studying Buddhist teachings and used this to justify his association with these women. To his way of thinking, his correspondence with Mei Danran epitomized his moral exemplarity and enlightenment. Not only did he continue to correspond with the Mei women; more important, the publication of *Questions of Guanyin* was a slap in the face of his attackers delivered before the reading public.

The same year that the controversial *Questions of Guanyin* went into print, Li Zhi drafted a list of principles concerning the management of his monastery and the performance of Buddhist rituals in the essay "An Agreement in Advance" (Yuyue), which he immediately circulated to his literati-official friends in and outside Macheng.[46] In this public document, he again employed the concept of the "real man" to discuss his association with Mei Danran:

> Mei Danran is an enlightened *zhangfu*. Although she was born a woman, men [*nanzi*] cannot easily surpass her. She has devoted herself to learning the Buddhist Way and has demonstrated accomplishment in this. I have no worries. She has never formally made me her mentor—she knows that I do not want to become a mentor, but she often sends people from thirty *li* away to ask me questions about Buddhism. How could I not respond even if I'd prefer not to! She self-effacingly treats me in the proper manner befitting a mentor. So even though I will not take in one single disciple, I can scarcely leave her requests unanswered. Therefore, in our correspondence on Buddhist learning, she calls me *shi* [master or teacher] and I address her as *Danran shi* [Master Danran] in order to avoid violating my principle of not mentoring.[47]

In this essay Li Zhi also refers to Mei Danran and some of the other Mei women with whom he communicated as bodhisattvas (*pusa*). He states that it is rare even among "extraordinary men" (*qi nanzi*) to demonstrate as much persistence as these women in their Buddhist study. They truly deserve respect. He blames his attackers for denying women's ability to learn: "Because these bodhisattvas were born as women, relatives who envy them spread gossip too disgraceful to listen to."[48] By defining the nature of this scandal as "family gossip" promulgated by men too ignorant to comprehend the Way, Li Zhi portrays himself as an innocent victim and urges readers of his texts to regard him as an enlightened master of unimpeachable moral standing. Curiously, he rarely promoted himself as a master for male disciples of Buddhism; instead he only discussed these exemplary women disciples. His usage of the category "real man" followed the same pattern. Thus, his publications and public letters might effectively reinforce the impression that he was interested only in pursuing opportunities to interact with gentry women.

Indeed, perceptions of Li Zhi's correspondence with gentry women were key to this textual-sexual scandal. It is interesting that the friendly narrative in the local history quoted earlier chooses to highlight the correspondence about Buddhist learning between the Mei father and daughter, a completely proper and admirable domestic interaction, while omitting the well-known correspondence between Li Zhi and Mei Danran. Likely an editorial effort to sanitize the reputation of the Mei family, this small detail reveals how sensitive the question of "correspondence" became in this scandal. A widespread story at the time about Li Zhi's attempt to approach a local female poet, Mao Yulong (n.d.), also drew attention to correspondence. In a biography of Li Zhi composed after his death, Qian Qianyi (1582–1664) quoted the following anecdote from the official Zhou Hongyue, the Macheng native we encountered earlier: "Madam [Mao] worshipped the Buddha in her later years. She followed the commandments and sought a life of compassion and tranquility. A master [Li Zhi] visiting this region riled up a lot of men and women by preaching transcendence and what he considered the most sophisticated Buddhist teachings. He informed Madam Mao that he wished to visit her in person. She rejected his proposal. He then asked to correspond with her. This she also refused."[49]

Although Zhou Hongyue thought Li Zhi's "deviant" behavior and his zeal for Buddhist learning would bring disaster upon society,[50] he did not object to women's pursuit of Buddhist studies or literary activities. According to the local gazetteer, from the mid-Ming on, this area produced many talented and exemplary women. Zhou's own wife, along with the poet Madam Mao, enjoyed respect and a high literary reputation.[51] What Zhou Hongyue—and authors like Qian Qianyi—passed along was a popular perception of Li Zhi as seeking opportunities to interact with women in the name of promoting Buddhist self-cultivation, and this image repulsed even those who considered women's learning and Buddhist pursuits legitimate. The emphasis on the chaste Madam Mao's refusal to correspond with Li Zhi in this anecdote is particularly revealing. A textual scandal made a sexual scandal seem likely.

Hence, the more Li Zhi wrote about these women and published accounts of his interactions with them, the more damaged his image became. Finally, the textual-sexual scandal surrounding the Mei women led to his forced exile from the Huang'an-Macheng area. From 1596 to 1600, Li Zhi traveled to Shanxi, Nanjing, and Shandong, where his patron-friends held important official positions and provided him with a comfortable material and intellectual environment. He composed many poems during this period, including flower poems, most of which, interestingly enough, evoked plum blossoms. These poems, with their conventional literary tropes, often situated him in a textually romantic relationship with plum flowers.[52] Considering that the Chinese name for plum flowers, *mei*, is the family name of Mei Danran, these poems undoubtedly sent a mixed message. Toward the end of this long trip away from Macheng, Li Zhi wrote four more flower poems directly to Mei Danran in response to her letters trying to persuade him to return to Macheng. One reads:

> Flying snow in the wind lightly brushes through
> Plum flowers wear the rain like rouge on a beautiful face
> Busy visitors at the door are not worth mentioning
> The cuckoo is calling Spring to return.

Another says:

> You are the Guanyin we long to see
> The lotus flower belongs to the beautiful one.[53]

Although these poems could easily be cited as damaging evidence against him, Li Zhi nonetheless included them in an expanded edition of *A Book to Burn*, which was published in Jiangnan in 1600 and became an instant hit in literati society. When he returned to Macheng months later, local opponents had rekindled the flames of persecution, based on the charge that "monks and nuns were engaging in immoral activities."[54] After they burned down his monastery, destroyed his pagoda, and forced him into hiding, he took refuge in the mountains until his patron-friend Ma Jinglun came to help. If earlier they had let him get away with outlandish rhetoric that could be "misread" by ignorant young men, this time, when Li Zhi publicly and persistently advertised his frequent interactions with gentry women, they could not tolerate such provocation. Not only did they insist that he should be deprived of the right to publish on the subject of women, but they also fulminated that he had to be expelled from the community for good.

The diversity of the late-Ming intellectual and spiritual world generated an ideal platform for new explorations but also put tremendous pressure on linguistic, rhetorical, and moral clarity. The prevalence of print and its operational patterns in the late Ming contributed to these developments. Li Zhi became a sensation by widely publicizing novel commentaries on Confucian classics, official histories, popular literature, and social phenomena as a way of diagnosing the causes and culprits of "moral decline" of his era. However, his effort to elucidate true moral teachings and ways to lead the life of an enlightened person reached most of his audience in printed segments or gossip. His iconoclastic writing style and strong desire to publicize his ideas met a perfect match in the "unruly" audience that freely interpreted and cited his words. As a result, his words and actions came under attack as the very cause and symptom of late-Ming moral decline.

In a sense, Li Zhi was caught in a perfect storm. Years of experimenting with names, terms, and methods of self-cultivation in writing as well as many best-selling, provocative publications of scholarship and personal correspondence did not amount to greater clarity or persuasion in his messaging. At the peak of his fame, he was fighting against the vast discrepancy between his claim of enlightenment and his perceived image as a moral threat—an irresponsible husband, a licentious womanizer disguised as an enlightened master. In the meantime, during the last decade of the sixteenth century, literati-officials who actively pursued Buddhism could face the serious criticism that Buddhist exploration prevented them from fully engaging in the study and practice of Confucian statecraft.[55] In addition, escalating political factionalism, made messier by print culture and the sensationalism it fed, compelled officials to scrutinize opponents' personal lives for any impeachable behaviors.[56]

It is particularly revealing that in the last months of his life, Li Zhi turned to the most conservative rhetoric of male self-discipline to fight for his life. Not long before his imprisonment, he wrote in an essay recalling a conversation with Yuan Zhongdao, "Throughout my life I have been obsessed with cleanliness. Things such as alcohol, sex, and money in the mundane world cannot pollute me one bit. I am seventy-five this year. I have done nothing that would cause me to fear the scrutiny of ghosts and deities."[57] This rhetoric of purity and lack of desire could be found in both Confucian and Buddhist discourses on self-cultivation. But painting Li Zhi as a Confucian moral exemplar became critical to his friends' efforts to defend him in an increasingly precarious situation. It was a key argument after his arrest, which quickly ensued once the censor Zhang Wenda submitted his famous memorial blasting Li Zhi as a threat to social order.[58]

The official Ma Jinglun, who made the greatest effort to rescue Li Zhi, emphasized Li's commitment to Confucian ethics. To his colleagues, Ma forcefully argued that a man like Li, who had devoted his life to intellectual and spiritual exploration, could not possibly have enjoyed inappropriate intimacy with women: "How can a man who dedicates all his energy to scholarly work and has published almost a hundred books indulge himself in sexual immorality? I need not mention his old age. Even a young man seriously engaged in study will not be interested in women. Young men who like women invariably dislike study. People consider Li Zhi's writing a crime; they charge him with sexual immorality. They criticize his head-shaving and accuse him of seduction. These charges contradict one another and are truly ridiculous!"[59] Ma Jinglun's defense presumed—and in effect helped perpetuate the idea—that a literatus's dedication to scholarly life in the company of fellow (male) scholars could not coexist with an interest in women and sex. Contradicting Li Zhi's own previous confession, Ma chose to ignore Li's sensational experiments and instead argued that his dedication to and passion for scholarship excluded the possibility of sexual indulgence.

Further, Ma's defense connected the masculine virtue of loyalty to self-discipline. In several letters addressed to colleagues on behalf of Li Zhi, he vehemently dismissed the charges against Li as vicious fabrications employed for political purposes. In a letter to an official in charge, he argued that the accusations of Li Zhi as "a deluder of society" (*huoshi*) who "blatantly engaged in sexual immorality" (*xuanyin*) were launched for political reasons.[60] He believed that the honorable official Mei Guozhen was the real target of the attacks and that Li Zhi was simply a convenient sideshow. Contrasting Li with womanizers and fame-chasers among his colleagues, Ma presented him as a true Confucian exemplar and model official: "Men in this world enjoy official positions as if they were candy. If they do not sleep with a woman for even a few days they feel as if they may expire. They even put on makeup, seeking to attract their superiors' attention if just briefly or to gain a moment's intimacy with their concubines. These habits have become the fashion; even worthy men succumb. Don't they feel any shame when they compare themselves to Li Zhi's spotless conduct?"[61]

Ma Jinglun's construction of this ideal image for Li Zhi is not as formulaic as it appears. Li Zhi was a vocal proponent of the cult of *qing* and was championed as a leading figure of this discourse, which also drew inspiration from Yangming neo-Confucianism.[62] His seemingly incoherent rhetoric in fact was quite consistent on one matter: the form self-cultivation took was less important to him than the sincere, meaningful pursuit of true enlightenment. Accordingly, he experimented in writing and everyday life, including reworking gendered vocabularies in Confucian and Buddhist cultures and exposing the superficiality of the existing moral curriculum by—at least rhetorically—breaking behavioral norms. In contrast, though heavily influenced by the Yangming School as well, Ma adopted an unmistakably ascetic approach. He advocated restraining one's desires and emotions and cultivating sagehood by cultivating *wuqing* (literally, "no desires" or "no emotions"). He once argued, "A great man who wants to succeed in great undertakings must keep his own body clean; a wife and concubines are the heaviest burden."[63] His vocabulary reflected an important internal development in seventeenth-century neo-Confucianism: scholars who shared many similarities with the radicals of the Yangming School theorized and practiced a new kind of "extreme moralism."[64] Ma's enthusiastic defense of Li, depicting him as a conventional exemplar of manly self-discipline, was in line with his own approach to self-cultivation. Although the efforts to "correct" Li Zhi's image eventually failed to save his life, the gendered moralistic rhetoric it employed helped create one of the images of Li Zhi that we have inherited from the seventeenth century.

The extraordinary friendship between Li Zhi and Ma Jinglun aptly illustrates the rich texture of history beneath the seemingly cliché image of the ideal Confucian man.[65] Indeed, nothing was straightforward in the colorful world of the late Ming, when the web of information and exchange became much more varied, dense, and intense than before. Precisely because of this, simplification became an inevitable, destabilizing part of life; so did polarization of the images of prominent men along the axis of gender. This paradoxical situation appears oddly familiar to us at this historical juncture.

NOTES

1 On these phenomena, see Ko, *Teachers of the Inner Chamber*; Handler-Spitz, *Symptoms*.

2 See, for example, Bai, introduction to *Fu Shan's World*; Yuming He, *Home and the World*.

3 Chapter 1 shows the inner tensions and contradictions in Li Zhi's discussion of genuineness. Additionally, Pauline Lee argues that the names Zhuowu and Duwu allowed him to embody an ethic of genuineness (*Li Zhi*, 22–24).

4 On the source of the names Wenling and Zhuowu, see chapter 2.

5 Li Zhi, *Chutanji*, in *LZ* 12:127, emphasis added.

6 Li Zhi, "*Chutanji* xu," in *LZ* 12:1, emphasis added.

7 Brook, *Praying for Power*, esp. ch. 2. See also chapter 9 of the present volume.

8 To preserve her son from likely disaster, Wuji's mother never revealed to him that the powerful Wang family had killed his father. Ban Zhao wisely chose to stay away from the emperor to avoid trouble in the imperial house. Sun Yi's wife plotted to kill the men who had murdered her husband. Li Xinsheng, a courtesan, tried to persuade her master not to follow a rebel. Li Kan's wife reproached him for not taking on the responsibilities of a county magistrate. Mother Lü of Haiqu spent all of her fortune over a period of some years, determined to recruit young men to kill the county official who had wrongfully executed her son.

9 Li Zhi, "Fufu lun si," in *LZ* 12:115.

10 Li Zhi, "Fufu lun er," in *LZ* 12:43.

11 Li Zhi, "Da yi nüren xue dao wei jianduan shu," in *LZ* 1:144. See also chapter 7.

12 Grant, *"Da Zhangfu,"* 186.

13 For example, in *The Libertine's Friend* Giovanni Vitiello has characterized the discourse on male-male relations in early modern Chinese literature as syncretic.

14 Li Zhi's comments in the section "Zhongcheng dachen," in *LZ* 5:95.

15 Lu Miaw-fen, *Xiao zhi tianxia*.

16 Again, on the genuine and the filial in Li Zhi's self-image, see chapter 2.

17 *Analects*, 1:6; Watson, *The Analects*, 16.

18 Geng Dingxiang, "Yu Zhou Liutang," in *Geng Dingxiang xiansheng wenji*, 3:54b–55b. See also see Li Zhi, "Da Geng Sikou," in *LZ* 1:71. On the correspondence between Geng Dingxiang and Li Zhi, see chapter 4.

19 Li Zhi, "Yu Zeng Jiquan," in *LZ* 1:129.

20 On Li Zhi's abandonment of his family, see chapters 2 and 3.

21 I adopt this term from Hawes, "Mundane Transcendence."

22 Li Zhi, "Fu Deng Shiyang," in *LZ* 1:27. For more on this question, see chapter 3.

23 Li Zhi, "Da Geng Sikou," in *LZ* 1:76–77. For a discussion on the question of male fidelity, see Hinsch, "The Emotional Underpinnings."

24 William Theodore de Bary suggests that Li Zhi appealed to "the taste for sensational and shocking literature" among the reading public of the late Ming ("Li Chih," 259). Also see Ge, *Zhongguo sixiang shi*, 2:328.

25 Li Zhi, "Da Zhou Erlu," in *LZ* 1:214. This letter was written around 1588. Li Zhi clearly invokes the *Daodejing* here.

26 Jin Jiang, "Heresy and Persecution," 14. It should be noted that the image of the layman Vimalakīrti in Chinese Buddhism had been transfigured to help reinforce the masculine virtues of the Confucian gentry and had had great appeal for literati since the early medieval period. See, for example, Ch'en, *Buddhism in China*, ch. 7.

27 De Bary, "Li Chih," 263.

28 De Bary, "Li Chih," 263–64. On Li Zhi's connections to Buddhism, see chapter 9.

29 Qian Qianyi, "Yiren san ren," in *Liechao shiji xiao zhuan*, 744. On Li Zhi's relationships to his teachers and students, see chapter 5.

30 For example, see Geng Dingxiang's letters to friends in *Geng Tiantai xiansheng wenji* (1970): "Yu Zhou Liutang," 314–69, and "Yu Wu Shaoyu," 377–93. In addition, his biographies of these men emphasize their deviance: Deng Huoqu did not return home to formally mourn his father's death, did not arrange his daughter's marriage, and instead indulged in a homosexual relationship with a young male servant surnamed Zhu. Geng Dingxiang

highlights that Fang Yilin too neglected his responsibility as a husband and abandoned his wife. Geng Dingxiang, "Lizhong san yiren," in *Geng Tiantai xiansheng wenji* (1970), 1621–48. Also see Shimada, "Ijin Tōkatsukyo ryakuden."

31 Geng Dingxiang, "Yu Zhou Liutang."

32 Geng Dingxiang, "Yu Zhou Liutang."

33 Li Zhi, "Da Geng Sikou." See also chapter 4.

34 Geng Dingxiang, "Da Zhou Liutang," in *Geng Tiantai xiansheng wenji* (Library of Congress), 3:54b. I thank Jiang Wu for an inspiring exchange on Buddhist elements in Li's writings.

35 Lin Haiquan, *Li Zhi nianpu kaolüe*, 226–27. Some historians argue that Geng Dingxiang (like many in the government and later the Donglin camp) increasingly tilted toward a moralistic stance in the face of the widespread social unrest and encouraged these attacks against Li Zhi. For example, Jin Jiang, "Heresy and Persecution."

36 Geng Dingxiang, "Yu Zhou Liutang," 3.57a–58b, emphasis added. Geng Dingxiang is referring to *Analects* 16.7, where Confucius says this about manhood: "There are three things which the superior man guards against. In youth, when his energies are not fully controlled yet, he guards against lust. When he is strong and the physical powers are full of vigor, he guards against quarrelsomeness. When he is old, and the animal powers are decayed, he guards against covetousness."

37 Huang Zongxi's intellectual history of the Ming points out that Geng Dingxiang never aimed to engage in the metaphysical aspect of Confucian studies. He believes that Geng tried to root his words firmly in the most fundamental and practical Confucian teachings when debating with Li Zhi's wild Chan Buddhism. However, he argues, because Geng did not fully think through some important philosophical issues, and because he could not adamantly repudiate Buddhism, he failed to defeat Li. Huang Zongxi, "Taizhou xue'an si" and "Gongjian Geng Tiantai xiansheng Dingxiang," in *Ming Ru xue'an* (1985), 815–16.

38 Geng Dingxiang, "Yu Wu Shaoyu" and "Yu neihan Yang Fusuo," in *Geng Tiantai xiansheng wenji*, 377–402.

39 See, for example, his letter "Yu Beitai jian," *Geng Tiantai xiansheng wenji* (1970), 564–65.

40 Brook, *The Confusions of Pleasure*, 233. See also chapter 4 of the present volume.

41 Whether Geng Dingxiang explicitly instructed his students and the local gentry to attack Li Zhi needs to be studied more carefully case by case. Geng Dingxiang wrote a public letter defending himself from accusations that he had incited his disciples to attack Li Zhi physically or verbally. Geng Dingxiang, "Qiu jing shu," in *Geng Tiantai xiansheng wenji* (1970), 696–98.

42 Yu Jinfang, *Minguo Macheng xianzhi qianbian*, 175, emphasis added.

43 Jian, *Mingdai funü Fojiao xinyang yu shehui guifan*, ch. 4; Zhou Yiqun, "The Hearth and the Temple."

44 Li Zhi, "Yu Zhou Youshan," in *LZ* 3:47.

45 Li Zhi, "Yu Zhou Youshan," in *LZ* 3:47.

46 Lin Haiquan, *Li Zhi nianpu kaolüe*, 310.

47 Li Zhi, "Yuyue," in *LZ* 2:105.

48 Li Zhi, "Yuyue," in *LZ* 2:105.

49 Qian Qianyi, "Liu Wenzhen mao shi," in *Liechao shiji xiao zhuan*, 771–72.

50 Shen Fu, "Li Zhuowu zhuan," cited in Lin Haiquan, *Li Zhi nianpu kaolüe*, 283.

51 Rowe has pointed out that almost all major social-political figures in this region at the time were interested in Buddhism, including those who disliked Li Zhi (*Crimson Rain*, ch. 3).

52 For example, a set of two poems composed during Li Zhi's visit to Mei Guozhen in the northern frontier, "Fu song mei," in *LZ* 2:276.

53 Li Zhi, "Que ji," in *LZ* 2:301.

54 Cited in Lin Haiquan, *Li Zhi nianpu kaolüe*, 386.

55 Brook, *Praying for Power*, ch. 2.

56 Zhang Ying, *Confucian Image Politics*.

57 Li Zhi, "Shu Xiaoxiu shoujuan hou," in *LZ* 3:201.

58 *Ming Shenzong shilu*, 6917–19.

59 Ma Jinglun, "Yu Zhangke Li Linye zhuan shang Xiao Sikou," in *Qian Ming Henandao jiancha yushi Chengsuogong wenji*, 36a–38b.

60 Ma Jinglun, "Yu Dangdao shu," 267.

61 Ma Jinglun, "Yu Zhangke Li Linye zhuan shang Xiao Sikou."

62 On Li Zhi and the discourse of *qing* in the late Ming, see Pauline Lee, *Li Zhi*, 70–71. On the cult of *qing*, see Ko, *Teachers of the Inner Chambers*; Epstein, *Competing Discourses*.

63 Ma Jinglun, "Yulu," in *Qian Ming Henandao jiancha yushi Chengsuogong wenji*, 1b–2a.

64 Wang Fansen, *Ming mo Qing chu de yi zhong daode yange zhuyi*.

65 See chapter 3. Additionally, for analysis of their friendship and how it resembled the legendary examples in history, see Zhang Ying, "Politics and Morality," ch. 1.

CHAPTER 7

NATIVE SEEDS OF CHANGE

Women, Writing, and Rereading Tradition

PAULINE C. LEE

LI ZHI'S INABILITY TO CONTROL HOW HE WAS READ AND HIS GROWing and severe "image problem" as a neglectful husband and licentious womanizer allowed his critics to manipulate and embellish upon both his lived stories and the texts he wrote (chapter 6). Similarly, he used the medium of writing to manipulate texts skillfully and propose a new vision of women's roles in society. When we examine the nuances of Li Zhi's writings—reading along the lines of what he describes as probing beyond mere skin, blood vessels, bones, and internal organs even into the "state of [the author's] whole being"[1]—we find scattered passages, poems, essays, commentaries, and letters that together begin to stake a new ground for a world where it is assumed that women travel freely, read widely, write and publish poetry and history, govern, marry (and remarry if they wish) partners of their own choosing, whose inner emotional lives matter, and whose deaths are recognized as irreplaceable losses.[2] Repeatedly Li Zhi tells us that his deepest pleasure is reading, and the meaning of his life is largely determined by the moral, spiritual, and aesthetic power of what he reads and the enduring legacy of the books he authors. Writing in old age and reflecting on his blessings, he comments, "My [antisocial] disposition is a blessing, for I have never enjoyed the company of ordinary people, and so from my early days to my old age, I have . . . devoted myself single-mindedly to reading."[3] Also, "What rots away is but the bones. / And these [books] alone will never fade."[4] Li Zhi writes in the same way that he reads: deeply, immersed in the finest of details, and with extraordinary mastery of his literary tradition. This chapter examines a few examples of how he makes powerful statements by attending to what might look like nothing more than minute details; he skillfully attributes new meaning to words, weaves his own work into the commentarial tradition, and subtly rewrites small bits of biographical history. Using these various techniques, he expands women's roles in the world by envisioning a society in which each woman can create and live her distinctive life. His strategy for achieving this focuses on the Confucian project of *self-cultivation* and, in particular, takes seriously tradition and the power of reading and writing—rather than legal change, activism, or changes in social structures, for example—to affect hearts and minds and substantively transform lives.

REREADING TERMS OF ART

Li Zhi begins one of his most widely read pieces on the subject of women, titled "A Letter in Response to the Claim That Women Are Too Shortsighted to Understand the Dao," with an affirming declaration to his correspondent: "Yesterday I had the opportunity to hear your esteemed teaching wherein you proclaimed that women, being shortsighted [*duanjian*], are incapable of understanding the Dao. Indeed this is so! Indeed this is so!"[5] At the outset, there is no indication of what "shortsightedness" refers to, whether Li is speaking of spiritual, intellectual, or another form of shortsightedness. We simply know that he appears to stand with his interlocutor: women are indeed incapable of understanding the Dao. However, further explanation immediately follows. Li asserts, "Women live within the inner chambers while men wander throughout the world."[6] With this artfully chosen line from *The Book of Rites* (Liji), Li writes and reads women into the literary tradition in two ways. First, he reinterprets a classical text to support the empirical claim that women are shortsighted but explains this as a result of contingent social circumstances. Second, he explicitly denies that this "shortsightedness" refers to any inherent, essential spiritual or intellectual deficiency in women. Again and again, Li skillfully works within his tradition and language to challenge existing notions of women's place in the social world and the reasons given for keeping women within one space or out of another. Women indeed are "shortsighted," he writes, but only because they have been prevented from developing their native capacities.

As students of late imperial China know, during the Ming and Qing periods, women, or at least elite women, were often confined to the "inner chambers" of a household, where their social interactions were generally limited to other women, children, servants, and close male relatives.[7] Li laments this practice, insisting that physical confinement unjustly stunts the development of women, who in fact possess capacities for reading, writing, governing, and spiritual attainment identical to those of men. Writing about "a person with a woman's body and a 'man's' vision," he states: "It may have been in hopes of encountering such a person that the Sage Confucius wandered the world, desiring to meet her just once but unable to find her; and for such a person to be dismissed as a 'shortsighted creature,' isn't this unjust?"[8]

Li agrees that short- and farsightedness exist, but he denies that the first is in any way essentially associated with women and the latter with men. Instead he writes, "I humbly propose that those who desire to discourse on short- and farsightedness should do as I have done. One must not stop," as his unidentified interlocutor presumably does, "at the observation that women are shortsighted." He continues, "To say that shortsightedness and farsightedness exist is acceptable. But to say that a man's vision is entirely farsighted [*yuanjian*] and a woman's is wholly shortsighted, once again, how can that be acceptable?"[9] Li agrees that women all too often are limited in their insights, but he insists that they are so simply and lamentably because they are physically confined within the four walls of the domestic chambers.[10]

WRITING AND READING WOMEN INTO THE COMMENTARIAL TRADITION

In "A Letter in Response to the Claim That Women Are Too Shortsighted," Li employs additional techniques to argue for and expand the space for women's self-expression. Toward the beginning of the letter, he refers the reader to a number of historical women who achieved excellence and attained fame for their work as writers, rulers, and spiritual savants: "From our present perspective we can observe the following: Yi Jiang, a woman, 'filled in the ranks,' being the ninth of King Wu's ministers. Nothing hindered her from counting as one of the 'ten able ministers' alongside Zhou, Shao, and Taigong. Mother Wen, a sagely woman, rectified the customs of the southern regions. Nothing prevented her from being praised along with San Yisheng and Tai Dian as one of the 'four friends' who helped King Wu in his difficulties."[11] Here, Li reflects on women throughout history and simply and powerfully points out that while for the most part women may be excluded from participating in spheres such as government or writing, there are nonetheless clear examples of women every bit as accomplished in arts conventionally reserved for men. If, as a Ming scholar would do, we look more closely and consider the earliest sources for these references to the "ten able ministers" or the "four friends" and how the commentarial tradition through the centuries interpreted and reinterpreted these allusions, we find Li Zhi doing even more.

The Book of Documents (Shujing) records that King Wu, founder of the Zhou dynasty, believed he could triumph over his enemy. Although the tyrant Shou had "hundreds and thousands of men," they were divided against each other. In contrast, King Wu had only "ten ministers capable of bringing order." However small in number, they were more powerful for being united in heart and spirit. While later commentators have suggested that the ten included Wu's nine brothers and either his consort (Yi Jiang) or his mother (Wen Mu),[12] *The Book of Documents* mentions no woman among these ten.[13]

In Confucius's *Analects*, once again we find reference to King Wu's ten ministers and, here, explicit reference to a woman. *Analects* 8.20 states:

> Shun had five ministers, and the empire was well governed. King Wu said, I have ten capable ministers.
>
> Confucius said, Talent is hard to find—true, is it not? In the time of Yao and Shun, talent flourished, [yet Shun had only five ministers. As for King Wu's ten ministers,] among the ten was a woman, so he had nine and that was all.[14]

For whatever reason, Confucius excludes the one woman from the "ten able ministers"; perhaps women were not allowed to serve in the public role of minister, or it was believed that women lacked the abilities to serve as ministers. Thus, the view is attributed to Confucius that King Wu in fact had no more than nine capable ministers.

In one of the most widely read and respected commentaries on the *Analects*, the *Collected Commentaries on the* Analects *by Mr. He and Others* (Lunyu Heshideng jijie)—a Wei-period work attributed to and compiled by He Yan (d. 249 CE)—He Yan cites the Han-period scholar Kong Anguo (d. ca. 100 CE) commenting that during the rule of Yao and Shun all was complete for the reason that there was ample talent. Kong restates what we find in the *Analects*, "Still, amongst the ten there was one woman. And so there were really only nine."[15]

Of particular interest to our argument, the great Confucian Zhu Xi (1130–1200), in his widely read commentary on the *Analects*—also one Li Zhi surely knew—provides an explanation that places Yi Jiang in a different but arguably equally significant sphere of influence as the nine men: "Nine people governed the 'public' or 'outer' sphere; Yi Jiang governed the 'inner.'" With all ten ministers, the public and domestic spheres both were ably governed. Unlike in the He commentary, Zhu Xi does not address Confucius's seeming exclusion of the one woman as a minister; instead, he simply notes that talent is hard to find: "Still, [King Wu] only had such a number [nine plus one] of people and no more. Talent is indeed difficult to find."[16]

In Li Zhi's own commentary on *Analects* 8.20 he says nothing about women.[17] But in "A Letter in Response to the Claim That Women Are Too Shortsighted," he affirms, following Zhu Xi, that King Wu's consort Yi Jiang was the tenth minister and indeed served effectively. Unlike Zhu, however, Li excludes the explanation that Yi Jiang governed in a separate sphere. He insists that she was absolutely capable and no different from the nine men. And so there were ten able ministers: "Yi Jiang, a woman, 'filled in the ranks' alongside King Wu's nine ministers. Nothing hindered her from counting as one of the 'ten able ministers' alongside Zhou, Shao, and Taigong."

Extracted from the context of the canonical and the commentarial tradition—Li Zhi's "horizon of significance"[18]—his assertion that a king's consort was a capable minister can be seen as expanding women's roles into the outer or public sphere of government. Against the larger literary context, his writing on Yi Jiang is even more noteworthy. Moving through the canon and commentarial tradition, we first read King Wu's ten ministers as all male (*The Book of Documents*); in the *Analects*, a woman is included but not considered truly a minister; with Zhu Xi, the woman minister is celebrated as different but equal; and with Li Zhi, Yi Jiang is named and described as no different from the other nine capable male ministers.

Returning to the text of our letter of interest, we find Li citing yet other historical (and, later in the letter, contemporary) examples of women who are just as competent as the most accomplished men in regard to their intellectual and spiritual capacities.[19] He writes, "Mother Wen, a sagely woman, rectified the customs of the southern regions. Nothing prevented her from being praised along with San Yisheng and Tai Dian as one of the 'four friends' who helped King Wu in his difficulties."[20] The locus classicus for the reference to the "four friends," whom Li Zhi claims include Mother Wen, is *The Book of Documents*, where we find reference to four loyal ministers, all men (Taigong, Nangong Shi, San Yisheng, and Hong Yao), originally serving King Wen and later his son King Wu. King Wu's mother, Mother Wen, is not listed among these four. Through consistent, nuanced misreading or misremembering—repeatedly telling the story ever so slightly differently from what is found in the classics—whatever Li Zhi's intentions, the effect is of amending his written world in a way that multiplies the roles available to women.

Throughout Li's writings he argues for and opens up space for women to express their distinctive selves by reworking words, retrieving stories from the classics, extending the commentarial tradition, reinterpreting or misreading classical texts, and more.[21] If we turn to Li Zhi's *A Book to Keep (Hidden)*, we can find examples where he skillfully extends the commentarial tradition on biographies from the great Han period historian Sima Qian's *Records of the Grand Historian* (Shiji). Sima Qian's lengthy biography of the poet Sima Xiangru (ca. 179–17 BCE) narrates his rise from obscurity to fame.[22] Within this piece are a few short paragraphs on his elopement with the young widow Zhuo Wenjun and her father's dismay at the news: "Zhuo Wenjun's father, Zhuo Wangsun, was in a rage. 'What a piece of trash—this daughter of mine!' he exclaimed. 'I have not the heart to kill her outright, but I will see to it that she never gets a penny of my money!'"[23] Later, when Sima Xiangru attains great fame, Zhuo Wangsun pays respect to and acknowledges Sima Xiangru as his son-in-law. Sima Qian writes, "When Sima Xiangru returned as a person of great honor . . . Xiangru's father-in-law, Zhuo Wangsun, as well as the various distinguished men of Linqiong, flocked to his gate with presents of meat and wine to express their warmhearted friendship. Zhuo Wangsun was filled with remorse that he had been so late in recognizing his daughter's marriage to Xiangru, and to make up for it he presented her with a generous portion of his estate, so that her inheritance equaled that of her brother."[24]

Li Zhi quotes Sima Qian's brief remarks on Zhuo Wenjun and extends Sima Qian's original biography in a way that celebrates Zhuo Wenjun's independence and defiance of conventions. He praises her ability to recognize the virtues of Sima Xiangru, a man who would eventually become one of the great poets of his time. Sima Qian notes that Zhuo Wangsun was initially "filled with shame" at the thought of his daughter with Sima Xiangru. Li balks at such condemnation and retorts, "In this world today those who know of Zhuo Wangsun's daughter, Zhuo Wenjun, appropriately see her to be a great joy for him. Why was he ashamed?" While in Sima Qian's narrative Zhuo Wangsun's friends all agreed "Wenjun . . . lost herself in eloping with Sima Xiangru," Li takes exception to such a judgment and counters, "She properly saved herself; she did not lose herself."[25]

Li Zhi's defense of Zhuo Wenjun contrasts sharply with positions toward widow remarriage put forth by many literati in his time. For example, the sixteenth-century literary critic Hu Yinglin (1551–1602) sums up well the prevailing moral condemnation of widow remarriage when he chastises Zhuo Wenjun: "Wenjun was a remarried widow . . . and Empress Zhen was not loyal to her first husband. Neither of these two women is worthy of emulation when it comes to the great norms of human behavior. But the historians tell us that Xu Shu did not remarry after [Qin] Jia's death and even disfigured her face to discourage potential suitors."[26] Hu considers the chaste widow Xu Shu a paragon of virtue, while he regards Empress Zhen and Li Zhi's heroine Zhuo Wenjun poetically gifted but morally weak.

The celebration of widow chastity can be traced in the Confucian tradition. Within the Chinese literary tradition oft-cited is the great neo-Confucian Zhu Xi's assertion: "Woman is born to serve others with her person; a wife should serve her husband and die together with him."[27] The influential neo-Confucian Cheng Yi (1033–1107) is famous for saying that it is a small matter for a widow and her children to die by starvation or exposure if she remains unwed and thus loyal to her deceased husband, but a calamity for her to lose her integrity by remarrying. Within the late-Ming cultural context, where marriages of literary giftedness were celebrated, whatever Li Zhi's intentions, the effect of including and embellishing upon the lives of Zhuo Wenjun and Sima Xiangru would be to affirm the practice of widow remarriage.

In a poem titled "Mourning the Precious Son" dated 1588 and written in Macheng, Li reaffirms his view of remarriage. The poem is addressed to the ghost of his deceased son, possibly born to Li Zhi's younger brother and subsequently adopted by Li so that he might have an heir.[28] Here Li brings his theoretical ideas to bear on his own personal life by advising that his bereaved daughter-in-law ought to have the opportunity to remarry. He writes:

> Your wife should remarry.
> Your son, he is my grandchild.
> Where has your spirit settled?
> Find refuge in the honorable world of the Buddha.[29]

While one might read Li Zhi as encouraging his daughter-in-law to remarry because, due to his own straitened financial circumstances, he would find it difficult to care for her, the combination of this poem and his commentary on Zhuo Wenjun suggest a consistent commitment to the support of widow remarriage. Following the line "Your wife should remarry" Li adds that his deceased son should "find refuge in the honorable world of the

Buddha," presumably rather than comfort in the fact that his wife would remain unmarried, thus loyal, after his death.[30]

NATIVE SEEDS OF CHANGE

In a letter to his student Wang Benke dated 1594, Li discusses writing strategies: "When ordinary people write, they begin from the outside and fight their way in; when I write, I start from the middle and fight my way out. I go straight for the enemy's defenses and moat, eat his grain, and command his troops; then, when I level my attack, I leave him utterly shattered. In this way I do not expend so much as a whit of my own energy and naturally have powers to spare."[31] With a quote from *The Book of Rites*,[32] reference to the legendary King Wu and his ten ministers,[33] allusion to the great historian Sima Qian's commentary on the widow Zhuo Wenjun, and more, Li Zhi situates himself at the heart of the literary canon. His acts of dissent work from within the *Ru* tradition, the world of writing and culture (*wen*), where effective strategies for social change include attending to words, characters, classical references, commentaries, genre, and canon. As we have seen, women too are part of Li's world and he holds that each woman ought to have greater opportunities for self-expression. Even Li, widely known as an iconoclast in Chinese cultural history, took the Confucian tradition absolutely seriously.

Writing about the late-Qing period, the authors of *The Birth of Chinese Feminism* persuasively argue against what they refer to as "the conventional view of the birth of Chinese feminism [as] a by-product of the introduction of liberalism."[34] One primary task in their book is to move beyond "the Western or male problem of origins" for Chinese feminisms by bringing to light the writings of the female Chinese feminist He-Yin Zhen (1884–ca. 1920).[35] Elegant and powerful, this work emphasizes global discourse rather than unidirectional influence. As the authors summarize their project, "He-Yin Zhen's feminist and anarchist radicalism allows us to complicate today's received narrative about the origins of Chinese feminism in a borrowed male liberal worldview."[36] A study of Li Zhi and his views on women aligns with such an aim, allowing us to complicate the inaccurate received narrative that Chinese feminism finds its origins in a borrowed liberal worldview. *The Birth of Chinese Feminism* further describes He-Yin Zhen as "debunking . . . the millennia-long classical textual scholarship and Confucian commentarial traditions" and engaging in a "totalistic rejection" of Confucianism.[37] But is He-Yin in her writings wholly rejecting

Confucianism? Or is she more like Li Zhi, who, I have argued, works cleverly with erudition within the millennia-long classical textual scholarship and Confucian commentarial tradition and stands in the middle and fights his way out?

While Li's strategy for bringing women into the world of men may seem unimaginative or limited, his writings reveal one example of a distinctive and valuable approach to social change rich with possibility. Rather than focusing on legal change, the ideals of autonomy and rights, the world of employment, or issues of private and public, he insists on the power of tradition forged through the acts of writing and reading.[38] We may wish that he had been able to consider difference rather than simply sameness between men and women.[39] Or we may want to move beyond his suggestions that for women to flourish they must be granted more opportunities for self-cultivation; instead, the structure of society must be changed, for example, so that women can truly move beyond the "inner chambers" and attain "farsightedness"—as men do.[40] I have argued that as early as the late Ming, one may already perceive a glimmer of the sorts of "native" or "indigenous" feminisms that would flourish in the late Qing. Further study of thinkers in early modern China may strengthen the view that Li's thought contributed to creating a nuanced, complex, and powerful discourse on gender relations and that in his writings we find native seeds of change.[41]

NOTES

I am grateful to Robert Hegel, Eric Hutton, Philip Ivanhoe, Haun Saussy, Ying Zhang, Brook Ziporyn, and especially Rivi Handler-Spitz for invaluable comments on this chapter.

1 Li Zhi, "'Dushule' bing yin," in *LZ* 2:240–43; Li Zhi, *A Book to Burn*, 211–14.

2 For instance, in chapter 2 Maram Epstein analyzes Li Zhi's response to his daughters' deaths.

3 Li Zhi, *A Book to Burn*, 211.

4 Li Zhi, *A Book to Burn*, 214.

5 Li Zhi, "Da yi nüren xue dao wei jianduan shu," in *LZ* 1:143–47; Li Zhi, *A Book to Burn*, 27–33.

6 See "The Pattern of the Family," in Legge, *Li Chi*, 471.

7 For discussion on women's social space in late imperial China, see Mann, *Precious Records*.

8 Li Zhi, "Da yi nüren xue dao wei jianduan shu," in *LZ* 1:143–47; Li Zhi, *A Book to Burn*, 27–33.

9 Li Zhi, "Da yi nüren xue dao wei jianduan shu," in *LZ* 1:143–47; Li Zhi, *A Book to Burn*, 29–33. Of interest, He-Yin Zhen (1884–1920?) in her essay "On the

Question of Women's Liberation" (Nüzi jiefang wenti) makes reference to Zhuo Wenjun and Cui Yingying and argues that cloistering women within the "inner chambers" in fact (for different reasons than Li Zhi argues) cripples women's virtue. See Liu, Karl, and Ko, *The Birth of Chinese Feminism*, 57.

10 For a discussion of how Li Zhi frames the term "orphaned" (*gu*), in his time most typically used to refer to a child who had lost his or her father even if the mother was still alive, see Pauline Lee, *Li Zhi*, 35–36. He uses the term to refer to himself when his birth mother died, even though his father at that time was still living. See also chapter 2.

11 Li Zhi, "Da yi nüren xue dao wei jianduan shu," in *LZ* 1:143–47; Li Zhi, *A Book to Burn*, 29–33.

12 For a list of the names of the ten ministers, see *LZ* 1:146n14. In the scholarly literature, there are suggestions that preceding the Sui period, commentators generally considered King Wu's mother to be the tenth minister; following the Sui, his consort Yi Jiang was considered the tenth.

13 Legge, *The Shoo King*, 292.

14 Watson, *The Analects*, 56–57, amended.

15 He Yan et al, *Lunyu Heshideng jijie*, 6b.

16 Zhu Xi, *Sishu zhangju*, 58.

17 Li Zhi, "Taibo diba," *Sishu ping*, in *LZ* 21:141.

18 See Taylor, *Ethics*.

19 Throughout the first chapter of Li's *Upon Arrival at the Lake* (Chutanji), he praises virtuous and courageous women as "real men" or "better than men." For analysis of this locution, see chapter 6.

20 Li Zhi, "Da yi nüren xue dao wei jianduan shu," in *LZ* 1:143–47; Li Zhi, *A Book to Burn*, 29–33.

21 For discussion of Li Zhi's strategies for reworking Buddhist texts and practices, see chapter 9.

22 See Sima, *Shiji* 117; Watson, *Records*, 297–342.

23 Watson, *Records*, 299.

24 Watson, *Records*, 325.

25 Li Zhi, "Sima Xiangru," *Cangshu*, in *LZ* 7:147–53; translated in Pauline Lee, "Li Zhi (1527–1602)," 247–51.

26 Idema and Grant, *The Red Brush*, 135, 85–91. Empress Zhen (183–221) was an accomplished poet first married to a son of one of the powerful rivals of the great warlord Cao Cao. After Cao Cao's military defeat of this rival, she was married off to his son Cao Pi (187–226). Xu Shu (b. middle of the second century CE), known as both a virtuous woman and a gifted writer, was well-matched in a marriage to Qin Jia. When Qin Jia died, her brothers pressured her to remarry, whereupon she mutilated her face and vowed her loyalty to her deceased husband.

27 See Zhu Xi, *Shiji zhuan*, 3:29; Raphals, *Sharing the Light*, 68, adapted. For further discussion of this text see Raphals, 205.

28 Of his seven children, all but his eldest daughter died in childhood. For further discussion on the adult son in this poem, see *LZ* 3:340n1.
29 See Li Zhi, "Ku gui'er," in *LZ* 3:340; translated in Pauline Lee, "Li Zhi (1527–1602)," 226.
30 See, for example, Yang Jisheng's insistence that upon his death, his childless concubine ought to be urged to remarry rather than remain a widow, discussed in Bossler, "Final Instructions," 123. Also see Ropp, "The Seeds of Change," 9–10, for reference to Gui Youguang (1506–1571) and Lü Kun (1536–1618), both of whom supported widow remarriage.
31 Li Zhi, "Yu youren lun wen," in *LZ* 3:21; Li Zhi, *A Book to Burn*, 245–46.
32 Li Zhi, "Da yi nüren xue dao wei jianduan shu," in *LZ* 1:143–47; Li Zhi, *A Book to Burn*, 29–33.
33 Li Zhi, "Da yi nüren xue dao wei jianduan shu," in *LZ* 1:143–47; Li Zhi, *A Book to Burn*, 29–33.
34 Liu, Karl, and Ko, *The Birth of Chinese Feminism*, 36.
35 Liu, Karl, and Ko, *The Birth of Chinese Feminism*, 38.
36 Liu, Karl, and Ko, *The Birth of Chinese Feminism*, 47.
37 Liu, Karl, and Ko, *The Birth of Chinese Feminism*, 20, 36.
38 For arguments against labeling Li Zhi an "individualist" and discussion of his relationship to late-Ming Confucian, literati, and mercantile culture, see chapters 2 and 8.
39 See MacKinnon, *Toward a Feminist Theory*, 215–34. Also see MacKinnon, "A Substantive Equality."
40 See Tong, *Feminist Thought*, 94–129. Also see the work of Kang Youwei (1858–1927), Mao Zedong (1893–1976), and He-Yin Zhen. For Kang's work on this subject, see *Book of Great Unity* (Datong shu).
41 See Ropp, "The Seeds of Change."

PART FOUR

TEXTUAL COMMUNITIES

CHAPTER 8

AN AVATAR OF THE EXTRAORDINARY

Li Zhi as a Shishang *Writer and Thinker in the Late-Ming Publishing World*

KAI-WING CHOW

IN ANTICIPATION OF HIS DEATH, LI ZHI GAVE THIS INSTRUCTION to the monks at the Zhifoyuan Monastery in 1596: "I love books! During seasonal sacrifices to me, books that I copied, edited, and commented on must be put on the right side of the altar."[1] Unlike other avid readers of his time, he was a prolific best-selling writer. Between 1604 and the 1620s no writer surpassed him in wit, pungency, and profundity.[2] He was the leading author in a vastly expanded pool of "mercantile literati" (*shishang*) writers, literary laborers who, while to varying degrees dependent on remuneration from publishers or patrons, continued to identify themselves with the literati (*shi*) and remained reticent about their pecuniary activities.[3] The popularity and ascendance of Li Zhi to the pantheon of literary masters should be understood in the context of burgeoning commercial publishing and the transforming social and intellectual contours of the late Ming. His involvement in and manipulation of commercial publishing as well as his powerful articulation of the emerging ethos of his time—*shishang* ethics—contributed to the massive appeal of his brush.

COMMERCIAL PUBLISHING AND THE ECONOMIC MODE OF *SHISHANG* WRITERS

Li Zhi is arguably best known as an outspoken iconoclast, a nonconformist, and an advocate of the extraordinary (*qi*). His reputation owed much to the publicity generated by commercial publishing as well as to the expansive ideological purview of his writings, which appealed to a burgeoning reading population with diverse interests, both ideological and practical. His strategic involvement in commercial publishing, astute use of satire, colloquial expressions, and ingenious use of paratexts transfixed readers.

A reader might encounter the name Li Zhi whether she was interested in fiction, drama, history, Confucian classics, Buddhist scriptures, or Daoist treatises. The inscription of his name on innumerable imprints spanning several literary genres no doubt contributed to his exceptional reputation as a prolific and versatile *shishang* writer. Amid the cutthroat competition of commercial publishing in the late Ming, publishers favored Li Zhi's works, many of which assumed the popular forms of "critical commentary" (*piping*) written in an increasingly simple and plain (*tongsu*) mode.[4]

Even though the direct and indirect participation of literati in commercial publishing reached unprecedented heights in the late Ming, their habitus transformed slowly due to a lack of discursive efforts to fashion a distinct literary identity for professional writers. The only social identity that educated elites were willing to embrace was that of the literatus (*shi*). Specific information about writers' interactions with publishers or their publishing careers is elusive and remains buried under allusions and metaphors in their personal writings. The common practice of deliberate "forgetting" of the positions the literati once occupied in the economic field further obscures the process by which they labored for economic benefit.[5] Despite the substantial amount of writing attributed to Li Zhi, authentic or otherwise, information about his involvement in commercial publishing remains scanty at best.[6]

Li's father was a private tutor who trained his son to excel in the increasingly competitive examinations. Li became a government student at about the age of sixteen.[7] After passing the provincial examination in 1552 at the age of twenty-six, he decided not to pursue the metropolitan degree and applied for a government position in 1555.[8] He was sent to Huixian, Henan as a lecturer (*jiaoyu*) at the government school, which marked the beginning of his twenty-some-year-long official career.[9] He unexpectedly retired from government in 1580 at the age of fifty-four. For the next twenty-two years, he eked out a meager living with the support of a few friends and admirers, pursuing his passion for reading and writing, as well as his religious goals.

Li Zhi's economic mode of existence after withdrawal from government service defies classification. He relied heavily on patronage of friends and devoted supporters and occasionally received remuneration for literary labor he expended for commercial publishers. But it does not seem that he depended on these sources of income as a major means of support, as did professional writers.[10] He occasionally worked as a tutor, grooming students for the civil service examination. These instructional responsibilities surely generated some income. Acceptance of invitations to visit or lecture customarily came with material and monetary compensation as well.[11]

After he relinquished his official career in 1580 and up until his suicide in 1602, he depended on the patronage of a few ardent followers, some of whom were high-ranking officials. Support might be offered in the form of direct financial assistance or material gifts. In Macheng, Zhou Sijiu and his brother Zhou Sijing, both official patrons, paid to build his residence at the Vimalakīrti Monastery.[12] Yet despite the generosity of Liu Dongxing, Mei Guozhen, and other friends, Li Zhi's economic position was precarious, and he may have found editing and publishing a satisfying way to supplement his income.

Li Zhi's passion for reading was intense and the range of his interests immense. While reading was indisputably his favorite and perhaps his only pastime in solitude, there are reasons to believe that reading was also a type of work critical to the production of publishable manuscripts. He did not just enjoy commenting on the books he read; he also authorized or abetted the publication of his reading notes as comments, whether as private publications or as commercial imprints.[13] He confided to Jiao Hong, "I have copied and commented on numerous writings of great men past and present. It's a pity that I cannot send all of them to you for comment!"[14] Once he finished writing, the manuscripts would be taken to a publisher. He joked that he could not prevent his notes from being published.[15]

LI ZHI AND THE CIVIL SERVICE EXAMINATION

In the late Ming, the market for books of all genres expanded dramatically, but books published for examinees and gentry indisputably dominated the market. The examination system continued to structure the field of literary production in Li Zhi's time even though commercial publishing had expanded to the point where reputations generated by a massive volume of imprints created positions of authority that came to challenge official, governmental authority over literary and exegetical standards.[16] Despite his invective against the civil service examination, Li Zhi did not call for the abolition of the institution nor the eight-legged essay.[17] Repulsed as he was by the pedantry with which his contemporaries approached Confucianism, he nonetheless found reasons—intellectual as well as economic—to publish his own readings of the Four Books. In his preface to the 1590 edition of *A Book to Burn*, he explained why he decided to publish controversial works like *A Book to Burn* and *A Book to Keep* (*Hidden*) (Cangshu), even though he expected opprobrium and persecution to follow. In contrast, his *Expositions of the Four Books* (Si shu ping, also known as Shuo shu) strove to illuminate the sublime meanings of the sages' remarks, rendering their teachings "quotidian and ordinary" (*riyong zhi pingchang*).[18] He published his essays on the Four Books in several editions of incremental length: the first edition of *Expositions of the Four Books*, published in Macheng, contained 20 percent of the entries included in the final edition.[19] This initial edition apparently consisted only of essays on questions on the *Great Learning* and the *Doctrine of the Mean*. He later published essays on the other two books: the *Analects* and the *Mencius*.[20]

Known for adopting a critical stance toward Confucian texts in his famous essay "On the Childlike Mind" (Tongxin shuo), Li Zhi considered *Expositions of the Four Books* a venue for voicing his disagreement with the official commentary by Zhu Xi and presenting his own understanding of the Four Books. According to Jiao Hong, Li Zhi considered *Expositions of the Four Books* one of his three most important books. But its publication served a more practical purpose. By his own account, his friends frequently asked him to read and comment on their eight-legged essays, and the book represented his accumulated efforts to help them write such compositions. Oddly enough, Li enjoyed writing model eight-legged essays. He often wrote them on examination questions (*ti*) and sent them to Jiao Hong for comment.[21]

Elsewhere, Li Zhi confided to Jiao Hong that the comments in *Expositions of the Four Books* were prompted by "students who did not comprehend the main ideas of examination questions."[22] Obviously many of his so-called friends (*you*) wrote to him seeking advice on how to write great essays so that they could distinguish themselves in the increasingly competitive examinations.[23] In order to ensure that his readers would not fail to appreciate this use of his *Expositions on the Four Books*, in the preface he added a note specifying that this text would "be beneficial to writing eight-legged essays."[24] These words would serve a promotional purpose, drawing readers' attention to the publication's value as an examination aid. Nonetheless, Li Zhi followed his remark with a caveat: "There are also many [essays in this book] that offer no assistance with writing eight-legged essays."[25] Such an adroit use of discursive space in paratexts allowed him to camouflage any economic desire he might have had for his publication. He did not mean to mislead his readers with commercial parlance concocted merely to court examinees.

It is important to note that Li Zhi was not opposed to eight-legged essays or to students dedicating themselves to preparing for the examinations. In fact, he believed that the best eight-legged essays were evidence of the talents and achievements of the examinees. In a preface to a collection of eight-legged essays he penned for a patron, he criticized those who disapproved of the essays as ineffective in producing competent civil servants. "Those who say that eight-legged essays [*shiwen*] can be instituted to recruit official candidates but those essays would be swiftly forgotten neither understand essay writing nor fathom the nature of time."[26] He ranked eight-legged essays among the best writings of all time (*gujin zhiwen*), which include works of vernacular fiction such as *Outlaws of the Marsh* (Shuihu zhuan) and dramas like *The Western Chamber* (Xixiang ji). He considered all these works creations of the "authentic mind" (*zhenxin*).[27]

After he moved to Macheng, Li Zhi took in a student, Wang Benke, who studied with him for nine years seeking to hone his skills writing eight-legged essays and deepen his understanding of Confucian texts. Reminiscing about a three-month stay at the Zhifoyuan Monastery in 1594, Wang stated, "During the day, I was taught how to prepare for the civil service examination and at night I studied one trigram of *The Book of Change*" (Rike juzi ye, ye du yi yigua).[28] When Li Zhi went to Beijing in 1597, Wang again went to study with him in the Temple of Bliss (Jile si). Li was somewhat disappointed in Wang, who was primarily interested in learning the craft of producing winning essays. Li voiced his discontent thus: "If *I were to teach you only* how to prepare for the examination, I would be a tutor specialized in grooming students for examinations, which I am not."[29] Li no doubt did not consider himself a petty career tutor. Even though he did not see writing eight-legged essays as incompatible with seeking the Way (*dao*), he still placed a premium on the latter.[30] His own priorities notwithstanding, he did take Wang's objective seriously, as a professional writer or instructor would. He sent him his *Expositions of the Four Books* and *Ancient Meanings of Examination Essays* (Shiwen guyi) to commit to memory.[31] Doubtless, both teacher and student understood that their short-term goal was Wang's success in the examinations.

When Li Zhi went to stay with Liu Dongxing in Shangdang, Shanxi in 1596, he instructed Liu's son in the *Great Learning* and the *Doctrine of the Mean*. Even though the conversations between them were published as *Illuminating Discussions of Antiquity* (Dao gu lu, also known as Mingdeng dao gu lu), which underscored Liu Dongxing's and his son's moral and personal quest for understanding Confucian truths, the contents of Li Zhi's lessons also coincided with the examination curriculum. Surely the father and son expected Li's intellectual and spiritual instructions to benefit the son's pursuit of examination success.[32] Li Zhi's reputation attracted examinees who wanted to learn to write winning essays, but few could or would make the trip to visit him in Macheng. Some sent him letters seeking advice on comprehending the Four Books.[33] These requests were customarily accompanied by some kind of remuneration, in the form of either gifts or money.[34]

Had his writings not met the examinees' practical needs, Li Zhi would not have gained such high visibility, for the examination not only structured the literary field; it also undergirded the patronage system. Examinees became increasingly involved in commercial publishing as readers, producers, and arbiters of literary excellence.[35] Li Zhi's reputation as a best-selling writer was itself part of that process. And he never lost sight of the largest reading public for his time: examinees. His *Expositions of the Four Books* exemplifies a new type of examination aid—a compendium of commentaries on the Four Books. His preface to that volume explicitly identifies the reader as an examinee. The paratexts of *A Book to Keep (Hidden)* and *The Collected Writings of Poxian* (Poxian ji) likewise emphasize literary skills one had to master in order to pass various examinations.[36]

Honing the skills requisite for writing eight-legged essays was the foremost responsibility of any examinee. The late Ming witnessed the unprecedented proliferation of new types of anthologies of actual examination essays as well as personal exercises and failed samples.[37] Anthologies of model essays flooded the book market as leading writers competed for the attention of examinees. Selecting and commenting on the best prose, including eight-legged essays, was always on Li Zhi's mind.

LI ZHI AND *SHISHANG* ETHICS

The enormous popularity of Li Zhi's books and the antipathy they evoked from orthodox literati epitomize the mixed reactions of readers who were dazzled by the words and deeds of an eccentric, nonconformist, and dissenting luminary. But did his popularity rest solely on his witty and entertaining iconoclasm and his adept manipulation of paratexts? Were his ideas truly idiosyncratic and uniquely at odds with conventional values?

As Wai-yee Li and Maram Epstein argue in this volume, Li Zhi's self-representation is fraught with tension and fragmentation. Wai-yee Li observes that Li Zhi's "true core remains opaque to others and perhaps even to himself." These characteristics typify not only his individual intellectual and psychological conditions, but also those of the emerging class of *shishang*. Thus, Li Zhi's popularity flourished in large part because his ideas and values resonated with those of the mercantile literati, a social class that developed out of the conjoining of career paths and social practices associated with conventional literati (*shi*) and merchants (*shang*). In contrast to William Theodore de Bary, who characterizes Li as "almost a classic case of alienation from his whole society and culture," I maintain that Li's ethics were congruent with the emerging values of a group that was gradually gaining dominance, the *shishang*.[38] The values he openly promoted and vociferously defended echoed and gave shape to a new ethics of the *shishang*, which cannot be classified neatly in terms of any of the conventional intellectual systems of Confucianism, Daoism, or Buddhism.

While the popularity of Li Zhi's writings is beyond any dispute, mapping his intellectual affinity has been challenging for his critics and admirers alike. De Bary considers Li Zhi an "arch-individualist," representing the zenith of the "tide of individualistic thought in the late Ming."[39] Keenly aware of the "problem of 'individualism'" as a Western concept, de Bary nonetheless cannot avoid using this concept to represent Li's ethics. De Bary's use of the phrase "public individualism" bespeaks the inapplicability of the term "individualism" to the study of Chinese thought. Moreover, the concept itself is problematic inasmuch as it glorifies the autonomous, isolated, and desocialized individual.[40] As Michel de Certeau has remarked, and Epstein also argues in this volume, "Individualism is a historical trope of occidental modernity."[41]

De Bary mistakes Li Zhi's advocacy of pursuing selfish desires for evidence of his "individualistic" ethics."[42] But "selfishness" does not adequately convey Li's idea of personal interests (*si*). His ethics is not individualism but a system of values focusing on what is important to the individual as a *social subject*. Unlike individualism—a self-centered, self-asserting concept, privileging the self over all other individuals in political, social, and economic relations—Li Zhi's ethics situates the self in a network of relationships. The well-being of the self includes—and even privileges—duties to and concerns for family members and friends. The Western ideology of individualism is incapable of articulating the change in discourse on the self in the late Ming, when change in the formation of the self involved not so much an individuation in socioeconomic and political practices as a reconfiguration of the self in different relational contexts: marriage, intergenerational relationships, personal identities, and relationships to the state. Michel Foucault's idea of "care of the self," which allows for these reconfigurations, may be applicable to this mode of ethical thinking, which is at odds with the liberal idea of individualism. Foucault subsumes at least three different conditions under the radiant icon of the self: "the individualistic attitude," "the positive valuation of the private life," and "the intensity of the relations to self."[43] Foucault's analysis lays bare the problem of glorification of the self in utter independence from social relations.

Li Zhi's ethics centers on the self's well-being, including its material, relational, spiritual, and intellectual interests. The fulfillment of an individual's "material" and "relational" needs is anchored in the affirmation and priority of one's personal needs. Personal interests (*si*) were denounced or diminished in conventional Confucian ethics, especially in Cheng-Zhu *daoxue*, which upheld rigorous moralism. In his comments on "Confucian Officials with Virtuous Achievements" (Deye Ruchen), Li Zhi remarks, "Selfishness is the heart-and-mind of man. Men must be selfish so that what is in their minds can be made known. If there is no selfishness, there is no mind."[44] In seeking to meet one's material and relational needs, one must be selfish, giving priority to oneself over others. But this "selfishness" is not a form of individualism that requires one to put oneself over other persons. The selfishness Li advocates, in fact, was materialized in a social network of relationships. This is the "relational" need that is integral to the care of the self. It is not indicative of an autonomous, isolated, desocialized subject. Li's understanding of the material and relational needs of the self is rooted in Confucianism.

Recall Li Zhi's emphasis on "ordinary, quotidian activities" (*riyong zhi pingchang*) as the core of Confucius's teachings. Elsewhere he glossed this idea as the basic needs of "wearing clothing and eating food" (*chuanyi chifan*). Nothing is more fundamental to a person's material existence. He proclaimed, "There can be no ethical relations beyond wearing clothes and eating food" (Chuque chuanyi chifan, wu lunwu yi).[45] All human relationships rest on our basic material needs, our sustenance. Morality and economics are fused, and economics becomes the criterion for fulfilling one's moral obligations. Unlike conventional literati who would not openly acknowledge the quest for material well-being as a priority, Li Zhi justified seeking it: "Wealth, high position, profit, and social advancement enrich the heavenly endowed five senses. They are necessarily so. Therefore, the sages follow these tendencies; and following these tendencies results in everyone's being contented. Hence, those who are greedy for wealth are given stipends. Those who hanker after positions are granted ranks, and those who are strong and powerful are given authority. Competent people are appointed officials; less capable ones are made to provide service."[46]

Striving for wealth and power are most natural and in fact necessary to "enriching one's five senses." Selfishness is redefined in relational and material terms. Since Li Zhi sees moral obligations as economic obligations, fulfilling one's moral duties requires pursuing material interests. There is nothing shameful about these worldly pursuits. And in pursuing wealth and power, everyone takes up the vocation that suits him best. All vocations are worthy insofar as they further these goals. In a letter to Geng Dingxiang, Li points out that everyone "plows to get food, [and] purchases land to cultivate; in building a house, one seeks safety; in studying, one desires examination degrees; and in government, one seeks promotion and fame. One goes after geomantic sites in order to benefit one's descendants. All these quotidian activities are undertaken for oneself and family, not one bit for others."[47] He dubbed all these "selfish" pursuits "simple and immediate words" (*eryan*). He was repulsed by the hypocrisy of Geng Dingxiang, who insisted upon preaching *daoxue* morality to the literati while seeking wealth and fame no less earnestly than an ordinary person. Rather, Li advocated talking openly about desire for wealth and social advancement. He deemed them legitimate concerns for all regardless of their vocation. In his letter to Geng's student Deng Lincai, he defended his preference for honestly and unaffectedly embracing the "quotidian life of the ordinary people" (*baixing riyong*). Folks "desire good products, beauty, diligence in study, and advancement; they amass gold and valuables, purchase estates for their descendants, and seek geomantic sites that will protect their progeny. Everyone craves and engages in economic production and enterprises; these are what they know and talk about. This is truly simple talk!"[48] His censure of Geng's ignominious conduct stems from his revulsion at dishonesty on the one hand and, on the other, Geng's censorious attitude toward ordinary people's pursuit of self-interest. Everyone, including Geng himself and all the officials and gentry, Li averred, strove for the same goal: a better life for themselves, or care of the self.[49]

The conflict between Li Zhi and Geng Dingxiang symbolizes two general positions of Confucian-educated literati. Geng upheld conventional Cheng-Zhu *daoxue* ethics, which privileged moral perfection as the primary goal. This position publicly defined the aspirations and conduct of the literati, since they were required to master *daoxue* teachings in their preparation for the civil service examinations. In contrast, Li's ethics underscored the pursuit of material interests and worldly success as fundamental to caring for the self and its relational needs. Consequently, Li relegated the pursuit of moral perfection and public service to the status of secondary activities.

Such ethics valorizes the pursuit of material well-being and worldly success as goals for all. As the normative goal of government service, inherent in Confucian education, became increasingly elusive, late-Ming literati could no longer dismiss out of hand the possibility of supplementing their incomes by engaging in pecuniary activities. The ideal of the Confucian gentleman (*junzi*) who speaks only of righteousness (*yi*), not profit, could no longer be sustained.

The gentry's extensive involvement in luxurious consumption, production, and trade accompanied attempts to renegotiate the value of commerce and the role of merchants in the hierarchy of social relations and values.[50] The career of a merchant was no longer deemed undesirable or secondary to that of a literatus (*shi*). Merchants were able to win respect and social prestige by financing projects important to their communities and even by purchasing degrees. It is no surprise that the social status of merchants rose most prominently in areas where commerce had been crucial in maintaining wealth and power for the local elites.[51]

This leveling out of social classes finds corroboration in the remarks of Xu Fang, an obscure figure, one of whose essays was nonetheless included in Huang Zongxi's colossal anthology of Ming writings, *Sea of Writings of the Ming* (Ming wenhai). Xu argued that there were only "three classes of people" in his time—farmers, artisans, and merchants—because in practice the *shi* class had disappeared long ago:

> When literati, brooding over their books, look up in reflection, they are not concerned with the truth of sages and worthies. They [studied] those books for social advancement. The teachings of father, elder brother, teacher, and friends do not aim to cultivate sages and worthies; they aim to produce wealthy and powerful persons. . . . Today there is no literatus who is not preoccupied with profit. How can they be called literati? I simply call them *shang* [merchants]. . . . If hundreds and thousands become merchants, how can we claim that there are literati? [We can] say that there are only "three classes" because the literati class disappeared long ago![52]

Two points here bear elaboration. First, Xu observed that the purpose of education for most people was dissociated from the quest for moral cultivation. Rather, they studied to get ahead in society by accumulating wealth and power. Any moral precepts they learned from books were merely incidental. Second, even those studying to become officials did so primarily to enrich themselves. In pursuing wealth, they were as obsessive as merchants. For Xu, the *shi* no longer had a moral calling; in practice they had become careerists just like members of other occupations. Xu explained that he did not mean to denigrate commercial careers. On the contrary, he recognized that merchants labored hard to earn a living, and this was not at odds with acting righteously.[53] His view accurately reflects the new social reality echoed in Li Zhi's writings.

Regardless of vocation, everyone was striving to enrich himself and his family in the late Ming. Educated elites, gentry, and officials, no less than merchants, scrambled for wealth and competed in lavish consumption as social distinctions became increasingly porous and markers of status came to be defined in terms of material wealth.[54] Materialism was the order of the day and engendered a discourse on luxury consumption (*she*) both as a solution for unemployment and as a justified practice of the rich.[55]

Li Zhi's decisions and experiences symbolize the emerging demand for adjustments to conventional Confucian ethics. He had to negotiate the length of his service to the government and his responsibilities toward his family. His frequent justifications of his pursuit of personal self-interest point to the growing difficulty with which literati had to contend as they sought to fulfill their dream of obtaining an official career. Increasing numbers of literati found it necessary to pursue careers as tutors, merchants, doctors, private secretaries, professional writers, publishers, and litigation masters. The growing trend in the merging and mixing of careers of the literati and merchants became all the more conspicuous in the sixteenth century.[56]

In castigating the hypocrisy of officials who engaged in moral lecturing while striving for wealth and fame, Li Zhi compared them to merchants. But like Xu Fang, he hastened to add that there was nothing shameful about real merchants, who labored diligently to make a meager living.[57] Li Zhi did not view merchants' pursuit of profit in terms of conventional morality. Like Xu Fang and many others, including later thinkers like Huang Zongxi (1610–1695) and Tang Zhen (1630–1704), Li regarded profit from trade and commerce as the worthy rewards of labor. And, to justify this pursuit of profit, he transformed the conventional dichotomy between "righteousness" and "profit" (*yili*)—the one morally sanctioned, the other condemned—into a single, morally neutral end toward which people of all vocations equally strove.

This ethics of the "quotidian life of ordinary people" fused profit-seeking and moral duties. Li Zhi both practiced this type of ethics and articulated his ideas in his widely read publications. His ethics underscores the legitimacy of material interests for both literati and merchants. Moreover, his ideas accorded with the values of the majority of literati and merchants, who increasingly intermingled. In plain language that everyone could understand, he powerfully verbalized and eloquently defended this transformation of the career structure and class stratification of late-Ming society.

For mercantile literati, care of the self involved fulfillment of the needs of the "five senses." Sensual needs underwent profound changes in the late Ming as commercial publishing produced huge quantities of imprints to meet the intellectual, spiritual, practical, and entertainment needs of multiple reading publics.[58] Large quantities of fiction and drama were produced to provide alternative reading materials for the educated elites. In terms of readership, literati and merchants overlapped considerably. From the publishers' perspective, many genres—practical manuals, travel guides, and entertaining publications—could target the two simultaneously. *Shishang* ethics grew from the common experiences of literati and merchants, which included education, travel, and interactions with officials. The titles and subheadings of many travel guides and practical manuals simply and directly addressed literati and merchants in the same breath. Titles such as *Classified Essential Knowledge for Literati and Merchants* (Shishang leiyao), *Essential Readings for Literati and Merchants* (Shishang yaolan), *Essential Rules for Literati and Merchants* (Shishang guilüe), and *Ten Essential Rules for Literati and Merchants* (Shishang shiyao) simply leave out the other two vocations: farmers and craftsmen.[59]

Contemporary vernacular fiction and drama attest to the growing resemblance, even the merging of literati's and merchants' quotidian experiences. Literati and merchants were often protagonists in fictional worlds that mimicked the social world. Li Zhi not only was an avid reader of this burgeoning literature but also a fierce and eloquent champion of its literary value. In his widely read essay "On the Childlike Mind," he cites a comment on the popular drama *The Western Chamber* to proclaim that "the child's mind is the authentic mind."[60] By "the childlike mind," he means that "the first thought of the original heart-mind is without dissimilation and sincerely authentic" (fu tongxin zhe, juejia chunzhen, zuichu yinian zhi benxin ye).[61] As Pauline Lee has observed, "Li's ethical view directly impact[ed] his literary criticism, and his assessment of literary and historical figures, as well as his views on aesthetics."[62] The idea is that "the child's mind" is the foundation of his literary view, which is egalitarian, pluralistic, historical, and aesthetic. Any writing that expresses the authentic is great literature. For him vernacular literary works were even more valuable than Confucian classics, since not all of the latter were the authentic words of the sages.[63] It bears pointing out that contemporary literary genres such as fiction, drama, and eight-legged essays provided *shishang* writers like Li Zhi with a new discursive space for articulating and justifying the practices and ethics of the *shishang*. These genres also created a supplementary economic foundation for such practices as commercial publishing in the sixteenth century, enabling literati to take up positions in the economic field as professional writers.[64] Li Zhi did not, however, redefine great literature simply in terms of expression, nor did he repudiate the Confucian view that literature should serve didactic and social purposes.[65]

Like millions of other *shishang*, he navigated a world in which consumerism, commercial expansion, and the blurring of social distinctions were calling for a new ethics that reflected the changing structure of social possibilities and accentuated material desires. The teeming public of readers—literati seeking official careers without a moral calling and merchants going after profits without a sense of moral deficiency—thirsted for literature of the quotidian world, a world in which their paths crisscrossed as they struggled to fulfill their personal goals in the care of the self. As a writer, Li Zhi offered them not only practical aids like model eight-legged essays but also amusing and satirical comments on their favorite novels and dramas. With his brush, he entertained them with tantalizing stories, many of which were autobiographical, enlightened them with penetrating censure of the hypocrisy and moral condescension of officials, and moved them with honesty and a relentless quest for personal spiritual improvement.

SHISHANG AND THEIR RELIGIONS

Unlike conventional literati, who were expected to embody Confucian ethics, *shishang* were free to seek spiritual meaning in any religion. The great variety of syncretic practices bringing together the Three Teachings were emblematic of this late-Ming intellectual milieu. Wang Yangming and many of his disciples, such as Wang Ji, Luo Rufang, Yuan Huang (1533–1606), Lin Zhao'en (1517–1598), and Li Zhi, his teacher Wang Bi, and friends like Jiao Hong, all exhibited an open and inclusive attitude toward different religious traditions.[66] Liberated from the moral strictures of Confucianism and its *daoxue* doctrinal censure of heresy (*yiduan*), *shishang* were free to pursue their personal religious interests, as religion in the late Ming had become immensely private and personal.

I would argue that despite his deep interest in Buddhism, Li Zhi's ethics were those of a *shishang* literatus, not a Confucian literatus, a Buddhist adherent, or a Daoist practitioner in the conventional sense. Li Zhi was a syncretist in the broadest sense. As the chapters in this volume by Wai-yee Li,

Maram Epstein, Miaw-fen Lu, and Jiang Wu show, Li Zhi, whether in his authorial or objectified mode of presentation, was genuinely devoted to his own vision of the three religions. In his intellectual and religious convictions, he was a Confucian, a Buddhist, and a Daoist. He might not openly advocate the union of the Three Teachings, as Wang Ji and Lin Zhao'en did, but he embraced all three as vehicles for transmitting the Way.

Li Zhi's embrace of all the Three Teachings was a factor in his conflict with Geng Dingxiang, an outspoken follower of Cheng-Zhu *daoxue*. Hostile to those who derided Buddhism, Li Zhi articulated an ethics akin to the common position of the *shishang*, who were free to create their own personal spiritual world.

Li Zhi's much publicized flirtation with Buddhism notwithstanding, he was, as Jiang Wu confirms in his chapter, not a Buddhist in the conventional sense. Jiao Hong once asked Li which of the books he had authored were his favorites. Li replied, "All of them; none should be neglected. *A Book to Keep* (*Hidden*) embodies my spirit, *A Book to Burn* registers my life experiences, and *Expositions of the Four Books* bears witness to my learning."[67] It is worthy of note that none of these texts focuses exclusively on Buddhism, although *A Book to Burn* does contain some Buddhist content.[68] Insofar as his literary legacy is concerned, his interests and values revolved around the quotidian life of the human world. To the extent it was important, Buddhism was but one of the Three Teachings or three paths (*dao*).

While Li Zhi considered the pursuit of worldly interests and success as worthy and justified for all, his own personal priorities lay elsewhere. For him, wealth and status were sources of unbearable suffering in his personal spiritual pursuits, even though he demonstrated a Confucian interest in just and peaceful governance.[69] His personal frustrations with endless demands from his family and kin led him to relinquish all ties with his family in Quanzhou by taking the tonsure. But he did not abandon his family for the same reasons that might have motivated a Buddhist monk to take this step. He had striven for years to fulfill his obligations toward his family, and only after he considered his duties fulfilled did he renounce his family.[70] They had become an obstacle to his pursuit of friendship, reading, writing, and the Way.

Government service was likewise a conventional duty of Confucian literati, but it was becoming more elusive, expensive, and unsavory. By retiring from office, Li Zhi attempted to free himself from the Confucian literatus's obligation to serve the government. At any rate, he had already fulfilled his obligation by working in the government for over twenty years.

In "Miscellaneous Remembrances" (Za shu), he lamented his agonizing experience as an official.[71]

Regarding government service as merely an obligation, Li Zhi did not abandon his other Confucian values. He continued to uphold Confucian social ethics, but as a participant and critic, not as a gatekeeper or master. Indeed, he was committed to many Confucian values essential for sustaining the social order. As a *shishang* whose world depended on good government as well as loyal and competent officials, he took a deep interest in statecraft and dynastic history. Even after he retired from the government and took the tonsure, he never gave up his interest in problems of governance (*jingshi*).

His profound interest in Buddhism and his shaved head notwithstanding, he was no ordinary Buddhist and, by conventional standards, not even a good Buddhist. His use of the expression "leaving the family" (*chujia*) when applied to himself was more social than religious. He used this phrase not to indicate his cutting off all social ties and living as a monk in a monastery, but instead to connote the mode of existence he cultivated—hovering between that of a Daoist hermit and a Confucian gentleman disinterested in government service but fully engrossed in the quotidian world and harboring no cravings for wealth or power.

As illustrated by the three of his own books he prized most highly—*A Book to Burn, A Book to Keep* (*Hidden*), and *Expositions of the Four Books*, all of which concern his life experiences and views on government, history, and the Confucian classics, he unmistakably did not advocate the Buddhist negation of the mundane world. In light of his view of "leaving the family," his writing and publishing these three works no longer appears incompatible with his interests in Buddhism. His idea of the Way encompassed aspects of Confucianism, Buddhism, and Daoism, which in infinite configurations were practiced by the educated, including literati and merchants alike, or simply the mercantile literati (*shishang*). Different configurations of *shishang* syncretism were practiced by his friends Jiao Hong and Tao Wangling (1562–1609) and other *shishang* writers like Tu Long (1543–1605) and Tang Xianzu (1550–1616).

CONCLUSION

The significance of Li Zhi's thought and experiences needs to be reckoned in terms of the distinctive practices in late-Ming society. Li Zhi was a practical, satirical, entertaining writer and social critic. He was also a champion and a defender of a new society in which the dominant social group was no longer the Confucian literati but the mercantile literati, the *shishang*. He articulated the ethics of this new group in his writings. Ethical relationships were redefined in material terms of the quotidian life, and worldly interests were legitimate pursuits of all regardless of their social and vocational positions. This ethics reconfigured the social hierarchy, elevating merchants to the status of literati, whose moral calling was in turn dissociated from its practical goal of worldly success. Both the literati and merchants, who were becoming indistinguishable in their career trajectories, sought wealth, power, and social distinctions as their legitimate and essential life goals. Moral perfection, government service, and spiritual pursuits were all optional, incidental, and the private concerns of the individual. To readers of his times, Li Zhi was truly an avatar of the extraordinary, but in the social world, he was a *shishang* writer for the quotidian world and a penetrating heroic thinker and critic of his times, who with supreme discernment and literary ingenuity blazed the trail along which modern Chinese society tumbled forward.

NOTES

1 Li Zhi, "Zaowan shouta," in *LZ* 2:103.

2 For an intellectual history approach to Li Zhi's ideas, see Pauline Lee, *Li Zhi*.

3 For the emergence of *shishang* culture, especially *shishang* involved in commercial publishing, see Chow, *Publishing*, especially chs. 3, 4, and 5.

4 Rolston, *Traditional Chinese Fiction*.

5 See Chow, *Publishing*, 100–102.

6 In a letter to Pan Shizao (1537–1600), Li Zhi mentioned that the living expenses had been paid for his stay in Xishan Temple. This is information rarely found in late-Ming literati writings. Li Zhi, "Yu Pan Xuesong," in *LZ* 3:123.

7 Lin Haiquan, *Li Zhi nianpu kaolüe*.

8 Li Ruiliang, "Li Zhi nianpu jianbian," in *LZ* 26:426.

9 Li Zhi, "Da Geng Sikou," in *LZ* 1:77.

10 For example, he wrote prefaces to an anthology of examination essays, a collection of memorials, and a study of Zhang Zai's *Book of Change* for patrons. He was the ghostwriter for a treatise on government. Li Zhi, "Lun zheng pian," in *LZ* 1:242; Li Zhi, "Li Zhongcheng zou yi," in *LZ* 1:318–19; Li Zhi, "Ji wu ji wen, dai zuo," in *LZ* 1:346–48.

11 See Li Zhi, "Da Li Weiqing," in *LZ* 3:73.

12 Li Zhi, *Fenshu*, in *LZ* 2:104. Zhou Sijing paid 70 taels for the construction of the Vimalakīrti Monastery. *Xu Fenshu*, 3:19. Li moved into the Zhifoyuan

Monastery on Dragon Lake east of the city in the fall of 1588. Li Ruiliang, "Li Zhi nianpu jianbian," in *LZ* 26:449. The expenses for constructing other buildings at this site were disbursed from funds raised by his friends in Beijing and Buddhist devotees. Li Zhi, "Yu Chenglao," *Xu Fenshu*, in *LZ* 3:62.

13 He was working on *Supplement to New Account of Tales of the World* (Shishuo xinyu bu). Li Ruiliang, "Li Zhi nianpu jianbian," in *LZ* 26:447.

14 Li Zhi, "Yu Jiao Ruohou," in *LZ* 3:106–7.

15 Li Zhi, "*Laorenxing* xu," in *LZ* 3:177.

16 Chow, *Publishing*, ch. 4.

17 For discussion of Li Zhi's dismissive attitude toward his own examination success, see chapters 1 and 2.

18 Li Zhi, "Zi xu," in *LZ* 1:1.

19 The first edition of *Expositions of the Four Books* was published in Macheng between 1585, when Li moved to Macheng, and 1590, when *Fenshu* was first printed.

20 Li Zhi, "Da Jiao Yiyuan," in *LZ* 1:17–18.

21 Li Zhi, "Fu Jiao Ruohou," in *LZ* 1:110; Li Zhi, "Yu Jiao Ruohou," in *LZ* 3:19; Li Zhi, "Yu Jiao Ruohou," in *LZ* 3:130.

22 Li Zhi, "Da Jiao Yiyuan," in *LZ* 1:17.

23 See, for example, Li Zhi, "Yu Jiao Ruohou," in *LZ* 3:130. For a general study of the civil service examination, see Elman, *A Cultural History*.

24 Li Zhi, "Zi xu," in *LZ* 1:1.

25 Li Zhi, "Zi xu," in *LZ* 1:1.

26 Li Zhi, "Shiwen houxu," in *LZ* 1:324. The editor of that anthology of eight-legged essays may have been Li Yuanyang, who is referred to in the preface as Dazhongcheng, an unofficial title for governor.

27 Li Zhi, "Tongxin shuo," in *LZ* 1:276.

28 Li Ruiliang, "Li Zhi nianpu jianbian," in *LZ* 26:460.

29 Li Ruiliang, "Li Zhi nianpu jianbian," in *LZ* 26:467, emphasis added.

30 Li Ruiliang, "Li Zhi nianpu jianbian," in *LZ* 26:467.

31 Li Zhi, "Yu Wang Dingfu," in *LZ* 3:137.

32 Liu Dongxing, "Shu Dao gu lu shou," in *LZ* 14:334.

33 For example, Li Zhi, "Da Jiao Yiyuan," in *LZ* 1:17; Li Zhi, "Da Geng Sikou," in *LZ* 1:74–76.

34 There are no direct or allusive records of payments by correspondents. But it was customary or *li* for seekers of assistance to provide some form of remuneration for the service. Even if there had been such information, it would have been excised during the editing process.

35 Chow, *Publishing*, ch. 4.

36 For instance, *A Book to Keep* (*Hidden*) provided new perspectives on major historical figures likely to appear in the section of the examination devoted to policy (*celun*). Li Zhi, "Yu Geng Zijian," in *LZ* 3:135.

37 Chow, *Publishing*, ch. 5.

38 De Bary, "Individualism," 203.
39 De Bary, "Individualism," 145–48, 188.
40 Kriegel, LePain, and Cohen, *The State*, viii.
41 De Certeau, *Heterologies*, 24.
42 De Bary, "Individualism," 199–201.
43 Foucault, *The History of Sexuality*, 42.
44 Li Zhi, "Deye Ruchen houlun," in *LZ* 6:526–27; de Bary, "Individualism," 200.
45 Li Zhi, "Da Deng Shiyang," in *LZ* 1:8.
46 Li Zhi, "Da Geng Zhongcheng," in *LZ* 1:41. See also Li Zhi, "Da Deng Mingfu," in *LZ* 1:94.
47 Li Zhi, "Da Geng Sikou," in *LZ* 1:72–73.
48 Li Zhi, "Da Deng Mingfu," in *LZ* 1:94.
49 On the conflict between Li and Geng, see chapter 4.
50 For a study of luxury consumption of the literati in the late Ming, see Wu Jen-shu, *Pinwei shehua*.
51 For instance, in the Huizhou area, careers in business were considered no less respectable than official positions. See Yu Ying-shih, "*Shi-shang*."
52 Huang Zongxi, *Ming wenhai*, 994–95.
53 Huang Zongxi, *Ming wenhai*, 995.
54 Wu Jen-shu, *Pinwei*; Clunas, *Superfluous Things*.
55 Wu Jen-shu, *Pinwei*, 36–39.
56 In the Song, merchants could become officials. Guo Dongxu, *Songdai fazhi yanjiu*, 386. For members of the same family taking up careers in trade and government service see Bossler, *Powerful Relations*, 203–12. For examples in the Ming, see Szonyi, *Practicing Kinship*, 56–89.
57 Li Zhi, "You yu Jiao Ruohou," in *LZ* 1:119.
58 See the essays in Brokaw and Chow, *Printing and Book Culture*; Chow, *Publishing*, 92, 123–26.
59 Chow, "The Merging."
60 Li Zhi, "Tongxin shuo," in *LZ* 1:276.
61 Li Zhi, "Tongxin shuo," in *LZ* 1:276.
62 Pauline Lee, *Li Zhi*, 10.
63 Li Zhi did not repudiate the Confucian classics in their entirety. He was actually criticizing the way in which phony lecturers used them. Li Zhi, "Tongxin shuo," in *LZ* 1:276–77.
64 For the application of Pierre Bourdieu's concept of the field to the study of the changing relationship between literary production and commercial publishing, see Chow, *Publishing*.
65 Li Zhi, "Hongfu," in *LZ* 2:133.
66 For studies of various forms of syncretism, see Berling, *The Syncretic Religion*; Brokaw, *The Ledgers of Merit*; Ch'ien, *Chiao Hung*.
67 Yuan Hongdao, *Yuan Hongdao ji jianjiao*, quoted in Zhang Jianye, "Li Zhi yanjiu ziliao huibian," in *LZ* 26:149.

68 Despite the diverse contents of his writings in *A Book to Burn*, in a letter to Jiao Hong he nonetheless characterized this work as records of his musings on Buddhism. Li Zhi, "Da Jiao Yiyuan," in *LZ* 1:17.

69 Li Zhi, "San jiao gui Ru shuo," in *LZ* 3:223–24.

70 When he sent his family back to Quanzhou in 1587, his daughter was already married.

71 Li Zhi, "Gankai pingsheng," in *LZ* 2:109–110. On Li Zhi's obligations and devotion to his family, see chapters 2 and 3.

CHAPTER 9

PERFORMING AUTHENTICITY

Li Zhi, Buddhism, and the Rise of Textual Spirituality in Early Modern China

JIANG WU

THE INFLUENCE OF BUDDHISM ON LI ZHI CANNOT BE UNDERESTIMATED. Not only did he adopt Buddhist dress and live in a monastery after retiring from his official career, he also expressed himself in Buddhist terms and frequently referred to Buddhist scriptures in his writings. Unlike the conventional approach to the history of ideas, which simply presents Buddhism as abstract "unit ideas" and "categorical labels,"[1] this chapter reexamines the relationship between Li Zhi and Buddhism by exploring his experiences of reading and writing texts related to Buddhism. His practices as a reader and writer provide insight into his spiritual life and his understanding of spiritual authenticity. His intimacy with texts fostered a special kind of "textual spirituality" that was shaped by reading, writing, and performing.

LI ZHI AND THE DAO LEARNERS (XUEDAOREN) IN THE LATE MING

Scholars have characterized Li Zhi as a follower of Wang Yangming's movement and labeled him a member of the Taizhou School, following Huang Zongxi's characterization in *Biographies of Ming Scholars* (Ming Ru xue'an). Needless to say, this labeling is too simplistic to explain the complexity of his thought and activities, especially his engagement with Buddhism. According to this Confucianism-centered paradigm, Li Zhi, a Confucian literatus, used Buddhism as a convenient means to express his "radical" ideas.

This paradigm neglects the broader intellectual changes during the time, which involved Confucian elites, "mercantile literati," low-level examination candidates, government clerks, educated commoners, and Buddhist and Daoist clergy who aspired to pursue spiritual goals across sectarian and doctrinal lines.[2] This group of "spiritual seekers," who often referred to themselves as "Dao learners," pursued the supreme truth of the Way (Dao) and were unconstrained by strict sectarian or social identities.[3] Their learning aimed to identify and recover the *primus fons* (prime source) of the universe and the human world through a "retrieval process," not only intellectually but also directly and experientially without mediation. In order to attain the supreme Dao, these learners valued the spiritual advice of teachers and friends and traveled constantly in search of spiritual communities. During their spiritual journey, they often dabbled in different religious traditions and developed eclectic views regarding the "teachings" they encountered. Because of their syncretic views and "stubborn" pursuit of truth, they often found themselves at the edge of society and had ambivalent social, cultural, and religious identities. They were frequently marginalized and viewed as "strange" or "heretical."

Although as a social and intellectual phenomenon the rise of the Dao learners was visible in the late Ming, so far there has been no substantial study of the genealogy of this category or its religious significance. References to Dao learning (Xuedao) are ubiquitous in earlier Chinese sources, especially in early Chan texts, but the formation of the Dao learners as a unique social group seems to have coalesced only during the Northern Song. It is especially prominent in the work of the Northern Song literatus Chao Jiong (951–1034), who used this category extensively. His *Record of the Scrap Gold from the Dharma Treasure* (Fazang suijin lu), *New Compilation at the Zhaode Estate* (Zhaode xinbian), and *Essentials from the Dao Cloister* (Daoyuan jiyao) are miscellaneous notes on his thoughts, which resemble Western "commonplace books" on spiritual matters. Chao Jiong clearly addressed his writings to what he called "Dao learners," individuals seeking to transcend the mundane world by "penetrating" the Dao.[4]

During the late Ming, however, the Dao learners emerged as a distinctive social group with extensive networks. References to the Dao learners were common in Ming writings and can be found in various sources. Li Zhi mentioned this category quite often and referred to his students and followers generically as Dao learners. He sometimes alluded to "true" spiritual seekers as "Dao learners with true color" (*bense xuedaoren*). For example, when in Tongzhou Yuan Zhongdao asked him about self-cultivation, Li Zhi suggested the method of using key phrase (*huatou*) contemplation. Emphasizing the role of doubt, as Chan masters did, Li remarked, "Doubt is a gem for 'Dao learners': The greater the doubt, the greater the enlightenment experience." Yuan Zhongdao concurred that "Dao learners these days" (*shi zhi xuedaozhe*) did not appreciate the true value of doubt.[5]

Dao learners clearly were not restricted to the ranks of literati and officials. Many of them, such as Wang Gen, He Xinyin, and Yan Jun and his disciples Han Zhen, Luo Rufang, and Deng Huoqu, whom Li Zhi admired the most, hailed from humble origins and may be regarded as Dao learners as well.[6] Deng Huoqu, for example, inspired by his teacher Zhao Zhenji, was determined to lead a wandering life in search of spiritual attainment. Dressing as a monk, he went to many places to find teachers and friends. He traveled to Yunnan and shaved his head to become a monk there in 1548. He died in a small Buddhist temple close to Beijing. Like Li Zhi, he was viewed as an outlier and was ridiculed as a "strange person" (*yiren*).[7]

Li Zhi's life fits the profile of a typical Dao learner. His primary goal was to pursue the Way, the ultimate source of spiritual truth, without sectarian or doctrinal constraints. Like many Dao learners, who immersed themselves in Buddhist teaching and practice, Li Zhi had a particular interest in Buddhism. He was an avid reader of Buddhist scriptures and compiled many anthologies of Buddhist literature. During his spiritual journey, Buddhism played an indispensable role in shaping his life and thought. By his own account, his interest in Wang Yangming's School of the Mind prompted him to turn to Chan Buddhism. Like many of Wang Yangming's followers, he believed in the unity of the Three Teachings, a real synthesis of all three without any differentiation or, in the words of Edward Ch'ien (Qian Xinzu), a syncretism of "non-compartmentalization."[8]

Not only did Li Zhi achieve tremendous understanding of spiritual teachings, he also attempted to live a life that embodied the Way. His retreat from his official career to the Macheng area can be read as a deliberate decision to devote himself to the pursuit of the Way.[9] His apparent seclusion from the mundane world symbolized his unity with the Way, both intellectually and experientially.

This seclusion, however, did not signify his complete renunciation of the outside world. Rather, he was connected to regional and national networks of like-minded friends and followers through constant epistolary communication and publishing activities. Friends, travel, and communities were crucial for the late-Ming Dao learners to develop spiritual insights.[10] To some extent, their spiritual pursuit was not a secluded, private enterprise but a public and collective effort relying on community support and the development of a "communication circuit" that helped to connect Dao learners in geographically disparate communities.[11]

His Nanjing period, from 1567 to 1577, was crucial to his later intellectual life: not only did he participate actively in "lecture-meetings" (*jianghui*), but he also built a strong network of like-minded Confucian literati such as Jiao Hong, Guan Zhidao, Fang Hang, and Luo Rufang. In his later life, he constantly drew upon this network for his livelihood and kept himself connected to the intellectual communities in Beijing and Nanjing. His meeting with Geng Dingli in 1572, for example, introduced him to the intellectual community in the Macheng area.

However, Li Zhi's pursuit of the Way created an enduring controversy about his identity, especially because of his decision to shave his hair and dress as a Buddhist monk. It was in the Zhifoyuan Monastery that he made the radical change in his appearance.[12] This decision, along with his choice to send his wife back to Fujian, brought criticism that he had "abandoned human relations," because in the Confucian tradition a grown man's keeping his hair symbolized his assuming familial and social responsibilities. Li Zhi defended himself as "having had no choice" other than to shave off his beard. He also claimed he was "old and afraid of death." He argued that he did not wish to shirk his moral duties; rather, he "wanted to fulfill them but was not able to" (*yu zhi er buneng*).[13]

Li Zhi was ambivalent about his decision because after he shaved his head many people considered him a Buddhist monk. He spent about twelve years at the Zhifoyuan Monastery, where he completed many of his works. Although other monks assumed that he had shaved his head because he believed that doing so was a prerequisite for engaging in Dao learning, he insisted that this was not the case. Nonetheless, despite his protestations, his iconoclastic behavior led Confucians and monks alike to view him as an outcast and a "charlatan" monk.[14]

It is against this background of the rising spiritual, intellectual, and social movement of the Dao learners that Li Zhi can be seen as one of its representatives. Instead of thinking through the lenses of the traditional division of the "Three Teachings," I emphasize the common characteristics among these Dao learners in order to gauge their impact on culture and society. One commonality is their engagement in reading and writing spiritual literature, in particular, Buddhist texts.

READING, WRITING, AND THE FORMATION OF TEXTUAL SPIRITUALITY

Dao learners like Li Zhi saw no need to differentiate among the Three Teachings since they perceived in each teaching just one side of the truth. Such a spiritual tendency toward syncretism and eclecticism nourished a large group of people, mostly Confucian literati, educated commoners, low-status examination candidates, and Buddhist and Daoist clergy who were connected through a national network of communication. To understand how Buddhism influenced the formation of their spirituality and why Li Zhi emerged as a leader, we have to understand how such a type of spirituality came into being.

"Textual spirituality" involved reading, writing, hand-copying, and printing religious books.[15] Books, as well as many other "superfluous things" (*changwu*), including stylish scholars' studios, strange rocks, and ancient vessels and utensils, had become indispensable components of literati leisure life. These objects were used for "pure enjoyment of cultured idleness."[16] A book-centered elite culture in the late Ming privileged reading, writing, publishing, and collecting. Li Zhi, in *Upon Arrival at the Lake* (Chutanji), listed four categories related to book culture: collecting (*jushu*), transcribing (*chaoshu*), reading (*dushu*), and writing (*zhushu*).[17] Gradually, a distinct social class emerged, which has often been referred to as "book readers" (*dushuren*).[18]

To a large extent, Dao learners can be treated as a subset of "book readers" because Dao learners shared a deep commitment to reading and writing. In addition to Confucian Classics, they read Buddhist and Daoist scriptures; in the late Ming, Buddhist scriptures such as the *Śūraṅgama Sūtra*, *Avataṃsaka Sūtra*, *Platform Sūtra*, and other Chan literature came to occupy a central position in their reading activities. This facilitated the immediate apprehension of "truth" by reading books rather than solely participating in devotional activities mediated by clergy or institutions. Moreover, the spiritual orientation of this group of spiritual seekers was to emphasize the supreme and sophisticated expression of philosophical and intellectual wisdom. Although they did not entirely dismiss faith and devotion, they did not consider them primary criteria for judging spiritual progress.

In addition to reading religious texts, Dao learners also engaged in writing, commenting, and anthologizing. As Paul Griffiths argues, the act of religious reading implies a set of epistemological views regarding the reader's attitude and knowledge and often entails religious writing, such as compiling anthologies and composing scriptural commentaries. Thus, religious writing reinforces the set of spiritual attitudes developed in religious reading.[19] In my book *Enlightenment in Dispute,* I give some evidence of this kind of religious reading and writing of Chan literature in the late Ming. Here, I focus on Li Zhi's reading and writing of Buddhist literature to illuminate the formation of his textual spirituality.

There is no evidence that Li Zhi studied Buddhist scriptures systematically. His understanding of Buddhism seems to have derived from a variety of sources, including popular morality books. According to his own account, he truly began to engage in reading Buddhist scriptures only in 1576, when he was fifty years old. It is not known, however, which scriptures he initially read. But the titles of the *Heart Sūtra,* the *Lotus Sūtra,* the *Combined Treatise on the Avataṃsaka Sūtra* (Huayan helun) by Li Tongxuan, and works of Chan literature such as the *Joint Collection of the Five Lamps* (Wudeng huiyuan; hereafter *Five Lamps Collection*) often appear in his writings.

His strategy for interpreting these pieces of Buddhist literature is most clearly stated in "The Outline of the *Heart Sūtra*" (Xinjing tigang), which was carved and printed in Huang'an. According to Li Zhi, the classics or scriptures were written in order to reveal the supreme truth, or Dao. His task as a commentator was to "explain" or "interpret" (*jie*). However, "explanation" is a double-edged sword: it can block the reader from apprehending the Dao; only if used correctly can it lead students to enlightenment:

> The Way is fundamentally great, but since the Way [is presumed to] rely on scriptures, one cannot clearly make it out. [Moreover], when seeking to clarify the Way by clarifying the scriptures, one can't discern the way because of the [attached scriptural] explanations. Thus, scriptures are robbers of the Way and explanations are barriers to the scriptures. So what use are they? Despite all this, good scholars penetrate the scriptures while bad ones are stuck clinging to them. Explanations enlighten the capable and mislead the incapable. And so it is appropriate that [scriptures and explanations] should be considered as robbers and barriers.[20]

Here, "explanation" is not the literal understanding of the meaning of words, as in the conventional Confucian and Buddhist commentarial tradition. (Actually there is little evidence that Li Zhi consulted these commentarial works.) Rather, "explanation" refers to the "subjective meanings" he imposed upon the texts, as Rivi Handler-Spitz has pointed out.[21]

Li Zhi had a leisurely reading life, which he describes in many places. He thoroughly enjoyed books and even wrote a poem to celebrate the joy of reading.[22] Residing at the Zhifoyuan Monastery, he used to "close and lock the door, and spend his days reading books."[23] Writing, commenting, and anthologizing were also part of his daily routine. Not only did he write commentaries on Chinese Classics,[24] but he also wrote commentaries on Buddhist scriptures such as the *Heart Sūtra*, the *Diamond Sūtra*, the *Śūraṅgama Sūtra*, and others. His writing philosophy has a strong individualistic tendency, which can be summarized in his own words: "In general, I write only to amuse myself, not for other people."[25] For him, a textual world centered on himself was created through writing, regardless of the existence of others and their opinions. This philosophy leads to a unique writing strategy: "When ordinary people write, they begin from the outside and fight their way in; when I write, I start from the middle and fight my way out."[26] Here, he highlights that good essays must rely on the author's own understanding and insight. His writing is also a direct expression of his feeling, even if the manner he used was direct, poignant, and "vulgar," in a way not conventionally acceptable. As Pauline Lee has pointed out, "When Li Zhi writes of writing, he speaks of 'spewing' (*pen*), 'spitting' (*tuo*), and 'pouring' (*su*) out one's feelings."[27]

Li Zhi established a routine of reading and writing that led him to compile anthologies. While reading, he selected and hand-copied passages he deemed worthy. Sometimes he asked his monk attendants to work for him. When they had completed their copying, he was ready to compile an anthology. After moving to the Zhifoyuan Monastery, he wrote to Jiao Hong, wanting to compile a book called *Confucian Chan* (Ruchan) to document the ideas of Confucians who spoke about Chan; he also mentioned publishing another volume, called *Clergy's Chan* (Sengchan), to collect monks' Chan sayings. He intended these two volumes to be published together, so that readers could gain access to "precise, pithy, and essential" teachings.[28] As a result, during his lifetime, Li Zhi compiled a variety of anthologies related to religion.[29]

Besides being a prolific writer and compiler, Li Zhi directly participated in the production process of his works. As Kai-wing Chow elaborates in chapter 8, Li Zhi was deeply engaged in printing activities, including publishing religious texts. In 1574, together with Jiao Hong, he published the famous morality book *Tract of the Most Exalted on Resonance and Response* (Taishang ganying pian), which might be his earliest foray into publishing.

In this book, he argues that the essential Buddhist teaching of causation was a corollary to the Confucian teaching of resonance response (*ganying*). The purpose of printing this book was to show that resonance response is not a hollow teaching but rather a profound truth.[30] Li Zhi seems to have responded to the printing request favorably and promptly, showing his eagerness to get his works publicized. In a letter to Jiao Hong dated 1588, he divulges interesting details about his involvement in publishing. His *Commentary on Three Classics* (Sanjing jie, most likely his commentaries on *Laozi*, *Zhuangzi*, and the *Heart Sūtra*) was carved in Jinhua, possibly by Pan Shizao (1537–1600). He compiled these anthologies rather quickly, in roughly nine days, by his own estimation. His comments on "The Outline of the *Heart Sūtra*" were added to a calligraphic rendering of this text, which he wrote for his friends. He did not expect to publish most of these works. Instead, he claimed to have written them simply for his own entertainment.[31]

Li Zhi's fondness for Chan literature led him to reprint several important Chan texts. While he was in Yunnan, he had the *Platform Sūtra* recarved at Mount Wuhua in Kunming.[32] He also arranged for the printing of the *Five Lamps Collection*, a text that he studied extensively. The preface he wrote for this printed work shows he was sensitive to the textual variations in different editions, especially the description of Tianhuang Daowu from the Yuan monk Yehai Ziqing's reprint.[33] As is well-known in Chan history, the identity of two Chan monks from different lineages in the Tang dynasty, Tianhuang Daowu and Tianwang Daowu, was the focus of a series of debates during the seventeenth century.[34] However, Li Zhi's preface to the reprinted *Five Lamps Collection* already contains important textual information related to the later Tianhuang and Tianwang debate. Li Zhi's investigation of the biography of Tianwang Daowu by Qiu Xuansu predated any polemical works about the debate. It may be the case that his substantial study of Chan literature influenced a group of literati and sparked the debate in the seventeenth century.

Not only did he engage in textual verification of Chan texts; he also attempted to rearrange the accepted Chan lineage based on his own understanding. In his "Treatise on the Five Lineages" (Wuzong shuo), written in 1598, he made a bold claim that the teaching styles of all the five Chan lineages actually resembled the style of Mazu Daoyi, whom he regarded as the spiritual source of all Chan traditions. His view resurfaced in the later debate on Chan lineage, which sought to rearrange the accepted Chan lineage by emphasizing Mazu's spiritual heritage.[35] What's more, he drew attention to Nanyang Huizhong and Yongjia Xuanjue because he thought even without dharma heirs, their superb understanding proved that they were the true heirs of the Sixth patriarch Huineng.[36] Clearly, Li Zhi placed his "interpretation" based on reading above the sectarian conventions established in Chan communities.

Evidence suggests that Li Zhi inhabited a world of textual spirituality constructed by intrinsic links among religious books. But when the issue of practice and devotion came to the forefront, he became equivocal and hesitant. Sure, he lived in a Buddhist monastery for a long time and was familiar with monastic routines; he even acted as abbot in the absence of Wunian Shenyou and set rules for monks.[37] He also once chanted the *Medicine King Sūtra* (Yaoshi jing) for an extensive period in the hope of recovering from asthma.[38] However, he remained at a remove from the genuine life of the monastic community and abstained from serious devotional practice. Even after he shaved his head, he continued to consume meat.[39]

It is a puzzle, however, that Li Zhi seems to have committed himself to Pure Land belief and practice, which appeared to be deeply devotional, in addition to Chan Buddhism. In 1593 he returned to Dragon Lake and built a Buddha hall. In 1597 he resided at Jilesi in West Mountain in Beijing and compiled *Essentials of Pure Land* (Jingtu jue) in three fascicles. This raises the interesting question of whether Li Zhi's spirituality was purely "textual." In fact, his discussions of Pure Land Buddhism are couched in the Chan rhetoric of spontaneity and nondualism. In his "Preface to *Resolving Doubts about the Pure Land*" (*Jingtu jue* qianyin), he declared, "Amitābha Buddha's Pure Land is no other than the Pure Land of one's own mind." Moreover, chanting Buddha's name and Chan investigation serve the same purpose of "purifying one's own mind."[40] As he also claimed in a letter to his friend Li Shihui, "There are many Buddha worlds. Wherever there is a world, there is Buddha. Wherever there is a Buddha, I would travel there and sojourn there. . . . If there is a Buddha in Heaven, I'd go there; if there is a Buddha in Hell, I'd go there as well. Why must I restrict myself to solely going to the inner court of the Tusita Heaven like Bai Letian [Bai Juyi] or being reborn in the Western Land like Tiantai Master Zhiyi and Chan master Yongming Yanshou?"[41] This passage mentions multiple descriptions of the Buddha Land, including the ones famous Buddhists such as Bai Juyi, Zhiyi, and Yongming Yanshou aspired to. However, for Li Zhi, these are all equal options with no differentiation or preference. The key point is to be with the Buddha no matter where he resides. Even here, where he is promoting Pure Land practice, he does not consider himself restricted by a devotional program aiming at rebirth in the Western Paradise. Rather, he conceives of Pure Land practice as simply one option for pursuing the supreme Way. In this sense, it was only one of the many practices subordinated to and supplementing his textual spirituality; his regular Buddhist practice could be considered auxiliary.[42]

PERFORMANCE AND AUTHENTICITY

The late Ming was a time of performance: drama, opera, and ceremonial rituals were staged in cities and villages and greatly enjoyed by people of all walks of life. Not satisfied with operating purely on the intellectual plane, late-Ming Dao learners sought to demonstrate their superior understanding of the truth through action. Wang Yangming's thought on the "unity of knowledge and action" (*zhixing heyi*) expressed such a tendency. The late-Ming "spiritual seekers" thus had a strong inclination to "do things" in order to demonstrate their "textual spirituality."

The performances I analyze here were largely enactments of Chan encounter dialogues (*jifeng wenda*), in which two or more interlocutors discuss spiritual matters.[43] The purpose of these performances was to demonstrate one's supreme understanding of authenticity (*benzhen*). In my book *Leaving for the Rising Sun*, I explain how the notion of authenticity as a spiritual, cultural, and political ideal became a hotly debated issue in early modern East Asia. The sharp contrast between ideal and reality stimulated an urge to search for "the real" in spiritual traditions. As I define it, authenticity is "the foundation of a tradition and the source for forming a coherent and consistent value system." Disbelief and doubt inevitably lead to what I call an "Authenticity Crisis."[44]

As is well known, authenticity is central to Li Zhi's thought and has been extensively studied.[45] Some argue that he advocated for a view of authenticity that included a full appreciation of human nature, especially pure, pristine, and genuine human feelings and desires as the basis of a full-fledged human life. He expected all Dao learners to cultivate themselves based on the notion of authenticity: "Dao learners should root themselves in authenticity [*jiaogenzhen*]. They must consider it their ultimate goal to be released from birth and death, to depart from the sea of suffering, and to avoid fear."[46]

Philosophically speaking, Li Zhi's view on authenticity can be summarized as a type of "radical nondualism." This hermeneutic strategy is consistent with the methods he used when commenting on the second fascicle of the *Śūraṅgama Sūtra*. He studied the scripture extensively and at one time may have attempted to write a commentary for the entire text. However, just one fragment of his commentary has been preserved; it can be found in *A Book to Burn*. This text contains his interpretation of the paragraph "Darkness as Void" (Huimei weikong), which provides a cosmological vision of the world. This paragraph points to the deluded ideas of common people and explains how the "darkness" of ignorance creates a "mental void" that becomes the source of dualistic thinking. Li Zhi explains as follows:

> How could the manifestation of the Mind be emptied! . . . Don't you know that everything, from my material [Rūpa] body to the mountains and rivers in the external world, the entire earth and all the space you can see is the material manifestation from my "Marvelously Illuminated True Mind" [Miaoming zhenxin]? All these are the natural manifestations of the Mind. Who can empty them? If the manifestation of the Mind is always the manifestation of the True Mind, is the True Mind situated within the Rūpa body? It is that all phenomena are but part of my True Mind, as the waves are floating bubbles of the great ocean. If the ocean could empty itself of bubbles, then the True Mind could empty itself of its phenomena as well. How self-delusional![47]

Here Li Zhi repeats a typical Mahāyāna trope about the unity of the Mind and its manifestations, noumena and phenomena, essence and function. His rhetoric of nonduality also echoes the key tenets of Wang Yangming's philosophy of the mind. However, what Li Zhi advocated was radically different from a mere reiteration of the rhetoric of nondualism, resulting in literary and philosophical exposition of the Mahāyāna teaching. Unlike most monastic and scholarly commentators, Li Zhi attempted to carry out in his real life the teaching of nondualism, and he sought to change the "corrupt" and "fake" reality he and his fellows criticized. This meant breaking down social boundaries, tearing up masks of hierarchy, and abolishing hypocritical "Daoxue" discourses, so as to return human existence to its "authentic" root, or in Li Zhi's words, so as to restore the "childlike mind." In his nondualistic world, the social divide between elite and commoner disappeared, and the differences among the Three Teachings could no longer hold. In other words, Li Zhi's teaching implies that the ideal of nondualism went beyond mere rhetoric and became part of an individual's knowledge of his own being. It held transformative power over a person's worldview, social behavior, and life experience. For Li Zhi, to embody the ideal of nondualism, the ultimate goal was to "penetrate, then transcend" (*toutuo*).

The most powerful display of such a radical understanding is performance. The type of performances in which Li Zhi engaged were natural extensions of his textual spirituality and depended heavily on his use of text. Just as Chan practitioners enacted encounter dialogues, groups of like-minded people, both Dao learners and later Chan masters, enacted their spiritual ideals by performing "scenes" recorded in Chan texts. These events, in turn, would be recorded in text format. After being collected, printed, and published, these textualized performances would be circulated among an even larger community, reinforcing a sense of "performatively created reality." Although the performances may appear to be "impromptu," or even "faked" and "forced," they originated from textual sources and remained "distinctively real" within the textual realm through anthologizing and publication.[48]

Such performances were often recorded in compilations of anecdotes, recollections, and memoirs as well as in anthologies, essays, and treatises, providing references to their origins in Li Zhi's life. His performances with his followers were recorded in collections such as *Conversations in the Oak Grove* (Zuolin jitan) and *Answers to Questions at Yongqing Temple* (Yongqing dawen). How to interpret them, however, poses a challenge. I suggest considering these documents as literary imaginings of performances based on actual happenings. Interpreting the texts in this way presupposes the existence of a community of performers, "audience members" who watched "live performances," and readers who encountered these performances on the printed page. Through such a communal link and exchange of ideas, consensus could be reached within this community. As in many kinds of theater, performances followed a "script," which could be repeated and duplicated. Very often, the voluminous Chan *gong'an* stories (Jpn. *kōan*), full of performative encounters, served as textual sources and models for Li Zhi's performative imitations.[49] As we will see, action and performance—the result of textual spirituality—took place in a networked community and largely followed the model of encounter dialogue in Chan Buddhism.

Li Zhi's enthusiasm for the performance of encounter dialogues can be seen in his comments on Yan Jun's famous "performance" of "rolling on the ground" (*dagun*). In his letter to Zhou Sijiu in 1588, Li Zhi remarked upon an anecdote about a commoner named Yan Jun who was inspired by Wang Yangming's learning. According to Geng Dingxiang's account, during a lecture meeting Yan attended, when the *Great Learning* was discussed, Yan suddenly began rolling on the ground and yelling, "Look at my 'pristine moral consciousness' [*liangzhi*]!" This episode became legendary and circulated widely among the literati.[50] However, the anecdote received mixed reviews. Apparently, some viewed Yan's rolling negatively and criticized it as the action of a mad Chan Buddhist. Li Zhi, however, viewed Yan's behavior positively. He said the following in response to Geng Dingxiang's negative characterization of the event:

> I don't know whether Shannong [Yan Jun] truly attained this state. I don't even know whether Shannong was actually capable of rolling on the ground for his entire life. I fear that even he may not have been able to do so. But if he did attain this level, then he is my teacher. How could I doubt this man's accomplishment simply because other people laugh at him? To base my opinion of him not on my own investigation but on other people's ridicule would be a mistake. It would oppose the principles of empirical investigation, of learning for one's self. These were the very source of Shannong's spontaneous intuition; it had absolutely nothing to do with "Chan [Zen] tricks." Shannong attained the highest level of "studying for one's own sake." That is why he was able to behave in such a way. Had any fraction of his mind been diverted by the desire to impress other people, he would not have been able to succeed.[51]

Let's take a close look at an example of such a performance between Li Zhi and the Buddhist monk Wunian Shenyou to illustrate how he demonstrated his "authentic" self through performance. Wunian, a local monk from Macheng, lived with Li for more than ten years. The two developed a deep bond, despite occasional conflicts due to differences in personality.[52] Through Li's network, Wunian came to be known among the literati as an eminent monk. The collection of epistolary correspondence between him and famous literati was preserved in the Jiaxing Buddhist canon (Jiaxingzang). The following conversation between the two occurred because Wunian was having trouble reaching enlightenment and felt perplexed about his self-cultivation. Here is the record from Wunian's biography:

> When he saw [Wunian], the layman [Li Zhi] asked: "How is your cultivation [*gongfu*]?" Master [Wunian] replied: "I have doubts." Li Zhi asked further: "What do you doubt?" The master said: "If I have insight I will know." Li Zhi became serious and remarked:

> "This is not your insight." The master was confused again. [Later], Li Zhi invited his friends to meet [Wunian] at Sima mountain. There was also a scholar-monk who came and joined the meeting. Sitting at night, Li Zhi asked: "How can the pure and original [mind] suddenly produce mountains, rivers and the earth?"[53] After the scholar-monk explained, the layman [Li Zhi] said: "Wunian, would you explain how?" When Wunian Shenyou was just about to open his mouth, Li Zhi pushed Wunian's knee and said: "How about this [*ni*]!" Wunian was suddenly awakened. When he returned to Dragon Lake, he practiced quiet sitting for several days and all he had learned in his lifetime disappeared completely. From that time on, all his doubts and anxieties disappeared forever.[54]

This encounter closely resembles Chan *gong'an* stories. Li and Wunian formed a teacher-student relationship, in which Li presented Wunian with a perplexing question. Readers well versed in Chan literature may also perceive resonances between the wording of this anecdote and phrases found in existing *gong'an* stories. For example, Li Zhi's use of the word *ni* is actually an imitation of the response of the Song Chan master Foyan Qingyuan in his encounter with the Song literatus Feng Ji (?–1153) preserved in a record of lamp transmission. It is recorded that the two one day walked through the dharma hall where a novice monk was reciting a phrase from a poem by the Tang monk Changqing Huiling: "Among all phenomena he revealed only his body" (Wanxiang zhi zhong du lushen). Upon hearing this, Foyan said to Feng, "Ni," exactly the same response Li Zhi used in his performance.[55]

Another example can be found in *Answers to Questions at Yongqing Temple* (Yongqing dawen), compiled in 1602. This document contains a precious record about Li Zhi and his conversation with his followers during his 1598 visit to Nanjing. Invited by She Changji and Wu Dechang, who were students of Yang Qiyuan, a student of Luo Rufang and an admirer of Chan Buddhism, Li Zhi resided in Yongqing Monastery in Nanjing. During the meeting, he was surrounded by his followers and acted like a Chan master.

Li Zhi's behavior and conversation in Yongqing Monastery in Nanjing, translated below, were also recorded in a way similar to the Chan encounter dialogues:

> Cheng Hunzhi from Haiyang came to see Li Zhi but did not have a single word with him. One day, he and Mr. Fang Ren'an

[Fang Hang] sat together with Li Zhi, who remained silent for a long time. The two [Cheng and Fang] [began to] converse with one another.

Mr. Fang said: "When Mr. Luo Rufang teaches students, he is full of energy."

Cheng replied: "Yes. Mr. Luo teaches students earnestly and honestly. He is truly a great, compassionate father."

Li Zhi suddenly turned to them and said: "If it is so, I am not [a great, compassionate father]. Let me ask you: why did you want to see me?"

Cheng replied: "To seek the Buddha."

Li Zhi said: "Where is the Buddha?"

Cheng said: "All over the dharma realm."

Li Zhi said: "What is your place among the Buddhas?"

Cheng said: "I am number one."

Li Zhi said: "Since the Buddhas are all over the place, how can you be number one?"

Cheng said: "Everyone is number one."

Li Zhi replied: "Is there such a thing as number one?"[56]

This encounter dialogue involves three people and begins with a conversation between Cheng Hunzhi and Fang Hang. Li Zhi remains in the background without saying a word. His silence hints at his superb understanding of the truth, like that of the Layman Vimalakīrti at the end of chapter 9 of the *Vimalakīrti Sūtra*. Li Zhi joins in only when the conversation between Cheng and Fang shifts to praising Luo Rufang. Li raises essential Buddhist questions about the number one Buddha. Cheng replies that Buddhas are everywhere and he himself is the number one Buddha. By declaring this, Cheng shows his understanding of the Mahāyāna teaching of the Buddha nature: All sentient beings are equal as they are endowed with the potential to become a Buddha. However, Li does not regard this as the ultimate teaching, and he is not satisfied with the logical contradiction in Cheng's answer that everyone is number one. The conversation ends with Li's negation: there is no such thing as the number one Buddha. He transcends the paradox of conventional thinking and comes to rest upon the state of nondualistic "emptiness." Readers familiar with Chan *gong'an* literature will immediately recognize the similarities. To a large extent, the structure of encounter stories like this resembles a joke: a long and paradoxical setup is created to highlight the revelation of the punch line. When the punch line,

Li Zhi's last remark, is revealed, the episode stops with the expectation that the enlightenment experience ensues in the silence of all participants.[57]

Li Zhi even used his highly dramatic death as a punch line. When a follower named Wang Keshou asked him, "What will your final act be?," Li Zhi replied, "I should benefit from people who don't know me. Dying in jail with honor should complete my life." He then clapped his hands and said loudly, "At the time [of my death] I will become famous throughout the world. How happy! How happy!" In this episode, both questions and answers follow a typical Chan *gong'an* style, as demonstrated by the phrases "final act" and "How happy! How happy!"[58]

Close reading of texts by and about Li Zhi reveals that performance constituted a major part of Li Zhi's spiritual life, which was characterized by his relentless pursuit of the ideal of authenticity. Such performances of authenticity, initiated by spiritual seekers such as Li Zhi and based on Chan literature, were transformed into textual anecdotes that circulated widely and had a profound impact on the intellectual, particularly the Buddhist community. As I explain in my book *Enlightenment in Dispute*, such performances first developed among Dao learners. Later, when they were reintroduced into the Chan community, they became part of the Buddhist revival in the seventeenth century.[59]

CONCLUSION

The complexity of Li Zhi's thought and behavior is difficult to explain. As many have pointed out, his writing is full of contradictions. The role that religion, especially Buddhism, plays is even more subtle and nuanced. Some previous scholarship, especially in Chinese and Japanese, labeled him in either Confucian or Buddhist terms so as to "classify teachings" (*panjiao*) and subtly elevate one teaching above the others. According to some scholars, Li Zhi either "synthesized" (*zarou*), "combined" (*huitong*), or "entered and exited" (*churu*) the Three Teachings, but in the end he "returned" (*guiyi*) to one of them.[60]

Unlike such scholarship, this chapter seeks to situate Li Zhi and his pursuit of Buddhist teaching in immediate life experience relevant to his thought. In my view, although his national notoriety and his embrace of extreme views set him apart from the majority of Dao learners, he was nonetheless first and foremost a member of this growing community. Like them, he read and wrote actively and fostered a kind of "textual spirituality" anchored in the notion of authenticity. For this reason, his involvement with Buddhism must be understood within this context. Familiar questions about his connection with Buddhism must be abandoned and a new question posed in their place: How did his reading and writing of Buddhist texts contribute to the formation of his textual spirituality and his continual performance of authenticity?

NOTES

1 The "unit idea" approach was most famously proposed by Arthur Lovejoy for the study of the history of ideas. See Lovejoy, *The Great Chain of Being*. On the confusion of using labels in Chinese religion, especially Daoism, see Sivin, "On the Word 'Taoist.'"

2 On Li Zhi's boundary-crossing as a mercantile literatus, see chapter 8 especially pp. 158–59.

3 They often called themselves *xuedaoren, xuedao zhiren, xuedaozhe*, or simply *xuezhe*. Because of the spiritual purpose of their pursuit of knowledge, I feel hesitant to use the word "student" or "scholar" to translate the term. It should be noted that in Li Zhi's writing the term *xuedao* takes on a meaning drastically different from the meaning of orthodox Confucian "Learning of the Way" (Daoxue), which he vehemently opposed.

4 Chao Jiong, *Zhaode xinbian* (*Siku quanshu* edition), *j.* 1, p. 5. For Chao Jiong's practice of religious reading, see Jiang Wu, *Enlightenment*, 54–56. See also Skonicki, "Getting It for Oneself."

5 Yuan Zhongdao, "Shu Yuegong ce," in *Kexuezhai ji, j.* 21, in *LZ* 26:164.

6 Li Zhi also published Deng's works and befriended Deng's disciples in Huang'an. According to Li, Deng Huoqu had a disciple named Li Shou'an who hailed from Huang'an, and two of his disciples were Wang Shiben (Ruowu) and Zeng Jiquan. See Li Zhi, "Zhenshi," in *LZ* 1:197–98; Li Zhi, "Gaojie shuo" (1589), in *LZ* 1:294–96. For a full translation, see Li Zhi, *A Book to Burn*, 121–24. In 1585, Li Zhi wrote a preface to Deng's *Nanxun lu* ("*Nanxun lu* xu," in *LZ* 3:191). On Li Zhi's relationships with his teachers and students, see chapter 5.

7 Li's intellectual opponent Geng Dingxiang described three intellectuals of his time as "strange people": Deng Huoqu, He Xinyin, and Fang Yilin. See Geng Dingxiang, "Lizhong san yi zhuan." For the conflict between Geng and Li, see chapter 4. See also Rowe, *Crimson Rain*, 95–103.

8 Ch'ien, *Chiao Hung*, 117–20.

9 Because of its geographical advantage, during the mid Ming the Macheng area, including the newly created Huang'an County, gradually rose to prominence as a transportation hub and commercial center, fostering education and culture. According to William Rowe, agricultural commercialization, lineage building, accumulation of wealth, and the formation of

a merchant network brought this area to regional prominence and allowed Buddhism to flourish. See Rowe, *Crimson Rain,* especially chs. 3 and 4.

10 See also chapters 4 and 8.

11 Here I have adopted the concept of the "communication circuit" from Darnton's "What Is the History of Books?"

12 Handler-Spitz, *Symptoms,* 79–87.

13 See Li Zhi, "Fu Deng Shiyang," in *LZ* 1:25, and the four poems he wrote about shaving his head (*LZ* 2:260). It is noteworthy that Li Zhi's tonsure was not accompanied by an ordination ceremony. Ordination was a serious, life-changing event, and historically Buddhist monks were supposed to accept three types of ordination ceremonies in succession: for novice, full precepts, and bodhisattva. The government usually controlled the official ordination platforms (*jietan*), which offered the full precepts ordination ceremony. However, during the 1560s, the Jiajing emperor ordered that official platforms be halted. This led to an unusual situation: ordained monks could no longer receive official recognition. The Triple Platform Ordination (Santan dajie), which is the commonly accepted ritual today, was not invented until the early 1600s. The silence about the ordination ceremony in Li Zhi's and other monks' writings during this period seems to corroborate this lack of a centralized ordination system at that time. On the reinvention of the ordination ceremony, see Jiang Wu, *Enlightenment,* 28–31; Jiang Wu, "Discipline." On Li Zhi's alleged renunciation of family ties, see chapters 2 and 3.

14 See chapter 6.

15 Jiang Wu, *Enlightenment,* 53–64.

16 Clunas, *Superfluous Things,* 18.

17 Li Zhi, "Shiyou er," in *LZ* 12:332–60.

18 Li Yu, "A History of Reading"; Cherniack, "Book Culture"; Thomas Lee, "Books and Bookworms."

19 Griffiths, *Religious Reading*; McDermott, *A Social History.*

20 Li Zhi, "Notes on the 'Outline,'" in *LZ* 1:280, translation adapted from David Lebovitz's in Li Zhi, *A Book to Burn,* 119.

21 Handler-Spitz, *Symptoms,* 130–52.

22 Li Zhi, "'Dushule' bing yin," in *LZ* 2:240–41; Li Zhi, *A Book to Burn,* 211–15.

23 Yuan Zhongdao, "Li Wenling zhuan," in *LZ* 26:158.

24 These works include exegeses of *The Book of Change* (Jiuzheng yiyin), *Laozi* (Laozi jie), *Zhuangzi* (Zhuangzi jie), and *Expositions of the Four Books* (Si shu ping). On Li Zhi's commentarial practices, see chapter 7, especially 135–39 and chapter 10.

25 Li Zhi, "Ji jingyou shu," in *LZ* 1:171–72, translation modified from Li Zhi, *A Book to Burn,* 20.

26 Li Zhi, "Yu youren lun wen," in *LZ* 3:21, translation adapted from Li Zhi, *A Book to Burn,* 245–46.

27 Pauline Lee, *Li Zhi*, 111. See also Rivi Handler-Spitz's discussion of Li Zhi's "provocative" style in *Symptoms*, ch. 6.

28 Li Zhi, "You yu Congwu Xiaolian," in *LZ* 1:208.

29 As a follower of Wang Yangming, he published Wang's selected works (Yangming xiansheng Daoxue chao) and chronological biography (Yangming xiansheng nianpu). He also published Wang Ji's selected writings (Longxi xiansheng wenlu chao). His Buddhist compilations include Dahui Zonggao's recorded sayings (Li Zhangzhe pixuan Dahui ji), *Records of Cause and Consequence* (Yinguo lu, also known as Ganying pian), *Commentary on Yao Guangxiao's* Daoyu lu (Li Zhuowu xiansheng pidian *Daoyu lu*), *Essay of Good Words* (Yanshan pian, also known as Sanjiao miaoshu), and more. He also published selections of popular religious texts such as *A Record of a Cart Full of Ghosts* (Kuichezhi) and the anthology *Unstringing the Bow* (Shuohuzhi).

30 It was reprinted in 1578, during the time Li Zhi was posted to Yunnan. This work later became known as *Yinguo lu* after he took up residence at Dragon Lake.

31 Li Zhi, "Da Jiao Yiyuan," in *LZ* 1:17–18.

32 He Shouzhuo, "Wenshusi beiji," in *LZ* 26:338–39.

33 Li Zhi, "Chongke *Wudeng huiyuan* xu," in *LZ* 3:180; Jiang Wu, *Enlightenment*, 319–23. It should be noted that the issue of the two Daowus was made public by Qu Ruji (1548–1610), who visited Li Zhi in 1595. It is possible that Li's note influenced Qu's compilation of *Zhiyue lu*.

34 The significance of this debate is that the biographers of these two monks claimed that the Chan monk Longtan Chongxin, from whom the two Chan lineages, Yunmen and Fayan, derived, was their dharma heir. The different attributions of the lineage affiliation of Longtan Chongxin would thus significantly alter the official lineage transmission system promoted in *Jingde chuandenglu* and *Wudeng huiyuan*. The earliest reference I have found to the dubious identity of these two monks was made by Qu Ruji in his Chan anthology *Pointing to the Moon* (Zhiyue lu) published in 1602. See Jiang Wu, *Enlightenment*, 198.

35 Jiang Wu, *Enlightenment*, 311–12.

36 Li Zhi, "Wuzong shuo," in *LZ* 3:218.

37 During Wunian Shenyou's absence, Li Zhi temporarily assumed the position of abbot and led a series of ritual events. He also helped to regulate the monastic assembly. See related essays in *Fenshu*, *j.* 3 and 4 (*LZ*, vol. 1) and *Xu Fenshu*, *j.* 4. (*LZ*, vol. 3). A number of these pieces are translated into English in Li Zhi, *A Book to Burn*, 172–85.

38 See Li Zhi, "Lisong Yaoshi gaowen" and "Lisong Yaoshi jing bi gaowen," in *LZ* 2:38 and 41. The assembly started on the fifteenth day of the tenth month and lasted for 120 days. Participants first chanted *Yaoshi jing* in forty-nine fascicles for Li Zhi's health. In total, they chanted nine scriptures.

39 Li Zhi, "Shu Xiaoxiu shoujuan hou," in *LZ* 3:201–3; Li Zhi, *A Book to Burn*, 267–69.

40 Li Zhi, *A Book to Burn*, 180.

41 Li Zhi, "Yu Li Weiqing," in *LZ* 1:149.

42 This is similar to what Charles Jones has classified as a type of Pure Land practice "subordinated to other practices." See Jones, "Toward a Typology of *Nien-fo*." Li Zhi's close associate Yuan Hongdao used similar rhetoric to justify Pure Land practice as a legitimate method of self-cultivation. See Jones, "Yuan Hongdao and the *Xifang helun*." Similar to Li, after compiling a major Pure Land anthology to defend its practice, Yuan did not convert to Pure Land Buddhism but remained committed to Chan Buddhism. See Jones, "Yuan Hongdao and the *Coral Grove*." For Yuan's connection with Li Zhi, see Zi, "Strolling in 'Coral Grove,'" 23–28. For analysis of a literati community with extensive links to Li Zhi, see Eichman, *A Late Sixteenth-Century Chinese Buddhist Fellowship*.

43 According to John McRae's definition, encounter dialogue "refers to the spontaneous repartee that is said to take place between master and student in the process of Ch'an training. This type of communication includes both verbal and physical exchanges that are often posed in the form of sincere but misguided questions from Ch'an trainees and perplexing, even enigmatic, responses from the masters" ("Encounter Dialogue," 340–41). For a recent study, see Van Overmeire, "Encounter Dialogue."

44 Jiang Wu, *Leaving*, 5–7. The issue of authenticity was a prevalent topic in seventeenth-century philosophy, literature, and art. See Bentley, *The Figurative Works*; Epstein, *Competing Discourses*.

45 See, for example, chapter 1. See also Pauline Lee, *Li Zhi*; Handler-Spitz, *Symptoms*.

46 Li Zhi, "Guanyin wen," in *LZ* 2:80.

47 Li Zhi, "Jiejing wen," in *LZ* 2:6. For a translation of the original texts in *juan* 2 of the *Śūraṅgama Sūtra*, see Hsüan Hua, *The Śūraṅgama Sūtra*, 52–53.

48 I have studied extensively how this type of performance was first enacted within the literati communities and later extended to the revived Chan communities. See Jiang Wu, *Enlightenment*, 160.

49 For understanding *gong'an*, see Sharf, "How to Think." For comprehensive studies of the *gong'an* tradition in East Asia, see also Heine and Wright, *The Kōan*.

50 Geng Dingxiang seems to be the only person who mentioned this anecdote. For a description of this episode in English, see Li Wai-yee, "The Rhetoric of Spontaneity." Yan Jun is a neglected "Taizhou" scholar who nurtured students such as He Xinyin, Luo Rufang, and Han Zhen. His complete collection, printed in 1855, was discovered only in the 1980s. Aside from Geng Dingxiang's reference to this anecdote, there is no reference to Yan Jun's rolling on the ground in this rediscovered collection. There is only one

similar account of his student's rolling on the ground. According to Yan Jun, once he traveled on a boat, his student Cheng Xueyan, after realizing the truth, rolled ten times on the cabin floor (*jiu gun cangban shizhuan*). See Yan Jun, "Cheng Shendao zhuan," in *Yan Jun ji*, 22.

51 Li Zhi, "Da Zhou Liutang," in *LZ* 1:220, translation adapted from Li Zhi, *A Book to Burn*, 72.

52 Wunian hailed from Macheng and became an eminent monk in his own right. His interactions with Li Zhi were extensive. Li's tensions with him and other monks in the Zhifoyuan Monastery reached their peak in 1594. Wunian left for Huangbo Mountain in neighboring Shangcheng County to build Fayan Monastery. For his relationship with Li Zhi, see Ling, "Wunian yu Li Zhi." There is a collection of his records, including a dozen letters exchanged with famous literati during this time. See *Huangbo Wunian Chanshi fuwen*, in *Mingban Jiaxing dazangjing* 20:6. For the CBETA online edition, go to http://tripitaka.cbeta.org/J20nB098_006. A punctuated edition was published recently in China. See Hou Suping, *Chan fei yizhihua*.

53 This is a quote from the *Śūraṅgama Sūtra*.

54 "Xingyou" (Biography of Wunian), *Huangbo Wunian chanshi fuwen*, in *Mingban Jiaxing dazangjing* 20:526 (traced through CBETA). My translation is adapted from my *Enlightenment*, 69–70.

55 *Taishō shinshū Daizōkyō*, 51:671b.

56 Li Zhi, *Yongqing dawen*, in *LZ* 18:337.

57 For the use of the joke structure to understand the teaching of nondualism, see Ziporyn, *Evil*, 154–57.

58 *Li Wenling waiji*, in *LZ* 26:84.

59 I have argued that the revival of Chan Buddhism in the seventeenth century should be considered an extension of late-Ming literati culture. See Jiang Wu, *Enlightenment* and *Leaving*.

60 There are numerous such categorizations in East Asian scholarship on Li Zhi. For a recent example, see Dai Jingxian, "Li Zhi yu Fojiao."

PART V

AFTERLIVES

CHAPTER 10

PERFORMING LI ZHI

Li Zhuowu and the Fiction Commentaries of a Fictional Commentator

ROBERT E. HEGEL

IT WOULD BE FASCINATING TO HAVE LOOKED OVER THE SHOULDER of the historical Li Zhi as he read what were to become known as the "four masterworks" (*si da qi shu*) of the Ming novel, all of which were in circulation during his lifetime. As a student of fiction I have searched for evidence of just how their original readers responded, any remarks or notations that might reveal their intellectual and emotional reactions when Ming readers encountered this new and largely unprecedented literary form, the extended vernacular prose narrative studded with poems. But unless a copy with extensive marginalia can somehow be identified, that goal is elusive.[1] Instead, we must be content with the rather more self-conscious commentaries that became a conventional feature of lengthy prose narratives around the turn of the seventeenth century.

One of those commentators was, ostensibly, Li Zhi. And yet very little of this body of commentary can be safely attributed to his brush.[2] The imaginary figure introduced here is the fictitious Li Zhi, conjured up using his style name (*hao*) Li Zhuowu as commentator for the novels *Loyal and Righteous Outlaws of the Marsh,* or *Water Margin* (Shuihu zhuan), *Romance of the Three Kingdoms* (Sanguo zhi yanyi), and *Journey to the West* (Xiyou ji). "Li Zhuowu" refers here only to the persona created as a literary commentator and critic, not the historical Li Zhi.

Scholars in China and the West began to treat indigenous Chinese fiction commentary and criticism as an area for serious study only in the 1980s. Some took the attribution of this commentary to Li Zhi as reliable and reflective of his presumed philosophy of the novel. Instead, my purpose here is to interrogate "Li Zhuowu" as a persona created to embody a model reader. I hope thereby to contribute to a larger sense of how readers during the late Ming appreciated the historical Li Zhi while drawing attention to the growing importance of commentary in Chinese literary history.

COMMENTARY ON THE VERNACULAR NOVEL

By around 1600 the Chinese vernacular novel was reaching its first stage of maturity, and commentators addressed reading audiences according to their presumed level of sophistication—suggesting that at least some readers were highly educated, and others simply were not.[3] Commentaries in his name and attributed to the historical Li Zhi gained a certain amount of literary authority, thereby appropriating his elite aura for the relevant novels. Commentaries in the name of renowned cultural figures ostensibly would insinuate vernacular fiction into the category of genres that appealed to the most highly educated and thus provide the reader with sophistication by association.[4] It is not surprising, then, that publishers would wish to associate Li Zhi's name with commentaries on three of the four major Ming-period novels, the "masterworks" that later became central texts in the literati novel tradition.

Commentaries played an important role in the development of vernacular fiction in China, both demonstrating and inviting participation in interpreting a text.[5] They elicited and modeled individual visions of what the narrative meant, or at least implied, inviting the reader to engage with the text emotionally as well as critically, to create *personal* versions of fictional tales. In addition, commentaries might also embody the not-always-positive evaluation of literary style from the position of a detached and critical observer. Moreover, beginning in the late sixteenth century, when commentary became a regular addition to most new novels, these paratexts suggested ways to improve one's own writing by studying their stylistic features. Attending closely to style—especially of the classics, of course—was a central practice in civil service examination preparation at the time, one that the historical Li Zhi encouraged.[6] Commentaries integrated fiction into mainstream writing practices by insisting on both the literariness and the didactic value of vernacular fiction. This was a crucial step in the development of the novel as a vehicle for literary and artistic expression for literate elites (*wenren*).

FICTION COMMENTATORS

The sixteenth century produced a number of now largely forgotten novels. Their authors were editors, printers, and professional writers. None of the sixteenth-century novels was an individual creative work; all—even the masterworks—were to some degree compiled and adapted from earlier texts, whether historical or religious or from the large, shaggy category of *xiaoshuo*. Many shared plot materials with contemporary plays and other oral performance forms as well. Scholars attribute the introduction of novel commentaries to purely commercial motives. Even so, the appearance of commentaries signaled a developing contest in the novel format between collective knowledge and shared, orthodox values, on the one hand, and the perspectives and evaluations of identified individuals, on the other. They also heralded and encouraged private, silent reading and authorized a range of personal emotional responses.

An early commentator, editor, and printer was the Fujian bookseller Yu Xiangdou (ca. 1555–after 1637), whose books exemplify the distinctive style of Jianyang, Fujian booksellers who printed illustrations in the top register of every page and text in the lower two-thirds. Sparse comments and explanations appear in the margin above the illustrations. Yu Xiangdou printed several early novels with his own commentary, including *Outlaws of the Marsh Chronicles, with Dense Commentary* (Shuihu zhizhuan pinglin, 1594) and *Chronicles of the Three Kingdoms, with Dense Commentary* (Sanguo zhizhuan pinglin, ca. 1600). He also printed an edition of *Romance of the Three Kingdoms* with commentary attributed to "Li Zhuowu."[7]

The Li Zhuowu commentaries played a pivotal role in the growth of fiction criticism, heralding the beginning of a second stage in its development.[8] They both expanded upon earlier commentarial practice, most notably by the bookseller Yu Xiangdou, and anticipated later developments by the better known literati fiction commentators Jin Shengtan (1608–1661), Mao Lun (1605?–1700?), his son Mao Zonggang (1632–after 1709), and Zhang Zhupo (1670–1698). In addition to *quandian*, the by then conventional marks of emphasis alongside lines of text, the Li Zhuowu figure favored *meipi* and *jiapi* (marginal and interlinear/interlineal comments, respectively), forms pioneered by his predecessors. These brief comments recorded seemingly spontaneous reactions to specific lines of text, as Yu Xiangdou had done.[9] But Li Zhuowu's extensive reliance on general observations (*zongping*) at the ends of chapters was an innovation in novel criticism. His model was most assuredly the sober reflections left by the great

Han-period historian Sima Qian (ca. 145–ca. 85 BCE) in his *Historical Records* (Shiji). As we will see, the tenor of Li Zhuowu's chapter postfaces is thoughtful and more complex than his terse exclamations within the text. In their degree of critical sophistication, these comments were also exceptional for the time; they set a standard avidly followed by subsequent generations of fiction commentators. To some degree, his marginal and interlineal comments also provided a new model. The literary historian Ye Lang concludes that Li Zhuowu was the true founder of novel criticism in China.[10]

WHO WAS LI ZHUOWU?

Despite his explicitly acknowledged fascination with *Outlaws of the Marsh*, the historical Li Zhi wrote very little about it that can be authenticated.[11] Instead, the commentaries produced for editions of various printing houses, especially Rongyutang in Hangzhou, were mostly written by one Ye Zhou (Ye Wentong, also known as Ye Yangkai, fl. 1595–1624), of Liangxi (modern Wuxi in southern Jiangsu, near Suzhou). A man of considerable learning, in 1594 he had studied with Gu Xiancheng (1550–1612), founder of the politically active Donglin Academy in Wuxi. Contemporary accounts portray this Ye Zhou as an eccentric, "a frustrated scholar addicted to wine who supposedly met his end at the hands of the husband of a woman he was having an affair with."[12] Qian Xiyan (fl. 1612) scornfully describes Ye as a poor scholar who drank too much and supported himself by ghostwriting. But several decades later the noted scholar-publisher Zhou Lianggong (1612–1672) pronounced Ye a man of broad knowledge despite his unconventional behavior. To later readers he was remarkable for his deep feeling and sharp wit, the source of a number of jokes that circulated among his friends.[13] Ye probably supported himself primarily by writing prefaces, commentaries, and the like, as did many others during the late-Ming period.[14] Rongyutang and other publishers must have been satisfied that his writing would attract customers. We might further conclude that his commentaries were successful in projecting an image that readers were content to identify with Li Zhi.[15]

Ye Zhou's Li Zhuowu commentaries included the three novels as well as *Red Duster* (Hongfu ji), *The Bright Pearl* (Mingzhu ji), *The Jade Case* (Yuhe ji), and other *chuanqi* plays. There is no question that he penned the comments on *Romance of the Three Kingdoms*; he identified himself as Ye Zhongzi (Second Son) in several chapter-ending comments. In style and content, these three Li Zhuowu commentaries closely resemble one another.

Modern scholars of Chinese fiction commentary have been careful to distinguish between what might safely be attributed to the historical Li Zhi and what seems to have been crafted by the commentator Li Zhuowu. Li Zhi's comments on *Outlaws of the Marsh* are recorded in his essay "On the Childlike Mind" (Tongxin shuo) and in his preface to *Outlaws of the Marsh*, both found in *A Book to Burn*; portions were copied into the Li Zhuowu prefaces to two subsequently quite influential imprints of the novel. These were the Rongyutang edition, which was printed in 1610, and the Yuan Wuya edition of 1612. If any comments are authentically Li Zhi's, they appear there.[16]

In "On the Childlike Mind," Li Zhi asserts that all the finest writings express authenticity and spontaneity; he singled out the Yuan play *The Western Chamber* (Xixiang ji) and the Ming novel *Outlaws of the Marsh* as prime examples of these values.[17] The ambiguity in precisely how authenticity is manifested becomes the starting point for the Li Zhi prefaces to *Outlaws of the Marsh*. There authenticity is interpreted as loyalty to the throne (*zhong*) and generosity, altruism, and righteousness toward one's comrades (*yi*). The *Outlaws* preface praises bandit leader Song Jiang for his supposed exceptional loyalty and righteousness, his outstanding strength and virtue (*li* and *xian*) in an age of corruption and weakness at court. In response to the ideology of his age, Li Zhi emphasizes the commanding presence of the strong leader and his unfailing influence over the others among the novel's 108 heroes. Thus he urges that at court and in the provinces, all persons in positions of authority should read and take inspiration from the virtues of Song Jiang and his band. The authors of the text were motivated by their outrage (*fen*) at the state of the Yuan rule, he asserts.[18]

COMMENTS ON *OUTLAWS OF THE MARSH*

The Li Zhuowu commentary on *Outlaws of the Marsh* discussed here is from the Rongyutang (1610) edition.[19] Ye Zhou's interests in *Outlaws* certainly include its literary aspects. In chapter 10 he repeatedly praises descriptions of the misadventures of the hero Lin Chong with interlinear comments composed of a single word, "[Like a] painting!" (*Hua*); in chapter 11 he does the same, again repeatedly, adding praise for the writing to that for his subject: "Marvelous in action and description!"[20] Of Lin Chong's slaughter and butchery of the childhood friend who betrayed him, a marginal comment declares, "What a happy killing! Had he stabbed him to death as he did the others, with one thrust of his spear, it would have held no interest." Once his enemies are dispatched, Lin Chong decapitates them, then ties the heads together by their hair and dumps them on the offering table before an image of the mountain deity in the temple where he had taken refuge from a storm. At that, Li Zhuowu comments, simply, "Interesting!" (*Qu*). On the hero's actions thereafter, the comments frequently read "Marvelous!" (*Miao*) or again "Like a painting!" When Lin catches a whiff of warm wine, Li's comment is "[What a] great idea!" (Hao xiangtou). When a group of farmers refuse to share their drink with Lin Chong he comments, "Detestable!" (*Wu*), "Boring!" (*Mei qu*), "Laughable!" (*Kexiao*), and "How rude!" (*Mei li*). Once the farmers have scattered and Lin Chong helps himself to their wine, a marginal comment reads, "Here it becomes interesting again" (Dao ci you you qu).[21] The Rongyutang chapter-end critique makes the commentator's concern with the art of writing even more explicit, albeit not theoretical: "The Bald Old Man says, 'The text of *Outlaws of the Marsh* is fundamentally fictitious, but all because it describes situations truthfully, it deserves to last as long as heaven and earth. As with Li Xiao'er and his wife in this chapter: their absurdity was as clear as a picture. When later you get to the "Creating Chaos in Heaven" array, it is so fake that it is hard to read no matter how much effort you put into it.'"[22]

What we see here initially is a rather subjective response to specific textual elements, with several general patterns: the commentator likes certain of its characters, and he enjoys the dense vernacular description of individuals and actions characteristic of the tales that compose *Outlaws of the Marsh*. The larger campaigns in the later parts of the novel that emphasize strategy and magic are of less interest. But the Li Zhuowu comments also reflect his views on what constitutes good fiction: the commentator's enthusiasm for particular characters and their struggles can be seen in the misadventures of Yang Zhi in chapter 12.[23] The commentator's interest in the individual seems focused on his moral reactions to challenges, wherein personal choices take on significance for both society and the state.

The commentator's position becomes more politically engaged once Song Jiang, the eventual leader of the Liangshan bandits, is introduced. In the critique following chapter 18, he declares, "In general there has been little difference between catching a thief and becoming a thief or arresting a robber and becoming a robber. In order truly to get rid of all thieves, the most important thing is to get rid of those constables" (340). In chapter 39 Song Jiang, in his cups, writes a rebellious poem on the wall of a wine shop. There the retired official Huang Wenbing sees it and uses it to curry favor with the local prefect. The Li Zhuowu chapter postface as printed in the Yuan Wuya edition reads, "Huang Wenbing copied down the rebellious poem in order to prove that Song Jiang's madness was a ruse. This was an evil intent, but he was not a man of no worth. It is just that he was trying to harm another person to get the attention of the magistrate, and so made himself detestable" (733).

In these two places, Li Zhuowu emphasizes the personal capacities needed by the administrator and the consequences of their absence. Moreover, he draws attention to the ways that concern for personal advantage can draw an otherwise laudable character into self-destructive acts.

One of the novel's more gruesome scenes occurs in chapter 41. Led by the naked, ax-wielding Li Kui (interlineal comment: "Truly loyal and righteous!"), seventeen of the nascent Liangshan outlaw band had rescued Song Jiang from the execution grounds in the previous chapter. Now Song enlists the Liangshan band to take revenge on Huang Wenbing for provoking the arrest. Although they leave his righteous brother and all of the villagers unmolested, they exterminate the rest of Huang's immediate family. On the slaughter of these innocents, Li Zhuowu comments, "Since he knows that [his arrest] had nothing to do with the common people of Wuweijun, he should also know that it had nothing to do with the forty or fifty men and women of his household; for what reason did he harm them as well?" Once captured, Song Jiang has Huang stripped and tied to a tree while the outlaws drink ("A fine diversion!"), cursing him roundly for the harm Huang brought him. (This is no wonder, since Song Jiang has no sense of propriety.) But the cruel punishment Song levies is ostensibly in response to Huang's (nicknamed "Huang the Stinger," Huang Fengci) running roughshod over the local population; Song aims to remove his stinger ("Interesting!" [*Qu*]), he claims. The work of carving the living victim's flesh is given over to Li Kui ("A Buddha!" [*Fo*]), who refuses Huang the speedy death he requests ("Interesting!"), but after the description of the agonized execution, the marginal comment reads "Excessive!" (*Tai shen*). And as the outlaws congratulate Song Jiang on his revenge, Li Zhuowu asks, "What is there to celebrate? This makes no sense!" At the end of the chapter he offers an impassioned critique of the whole episode: "Huang Wenbing was also an intelligent man, a man of use to the state. Having seen the rebellious poem, how could he not have been alarmed? Song Gongming should not have blamed him for it. The raid on the execution grounds at Jiangzhou was all for the rescue of the two lives; it was unavoidable. But as for [the raid on] Wuweijun: in the end how could someone so understanding carry out such acts? A grave wrong, a grave wrong!"[24]

Thus in an intense section of the novel, we see Li Zhuowu responding somewhat inconsistently, but his comments regularly record an immediate, very personal and emotional response to the text.

We also see an impatient, even irascible face of the commentator when he critiques the positions of his predecessors. In the postface for chapter 52, Li Zhuowu scorns a previous commentator's reproof of Li Kui's killing Luo Zhenren as simplistic: "These words are just so much gas!" By contrast, Li Zhuowu then explains his position on *Outlaws of the Marsh* as fiction: "Every action, every word can be interesting. Every piece of writing in the world should take interest as its highest priority. If it is interesting, what matter that the event or the person should be wholly fictitious?" (984).[25]

COMMENTARY ON *ROMANCE OF THE THREE KINGDOMS*

The first edition of the perennially favorite historical novel *Romance of the Three Kingdoms*, presumably completed during the late fifteenth century, was published in 1522, making it the earliest of the "four masterworks" and, indeed, the progenitor of the entire novel tradition in China. By the 1550s book printers in Fujian were producing a discontinuous fictional history of China from time immemorial through the founding of the Ming in compilations that centered primarily on individual dynastic periods.[26] *Three Kingdoms* was the model, but few approached that level of literary sophistication in theme, characterization, and style of language. Except for reconceiving its chapter divisions and relatively minor editing by the father-and-son team Mao Lun and Mao Zonggang in the 1660s, no later editor made significant changes to the text: it remains a largely untouchable classic—in marked contrast to other early novels that were regularly rewritten and extensively adapted from their first appearance through the twentieth century.[27]

The Li Zhuowu commentary in *Romance of the Three Kingdoms* is certainly the work of Ye Zhou.[28] His comments here again take the form of chapter-ending general critiques (*zongping*) and laconic exclamations scattered throughout each chapter, either as comments in the upper margin of the page or, more frequently, placed within or between the lines of text.[29] Generally the novel is not heavily annotated; Ye Zhou's persona passed over without explicit notice many elements of the text that would attract extensive attention from subsequent readers and commentators.

The tenor of the Li Zhuowu comments clearly varies according to their location within the text. Some chapter-end critiques often seem flippant, suggesting ways to cut the annotated text rather than how to interpret it, as other Ming literary commentators would later do.[30] At one point Li Zhuowu quotes himself (chapter 117); in chapter 105 he quotes a quip he made in response to another person's question, as if recording a conversation among friends about the novel. Yet at novel's end he comments gravely on the transience of all grand endeavors.[31]

By contrast, in his interlineal comments he explains events and the factors that provoked them as if for the benefit of less conscientious readers. Among his first is a sardonic comment on Liu Bei. When Liu is described as a "hero" who "was not particularly fond of reading," Li Zhuowu responds, "Taking no joy in reading is the mark of a hero." Li Zhuowu regularly comments on the events narrated in ways that reveal his emotional engagement with the text and its characters. Clearly the commentator did not like General Cao Cao; he frequently criticizes him for his vaunting ambition and his vanity.[32] When Cao Cao finally realizes that he is dying, the interlineal comment reads, "Finally the old traitor understands. Were he alive today, who knows how many scandalous acts he would have committed!" Such bleak humor is more regularly visible here than in the *Outlaws of the Marsh* commentary.

Li Zhuowu takes the side of Liu Bei in his quixotic efforts to restore the falling Han imperial house. Liu's general Guan Yu is a favorite. "Guan Yunchang [Yu] has the compassion of a saint or a Buddha and thus could not [kill Cao]," the commentary says, with apparent enthusiasm. His remarks about the ferocious general Zhang Fei are almost affectionate. In chapter 45, when Zhang Fei comes with an unneeded rescue mission in case Liu Bei had fallen afoul of a plot on his life, Li Zhuowu writes, "That old Zhang: always acting rashly!" (568).

Often the commentator criticizes characters harshly, commenting, "Fool, fool!" (*Chiren, chiren* [619]). But he can also respond positively. In chapter 117, after Zhuge Chan falls in a hail of arrows and slits his own throat with a sword, his son Zhuge Shang makes a suicidal foray into the besiegers of his city to die with his father. The commentator praises him for his action: "A loyal subject, a filial son, a benevolent grandson!" (1420). In chapter 45, when Zhou Yu in his frustration orders a messenger from Cao Cao beheaded in violation of the rules of warfare, he is stopped by his officer Lu Su, who rebukes him: "When two states go to war, they do not execute emissaries." Zhou Yu retorts, "Behead this emissary to show our mettle!" "Just right! Just right!" (*Da shi, da shi* [569]) Li Zhuowu applauds interlineally.

One episode particularly engaged this commentator's attention: Liu Bei's famous three visits to Zhuge Liang's thatched hut to enlist his aid as a strategist in preserving the Han Empire. In chapter 37, on their first visit, Liu gives the houseboy a long list of his titles in introducing himself. The boy replies, "I can't remember so many names!" Li Zhuowu comments, "This boy is one marvelous fellow!" (Tongzi bian shi miao ren le [464]).

Following a description of the area around the hut as Liu Bei sees it, the commentary reads, "He is also excellent at elements of scene, indeed a marvelous writer! (Yi shan shu jingwu. Gu shi miaoshou [464]). When Zhang Fei explains that he is concerned only that Liu Bei is wasting his time, Li Zhuowu chuckles, "A Buddha—Zhang is a Living Buddha!" (Fo: Zhang Huofo [466]).[33] Similarly inconsequential remarks continue throughout the episode, revealing a reader who is relishing the text more than he is carefully analyzing it, presenting his preferences rather than seeking to discover the art of fiction.

Most irreverently, on the eve of the great Red Cliffs naval battle that ultimately decides the fate of the realm, as Liu Bei and his allies worry about whether there will be a southerly wind to aid their attack, the Li Zhuowu comment reads, "The 'southern wind' [*nanfeng*] has always prevailed; we need not worry about it" (613). One can only assume that he was not referring only to movements of air masses from the south but also to the "fashion" among literati for romantic involvement with boys and young men (*nanfeng* or the "southern" or, by pun, "male fashion"). He attributes this observation to a monk named Riniu.[34]

However, in the chapter-end evaluative commentaries the commentator perhaps most frequently presents himself as a somewhat curmudgeonly older man who has seen through most of the foibles of his age. At the end of chapter 105, as Li Zhuowu he quotes comparisons of a major historical figure, Zhang Liang (d. 186 BCE), chief strategist for the Han dynasty founder, with Zhuge Liang as a means to reinforce his sense of Zhuge's greatness in attempting to restore the Han Empire. But the person quoted here is the real commentator Ye Zhou, a private joke for readers who knew his true identity. Then he continues, disparaging any alternative interpretations of historical as well as fictional characters, "Would not a couple of comments made recently by [Ye] Zhongzi of Liangxi be relevant in relation to these two gentlemen? I append them here. Zhongzi said, 'Zifang was a knowledgeable sort of person and Kongming was a sincere sort.' The imperceptive foolishly say that Zifang was false and Kongming was true. Dear me! How could such people be fit to discuss those two gentlemen with!"[35]

At the end of chapter 112, the Li Zhuowu persona further endorses his own insights by making a sarcastic comment about what he considers a lack of originality. Referring to the literal meaning of the title *Romance of the Three Kingdoms*, he observes, "Since [similar events] were narrated previously, this does nothing more than change the names to pad out the narrative. How irritating! This is why it is an 'elaboration' [*yanyi*] of the *Chronicles of the Three Kingdoms* [*Sanguo zhi*]. Laughable!" (1367).

Elsewhere he also sympathizes with the need for fictional elaboration. At the end of chapter 21 in reference to Liu Bei's dropping his chopsticks, Li Zhuowu observes, "This [episode] was added in by some later person and is not to be taken as authentic. Anyone who reads the *Popular Romance of the Three Kingdoms* must first distinguish such things. Even so, this is a 'popular romance' [*tongsu yanyi,* more literally, a 'popular elaboration'] and not official history. If it were not so [embellished], then how could it be 'popular'?" (265).

Ye Zhou in the guise of Li Zhuowu makes critical observations on his contemporaries as well: praising the sterling qualities of Liu Bei and Zhuge Liang for their acknowledgment that Cao Cao must be allowed to live, he observes that they are "not like people nowadays who would hate [Cao Cao] and wish him dead" (618). Here again, Li Zhuowu is presented as a reader who appreciates the text, an interpreter and appropriate model for readers unfamiliar with the form. Despite his sharp tongue, he generally provides thoughtful, personal interpretations, with empathy for and understanding of these fictional characters.

COMMENTS ON *JOURNEY TO THE WEST*

In the rush among China's new generation of scholars in the 1920s to identify individual creators for all of China's great works of popular literature, Hu Shi (1891–1962) was the first to identify Wu Cheng'en (ca. 1500–ca. 1582) as the author of *Journey to the West.*[36] The evidence he cited was slight and dated long after Wu's death. In recent decades, scholars have become less confident in this attribution; the novel is now often considered a work of collective authorship, as are *Romance of the Three Kingdoms* and *Outlaws of the Marsh.* In large part this is because an increasing number of textual sources have been identified for the novel, ranging from local tales of extraordinarily human-like monkeys in Hangzhou to Chinese-language summaries of the great Indian epic *Rāmāyaṇa.*[37] Even so, because the earliest extant version, the 1592 Shidetang edition, is so highly polished, its various parts so skillfully adapted and smoothly integrated, it could have reached this stage only through the concerted efforts of one or a very small number of tremendously creative writers working together over a relatively long period of time.[38]

The edition known as the *Journey to the West with Mr. Li Zhuowu's Commentary* (Li Zhuowu xiansheng piping Xiyou ji) for the most part follows the text of the 1592 edition and carries a prefatory comment (tici) written by the playwright and novelist Yuan Yuling (1592–1674) seemingly dating from the 1620s. There are relatively few "eyebrow" comments (*meipi*) in the upper margins of pages scattered through the text. Here as in the other novels, many comments within the text consist of only a single word: "Interesting!" (*Qu*), "Fantastic!" (*Huan*), or "That ape!" (*Hou*). The original "General Principles" (Fanli)—perhaps also penned by Ye Zhou—cautions that the novel will force the reader to "hold his sides with laughter" (*pengfu*) even as its message "seeps into his heart" (*qinxin*); the general critiques embody the subtlety of all the Daoist masters in transferring anguish into hilarity and scorn, it observes. The "General Principles" also explain that these laconic interjections draw attention to the narrative's philosophically important subtexts. For his part, Yuan Yuling lauds its indirection, praising the "fantastic" (*huan*) elements of the novel as composing its "truth" (*zhen*) and directing the reader to pursue its subtle implications. As the editors of this volume describe them, the commentator's concerns are with the emotional relationship between the individual mind and the world, with explaining points of literary excellence, and with castigating the foibles of his contemporaries.[39]

As we have seen in the other novels, Li Zhuowu here again points out particularly excellent writing as a model for his contemporaries. For example, in chapter 30 a demon has transformed the monk Tripitaka into a tiger, and their faithful horse (a magically transformed dragon)—desperate to save their master—changes himself into a beautiful girl to get the demon drunk so that he can be killed. When his plan fails, the wounded horse changes back into a dragon in order to hide. In the general critique at chapter's end, the commentator says, "For the Tang Monk to change into a tiger and the white horse to transform into a dragon is the most inspired, the most wonderful example of imagination, the most extraordinary, the most fanciful piece of writing. How could some bachelor's-level student studying for the next examination have written something like this?"[40]

In chapter 17 a marginal comment on an invitation from one monster to another shows his love of reading: "What an extraordinary imagination at work here—just extraordinary!" (220; *JW* 1.356).

More commonly the Li Zhuowu commentary here is rather provocative, often quite distinctive for its sardonic wit and philosophical insights—reminiscent of one of the Daoist masters to whom the "General Principles" likens the commentator. For example, in chapter 14 after the Monkey King kills the Six Bandits (*liuzei*, symbolic representations of the six sense organs, including the mind), the chapter-end comment reads, "I wonder whether in today's world people kill off the Six Bandits, or are killed off by those Six Bandits?" (183). Reflecting on chapter 76, Li Zhuowu comments,

"Monsters frequently seem to respond very much like real people, whereas real people very frequently have feelings like monsters" (1034). And again, "A marvelous aspect of *Journey to the West* is simply that it speaks of the false as if it were true, causing one to smile" (1272).

In a more philosophical vein: "The East [the pilgrims' destination] is not far—it is your own home. One would think that you should go home" (183). And when Guanyin offers a profound explanation in chapter 17, "Wukong, the Bodhisattva, and the monster—they both exist in a single thought. Considered in terms of their origin, they are all nothing." Li Zhuowu observes, "She explained it directly!" (Shuo chu).[41] One of his more profoundly philosophical comments is in chapter 58 (in which the Monkey assumes three forms of himself), a response to a lesson by the Buddha:

> Form has no fixed form;
> Thus form is emptiness.
> Emptiness has no fixed emptiness;
> Thus emptiness is form.

To this Li Zhuowu comments: "Extraordinary writing about illusion and form—it all leads up to this!" (781; *JW* 3.113).

In chapter 60, when a local spirit reveals that he had been banished for misbehaving in Heaven, the commentator remarks enigmatically, "This is absurd but it seems like reality" (801; *JW* 3.133). In chapter 73 the Monkey battles a monster who appears to have a thousand eyes attached to his ribs that all emit golden rays. With the help of a mountain deity the Monkey defeats the monster, who turns out to be a gigantic centipede. At chapter's end Li Zhuowu comments, "At first the Centipede was called the Demon Lord of a Hundred Eyes, but in the end he became a blind man. When one exhausts his intelligence, he indeed becomes a great fool." Then he gives an allegorical interpretation of the monsters as one's own misguided mind: "Seven big spiders and one old centipede: people consider them strange and poisonous. How could they know that these are nothing but nicknames for the reckless mind—it is just that this is not visible from the outside" (992).[42] In both cases Li Zhuowu draws attention to the wit and craft of writing in this novel.

Yet the commentator takes pains to point out the novel's didacticism by reference to the general precepts of the "Three Teachings" taken as a whole.[43] By doing so he confirms the reading of the novel identified by Yuan Yuling in his "Prefatory Remarks" to that edition. At the end of chapter 2, in which the Monkey King goes traveling to find a way to escape death, the commentary reads, "Refusing to study all manner of things and yet focusing on long life—if even monkeys are like this, how much more so humanity?" He continues, "But people in this world do not only study how to achieve longevity; they also study how to shorten life. How so? [Indulgence in] wine, lust, greed, and anger are all methods to shorten life. Who among the people of this world can separate himself from these four? . . . *Journey to the West* is filled with parables; the reader ought not to pass them off lightly" (27). And then, perhaps not without tongue in cheek, he extols the truth of common aphorisms. In the critique for chapter 74, Li Zhuowu endorses an aphorism and roasts his contemporaries at the same time—but in conventional moralistic terms: "It is too bad that people of the world throw themselves into the web of desire and occupy the prison of emotion" (1006).

Some comments are simply fun, expressing the commentator's delight with the narrative. At the end of chapter 19, when the Monkey King takes on the form of the Pig's wife in order to subdue him, the final commentary says, "What a truly fine couple they made, but in the end the old lady was stronger than the old man. Generally speaking, in the world today either we have old pigs acting as husbands, or we have old monkeys acting as wives to subdue them. So how can we not fear our old ladies? How can we not fear our old ladies?!" (395). And in chapter 73, when the Monkey is told about a Thousand Flowers Cave, Li Zhuowu comments, interlineally, "What a great name for a cave!" (989). Surely there is neither serious moralization nor pointed social critique in comments such as these.

CONCLUSIONS

When taken as a whole, there emerges from the Li Zhuowu commentaries a consistent image of the critic of the vernacular novel. For each of the three novels, emotive interjections of one to four characters printed within lines of the text or in the upper margin of the page were produced in this name. In his degree of critical evaluation, Li Zhuowu seems to have set a new standard for the pithy observation.[44] His chapter-ending commentaries range from the dismissive to the laudatory and take up matters of writing as well as evaluations of individual behavior. As he often repeated, he enjoyed narrative turns that struck him as lifelike. Not only did he approve of realistic action, but he also praised telling details that revealed the mentality and complex emotions of fictional characters. But he also held a negative attitude toward the women in all three novels.[45]

Various scholars have objected to attributing some of the Li Zhuowu chapter-ending comments to Li Zhi because they seem crude in style and intellectually pedestrian, beneath the standards of the historical philosopher.[46] On the other hand, with his identifiably sophisticated observations on life and art, Li Zhuowu raised the bar for novel commentary with his critique of both contemporary morals and the craft of writing. Moreover, his comments seem consistent in his admiration (at times ironic, at other times ostensibly quite serious) for the spontaneous, the unaffected, and the authentic responses of fictional characters. This is why he champions Lu Zhishen, Zhang Fei, and Sun Wukong in these three novels: in his interpretation, they have none of the absorption with self that higher status characters so frequently do. It also explains his attribution (especially in the Rongyutang edition of *Outlaws of the Marsh*) of treachery and banditry to the imperial court in contrast to the "outlaws" he admires.[47]

In terms of his aesthetic standards, the Li Zhuowu critic was the first to insist that good fiction is based on reality—of type, if not of specific incident, as he explained in comments to chapter 100 of *Outlaws of the Marsh*. Marxist-inspired literary historians observe that he praised social realism in writing, a product of his materialist perspective; this explains his disparagement of descriptions of dreams, fabulous creatures, and magical battle arrays. Despite this anachronistic interpretation, from the Li Zhuowu perspective fiction should not *record* reality but should evoke "interest" or "fascination" (*qu*) in the reader by *reflecting*—perhaps concentrating—real life, real emotions.[48] This tendency is most clearly revealed in his responses to characterization. Using such terms as "model" (*moyang*) and "identity" (*shenfen*), Li Zhuowu praised characters who fulfilled particular conventional types, such as the violent hero or the envious and petty person. At the same time, he emphasized descriptions that individualized these characters, endowing them with unique backgrounds, interests, and personality traits. Further, Li Zhuowu praised such scenes as the interchanges among Song Jiang, Yan Poxi, and her mother in *Outlaws of the Marsh* not only for conveying their thoughts but also for what was implied in their words and actions: motivations not available to the characters themselves. In this he compares the skill of the novelist to the greatest of painters, Gu Kaizhi (344–406) and Wu Daozi (680–759), both famous for their ability to look beyond physical likeness to capture the spirit (*shen*) of their subjects. Among his brief comments, the word "[like a] painting" (*hua*) occurs repeatedly.[49]

So what, if anything, do these writings that were attributed to Li Zhi tell us about this author's image? First, we can agree with David Rolston that these commentaries were a "labor of love" for their sheer volume and the range of responses they reflect. They could not have been merely a way to earn a living, as Qian Xiyan opined four hundred years ago. We know that Li Zhuowu was a devoted reader, and he played the role with gusto.[50] Clearly the Li Zhi being performed and projected through these comments was a reader of integrity, one who sought responsibility for moral standards as well as artistic concerns in this new literary form, the novel. He possessed acerbic wit and did not hesitate to chastise his contemporaries as fools and worse. He was a man who could be very serious in his philosophical pronouncements while maintaining his objectivity, one who clearly distinguished the purposes of fiction from other kinds of narrative, history in particular. He could make jokes, some of them fairly coarse, about common human foibles.

That this Li Zhuowu challenged the texts he read on both didactic and literary grounds suggests that Ye Zhou and his publishers—and, most likely, his educated readers as well—saw reasonable parallels between the iconoclastic thinker and a serious critic for the new and creative form that was becoming the literati novel. As a *Romance of the Three Kingdoms* comment declares, one cannot expect that novels (*yanyi*) should serve the same purposes as historical accounts; fiction should be appreciated as just that, good stories, especially when it disagrees with what the historians have written. This accords well with the image of Li Zhi as both conservative and iconoclastic.[51] Interestingly, when the commentaries are read in the order presented here—which probably does reflect the order in which they were written—we see a progression in Li Zhuowu's critical perspective. The level of humor increases from *Outlaws of the Marsh* to *Journey to the West*; there is more flippant commentary in the chapter-end critiques and a greater sense of detachment (a prerequisite for witty sarcasm) from the actions and characters in the literary texts. The same might well be true for how the real Ye Zhou conceived of his role. However, given his consistent devotion to *performing* in the role he created for the deceased Li Zhi, what Ye Zhou personally thought about the art of fiction is not so clear. Given the role he was assigned to play—and that he performed very well—we cannot uncritically assign the values expressed by Li Zhuowu to the real Ye Zhou, as many students of fiction have done. This would be tantamount to equating the values of a character in a play to the actor who impersonates him: there probably were significant similarities, but it would be fallacious to assume a simple identity between them. Yet when Li Zhuowu quotes "Ye Zhou's" comments on *Romance of the Three Kingdoms*, the real Ye Zhou may or may not reveal a glimpse of his own thoughts; at the least, appearing to quote himself confirms that Li Zhuowu is merely a costume Ye wears.

In sum, this Li Zhuowu commentator appears as a worldly-wise and tremendously experienced reader, sensitive to his texts and responsive to his role as potential teacher in the arts of reading. But he does not come across as a thinker upholding a particular set of ethical or rational principles. Instead he appears as a fairly developed fictional character, one whose primary characteristic is that he reads emotionally. Even when commenting on a matter of style, he does so with passion. To judge from this fictitious Li Zhuowu, the historical figure was considered to be a man of intense feelings. In this, and in the rough characters he praised, Li Zhi's basic authenticity might indeed be expressed.[52] One sees in the commentator Li Zhuowu the spontaneous expression of emotions generally concordant with the outlook of Wang Yangming's School of the Mind. Whether these comments reflect the more specific philosophy of Li Zhi, I must leave to readers who know more about this real man. My concern has been with a performance by an actor using a writing brush; we cannot expect him to be presented as so intellectual as the historical person himself. Nor can I have hoped to do more than simply whet your appetite for the fun of reading fiction commentaries right along with the novels themselves—as presumably an educated seventeenth-century reader would have done.

NOTES

1 Europeanists such as Steven Zwicker in "The Reader Revealed" have explored the extensive comments left by famous persons in the margins of the books they read. I know of no such study of marginalia on a Chinese novel.

2 Rolston, *Traditional Chinese Fiction*, 3; Rolston, *How to Read*, 356–58.

3 Lin Yaling, *Yu Xiangdou*, 77, 343ff., identifies a primary goal of the Yu family of printers as popularizing reading, especially the reading of fiction, while providing needed cultural information to the newly emerging urban reading audience.

4 Martin Huang, "Author(ity) and Reader," 47–50, explains the appeal to the more highly learned reader made by commentary and editing practices. For Rolston's essay "Formal Aspects of Fiction Criticism and Commentary," see *How to Read*, 42–74. The most extensive study of Yu Xiangdou available is Lin Yaling, *Yu Xiangdou*. Lin (77, 239, etc.), too, clearly indicates how Yu attempted to encourage wide readership because of the commercial nature of his printing establishment.

5 Huang, "Author(ity) and Reader," 41.

6 See Rolston, *How to Read*, 22–24, for the historical development of literary commentary through the relationships, presumed and real, between commentary, examination essays, and drama. Significantly, there is no parallel commentarial tradition for short vernacular fiction, *huaben* stories. On Li Zhi's attitude toward examination preparation, see chapter 8.

7 Yu left his personal mark on *Journey to the North* (Beiyou ji, 1602) and *Journey to the South* (Nanyou ji) in the form of poems within the texts expressing his reaction to specific passages. Lin Yaling, *Yu Xiangdou*, 215–31, 243, etc., cites numerous instances in which Yu wrote his commentary in the form of poems. See also Ma Youyuan, "Cong pinglin ben."

8 Rolston, *Traditional Chinese Fiction*, 2. Rolston traces the development of fiction commentary in this masterful study.

9 Lin Yaling, *Yu Xiangdou*, 231–39, comments on the subjectivity of his views.

10 Ye Lang, "Ye Zhou pingdian," esp. 298.

11 Rolston, "The Authenticity of the Li Chih Commentaries," 356, notes that in 1592 Yuan Zhongdao saw one of Li Zhi's disciples copying out the *Outlaws of the Marsh* text with Li's commentary. It seems no copy of that version has survived.

12 Rolston, *Traditional Chinese Fiction*, 3.

13 Liu Haiyan, *Ming Qing Sanguo zhi yanyi*, 108–10. Qian's comments appear in his collection *Xixia*, 3.23ab, that carries a preface dated 1613; Zhou Lianggong's are in *Yinshuwu shuying*. Both are quoted in Ye Lang, "Ye Zhou pingdian," 280–81. See also Lin Yaling, "Ye Zhou xiaoshuo," 104–6; Rolston, *How to Read*, 38–39; Rolston, "The Authenticity of the Li Chih Commentaries," 356–63; and Plaks, *The Four Masterworks*, 513–17.

14 See Rolston, *Traditional Chinese Fiction*, 31–32.

15 The editions of *Romance of the Three Kingdoms* with the Li Zhuowu commentaries were frequently reprinted. For a detailed comparison of various versions, see Liu Haiyan, *Ming Qing Sanguo zhi yanyi*, 97–148. Rolston, *How to Read*, 38–39, has summary comments on Ye Zhou as commentator. See also Plaks, *The Four Masterworks*, 288–89.

16 Lin Yaling, "Ye Zhou xiaoshuo," 102n4 summarizes current scholarly thinking on this question, concluding that the most authoritative is that of Ye Lang, "Ye Zhou pingdian." Ye concludes that the Yuan Wuya edition incorporates comments by Li Zhi, Xu Zichang, and Feng Menglong. Lin Yaling (105n13) observes that some consider Xu Zichang just another penname used by Ye Zhou; Ye Lang, "Ye Zhou pingdian," 296–97, credits Ye Zhou with composing a book in Xu Zichang's name; see n. 28 below.

17 Li Zhi, "Tongxin shuo," in *LZ* 1:276–79. Lin Yaling, "Ye Zhou xiaoshuo," 106, cites Huang Lin's argument that *The Western Chamber* commentary was also penned by Ye Zhou.

18 *Zhongyi Shuihu zhuan*, Li Zhi preface; the identical text is to be found in Li Zhi's *Fenshu*, *j*. 3. Rolston, *How to Read*, 36–38, notes its relative superficiality. For a translation, see Li Zhi, *A Book to Burn*, 125–28.

19 The filiation of the textual lines of *Outlaws of the Marsh* is complicated, with 120, 110, and 100 chapter versions in circulation by around 1600. Both the 1589 Tiandu waichen (Wang Daokun) edition *Loyal and Righteous Outlaws of the Marsh* (Zhongyi Shuihu zhuan) and the Rongyutang edition of 1610 have 100 chapters; the Yuan Wuya edition of 1612–14 also carries commentary attributed to Li Zhi but has 120. Lin Yaling, "Ye Zhou xiaoshuo," 102, 102n6; Ma Tiji, *Shuihu shulu* and *Shuihu ziliao huibian* suggest that the Yuan Wuya edition was based on the manuscript that Yuan Zhongdao saw Li Zhi himself working on. The standard study was for years Yan Dunyi, *Shuihu zhuan de yanbian*. For descriptions of these several versions, see He Xin, *Shuihu yanjiu*; Rolston, *How to Read*, 404–30; and Plaks, *The Four Masterworks*, 280–89. There are translations by Pearl S. Buck, *All Men Are Brothers* (1933); J. H. Jackson, *The Water Margin* (1937); Sidney Shapiro, *Outlaws of the Marsh* (1981); and John and Alex Dent-Young, *The Marshes of Mount Liang* (1994–2002).

20 Lin Yaling, *Yu Xiangdou*, 215, notes that Yu Xiangdou's comments are similarly emotive, many composed of merely one or two words. Wu Yinghui, "Commentary," 51, notes that the Li Zhuowu commentaries to the famous plays *The Lute* (Pipa ji) and *The Western Chamber* in their Rongyutang editions give the impression of "spontaneity and immediacy" and appear to be the product of "a dynamic process in which the commentator enacts a reader who would cry at one moment and laugh at another, slapping the desk and kicking his heels. . . . The person behind 'Li Zhuowu' is highly conscious of and deeply invested in creating a dramatized, appealing image." See also nn. 48 and 52 below.

21 See *Shuihu zhuan huipingben*, 201 (ten times!), 206, 208, 209, 211, 214, 215 216, 217; all are comments from the Rongyutang edition and thus all by Ye Zhou. Page references are to this edition.

22 *Shuihu zhuan huipingben*, 218; the battle array appears in the band's collective campaign against the Liao Kingdom in the north in chapters 88–89 of the 100-chapter version. Li Zhuowu expresses repeated enthusiasm for the clever plot twists in the "Taking the Birthday Presents by Guile" episode in chapter 16, 294–303.

23 For the Li Zhuowu comments, see *Shuihu zhuan huipingben*, 239–40. Praise for characterization is even more pronounced in his response to the character Lu Zhishen in chapter 9's final evaluative comment.

24 Wu Yinghui, "Commentary," 51, comments insightfully that in his play commentaries Ye Zhou's "predilection for over-the-top reactions and straightforward dirty words often make the little drama he was performing at the margin of the text outshine the main drama in the play text."

25 For a similar comment, see ch. 22, 480. Lin Yaling, *Yu Xiangdou*, 325–26, etc., notes that this comment was directed at Yu Xiangdou, whose view of fiction, its function, and its art differed significantly from later commentators.

26 Lin Yaling, *Yu Xiangdou*, 283.

27 For its textual history, see Rolston, *How to Read*, 430–39; and Plaks, *The Four Masterworks*, 535–36. The novel has been consistently known in English as *Romance of the Three Kingdoms*, with full translations by Brewitt-Taylor (1924) and Roberts, *Three Kingdoms: A Historical Novel* (1991).

28 Ye Lang gives convincing evidence that Ye Zhou also wrote the collection of anecdotes *Leisurely Notes from Useless Wood Studio* (Shuzhai manlu, 1612) attributed to the Suzhou playwright and printer Xu Zichang (fl. 1596–1623); there, too, Ye Zhou quotes his own witty comments in ways that a third-person writer would not have done. Ye Lang, "Ye Zhou pingdian," 296–97, concludes that Xu and Ye might have collaborated. See Rolston, *How to Read*, 358–59. See n. 17 above.

29 Detailed surveys: Wei An, *Sanguo yanyi banben kao*; Nakagawa Satoshi, *Sanguo zhi yanyi banben yanjiu*; and Liu Haiyan, *Ming Qing Sanguo zhi yanyi*. For a history of editions with the Li Zhuowu commentary, see Hegel and Sibau, "Introduction."

30 Rolston, *Traditional Chinese Fiction*, 3.

31 *Sanguo yanyi huipingben*, 1457. Unless otherwise noted, all page numbers in parentheses are from this edition.

32 In his evaluative comment on chapter 105 Li Zhuowu even comments on his own dislike for Cao Cao; see *Sanguo yanyi huipingben*, 1292.

33 As Rolston, *Traditional Chinese Fiction*, 222n28, points out, Ye Zhou regularly chides Liu Bei for hypocrisy. Interestingly Li Zhuowu refers to both Li Kui and Zhang Fei, the two most violent warriors in *Outlaws of the Marsh* and *Three Kingdoms*, respectively, as "Buddhas."

34 Both in *Li Zhuowu yuan ping xiuxiang guben Sanguo zhi* 49.41 and in *Sanguo yanyi huipingben*, 613, the monk's name is clearly *Ri*niu. However, in the chapter 21 postface, he quotes Monk Bainiu, who was a noted early Qing calligrapher. Hence the import of this attribution is unclear. See *Sanguo yanyi huipingben*, 265. Rolston, *How to Read*, 69, observes, "Lighthearted comments were an important part of the [commentary] tradition from the beginning." Most of the comments in these novels are not particularly jocular, however.

35 *Sanguo yanyi huipingben*, 1292. He continues here by quoting the sarcastic comment of "a friend," again as if these evaluative comments reflect conversations about the novel during social occasions.

36 See Hu Shi's 1923 essay "*Xiyou ji* kaozheng" and the response from historian Dong Zuobin in Hu Shi, *Zhongguo zhanghui xiaoshuo kaozheng*, 219–58.

37 Anthony Yu, *Journey to the West* (hereafter *JW*), 1.1–17, surveys these diverse sources.

38 See Xu Shuofang's introduction to *Li Zhuowu pingben Xiyou ji*, edited by Chen and Bao (page references are to this edition as *LXYJ*), 1–4.

39 *LXYJ*, "Tici," 1; "Fanli," 1; "Qianyan," 6. The single words that appear in the comments are stressed both by Yuan Yuling in his "Prefatory Remarks" and by the editor (Ye Zhou? Yuan Yuling? the printer?) of the "General Principles." Interestingly, the "General Principles" explains the meaning of "interesting" (*qu*) as having been established by the popular late-Ming poet Yuan Hongdao in his collected writings, *Yuan Zhonglang ji*, but many writings were spuriously attributed to Yuan.

40 *LXYJ*, 1.398, the chapter-end comment, in this novel called *zongpi*. Rolston, *How to Read*, 18, presents this comment somewhat differently.

41 *LXYJ*, 1.225; translation from *JW*, 1.363. Ye Zhou makes the same comment in ch. 16, 1.210. This is a Chan Buddhist term for a profound comment that reveals insight into the true nature of reality.

42 This echoes Yuan Yuling's statement in his "Prefatory Remarks": "The monsters are none other: they are our very selves." One wonders what the relationship was between Yuan Yuling and Ye Zhou: did they work on the text at the same time? Did they discuss the text and collaborate on editing it? Or was the commentary complete when the printer invited Yuan to write this preface, and so there was no contact between them? Information on such practical matters would greatly benefit scholarly understanding of the novel production process.

43 On the historical Li Zhi's engagement with "Three Teachings" values, see chapters 2, 6, 9, and 11 in this volume.

44 Lin Yaling, "Ye Zhou xiaoshuo," 108–9. By comparison, evaluations of writing style in the Yuan Wuya edition of *Outlaws of the Marsh*, chs. 4, 5, 9, more likely to have been based on Li Zhi's evaluations, tend to be significantly longer, eight or more characters each. In length and content, they reflect late-Ming examination essay criticism; Ye Zhou's brief comments do not, according to Lin.

45 As Ye Lang, "Ye Zhou pingdian," 286, points out. This contrasts with positive views of women articulated by Li Zhi, as Pauline Lee demonstrates in chapter 7.

46 Ye Lang, "Ye Zhou pingdian," 293, noting that some reflect both substance and style of Fujian printer Yu Xiangdou and may have been adapted from Yu's comments.

47 See Ye Lang, "Ye Zhou pingdian," 298–99.

48 Ye Lang, "Ye Zhou pingdian," 300, referring to the general comment at the end of *Outlaws of the Marsh*, ch. 50.

49 Lin Yaling, "Ye Zhou xiaoshuo," 114, counts more than forty *hua* comments in *Shuihu zhuan* ch. 9 and more than eighty in ch. 20. On Ye Zhou's focus on individuality in characterization, see 115–18. Interestingly, in a 1592 essay, "Za shuo," Li Zhi draws a contrast between the consummate artistry (*huagong*) of

the excellent writer and the creative genius (*huagong*) that makes some works even more outstanding; see Li Zhi, *A Book to Burn*, 102–5. Thanks to Rivi Handler-Spitz for pointing this out.

50 Rolston, *Traditional Chinese Fiction*, 31; Qian Xiyan, *Xixia*, 3.23a.

51 Yu, *JW* 1.24, maintains that the *Journey to the West* commentaries were written by Li Zhi: "The remarks themselves, usually appearing in 'end-of-chapter overall commentary,' . . . [are] consistently sardonic and witty enough to recall aspects of Li's rhetoric and style"; they "hardly hew . . . to the line of later criticism that tends to exalt either Neo-Confucianism or Quanzhen Daoism, a conscientiously syncretistic blend of Chan Buddhist and Daoist ideas advocated by the lineage." Yu does not consider questions of dating or comparisons with other Li Zhuowu comments that show the consistent work of Ye Zhou cited earlier.

52 Wu Yinghui, "Commentary," 48, observes, "A large portion of the commentary [on *The Western Chamber*] reveals moments of the author's mind and the characters' mind stirred by pure *qing* and unobstructed by learning or pretension." This too supports a general identification between Li Zhuowu and the real Li Zhi.

CHAPTER 11

THE QUESTION OF LIFE AND DEATH

Li Zhi and Ming-Qing Intellectual History

MIAW-FEN LU

THE QUESTION OF LIFE AND DEATH PREOCCUPIED LI ZHI AND MANY other late-Ming literati and motivated them to study the Dao. But as no consensus emerged on how best to do so, questions of method sparked many intellectual debates. Li Zhi's thought can be seen not simply as a general system of ideas but, more important, as an outgrowth of and a response to ideological discussions and conflicts taking place among Confucian scholars of his time.

THE QUESTION OF LIFE AND DEATH AND LI ZHI'S PURSUIT OF THE DAO

After Li Zhi returned to Dragon Lake from Wuchang in 1593, when he was sixty-seven years old, he renovated a local monastery and built a pagoda called Buried Bones (Maiguta). Living in the monastery, he pondered death intensively, perhaps because he felt his own death approaching.[1] According to the modern scholar Xu Jianping, Li Zhi's ideas about life and death changed several times: as a young man he espoused a Confucian viewpoint; in middle age he embraced a Daoist position; and at the end of his life he advocated for a Buddhist one. But he never completely gave up Confucian and Daoist concepts.[2] Even when he first encountered the works of Wang Yangming and Wang Ji, when he was about forty, the message that caught his eye was "A true man who attains the Dao will never die, and this achievement is equal to that of Buddha and the Daoist immortals."[3] He was not satisfied with Confucian ideas of worth, words, and works as means for overcoming death, nor did he entirely subscribe to the wisdom of seeing both life and death as intrinsic to the Dao. Instead, he contemplated such questions as: What happens to an individual after death? Does any part of life remain after a person dies? Does perception endure after death? Does a man really reap as he sows? Does the Western Paradise (Pure Land) really exist?

Li Zhi admitted that he was terrified of death, but he also endowed this fear with a positive meaning. He said, "If one takes the fear [of death] as the basis of learning, one's ultimate goal will be to free oneself from life and death, to escape the sea of bitterness, and to avoid fear."[4] He further averred, "The only reason why sages tried desperately to understand the cause of life and death was that they greatly feared death. They therefore could not stop [seeking its cause] until they had grasped the non-duality of life and death."[5]

Li Zhi's perplexity toward the question of life and death, and his fear of death, compelled him, like the sages, to pursue the Dao. Although the phrases "to free oneself from life and death" and "to escape the sea of bitterness" contain Buddhist connotations, he considered the term "sages" to include not only Buddhist sages but also Daoist and Confucian ones. He viewed the sages of the Three Teachings as equals to those who had attained enlightenment through spiritual self-cultivation. This view was popular among late-Ming literati. As the Japanese scholar Araki Kengo has pointed out, many late-Ming literati were tolerant of synthesis; they tended to believe in the existence of a transcendental common ground or shared origin of the Three Teachings and maintained that this origin could be accessed by self-cultivation based on one's mind-nature (*xinxing*).[6] Zhou Rudeng (1547–1629), for example, said, "Although the teachings of Confucianism and Buddhism differ, there is no difference in the root nature of the mind."[7] Similar viewpoints appeared in Du Wenhuan's (b. 1581) project to synthesize the Three Teachings (*huizong sanjiao*).[8] As Jiang Wu shows in chapter 9, this period saw the emergence of a group of Dao learners who, downplaying social, institutional, and cultural boundaries, maintained that distinguishing among different religions was less important than engaging in sincere self-cultivation.

This intellectual context is essential for understanding Li Zhi. He said "Confucianism, Daoism, and Buddhism are the same. All the Three Teachings have the same goal, which was to know the Dao."[9] He thought that the most important thing in life was to cultivate one's own spirit-and-nature (*xingming*), because one's body would perish after death, while spirit-and-nature would endure forever. The sages of the Three Teachings dedicated themselves to cultivating spirit-and-nature and all attained the Dao, even though their representations of it differed. Li Zhi emphasized that "the differences [among the Three Teachings] were only superficial."[10] He consequently proclaimed that a wise person should not overemphasize the differences, and neither should he try to erase them. On the contrary, he urged people to pay attention to the "sameness" among these teachings: "If one learns to see the sameness of them, one will see that not only is there no difference among the sages of the Three Teachings, but there is also no difference under heaven."[11]

Li Zhi was dissatisfied with the idea that one should not expound upon the nature of the afterlife. He was inclined to believe in retribution, reincarnation, and the existence of ghosts.[12] He said, "If there is no such thing as reincarnation or ghosts, then there is no reason to study the Dao. So what the sages of the Three Teachings did was all in vain."[13] He believed that an individual's identity continues beyond death and, when he spoke with Matteo Ricci (1552–1610), expressed his interest in and curiosity about "heaven."[14] However, he did not have a clear idea of what heaven was, nor did he set heaven (or the Pure Land) as his goal. When Li Shihui suggested that Li Zhi should strive to dwell in the Western Paradise, Li Zhi replied that he would not like to dwell forever in the Western Paradise: "If Buddha is in heaven, I will go to heaven; if he is in hell, I will go to hell." Since everything is impermanent, rebirth in the Western Paradise too should be impermanent.[15] Rather than set as his ideal goal an everlasting realm described by a religious doctrine, Li Zhi pursued the fullness of life, which had more to do with the living embodiment of the Dao than with any established religious ideology. He wouldn't allow himself to be restricted by conventional rules or institutional ideology. He was an extreme individualist, as William Theodore de Bary and Mizoguchi Yūzō have pointed out.[16] His identity was more fluid and unstable than those of other literati, even those who shared his omnivorous intellectual appetite. He praised the sages of the Three Teachings as models of self-cultivation, but he did not consistently identify himself with any institutional religion. His method of seeking the Dao and his inability to adhere to any institutional or conventional wisdom made him an outcast. But his passionate devotion to personal freedom also granted him the ability to appreciate people and things differently from his contemporaries.

THE QUESTION OF LIFE AND DEATH IN NEO-CONFUCIANISM FROM LATE MING TO QING

Li Zhi was not alone in his obsession with the question of life and death. During the late Ming, not only did Buddhism and Daoism offer their answers to this question; even Confucianism provided insights and produced rich discussions on it. The Song dynasty neo-Confucians Cheng Yi and Zhu Xi criticized Buddhists for being afraid of death and cravenly clinging to life. They distinguished themselves from Buddhists by not saying much on this issue. Unlike Cheng Yi and Zhu Xi, late-Ming Confucians were obsessed with the subject of life and death. In many ways—including techniques of self-cultivation, images of the sage, and biographical writings—this phenomenon was closely related to Buddhist culture. Its advocates claimed that understanding the meaning of life and death was the ultimate goal of Confucian sagely learning, and they took this phrase from the *Analects*, "If a man hears the Dao in the morning, he may die in the evening without regret," as evidence that Confucius taught people to ponder the meaning of life and death.[17] They thus claimed that the question of life and death was the ultimate concern of learning.[18] Some even emphasized the importance of being able to meet one's death peacefully, which they considered proof of having understood the Dao.[19]

From late Ming to early Qing, we see a sharp decline in Yangming learning and a surge of Confucian criticism of Buddhism. Early-Qing neo-Confucians tended to distinguish "true" neo-Confucianism from pseudo-Confucianism and Chan Buddhism. They often viewed Yangming learning, and sometimes even all neo-Confucianism, as poisoned by Buddhism and Daoism. In this intellectual milieu, however, the question of life and death remained attractive to Confucians.

Rejecting Buddhist theory about reincarnation, Song neo-Confucians like Zhang Zai (1020–1077), Cheng Yi, and Zhu Xi adopted a theory of the transformation of *qi* to explain the existence of life. They speculated that life arises when *qi* congeals and that death occurs when *qi* disperses. In general, they did not mention the existence of an individual soul or the continued existence of the individual after death. For example, Zhu Xi said:

> The *qi* of gods always extends and exists, but the *qi* of dead people disperses entirely. The speed of dispersion, however, differs according to the dead person. Some people do not submit willingly to death. As a result, their *qi* does not disperse after they die, and they became monsters or sinister beings. [For instance] the *qi* of people who die violent deaths does not disperse. This has also happened in the case of some Buddhist and Daoist monks. As for Confucian sages, they have all been able to embrace death peacefully. Has any one of them tried to hold onto his *qi* so as to become any sort of spiritual being?

> Certainly not! I have never heard that sages like Huangdi, Yao, or Shun became spiritual beings or monsters after death.[20]

According to Zhu Xi, the *qi* of the dead naturally disperses, and as this happens, one's individual identity fades. In other words, one's *qi* disperses after death and rejoins the great *qi* of the cosmos. This process follows the Dao.[21] In the Confucian Classics, however, there are some stories in which the dead return to life to exact revenge or individual spirits persist into the afterlife. Zhu Xi did not deny these phenomena. He admitted the possibility that one's *qi* might not disperse after death, but he claimed that this situation was not an ideal postmortem state for human beings. On the contrary, it was unnatural and was often caused by great injustice. The preservation of *qi* and individual identity were often related to ghosts and demons seeking to avenge a wrong perpetrated against them. The other possibility that Zhu Xi mentions is a result of Buddhist or Daoist cultivation, which he also thought unnatural and a betrayal of the Dao. As for Confucian sages, Zhu Xi believed that their *qi* would completely disperse and return to the great cosmic *qi*. Confucian sages wouldn't even try to preserve their *qi*, since they truly understood the Dao. Therefore, like Zhang Zai, Zhu Xi proposed that one should live according to the Dao and embrace death peacefully (*cunshun moning*). This view of the afterlife suggested that there was no fundamental difference between the postmortem fates of sages and of common people. Or, if there was, these differences did not occupy the minds of Song neo-Confucians.

Due to the orthodox role of Cheng-Zhu learning and its obvious difference from Buddhism and Daoism, this view of the afterlife was widely accepted by later Confucian literati. They saw no need to ponder the matter deeply, since ancient sages did not say much about it. Nevertheless, not everybody felt satisfied with this attitude, as the following dialogue, recorded by the Taizhou School scholar Deng Huoqu, demonstrates:

> Someone asked Liu Bangcai: "When one who has truly engaged in learning dies, where does he go?" Bangcai answered: "He returns to the Great Void [*Taixu*]." His interlocutor asked again: "How about one who has never engaged in learning? Where does he go after death?" Bangcai answered: "He returns to the Great Void." Someone asked Deng Huoqu's opinion about this. Deng Huoqu said: "Those who have truly engaged in learning did not dare to act rashly, but those who did not engage in learning did

all manner of evil. If both kinds of people return to the Great Void after death, why don't we just imitate those who did all manner of evil?"[22]

Liu Bangcai espoused a view of the afterlife that resembled Zhu Xi's, while Deng Huoqu, whom Li Zhi deeply respected, represented another opinion that gradually became popular in late-Ming and early-Qing Confucian discourse. Deng Huoqu posed an important question about justice and the value of Confucian moral cultivation. Apart from the legacy of words, work, and historical memory an individual left behind, was there any way to live on after death? If a person's moral achievement had nothing to do with his postmortem fate, wherein lay the value of Confucian morality? If in the end all human beings returned to the Great Void, what did justice mean for Confucianism?

Deng Huoqu was not alone in pondering these questions. Many of his contemporary Confucians had similar concerns and tried to offer their insights. One point they insisted on was that it was essential to differentiate between the postmortem condition of mortals and immortals. Gao Panlong (1562–1626), Chen Longzheng (1585–1645), Sun Qifeng (1585–1675), Huang Zongxi (1610–1695), Wang Fuzhi (1619–1692), Wang Sihuai (b. 1620), and many others emphasized this principle, although they did not have a consensus theory.[23] They believed that truly moral persons would be able to preserve certain elements of their individual identity after death. "Who dares say that [Sage King] Shun and [Robber] Zhi ended up the same?" they quipped. They criticized Cheng Yi and Zhu Xi for overlooking the similarities between Confucianism and Buddhism and implying that all lives, whether wise or foolish, good or bad, are completely extinguished. They believed that this idea would bring harm to moral education and customs.[24]

The early-Qing Confucian Ying Huiqian (1615–1683) also argued against the idea that an individual's *qi* disperses after death. He wondered why Confucian sages would continuously strive to improve their morality throughout their lives if they would end up no different from rotten, withered grass. He said that embracing the idea that *qi* disperses after death is like saying "Immediately after finishing the construction of a grand mansion, the mansion is burned to ashes." Ying Huiqian avowed that the idea was repugnant to common sense and thus could not be true. He also said:

> Confucians often say that because Buddhists and Daoists do not submit willingly to death, their *qi* doesn't disperse after death,

> and because Confucian sages do not crave life, their *qi* disperses after death. But all human beings love life and hate death. How could the teachings of the Confucian sages oppose this universal sentiment? Moreover, when the sages established the rites, they viewed death as inauspicious. But they regarded life as the greatest value of all. If Buddhists and Daoists possessed spiritual efficacy after death while Confucian sages rotted immediately [like grass], no wonder people rush to join the Buddhists and Daoists.[25]

Ying Huiqian thus claimed that Cheng Yi's and Zhu Xi's ideas about life and death betrayed the teachings of the sages. He believed that if Confucians continued to uphold Cheng-Zhu theory, people would be forced to abandon Confucianism altogether and convert to Buddhism or Daoism.

To sum up, many early-Qing neo-Confucians, following late-Ming discourse, continued to ponder the issue of life and death. Like Cheng Yi and Zhu Xi, they rejected Buddhism and Daoism. Nonetheless, they disagreed with Cheng Yi and Zhu Xi in that they tended to believe that moral cultivation should decisively influence a person's afterlife. The spirits of sages, unlike those of ordinary people, should continue to exist, to perceive, and to resonate with the minds of those who truly dedicated themselves to sagely learning while alive. By and large, Confucians of this period rejected the Buddhist concepts of heaven (Pure Land) and hell, but they tended to believe in a Confucian heaven. Instead of describing hell, they often talked about how commoners would perish like withered grass. As for Confucian heaven, it was often imagined as the court of the supreme God (*shangdi*), in which the spirits of all sages would join in fellowship, as *The Book of Poetry* (Shijing) states, "on the left and right of God [*zai di zuo you*]."[26] It is worth mentioning that in the same period this phrase was also often quoted by Jesuits to argue for the existence of a Christian heaven. Many Qing Confucians emphasized that sages and worthies were able to enter the heavenly court and enjoy spiritual fellowship with all Confucian sages.[27] In contrast to the common impression that Confucians cared mostly about worldly affairs, these scholars, like Li Zhi, were not satisfied with Confucian ideas of worth, words, and works as means for overcoming death. They tended to believe that some vestige of life would remain after death and that an ideal postmortem state existed for those who attained sagehood through self-cultivation. In short, Li Zhi's preoccupation with the question of life and death was shared by many of his contemporary literati.

DIFFERENT APPROACHES TOWARD LEARNING

If Li Zhi's views were not unique, what made him so controversial? As previously noted, no one disputed the importance of studying the Dao; the difference lay in practice. Many serious debates and criticisms derived from different views on the methods of sagely learning. Two different approaches toward sagely learning help explain why Li Zhi was so hotly debated in Ming-Qing intellectual history.

Li Zhi's quarrels with Geng Dingxiang afflicted Li greatly. Their falling-out sharpened Li's critique of literati culture and shaped his ideas of "genuineness" (*zhen*) and the "childlike mind" (*tongxin*). But in fact, as Timothy Brook argues in chapter 4, Li Zhi and Geng Dingxiang shared many similarities. Both studied the ideas of Wang Yangming and read texts representing all three teachings. They were friends too. They were, nevertheless, very different in personality and thought, which made their later quarrels almost inevitable.

As a prominent Confucian scholar and official, Geng Dingxiang represented conventional Confucian wisdom. In contrast, Li Zhi was harsh, cynical, and arrogant, even though his message was not without merit. Because of his irascible personality, it was difficult for the majority of literati to appreciate him. Nevertheless, those who befriended both men recognized the advantages of their different visions. For example, Zhou Sijiu pointed out that their differences lay chiefly in their attitudes toward Confucian ethical norms (*mingjiao*) and genuine spirit (*zhenji*).[28]

The following example illustrates the differences between the two men. Geng Dingxiang once debated with his brother Geng Dingli which phrase best encapsulated the meaning of the Four Books. Dingxiang advocated for a phrase from the *Mencius*, "The sages are the culmination of humanity" (*renlun zhi zhi*), while Dingli preferred the phrase "a state of equilibrium before any emotion has stirred" (*weifa zhi zhong*) from *the Doctrine of the Mean*.[29]

Commenting on the brothers' disagreement, Li Zhi remarked, "'The culmination of humanity' is precisely 'a state of equilibrium before any emotion has stirred.' How could one who has not experienced this state of equilibrium attain the culmination of humanity? Perfection is attained when the Dao achieves equilibrium."[30] Here Li Zhi tried to reconcile the two statements by linking the moral agent's state of mind to his behavior. Li's comments focus on the brothers' shared understanding of the ultimate goal of learning, but what he fails to account for is the fundamental incompatibility between the methods the two brothers proposed for approaching their common goal. The statements the Geng brothers favored implied two different stances toward sagely learning. Dingxiang defended the values of Confucian ethical norms, while Dingli was concerned with the subtle condition of the heart-mind. Li Zhi sided with Dingli. He explains why his quarrels with Dingxiang worsened: "Dingxiang, for his part, tenaciously set his heart on the phrase 'The sages embody the culmination of humanity.' He constantly feared that, in relinquishing worldly affairs, I had committed an error. For my part, I tenaciously insisted on the phrase 'a state of equilibrium before any emotion has stirred' and feared that perhaps he had failed to perceive the origin of things or to investigate the source of their principles. We debated back and forth, never pausing, and our debate turned into a quarrel that continues even to the present day."[31] Li Zhi considered his quarrels with Geng Dingxiang mainly a philosophical problem concerning the correct method for studying. He also said in another essay, "Geng Dingxiang and I argued over learning."[32] This helps us to understand why Li Zhi wouldn't give up easily; he insisted because he was arguing over the essence of Confucian learning.

The differences between Li Zhi's and Geng Dingxiang's approaches to learning should also be examined in a broader intellectual context. Some Confucians like Geng emphasized the value of ethical norms, which were said to be inherent in human nature and congruent with heavenly principles. Confucians who held this belief intended to defend the validity of these ethical norms as well as the objective moral judgments that formed the basis of society. They insisted that, no matter how great and unfathomable the Dao was, if it was to serve as a moral compass, it needed to be represented to the people clearly and concretely.

On the other hand, Confucians rejected moral lessons learned by observing external rules alone. Instead of emphasizing moral behavior itself, they stressed the moral agent's motivation and state of mind. A famous phrase from the *Mencius* expressed this idea clearly: "[A person should] follow [the path of] morality. He should not just put morality into practice."[33] Ideally, one's behavior should accord with one's inner mental state, just as "rites/propriety" (*li*) were defined as external manifestations of heavenly principles within human nature. In practice, however, it was difficult to judge a person's motivation by his behavior, and "proper behavior" was not easy to discern since it needed to adapt to various situations. Confucians, therefore, more often encouraged people to examine themselves and follow their own moral judgments than merely to observe fixed rules or judge others' motivations.

The "pristine moral consciousness" (*liangzhi*) of Yangming learning, which both Li Zhi and Geng Dingxiang studied, attempted to bring to light questions regarding a moral agent's mental state as well as his adherence to social norms. Wang Ji and a number of other Taizhou scholars to whom Li Zhi felt akin adopted the more radical position of fully believing in each individual's *liangzhi*. Wang Ji proposed the theory of "ready-made *liangzhi*" (*xiancheng liangzhi*), by which he meant that one's *liangzhi* was in a constant state of readiness and fullness. No practice was needed to improve one's *liangzhi*. Neither should one adhere to any fixed practice, because every move should follow from *liangzhi* and adapt to the unfolding situation. This theory did not deny the importance of self-cultivation but rather emphasized practice at every moment, in all situations, guided by perfect *liangzhi*. This theory, however, worried many scholars and provoked serious criticism. A common criticism was that it led people to cherish the sense that they had already attained enlightenment and to neglect true moral cultivation.

The thought of ready-made *liangzhi* consequently de-emphasized the importance of rites and social norms in theory, although it did not necessarily do so in practice. It also raised doubts about the correspondence between name and reality, a Confucian ideal. During the late Ming, some doubted whether the reputations of certain public figures truly reflected their state of morality. "Name" or reputation (*ming*) not only did not necessarily reflect reality, but also could become the subject of power struggles and an obstacle to true moral cultivation. Therefore, some neo-Confucians asserted that true gentlemen should sincerely and continuously engage in ethical self-cultivation, even if doing so meant forgoing public recognition. Some upheld the idea of "cutting the roots of fame" (*duan minggen*) and "breaking through the obstacle of reputation" (*dapo huiyu guan*). These efforts aimed to encourage sincere self-cultivation. For example, Yang Qiyuan (1547–1599) said, "One's reputation does not reflect one's achievements, nor does one's social status indicate whether one has comprehended the Dao. There are some who have hidden virtues and unknown merits. People unknowingly benefit from their help. This is how sagely learning ought to be."[34] All these sayings emphasize the value of true moral motivation and demonstrate that one need not make others' opinions the barometer of one's own self-worth.

This viewpoint was quite popular among those who sympathized with Wang Ji and the Taizhou scholars, including Li Zhi. However, it became a target of criticism for orthodox scholars, such as those of Donglin and Jiangyou (Jiangxi Province). Donglin and Jiangyou scholars stressed the role of rites, even though they also recognized the importance of achieving enlightenment through the cultivation of *liangzhi*.[35] They believed in the correspondence between names and reality (*ming shi xiang fu*). Wang

Shihuai (1522–1605) analogized the view of Wang Ji and other adherents to the Taizhou School to fierce floods and savage beasts:

> Acting arbitrarily was considered following one's nature. Fawning on the world was considered being at one with the myriad things. Transgressing the precepts was considered not craving reputation. An unrestrained attitude was considered the state of joy achieved by Confucius and his favorite student, Yan Hui. Empty vision was considered transcendental enlightenment. Behaving shamelessly was considered possessing an untrammeled heart. Neglecting one's heart and not seeking the Dao was considered never expending any artificial effort. Alas, there are so many people who behave like this nowadays.[36]

Wang Shihuai considered the potential negative influences of claiming that words and reputations do not necessarily reflect reality. By disrupting the correspondence between names and reality, one risked upsetting social norms and losing the ability to make any objective judgment. Moral confusion and social disorder were the expected results. Furthermore, people who held such an opinion might even satirize those who scrupulously abided by rites and laws. Luo Hongxian (1504–1564) and Wang Shihuai, for example, complained that their contemporaries liked to deride as fame seekers those who strictly adhered to the rites.[37] All these criticisms might remind us of Li Zhi both because he was accused of being a fame seeker and because he too accused others of seeking fame.

CONTROVERSIES SURROUNDING LI ZHI

In debates about the correspondence between name and reality, Li Zhi's views resembled those of Wang Ji and the Taizhou scholars. However, his views about name and reality led him not only to advocate engaging in authentic moral cultivation but also to attack others. These actions, in turn, generated negative responses from his contemporaries. He bragged about himself, saying, "When I measure myself, I find no evil in my heart, no error on my person, no dirt on my form, and no dust on my shadow. There is an old saying 'neither blushing nor ashamed.' I truly embody it."[38] He also said, "People like me are very different from the majority of people in the world. If I harbored even the slightest deceitful thought or committed a minor transgression, I would feel deeply ashamed for a long time. . . . I am a person of the utmost self-discipline, whom no one could rival. However, I am strict only with myself, and very lenient with others. I have disciplined myself assiduously for seventy years. As I look around at all the people in the wide world, I find no one who can compare with me."[39] Although these words were spoken in self-defense, the arrogant tone is obvious. More damaging, Li Zhi harshly criticized the hypocrisy widespread throughout contemporary literati culture: "Those who claim to learn from Masters Zhou, Cheng, Zhang, and Zhu all like to talk about morality, but their real concerns are high-ranking official positions and enormous wealth. After they have gained a high position and are garnering enormous wealth, they continue talking about morality, benevolence, and righteousness. They garrulously tell people: 'My purpose is to rectify social practice and improve customs.'"[40]

Li Zhi despised many literati and accused them of seeking wealth and rank while talking about morality. He derided them for doing so only because he believed that they lacked the true talent necessary to succeed.[41] Yet by bragging about himself, he failed to engage in the kind of intense self-scrutiny the Confucian tradition demanded. His attacks on contemporary literati were unbearable to many. Qian Qianyi said that the reason contemporary literati hated Li Zhi so much was that he accused almost all of them of hypocrisy.[42] And Fang Yizhi (1611–1671) accused Li Zhi of being a fame seeker:

> I always feel sorry that Li [Zhi] was such a vain person, who, with little wit or talent, gave free rein to his own prejudices. He tried to smear all under heaven by his hand, and honored himself as the most outstanding person in the world. Because he could not reach his aspirations through officialdom, he allowed himself to spew venom at others. . . . Thus he specialized in scolding people for seeking fame, but in fact, he himself was seeking fame. Since he praised people like Wu Zetian and Feng Dao, he became a chief offender in breaking the code of ethics and he wrought chaos in the world. He sinned against heaven and earth, and people criticized him for unorthodoxy. However, it turned out that this was what he hoped for. He knew that his sinister and diabolic ways would not only satisfy the desires of those who coveted strange and new things, but would also provoke more criticism from the world, and this would make him more famous.[43]

We don't have to agree with Fang Yizhi in seeing Li Zhi as a fame seeker, but his view that Li was a "chief offender in breaking the code of ethics [and] wrought chaos in the world" reflected popular opinions in his time.

In short, when reading Li Zhi's life story, we cannot stop wondering why a person with such lofty moral standards and the sincere intention to engage in serious study became a target of public attacks. It seems that his outlandish way of humiliating his contemporary literati was the main cause. Li Zhi's rejection of the correspondence between name and reality, his repudiation of objective moral rules, and his fluid identity also contributed to creating the tragedy he endured.[44] All of these made him an iconoclast and a highly self-conscious thinker in late imperial Chinese history.

PERCEPTIONS OF LI ZHI FROM LATE MING TO QING

As previously noted, Li Zhi and Geng Dingxiang held different views of practice, which reflected differences of opinion among the followers of Wang Yangming. From the late Ming onward, Yangming learning was greatly criticized for too closely resembling Buddhism and Daoism. To rectify this perceived problem, many Confucians completely abandoned the idea of *liangzhi*. Most Yangming scholars, no matter what branch of his philosophy they belonged to, held *liangzhi* to be the key to ethical attainment. Either maintaining that individuals must act according to their ready-made *liangzhi* or advocating that individuals must cultivate and preserve their *liangzhi* by quiet sitting, late-Ming Yangming scholars tended to engage in a certain kind of inward practice with regard to mind-nature, the so-called first order of practice. They claimed that if one acted according to *liangzhi*, one's behavior would naturally conform to proper norms, and one's human relationships would become peaceful and well regulated. On this point, Li Zhi and Geng Dingxiang agreed: both endorsed the cultivation of *liangzhi*.

However, Qing Confucians tended to oppose the inward practice of the heart-mind (meditation and the pursuit of enlightenment) and focused instead on concrete actions such as building human relationships and fulfilling ethical obligations in everyday life (*riyong renlun*). For example, Xie Wenjian (1615–1681), who was a follower of the Cheng-Zhu School, disagreed with Zhu Xi and Cheng Yi insofar as he rejected all types of inward practice of the heart-mind. Alleging that such practices had been contaminated by Buddhism, he instead proposed that morality be practiced in daily life, and he asserted that Confucian sages should be able to follow their nature while adhering to the five cardinal relationships: ruler-minister, father-son, husband-wife, elder brother–younger brother, and friend-friend.[45] Similarly, Pan Pingge (1610–1677) emphasized the importance of restoring one's own nature and seeking benevolence (*qiuren*) or substance (*benti*). He often talked about the unity of the myriad things (*wanwu yiti*), and in many ways he was an inheritor of late-Ming Yangming learning.[46] Pan, however, opposed the practice of preserving reverence through quiet sitting and the practice of "observing *qi* before the feelings of pleasure, anger, sorrow, or happiness arise" (*guan weifa qixiang*). He criticized the neo-Confucian teachings of Cheng Yi, Zhu Xi, Lu Jiuyuan, and Wang Yangming for having betrayed the precepts of the ancient sages, which, he thought, were able to bring about peaceful governance and inspire people to live according to the cardinal relationships. The following dialogue between Pan Pingge and his friend demonstrates the value he placed on filial obligations:

> To encourage the people in the hall, a friend quoted Master Yangming, saying: "Everyone in this hall is a sage." Master Pan said: "Everyone in this hall is somebody's son." The friend said: "Everyone should learn to become a sage." Master Pan said: "Pingge only hopes that everyone can learn to become a filial son and a loving brother." The friend then expounded the *Western Inscription* [Ximing], saying: "*Qian* is father and *Kun* is mother. We need to understand that heaven and earth are our great parents. Only then can we understand the meaning of Unity." Master Pan said: "Pingge only wishes that everyone will know his own parents, and this will naturally lead to the great Unity."[47]

Pan Pingge tried hard to ground the lofty discussions of "the great Unity" and "the heavenly great parents" in concrete ethical obligations to parents and brothers. He did not deny the teachings of the famous Song dynasty text the *Western Inscription* on the unity of the myriad things, but he rejected the notion that one should abandon daily familial obligations in order to pursue the Dao.

Similar opinions were popular in early Qing neo-Confucianism. Confucian scholars such as Chen Que (1604–1677), Lu Shiyi (1611–1672), Mao Xianshu (1620–1688), Zhu Yongchun (1617–1688), Xu Sanli (1625–1691), Lu Longqi (1630–1692), and Yan Yuan (1635–1704) criticized the inward focus on the heart-mind and argued that fulfilling ethical obligations was the basic requirement for sagely learning. According to their arguments, one could learn to become a sage only within the context of one's family. This thesis was also often invoked to distinguish Confucianism from other religions.

Corresponding to this argument, Qing scholars likewise asserted that all Confucian sages must have been great filial sons. They tried hard to argue that not only those whose filial behavior had been recorded in history, such as Sage King Shun, King Wen of Zhou, and Confucius's disciple Zengzi, deserved recognition, but so did many who had no particular reputation for filiality, such as Confucius himself and his student Yan Hui. Because these Qing scholars viewed filial piety as the foundation of all virtues, they believed that in order for a person to be benevolent, he must also be filial.[48] Geng Jie (1623–1693), a Henan neo-Confucian, stated this point clearly: "Anyone who would like to learn to become a sage must first learn to become a filial son."[49]

In sum, from the late Ming to the early Qing, the intellectual ethos had shifted away from the debates within the Yangming School, which in some sense were represented by the differences between Li Zhi and Geng Dingxiang, to conversations that generally rejected the ideas put forth by members of the Yangming School. Most early-Qing neo-Confucians agreed that those engaged in sagely learning had to abide by ethical norms; moral cultivation could be realized only by adhering to familial obligations. Therefore, although Qing neo-Confucians did not necessarily agree with Geng Dingxiang's inclination toward Yangming learning, there was no doubt that, if they had had to take sides in the dispute between Li Zhi and Geng Dingxiang, they would certainly have sided with Geng.

Along with these intellectual changes, perceptions of Li Zhi also changed. From the seventeenth to the eighteenth century, his negative image became more and more entrenched, while the "controversies" surrounding him subsided. In the late Ming, although severe criticisms of Li Zhi continued to proliferate, quite a few literati publicly spoke out on his behalf. People lamented his death and tried to rehabilitate his name. He was controversial but did not lack supporters.

During the early Qing, however, the criticism intensified. Writings by Wang Fuzhi, Peng Shiwang, and Lü Liuliang (1629–1683) attest to the literati's strong desire to rectify their culture and preserve it from Li Zhi's potentially deleterious influence. Eighteenth-century attitudes toward Li Zhi remained critical, but perhaps because his influence was on the wane, debates over his ideas receded. Few wrote to catalogue his misdeeds in detail. Rather, they considered him as representing the perversion and corruption of late-Ming culture. As Yuan Mei (1716–1797) said, Li Zhi was "an evil person recognized by all" (*ren suo gongshi de yaomei*).[50]

The eighteenth-century image of Li Zhi is clearly evident in the editorial synopses of the *Four Treasuries* (Siku quanshu), where he is portrayed not only as a representative of the corrupt literati culture of the late Ming but also as a touchstone for moral and cultural values. Phrases such as "the manner of Li Zhi" (*Li Zhi zhi xiqi*) and "the sort of person like Li Zhi"

(*Li Zhi zhi liu*) are often used pejoratively to describe other authors and scholarship.[51] Any positive words about him or any quotation from him is taken as evidence of bad scholarship. For example, the synopsis of *Leisurely Notes Composed during a Spring Chill* (Chunhan xianji) states, "The book contains many good stories and wise words of people in history; however, it conveys high regard for Li Zhi."[52] Here, "convey[ing] high regard for Li Zhi" obviously was meant as criticism. Similarly, the synopsis of the *Fragmentary Writings of Master Mao* (Maoshi canshu) mentions a preface written by the author Mao Yuchen, who praises Li Zhi. Based on this, the synopsis comments, "We therefore know that the source of Mao's learning was not correct."[53]

Another example is the synopsis of the *Biographies of Three Extraordinary People* (San yiren zhuan). The book consists of works by Fang Xiaoru (1357–1402), Yu Qian (1398–1457), and Yang Jisheng (1516–1555), selected by Li Zhi. Fang, Yu, and Yang were famous loyal officials, and the book contains their ethical teachings, but the synopsis warns, "Li Zhi transgressed ethical norms and poisoned the minds of later generations. Since he selected and edited these three men's writings, the collection won't honor them but rather will bring them shame."[54]

Not only was it considered intolerable to show favor for Li Zhi, but anything associated with him was considered shameful and humiliating. This viewpoint reflected the official perspective on Li Zhi throughout the eighteenth century. Sometimes along with Tu Long (1543–1605) or He Xinyin, Li Zhi was reviled as a symbol of the decadence of late-Ming literati culture, especially the part disfavored by orthodox Qing Confucians. Repeated references to his writing style, his personality, and his zealous pursuit of religion helped to shape Li Zhi as a stereotype of the Chinese iconoclast, and this fixed image remained unchallenged throughout the nineteenth century.

It was not until the twentieth century that the image of Li Zhi began to change. Liu Shipei (1884–1919) published a study of Li in Japan in 1907, and the Institute for the Preservation of Chinese Learning (Guoxue baocunhui) reprinted Li's *A Book to Burn* in Shanghai in 1908. Amid the anti-Manchu sentiment of the time, Li was transformed into a noble and insightful thinker. The *Guocui xuebao* (1905) praised his teachings as "exceedingly noble, refined, and independent of conventional views." The same newspaper extolled the courage with which he rejected the teachings of Confucius.[55] His thought was considered progressive and was even favorably compared to Western philosophy.[56] These tremendous changes marked a new era in the study of Li Zhi in the context of modern Chinese history.

CONCLUSION

Spurred by his yearning to understand the meaning of life and death, Li Zhi embarked on the study of the Dao. Many late-Ming literati shared his concern and his dedication to learning, but his thought and personality made him special. He believed that one could attain the Dao only by self-cultivation. He trusted his own experience more than any institutional guidelines and consequently downplayed the importance of social norms. Although he shared ideas with scholars such as Wang Ji and Luo Rufang, his identity was far more fluid than theirs.[57] The freedom with which he crossed boundaries and the ferocity with which he attacked those who disagreed with him prevented him from being accepted by mainstream Confucian scholars.

Throughout the late Ming and early Qing, Confucian scholars continually debated the issue of life and death. Like their Ming predecessors, Qing scholars emphasized the value of moral accomplishment and the preservation of individuality. But they tended to advocate methods for attaining these ends that differed from those endorsed by their Ming forebears. During the late Ming, a general consensus emerged that *liangzhi* must play a key role in moral practice, even though scholars such as Li Zhi and Geng Dingxiang emphasized different approaches toward learning. In the early Qing, however, many rejected the previous consensus and attempted to restore "true Confucianism" by claiming ethical norms as a basic requirement for sagely learning. In this latter period, Li Zhi and his ideas were further condemned and viewed as representing the heterodoxy of late-Ming literati culture. During the eighteenth century, his image as an iconoclast became more entrenched. It was not until the intellectual and political sentiment shifted to oppose the Manchu state that Li Zhi and his free spirit were finally rediscovered and appreciated. This time, due to a similar distortion of history, he was transformed into a harbinger of the Chinese Enlightenment.

NOTES

1 Xu Jianping, *Li Zhuowu zhuan*, 253–67.

2 Xu Jianping, *Li Zhi sixiang yanbianshi*, 351–66. Also see Liu Zhiqing, "Li Zhi." On Li Zhi's religious commitments, see chapter 9 in the present volume.

3 Li Zhi, "Wang Yangming xiansheng nianpu houyu," in *Wang Yangming quanji*, 1604.

4 Li Zhi, "Guanyin wen, you," in *LZ* 2:80.
5 Li Zhi, "Da Zixin, you," in *LZ* 2:84.
6 Araki, *Mingmo Qingchu de sixiang yu Fojiao*, 189–214.
7 Zhou Rudeng, *Dongyue zhengxue lu*, 575.
8 Du Wenhuan, *Sanjiao huizong*. For the thought of Du Wenhuan, see Lu Miaw-fen, "Du Wenhuan huizong sanjiao."
9 Li Zhi, "San jiao gui Ru shuo," in *LZ* 3:223.
10 Li Zhi, "Da Ma Lishan," in *LZ* 3:1.
11 Li Zhi, "Da Ma Lishan," in *LZ* 3:1.
12 Li Zhi, *Yinguo lu*, in *LZ* 18:9–12.
13 Li Zhi, *Yinguo lu*, in *LZ* 18:11.
14 Bernard and Wang, "Li Madou siduo he dangdai Zhongguo shehui."
15 Li Zhi, "Yu Li Weiqing," in *LZ* 1:148–49; Yuan Guangyi, *Li Zhuowu xinlun*, 95.
16 De Bary, *The Liberal Tradition*, 79–80; Mizoguchi, *Zhongguo qianjindai sixiang*, 111–93. See chapter 8 for an argument against identifying Li Zhi as an individualist.
17 Zhu Xi, *Sishu jizhu*, 2:12a.
18 For example, see Zhou Rudeng, *Dongyue zhengxu lu*, 210, and Wang Ji, "Zisong wenda," in *Longxi Wang xiansheng quanji*, 15:26b.
19 Lu Miaw-fen, "Rushi jiaorong de shengren guan."
20 Li Jingde, *Zhuzi yulei*, 3:39.
21 Li Jingde, *Zhuzi yulei*, 3:43–44, 46.
22 Deng and Deng, *Nanxun lu jiaozhu*, 26–27.
23 For detailed discussion, see Lu Miaw-fen, *Chengsheng yu jiating renlun*, ch. 1.
24 Gao Panlong, *Gaozi yi shu*, 1:20–21.
25 Ying Huiqian, *Xingli dazong*, 23:26–30.
26 Karlgren, *The Book of Odes*, 185.
27 Lu Miaw-fen, *Chengsheng yu jiating renlun*, ch. 1.
28 Huang Zongxi, *Ming Ru xue'an* (1987), 827.
29 For a complete translation of this essay, see Li Zhi, *A Book to Burn*, 166–71.
30 Li Zhi, "Geng Chukong xiansheng zhuan," in *LZ* 2:21; Li Zhi, *A Book to Burn*, 168.
31 Li Zhi, "Geng Chukong xiansheng zhuan," in *LZ* 2:22; Li Zhi, *A Book to Burn*, 169–70.
32 Li Zhi, "Da laishu," in *LZ* 3:56.
33 Lau, *Mencius*, 131.
34 Yang Qiyuan, *Taishi Yang Fuso xiansheng zhengxue bian*, 1:31a.
35 Lu Miaw-fen, *Yangming xue shiren shequn*, ch. 9.
36 Wang Shihuai, *Tangnan Wang xiansheng youqingtang hegao*, 4:18a.
37 Luo, "Ji Yu Jiong zhai," in *Nian'an wenji*, 3:67a–b; Wang Shihuai, "Yu Wang Simo," in *Tangnan Wang xiansheng youqingtang hegao*, 1:29b.
38 Li Zhi, "Yu Zhou Youshan," in *LZ* 3:47.
39 Li Zhi, "Yu Ma Boshi," in *LZ* 3:82.

40 Li Zhi, "You yu Jiao Ruohou," in *LZ* 1:119.
41 Li Zhi, "San jiao gui Ru shuo," in *LZ* 1:223–24.
42 Qian Qianyi, *Leichao shiji xiao zhuan*, 6277.
43 Fang Yizhi and Pang, *Dongxi jun*, 256–57.
44 For discussion of Li Zhi's image trouble, see chapter 6.
45 Xie Wenjian, *Xie Chengshan ji*, 9:23b.
46 Lu Miaw-fen, *Xiao zhi tianxia*, 182–87.
47 Pan Pingge, *Panzi qiurenlu jiyao*, 140.
48 Lu Miaw-fen, *Chengsheng yu jiating renlun*, ch. 2.
49 Geng Jie, *Jingshutang wenji*, 340–41.
50 Yuan Mei, *Xiaochang shanfang shiwenji*, 1540.
51 Yong, *Siku quanshu zongmu*, 125:12b, 16a.
52 Yong, *Siku quanshu zongmu*, 118:30b.
53 Yong, *Siku quanshu zongmu*, 129:20b–21a.
54 Yong, *Siku quanshu zongmu*, 192:35a–b.
55 *Guocui xuebao*, 2:1388.
56 Pei-kai Cheng, "Continuities in Chinese Political Culture."
57 On Li Zhi's complicated relationships to these two masters, see chapter 5.

GLOSSARY

ai 愛
Anle wo 安樂窩

baguwen 八股文
Bai Juyi 白居易 (*zi*: Letian 樂天)
Bai Letian. See Bai Juyi.
Bainiu 白牛
Baiquan Jushi 百泉居士
Baiquan Ren 白泉人
Baiquan shan 百泉山
Baixia 白下
baixing riyong 百姓日用
Baizhai gong 白齋公
Ban Zhao 班昭
baofang 報房
Beiyou ji 北遊記
benlai zhenxing 本來真性
bense xuedaoren 本色學道人
benti 本體
benxin 本心
benzhen 本真
Bijing lao jian mingbai. Ruo jinren buzhi zuo xuduo chou tai ye. 畢竟老奸明白。若今人不知作許多醜態也
bingfu zhi ziran 稟賦之自然
bixian 避嫌
Bo Ya 伯牙
Bo Yi 伯夷
bu dongxin 不動心
bu xianggan 不相干
budeyi 不得已
burong ziyi 不容自已
bushi daoli 不是道理

Cangzhou 滄州
Cao Pi 曹丕
celun 策論
Cen Cen 岑參 (ca. 715–770)
Chan 禪
Changqing Huiling 長慶慧稜
changwu 長物
Chao Jiong 晁迥 (951–1034)
chaoshu 抄書
chaotuo 超脫
Chen Longzheng 陳龍正 (1585–1645)
Chen Que 陳確 (1604–1677)
Cheng Hunzhi 程渾之
"Cheng Shendao zhuan" 程身道傳
Cheng Xueyan 程學顏
Cheng Yi 程頤 (1033–1107)
Cheng-Zhu daoxue 程朱道學
chiren, chiren 癡人癡人
"Chiren yu lijao" 吃人與禮教
chizi zhi xin 赤子之心
chuan shen 傳神
chuanqi 傳奇
Chuanxi lu 傳習錄
chuanyi chifan 穿衣吃飯
chujia 出家
Chunhan xianji 春寒閒記

chuque chuanyi chifan, wu lunwu yi 除卻穿衣吃飯，無倫物矣
churu 出入
churu yu huajie liushi zhijian 出入于花街柳市之間
chushi 出世
Cui Yingying 崔鶯鶯
cunshun moning 存順歿寧

da maimai 大買賣
da shi, da shi 大是，大是
da zhangfu 大丈夫
dagun 打滾
Dahui Zonggao 大慧宗杲
"Dai Hushang shu" 代湖上疏
Dao 道
dao ci you you qu 到此又有趣
Dao gu lu 道古錄
Daodejing 道德經
Daoxue 道學
daoxue xiansheng 道學先生
daoxue zhu junzi 道學諸君子
Daoyuan jiyao 道院集要
dapo huiyu guan 打破毀譽關
daren 大人
Datong shu 大同書
Da xue 大學
Dazhongcheng 大中丞
Deng He 鄧鶴 (*zi*: Huoqu 豁渠; *hao*: Taihu 太湖; 1498–1569
Deng Huoqu 鄧豁渠 (*ming*: 鶴; dharma name: Huoqu 豁渠; *hao*: Taihu 太湖; 1498–ca. 1569)
Deng Lincai 鄧林材 (*zi*: Zipei 子培; *hao*: Shiyang 石陽; *juren* 1561)
Deng Shiyang. See Deng Lincai.
"Deye Ruchen" 德業儒臣
dizi 弟子
dizi ru ze xiao, chu ze ti 弟子入則孝，出則悌
dizi zhi 弟子職
Dong Zuobin 董作賓
Donglin 東林
Donglin shuyuan 東林書院
Du Fu 杜甫 (712–770)
"Du Li Zhuowu yu Wang seng Ruowu shu" 讀李卓吾與王僧若無書
Du Wenhuan 杜文煥 (b. 1581)
"Du Yuanming zhuan" 讀淵明傳
duan minggen 斷名根
duanjian 短見
dushu 讀書
dushuren 讀書人
Duwu 篤吾

eryan 邇言

Fang Hang 方沆 (*zi*: Ziji 子及; *hao*: Ren'an 訒菴; 1542–1608)
Fang Ren'an. See Fang Hang.
Fang Xiaoru 方孝孺 (1357–1402)
Fang Yilin 方一麟 (alternate *ming*: Yushi 與時; *hao*: Zhanyi 湛一)
Fang Yizhi 方以智 (1611–1671)
Fang Yushi 方與時
Fang Zhanyi. See Fang Yilin.
"fanli" 凡例
Fayan Monastery 法眼寺
Fazang suijin lu 法藏碎金錄
fen 憤
Feng Ji 馮楫 (?–1153)
Feng Menglong 馮夢龍 (1574–1646)
Feng Yingjing 馮應京 (1555–1606)
Fo 佛
Fo. Zhang Huofo 佛。張活佛
Foyan Qingyuan 佛眼清遠
Fu Sinian 傅斯年 (*zi*: Mengzhen 孟真 1896–1950)
fu tongxin zhe, juejia chunzhen, zuichu yinian zhi benxin ye 夫童心者，絕假純真，最初一念之本心也
fufu 夫婦
Fujian 福建
"Fulu er" 附錄二

ganying 感應
Ganying pian 感應篇. See also *Yinguo lu*.
Gao Panlong 高攀龍 (1562–1626)
Geng Dingli 耿定理 (*zi*: Ziyong 子庸; *hao*: Chukong 楚倥; 1534–1584)
Geng Dinglih 耿定力 (1541–1607)
Geng Dingxiang 耿定向 (*zi*: Zailun 在倫; *hao*: Chutong 楚侗, Tiantai 天台; 1524–1596)
Geng Jie 耿介 (1623–1693)
gong 公
gong'an 公案
Gongcheng 共城
gongfu 功夫
"Gongjian Geng Tiantai xiansheng Dingxiang" 恭簡耿天臺先生定向
gongwen 公文
gu 孤
Gu Kaizhi 顧愷之 (344–406)
Gu Tongzhou 顧通州. See Gu Yangqian
Gu Xiancheng 顧憲成 (1550–1612)
Gu Yangqian 顧養謙 (1537–1604)
Gu Yanwu 顧炎武 (1613–1682)
guan weifa qixiang 觀未發氣象
Guan Zhidao 管志道 (1537–1608)
Guangong 關公
guben 古本
Gui Youguang 歸有光 (1506–1571)
guiyi 歸依
gujin zhiwen 古今至文
Guocui xuebao 國粹學報
Guoxue baocunhui 國學保存會

Haiqu Lü mu 海曲呂母
Haiyang 海陽
Han Zhen 韓貞 (1509–1585)
hao 號
hao dong ming 好洞名
hao xiangtou 好想頭
hao xiaoqian 好消遣
He Xinyin 何心隱 (*ming*: Liang Ruyuan 梁汝元; 1517–1579)
He Yan 何晏 (d. 249 CE)
Henan 河南
He-Yin Zhen 何殷震 (1884–ca. 1920)
Hong Yao 閎夭
Hongfu. See Li Zhi.
Hongfu ji 紅拂記
Honglou meng 紅樓夢
hou 猴
Hu Shi 胡適 (1891–1962)
Hu Yinglin 胡應麟 (1551–1602)
hua 畫
huaben 話本
huagong 化工
huagong 畫工
huan 幻
Huang Chao 黃巢
Huang Fengci 黃蜂刺
Huang Furen 黃夫人 (1533–1588) (Madame Huang)
Huang Lin 黃霖
Huang Zongxi 黃宗羲 (1610–1695)
Huang'an 黃安
Huangbo shan 黃檗山
Huangbo Wunian Chanshi fuwen 黃蘗無念禪師復問
Huanggang 黃岡
Huangzhou 黃州
huatou 話頭
Huayan helun 華嚴合論
Hubei 湖北
Huguang 湖廣
Hui of Liang, King梁惠王
Hui County 徽州
"Huimei weikong" 晦昧為空
Huineng 惠能
huitong 會通
Huixian 輝縣
Huizhou 徽州
huizong sanjiao 會宗三教
Huoqu. See Deng He.
huoshi 惑世
Hushang yulu 湖上語錄

jia 家
jia fo 假佛
Jiajing 嘉靖
Jiangcun 姜村
jianghui 講會
Jiangsu 江蘇
jiangxue 講學
Jiangyou 江右
Jianyang 建陽
Jiao Hong 焦竑 (*zi*: Ruohou 弱侯, Congwu 從吾, Shudu叔度; *hao*: Danyuan 澹園, Yiyuan漪園; 1540–1620)
jiaogenzhen 腳跟真
jiaoqing 矯情
Jiaoshi leilin 焦氏類林
jiaoyu 教諭
jiapi 夾批
jiaren 假人
jiashi 假事
jiawen 假文
Jiaxingzang 嘉興藏
jiayan 假言
"Jiazu zhidu wei zhuanzhizhuyi zhi genju lun" 家族制度為專制主義之根據論
jie 解
jietan 戒壇
jifeng wenda 機鋒問答
Jile si 極樂寺
Jin Shengtan 金聖嘆 (1608–1661)
Jinbu zazhi 進步雜誌
Jingde chuandenglu 景德傳燈錄
jingshi 經世
Jingtu jue 淨土訣
"Jingtu jue qianyin" 淨土決前引
Jinhua 金華
Jinjiang 晉江
Jinling 金陵
Jinshu 晉書
jiu gun cangban shizhuan 就滾倉版十轉
Jiuzheng yiyin 九正易因
juan 卷
junzi 君子
jushi 居士
jushu 聚書

Kang Youwei 康有為 (1858–1927)
kexiao 可笑
koan. See gong'an.
Kong Anguo 孔安國 (d. ca. 100 CE)
Kong Ruogu 孔若谷
kuang 狂
kuangjuan 狂狷
Kuichezhi 睽車志

Lanxi 蘭谿
Lao Qida 老乞大
Laozi 老子
Laozi jie 老子解
li 利 (profit)
li 禮 (ritual)
li 力 (strength)
Li 李 (surname Li)
Li Cai 李材 (1520–ca. 1606)
Li Gong 李塨 (1651–1733)
Li Kan 李侃
Li Kui 李逵
Li Laozi 李老子
Li Shihui 李時輝 (*zi*: Weiqing 惟清)
Li Shou'an 李壽庵
Li Tongxuan 李通玄
Li Weiqing. See Li Shihui.
Li Weizhen 李維楨 (1547–1626)
"Li Weizhen xu" 李維楨序
Li Wenling waiji 李溫陵外紀
"Li Wenling zhuan" 李溫陵傳
Li Xinsheng 李新聲
Li Yuanyang 李元陽 (*zi*: Renfu 仁甫; *hao*: Zhongxi 中谿; 1497–1580)
Li zhangzhe pixuan Dahui ji 李長者批選大慧集
Li Zhi 李贄 (*zi*: Hongfu 宏甫; *hao*: Li laozi 李老子, Sizhai Jushi 思齋居士, Wenling Jushi 溫陵居士, Zhuo lao

卓老, Zhuowu 卓吾, Zhuowu zi 卓吾子; 1527–1602)
"Li Zhi Jiao Hong liezhuan" 李贄焦竑列傳
"Li Zhi shengping zhuanji ziliao huibian" 李贄生平傳記資料彙編
Li Zhi zhi liu 李贄之流
Li Zhi zhi xiqi 李贄之習氣
Li Zhicai 李之才 (980–1045)
Li Zhuowu. See Li Zhi.
Li Zhuowu xiansheng pidian Daoyu lu 李卓吾先生批點道余錄
"Li Zhuowu zhuan" 李卓吾傳
Liangxi 梁溪
liangzhi 良知
Liezi 列子
Liji 禮記
Lin 林
Lin Shu 林紓 (1852–1924)
Lin Xiangru 藺相如 (ca. 179–17 BCE)
Lin Zhao'en 林兆恩 (1517–1598)
Linqiong 臨邛
Liu Bangcai 劉邦采 (*zi*: Junliang 君亮; *hao*: Shiquan 獅泉; *juren* 1528)
Liu Dongxing 劉東星 (*zi*: Ziming 子明; *hao*: Jinchuan 晉川; 1538–1601)
Liu Shipei 劉師培 (1884–1919)
"Liu Wenzhen mao shi" 劉文貞毛氏
Liu Yongjian 劉用健
Liu Yongxiang 劉用相
liuzei 六賊
lizhi 立志
"Lizhong san yi zhuan" 里中三異傳
Longhu 龍湖
Longqing 隆慶 (emperor; r. 1567–1572). See also Zhu Zaihou.
Longtan Chongxin 龍潭崇信
Longtan hu 龍潭湖
Longxi xiansheng wenlu chao 龍溪先生文錄抄
Lu Jiuyuan 陸九淵 (1139–1192)
Lü Kun 吕坤 (1536–1618)
Lü Liuliang 呂留良 (1629–1683)
Lu Longqi 陸隴其 (1630–1692)
Lu Shiyi 陸世儀 (1611–1672)
lun 論
"Lun Xie An jiaoqing" 論謝安矯情
Lunyu 論語
Lunyu Heshideng jijie 論語何氏等集解
Luo Hongxian 羅洪先 (1504–1564)
Luo Rufang 羅汝芳 (*zi*: Weide 惟德; *hao*: Jinxi 近谿; 1515–1588)

Ma Jinglun 馬經倫 (*zi*: Zhuyi 主一; *hao*: Chengsuo 誠所; 1562–1605)
Macheng 麻城
Maiguta 埋骨塔
maizhe 買者
Mao Lun 毛綸 (1605?–1700?)
Mao Xianshu 毛先舒 (1620–1688)
Mao Yuchen 毛羽宸
Mao Yulong 毛鈺龍 (n.d.)
Mao Zedong 毛澤東 (1893–1976)
Mao Zonggang 毛宗崗 (1632–after 1709)
Maoshi canshu 毛氏殘書
Mazu Daoyi 馬祖道一
mei 梅
Mei Danran 梅澹然
Mei Guozhen 梅國楨 (*zi*: Kesheng 客生 and 克生; *hao*: Hengxiang 衡湘; 1542–1605)
mei li 沒禮
mei qu 沒趣
meichen yaoshi 美疢藥石
meipi 眉批
Meng Zhen 孟真
Mengzi 孟子
miao 妙
Miaoguta 埋骨塔
Miaoming zhenxin 妙明真心
ming 名
"Ming Li Zhuowu biezhuan" 明李卓吾別傳
Ming Ru xue'an 明儒學案
ming shi xiang fu 名實相符

Ming wenhai 明文海
Mingdeng dao gu lu 明燈道古錄. See *Dao gu lu*.
mingjiao 名教
Mingzhu ji 明珠記
mo zhi suo zhang 莫知所長
moyang 模樣
Mudan ting 牡丹亭

nanfeng 南風 (southern wind)
nanfeng 男風 (male fashion)
Nangong Shi 南宮適
Nanjing 南京
Nanyang Huizhong 南陽慧忠
Nanyou ji 南遊記
nanzi 男子
neidan 內丹
Neijiang xianzhi 內江縣志
ni 譨
Ningbo 寧波
Ningzhou 寧州
"Nüzi jiefang wenti" 女子解放問題

Pan Pingge 潘平格 (1610–1677)
Pan Shizao 潘士藻 (*zi*: Quhua 去華; *hao*: Xuesong 雪松; 1537–1600)
Pan Zenghong 潘曾竑 (1559–1627)
panjiao 判教
pen 噴
Peng Shiwang 彭士望
pengfu 捧腹
piaohao 票號
Pingshang 坪上
Pipa ji 琵琶記
piping 批評
Poxian ji 坡仙集
pusa 菩薩

qi 奇 (extraordinary)
qi 氣 (psychophysical stuff)
Qi 齊 (state)
qi nanzi 奇男子
qi renlun 棄人倫
qi renlun li qishi 棄人倫離妻室
Qian Qianyi 錢謙益 (1582–1664)
Qian Tongwen 錢同文
Qian Xinzu 錢新祖 (1940–1996)
Qian Xiyan 錢希言 (fl. 1612)
"Qianyan" 前言
Qin Jia 秦嘉
Qin Shihuang 秦始皇 (259–210 BCE)
qing 情
Qin shi 琴史
qinxin 沁心
"Qiu jing shu" 求儆書
Qiu Xuansu 丘玄素
qiuren 求仁
qu 趣
Qu Ruji 瞿汝稷 (1548–1610)
quandian 圈點
Quanzhou 泉州

ren suo gongshi de yaomei 人所共識的妖魅
renlun zhi zhi 人倫之至
rike juzi ye, ye du yi yigua 日課舉子業，夜讀易一卦
Riniu, monk 日牛和尚 (a.k.a. Bainiu 白牛)
riyong renlun 日用人倫
riyong zhi pingchang 日用之平常
Rizhai 日在
Rongyutang 容與堂
Ru 儒
Ruchan 儒禪
Ruowu. See Wang Shiben.

San yiren zhuan 三異人傳
San Yisheng 散宜生
Sanguo yanyi 三國演義
Sanguo zhi yanyi 三國志演義
Sanguo zhizhuan pinglin 三國志傳評林
Sanjiao miaoshu 三教妙述. See also *Yanshan pian*.
Sanjing jie 三經解
Santan dajie 三壇大戒

Sengchan 僧禪
Shade kuaihuo. Shade kuaihuo. Ruo ru neiliange ye yiqiang cuosi bian meiqu le 殺得快活。殺得快活。若如那兩個也一槍戳死便沒趣了
shang 商
Shangcheng 商城
Shangdang, Shanxi 上黨，山西
shangdi 上帝
Shannong. See Yan Jun.
Shao Yong 邵雍 (1011–1077)
she 奢
She Changji 佘常吉 (*zi*: Yongning 永寧)
she ru jiu shang 捨儒就商
She Yongning 佘永寧
shen 神
Shen Fu 沈鈇 (1550–1634)
Shen Yiguan 沈一貫 (1531–1615)
shenfen 身份
Sheng Yusi 盛於斯
shengji 勝己
shengsi zhi jiao 生死之交
shengtai 聖胎
shi 士 (literati)
shi 實 (actuality)
shi 師 (teacher)
Shi Jingxian 史旌賢 (*zi*: Tingjun 廷俊)
shi li zhi xin 勢利之心
shi zhi xuedaozhe 世之學道者
Shi zhongchen, shi xiaozi, shi cisun. 是忠臣。是孝子。是慈孫
Shidetang 世德堂
Shiji 史記
Shijing 詩經
Shikui shu 石匱書
shishang 士商
Shishang guilüe 士商規略
Shishang leiyao 士商類要
Shishang shiyao 士商十要
Shishang yaolan 士商要覽
Shishuo xinyu 世說新語
Shishuo xinyu bu 世說新語補
shiwen 時文
Shiwen guyi 時文古義
shiyou 師友
Shou 受
Shu Qi 叔齊
"Shu Yuegong ce" 書月公冊
"Shu *Zuolin jitan*" 書柞林紀譚
Shuihu zhizhuan pinglin 水滸志傳評林
Shuihu zhuan 水滸傳
Shujing 書經
Shun 舜
shuo chu 說出
Shuo shu 說書
"Shuo xiao" 說孝
Shuohuzhi 說弧志
Shuzhai manlu 樗齋漫錄
si 私
si da qi shu 四大奇書
Si shu ping 四書評
Sichuan 四川
sifang qiuyou wendao 四方求友問道
Siku quanshu 四庫全書
Sima Qian 司馬遷 (ca. 145–ca. 85 BCE)
Sima Xiangru 司馬相如 (ca. 179–17 BCE)
siwu 私物
Sizhai 思齋
Sizhai Jushi. See Li Zhi.
sou 叟
su 訴
sui 歲
Suiyuan 隨園
Sun Qifeng 孫奇逢 (1585–1675)
Sun Yi 孫翊
sushi 俗事

Tai Dian 太顛
tai shen 太甚
Taigong 太公
Taishang ganying pian 太上感應篇
taixu 太虛
Taizhou 泰州
"Taizhou xue'an si" 泰州學案四

Taizu 太祖
tanci 彈詞
"Tang wen" 湯問
Tang Xianzu 湯顯祖 (1550–1616)
Tang Zhen 唐甄 (1630–1704)
Tao Qian 陶潛 (*zi*: Yuanming 淵明; 365–427)
Tao Wangling 陶望齡 (1562–1609)
Tao Yuanming. See Tao Qian.
ti 題
"Tian dao" 天道
Tian yu hua 天雨花
Tiandu waichen. See Wang Daokun.
Tianhuang Daowu 天皇道悟
tianli 天理
Tianwang Daowu 天王道悟
tianxing 天性
"tici" 題辭
tongsu 通俗
tongxin 童心
tongzhi 同志
Tongzhou 通州
Tongzi bian shi miao ren le 童子便是妙人了
toutuo 透脫
Tu Long 屠隆 (1543–1605)
tuo 唾
tuyi jiejiao qinmi zhe wei zhi you 徒以結交親密者謂之友

waidan 外丹
"Waiwu" 外物
Wang Benke 汪本鈳
Wang Bi 王襞 (1511–1587)
Wang Daokun 汪道昆 (*zi*: Boyu 伯玉; *hao*: Tiandu waichen 天都外臣; 1525–1593)
Wang Fuzhi 王夫之 (1619–1692)
Wang Gen 王艮 (*zi*: Ruzhi 汝止; *hao*: Xinzhai 心齋; 1483–1541)
Wang Ji 王畿 (*hao*: Longxi 龍谿 or 龍溪; 1498–1583)
Wang Keshou 汪可受 (1559–1620)
Wang Qiyuan 王啓元 (b. 1599)
Wang Shiben 王世本 (dharma name Ruowu 若無)
Wang Shihuai 王時槐 (1522–1605)
Wang Shouren 王守仁 (zi: Boan 伯安; *hao*: Yangmingzi 陽明子; 1472–1529).
Wang Sihuai 王嗣槐 (b. 1620)
Wang Yangming. See Wang Shouren.
wanwu yiti 萬物一體
wanxiang zhi zhong du lushen 萬象之中獨露身
Wei-Jin 魏晉 (220–589)
weifa zhi zhong 未發之中
Weimo an 維摩庵
weisi 未死
weiwangren 未亡人
wen 文
Wen Mu 文母 (Mother Wen)
Wenling Jushi. See Li Zhi.
wenren 文人
wu 惡
Wu Cheng'en 吳承恩 (ca. 1500–ca. 1582)
Wu Daozi 吳道子 (680–759)
Wu Dechang 吳得常 (*zi*: Shizheng 世徵)
Wu Shizheng 吳世征
Wu Yu 吳虞 (1872–1949)
Wu Ze 吳澤 (1913–2005)
Wu Zetian 武則天 (624–705)
Wuchang 武昌
Wudeng huiyuan 五燈會元
Wuhua shan 五華山
Wuji's mother 無忌母
wulun 五倫
Wunian Shenyou 無念深有 (1544–1627) See Xiong Shenyou.
wuqing 無情
Wuxi 無錫
"Wuzong shuo" 五宗說

xiaji zhi shi 狎妓之事
xian 賢

xiancheng liangzhi 現成良知
xiang'ai 相愛
xiangyuan 鄉愿
xiangzhi 相知
xiaoshuo 小說
Xie An 謝安 (320–385)
Xie Wenjian 謝文洊 (1615–1681)
Ximing 西銘
Xin ershisi xiao 新二十四孝
xin zhong ningju 心中凝聚
xindan zhi jiao 心膽之交
xingle sanshi yeyuan 幸了三世業緣
xingming 性命
"Xingyou" 行由
Xinjing tigang 心經提綱
xinxing 心性
xinxue 心學
Xiong Shenyou 熊深有 (dharma name Wunian 無念; 1544–1627)
Xishan Temple 西山寺
"Xiu'an yingyu, Xiyouji wu" 休庵影語西遊記誤
Xixiang ji 西廂記
Xiyou ji 西遊記
"*Xiyou ji* kaozheng" 西遊記考證
"*Xu Cangshu* xu" 續藏書序
Xu Fang 徐芳 (n.d.)
Xu Guangqi 徐光啟 (1562–1633)
Xu Sanli 許三禮 (1625–1691)
Xu Shu 徐淑
Xu Shuofang 徐朔方
Xu Yongjian 徐用檢 (1528–1611)
Xu Yue 徐樾 (d. 1551)
Xu Zichang 許自昌 (fl. 1596–1623)
xuanyin 宣淫
xuedao 學道
xuedao zhiren 學道之人
xuedaoren 學道人
xuedaozhe 學道者
xuezhe 學者
xuhuai ruogu 虛懷若谷
yaliang 雅量
Yan Hui 顏回 (*zi*: Yan Yuan 顏淵 and 子淵) (disciple of confucius)
Yan Jidao 晏幾道 (1030–ca. 1106)
Yan Jun 顏鈞 (*zi*: Zihe 子和; *hao*: Shannong 山農; 1504–1596)
Yan Yuan. See Yan Hui.
Yan Yuan 顏元 (1635–1704)
yang 陽
Yang Dingjian 楊定見 (*hao*: Fengli 風里; n.d.)
Yang Jisheng 楊繼盛 (1516–1555)
Yang Qiyuan 楊起元 (*zi*: Zhenfu 貞復; *hao*: Fusuo 復所; 1547–1599)
Yang Zhu 楊朱
Yangming xiansheng Daoxue chao 陽明先生道學鈔
Yangming xiansheng nianpu 陽明先生年譜
"Yangshengzhu" 養生主
Yangzi River 揚子江(長江)
Yanshan pian 言善篇. See also *Sanjiao miaoshu.*
yanyi 演義
Yao 堯
Yao Guangxiao 姚廣孝
Yao'an 姚安
Yaoshi jing 藥師經
Ye Zhongzi 葉仲子
Ye Zhou 葉晝 (*zi*: Wentong 文通; *hao*: Yangkai 陽開; fl. 1595–1624)
Yehai Ziqing 業海子清
yi 義
Yi Jiang 邑姜
Yi shan shu jingwu. Gu shi miaoshou 亦善敘景物。固是妙手
Yi Yin 伊尹 (1649–1549? BCE)
yiduan 異端
Yijing 易經
yili 義利
yin 陰

Ying Huiqian 應撝謙 (1615–1683)
yingling hanzi 英靈漢子
Yinguo lu 因果錄. See also *Ganying pian*.
Yinshuwu shuying 因樹屋書影
yiren 異人
"Yiren san ren" 異人三人
Yongjia Xuanjue 永嘉玄覺
Yongming Yanshou 永明延壽
Yongqing dawen 永慶答問
you 友 (friend)
you 有 (to have)
youxin 有心
"Yu Beitai jian" 與北臺諫
"Yu Dangdao Shu" 與當道書
"Yu neihan Yang Fusuo" 與內翰楊復所
Yu Qian 于謙 (1398–1457)
"Yu Wu Shaoyu" 與吳少虞
Yu Xiangdou 余象斗 (ca. 1555–after 1637)
"Yu zhangke Li Linye zhuan shang Xiao sikou" 與掌科李麟野轉上蕭司寇
yu zhi er buneng 欲之而不能
"Yu Zhou Liutang" 與周柳塘
"Yu Zhou Liutang (you)" 與周柳塘（又）
Yuan Hongdao 袁宏道 (*zi*: Zhonglang 中郎; *hao*: Shigong 石公; 1568–1610)
Yuan Huang 袁黃 (1533–1606)
Yuan Mei 袁枚 (1716–1797)
Yuan Wuya 袁無涯
Yuan Yuling 袁于令 (1592–1674)
Yuan Zhongdao 袁中道 (*zi*: Xiaoxiu 小修; *hao*: Chaizijushi 柴紫居士; 1570–1623)
Yuan Zhonglang ji 袁中郎集
Yuan Zongdao 袁宗道 (*zi*: Boxiu 伯修; *hao*: Yupan 玉蟠; 1560–1600)
yuanjian 遠見
Yuhe ji 玉合記
yulu 語錄
Yunmen 雲門
Yunnnan 雲南
Yuzhang 豫章
zai di zuo you 在帝左右
zaijia chujia 在家出家
zaijia xiuxing 在家修行
Zaizhi 載贄
zarou 雜糅
Zeng Jiquan 曾繼泉
Zeng Zhongye 曾中野 (n.d.)
Zhang Dai 張岱 (1597–1685)
Zhang Juzheng 張居正 (1525–1582)
Zhang Liang 張良 (d. 186 BCE)
Zhang Wenda 張問達 (d. 1625)
Zhang Zai 張載 (1020–1077)
Zhang Zhupo 張竹坡 (1670–1698)
zhangfu 丈夫
zhangzhe 長者
Zhao E 趙娥
Zhao Zhenji 趙貞吉 (*zi*: Mengjing 孟靜; *hao*: Dazhou 大洲; 1508–1576)
Zhaode xinbian 昭德新編
"Zhegu tian" 鷓鴣天
zhen 真
zhen fo 真佛
Zhen Huanghou 甄皇后 (Empress Zhen)
zhen nanzi 真男子
zheng fenghua 正風化
Zhengtu yugong 征途與共
zhenji 真機
zhenxin 真心
Zhi 跖 (Robber Zhi)
"Zhi Cai Heqing shu" 致蔡鶴卿書
Zhifoyuan 芝佛院
zhixing heyi 知行合一
Zhiyi 智顗
zhiyin 知音
Zhiyue lu 指月錄
zhong 忠
Zhong yong 中庸
zhongdao 重道 (realize the importance of the Way)
Zhongyi Shuihu zhuan 忠義水滸傳
zhongyou 重友
Zhongzi Qi 鐘子期
Zhou dynasty 周代

Zhou Hongyue 周弘禴 (*hao*: Erlu 二魯)
Zhou Lianggong 周亮工 (1612–1672)
Zhou Rudeng 周汝登 (1547–1629)
Zhou Sijing 周思敬 (*zi*: Zili 子禮; *hao*: Youshan 友山; *jinshi* 1568; d. 1597)
Zhou Sijiu 周思久 (*hao*: Liutang 柳塘; *jinshi* 1553; 1527–1592)
Zhou Youshan. See Zhou Sijing.
Zhu Xi 朱熹 (1130–1200)
Zhu Yongchun 朱用純 (1617–1688)
Zhu Zaihou 朱載垕 (r. 1567–72). See also Longqing.
zhuan 傳
Zhuang Chunfu. See Zhuang Fengwen.
Zhuang Fengwen 莊鳳文 (*zi*: Chunfu 純夫, 純甫; 1554–1606)
Zhuangzi 莊子
zhuo 卓
Zhuo lao. See Li Zhi.
Zhuo Wangsun 卓王孫
Zhuo Wenjun 卓文君
Zhuowu. See Li Zhi.
Zhuowu zi. See Li Zhi.
zhushu 著書
Zigong 子貢 (Duanmu ci 端木賜; 520–446 BCE)
zide 自得
"Zisong wenda" 自訟問答
ziwen 自文
zongping 總評
Zuolin jitan 柞林紀譚
zuowei 作偽
Zuozhuan 左傳

BIBLIOGRAPHY

ABBREVIATION

LZ Li Zhi 李贄. *Li Zhi quanji zhu* 李贄全集注. Edited by Zhang Jianye 張建業 et al. 26 vols. Beijing: Shehui Kexue Wenxian Chubanshe, 2010.

WORKS BY LI ZHI

A Book to Burn and a Book to Keep (Hidden): Selected Writings. Translated by Rivi Handler-Spitz, Pauline C. Lee, and Haun Saussy. New York: Columbia University Press, 2016.

"Ba wu" 八物. *Fenshu*. In *LZ* 2:59–68.

Cangshu 藏書. In *LZ*, vols. 4–8.

"Chongke *Wudeng huiyuan* xu" 重刻《五燈會元》序. *Xu Fenshu*. In *LZ* 3:180–83.

"*Chutanji* xu" 初潭集序. In *LZ* 12:1–3.

Chutanji 初潭集. In *LZ*, vols. 12–13.

"Da Deng Mingfu" 答鄧明府. *Fenshu*. In *LZ* 1:37–40.

"Da Deng Mingfu" 答鄧明府. *Fenshu*. In *LZ* 1:94–101.

"Da Deng Shiyang" 答鄧石陽. *Fenshu*. In *LZ* 1:8–10.

"Da Geng Chutong" 答耿楚侗. *Xu Fenshu*. In *LZ* 3:143.

"Da Geng Sikou" 答耿司寇. *Fenshu*. In *LZ* 1:71–94.

"Da Geng Zhongcheng" 答耿中丞. *Fenshu*. In *LZ* 1:40–46.

"Da Geng Zhongcheng lun dan" 答耿中丞論淡. *Fenshu*. In *LZ* 1:58–61.

"Da Jiao Yiyuan" 答焦漪園. *Fenshu*. In *LZ* 1:17–22.

"Da laishu" 答來書. *Xu Fenshu*. In *LZ* 3:56–57.

"Da Li Weiqing" 答李惟清. *Xu Fenshu*. In *LZ* 3:73.

"Da Liu Fangbo shu" 答劉方伯書. *Fenshu*. In *LZ* 1:130–32.

"Da Liu Jinchuan" 答劉晉川. *Xu Fenshu*. In *LZ* 3:128.

"Da Liu Jinchuan shu" 答劉晉川書. *Fenshu*. In *LZ* 1:140–41.

"Da Liu Xianzhang" 答劉憲長. *Fenshu*. In *LZ* 1:61.

"Da Ma Lishan" 答馬歷山. *Xu Fenshu*. In *LZ* 3:1–9.

"Da Mei Qiongyu" 答梅瓊宇. *Xu Fenshu*. In *LZ* 3:73–75.
"Da Shen Wang" 答沈王. *Xu Fenshu*. In *LZ* 3:128–29.
"Da xiao" 大孝. *Fenshu*. In *LZ* 1:194–97.
"Da yi nüren xue dao wei jianduan shu" 答以女人學道為見短書. *Fenshu*. In *LZ* 1:143–47.
"Da Zhou Erlu" 答周二魯. *Fenshu*. In *LZ* 1:214–18.
"Da Zhou Liutang" 答周柳塘. *Fenshu*. In *LZ* 1:218–26.
"Da Zixin, you" 答自信 又. *Fenshu*. In *LZ* 2:84–85.
Dao gu lu 道古錄. In *LZ* 14:223–334.
"*Dao gu lu* yin" 道古錄引. *Dao gu lu*. In *LZ* 14:227–31.
"Daxiao yishou" 大孝一首. *Fenshu*. In *LZ* 1:194–97.
"Deye Ruchen houlun" 德業儒臣後論. *Cangshu*. In *LZ* 6:526–29.
"Du Ruowu mu jishu" 讀若無母寄書. *Fenshu*. In *LZ* 2:19–20.
"'Dushule' bing yin" 讀書樂並引. *Fenshu*. In *LZ* 2:240–43.
Fenshu 焚書. In *LZ*, vols. 1–2.
"Fu Deng Shiyang" 復鄧石陽. *Fenshu*. In *LZ* 1:24–33.
"Fu Geng Tong Lao shu" 復耿侗老書. *Fenshu*. In *LZ* 1:147–48.
"Fu Geng Zhongcheng" 復耿中丞. *Fenshu*. In *LZ* 1:212–14.
"Fu Gu Chong'an weng shu" 復顧沖庵翁書. *Fenshu*. In *LZ* 1:185.
"Fu Gu Chong'an weng shu, you shu" 復顧沖庵翁書, 又書. *Fenshu*. In *LZ* 1:186.
"Fu Jiao Ruohou" 復焦弱侯. *Fenshu*. In *LZ* 1:110–18.
"Fu Jiao Ruohou" 復焦弱侯. *Xu Fenshu*. In *LZ* 3:34–35.
"Fu song mei" 賦松梅. *Fenshu*. In *LZ* 2:276.
"Fufu er" 夫婦二. *Chutanji*. In *LZ* 12:39–56.
"Fufu lun" 夫婦論. *Fenshu*. In *LZ* 1:251–54.
"Fufu pian zonglun" 夫婦篇總論. *Chutanji*. In *LZ* 12:1–3.
"Fufu si" 夫婦四. *Chutanji*. In *LZ* 12:112–29.
"Gankai pingsheng" 感慨平生. *Fenshu*. In *LZ* 2:108–20.
"Gaojie shuo" 高潔說. *Fenshu*. In *LZ* 1:294–97.
"Geng Chukong xiansheng zhuan" 耿楚倥先生傳. *Fenshu*. In *LZ* 2:21–26.
"Guanyin wen" 觀音問. *Fenshu*. In *LZ* 2:76–96.
"Guanyin wen, you" 觀音問 又. *Fenshu*. In *LZ* 2:80–81.
"He Xinyin lun" 何心隱論. *Fenshu*. In *LZ* 1:245–51.
"Hongfu" 紅拂. *Fenshu*. In *LZ* 2:133–34.
"Huiqi xiaoqi" 會期小啟. *Fenshu*. In *LZ* 1:181.
"Ji Jiao Ruohou" 寄焦弱侯. *Xu Fenshu*. In *LZ* 3:29–32.
"Ji jingyou shu" 寄京友書. *Fenshu*. In *LZ* 1:171–72.
"Ji wu ji wen, dai zuo" 祭無祀文，代作. *Fenshu*. In *LZ* 1:346–48.
"Jida Geng Da Zhongcheng" 寄答耿大中丞. *Fenshu*. In *LZ* 1:103–7.
"Jiejing wen" 解經文. *Fenshu*. In *LZ* 2:5–9.
"Jingtu jue qianyin" 淨土決前引. In *Wanxu zangjing* 卍續藏經 reprint, vol. 108, 357.a1–a17. Taipei: Xinwenfeng, 1983.
Jiuzheng yiyin 九正易因. In *LZ*, vol. 15.

"Ku gui'er" 哭貴兒. *Xu Fenshu*. In *LZ* 3:340.
"Ku Huang yiren" 哭黃宜人. *Fenshu*. In *LZ* 2:262–65.
"Langzhong Wang gong" 郎中王公. *Xu Cangshu*. In *LZ* 11:111–20.
"*Laorenxing* xu" 老人行敘. *Xu Fenshu*. In *LZ* 3:177–80.
Laozi jie 老子解. In *LZ* 14:1–103.
"Li sheng shijiao wen" 李生十交文. *Fenshu*. In *LZ* 1:354–56.
"Li Zhongcheng zou yi" 李中承奏議. *Fenshu*. In *LZ* 1:318–22.
"Li Zhuowu xiansheng yiyan" 李卓吾先生遺言. *Xu Fenshu*. In *LZ* 3:314–17.
"Lisong Yaoshi gaowen" 禮誦藥師告文. *Fenshu*. In *LZ* 3:38–39.
"Lisong Yaoshi jing bi gaowen" 禮誦藥師經畢告文. *Fenshu*. In *LZ* 2:41–42.
"*Longxi xiansheng wenchao lu* xu" 龍溪先生文抄錄序. In *LZ* 1:327–29.
"Lun zheng pian" 論政篇. *Fenshu*. In *LZ* 1:242–45.
"Luo Jinxi xiansheng gaowen" 羅近谿先生告文. *Fenshu*. In *LZ* 1:338–46.
"*Nanxun lu* xu" 南詢錄序. *Xu Fenshu*. In *LZ* 3:191–93.
"Qiongtu shuo" 窮途說. *Xu Fenshu*. In *LZ* 3:210–12.
"Que ji" 卻寄. *Fenshu*. In *LZ* 2:301–2.
"San jiao gui Ru shuo" 三教歸儒說. *Xu Fenshu*. In *LZ* 3:223–26.
"Shiwen houxu" 時文後序. *Fenshu*. In *LZ* 1:324–25.
"Shiyan sanshou" 失言三首. *Fenshu*. In *LZ* 1:199–200.
"Shiyou er" 師友二. *Chutanji*. In *LZ* 12:332–74.
"Shu Changshun shoujuan cheng Gu Chong'an" 書常順手卷呈顧沖庵. *Fenshu*. In *LZ* 1:230–31.
"Shu Huang'an er Shangren shouce" 書黃安二上人手冊. *Fenshu*. In *LZ* 1:362–64.
"Shu Xiaoxiu shoujuan hou" 書小修手卷後. *Xu Fenshu*. In *LZ* 3:201–3.
Si shu ping 四書評. In *LZ*, vol. 21.
"Sima Xiangru" 司馬相如. *Cangshu*. In *LZ* 7:147–53.
"Taibo diba" 泰伯第八. *Sishu ping*. In *LZ* 21:134–42.
"Ti Kongzi xiang yu Zhifuoyuan" 題孔子像於芝佛院. *Xu Fenshu*. In *LZ* 3:309–10.
"Tongxin shuo" 童心說. *Fenshu*. In *LZ* 1:276–79.
"Wang Longxi xiansheng gaowen" 王龍溪先生告文. *Fenshu*. In *LZ* 1:335–38.
"Wusi pian" 五死篇. *Fenshu*. In *LZ* 2:68–72.
"Wuzong shuo" 五宗說. *Xu Fenshu*. In *LZ* 3:218–20.
"*Xinjing* tigang" 心經提綱. *Fenshu*. In *LZ* 1:280–84.
"Xun Qing, Li Si, Wu Gong" 荀卿李斯吳公. *Fenshu*. In *LZ* 2:209–10.
Yinguo lu 因果錄. In *LZ* 18:1–102.
Yongqing dawen 永慶答問. In *LZ* 18:329–42.
"You da Geng Zhongcheng" 又答耿中丞. *Fenshu*. In *LZ* 1:46–48.
"You da Shiyang Taishou" 又答石陽太守. *Fenshu*. In *LZ* 1:10–11.
"You shu shi Tongzhou shi hou" 又書使通州詩後. *Fenshu*. In *LZ* 1:187–89.
"You yu Congwu Xiaolian" 又與從吾孝廉. *Fenshu*. *LZ* 1:207–12.
"You yu Jiao Ruohou" 又與焦弱侯. *Fenshu*. In *LZ* 1:118–23.
"Yu Chenglao" 與城老. *Xu Fenshu*. In *LZ* 3:62–65.
"Yu Fang Ren'an" 與方訒菴. *Xu Fenshu*. In *LZ* 3:23–27.

"Yu Fengli" 與鳳里. *Xu Fenshu*. In *LZ* 3:115–16.
"Yu Geng Kenian" 與耿克念. *Xu Fenshu*. In *LZ* 3:65–66.
"Yu Geng Sikou gaobie" 與耿司寇告別. *Fenshu*. In *LZ* 1:66–70.
"Yu Geng Zijian" 與耿子健. *Xu Fenshu*. In *LZ* 3:135–36.
"Yu Jiao Ruohou" 與焦弱侯. *Fenshu*. In *LZ* 1:5–6.
"Yu Jiao Ruohou" 與焦弱侯. *Fenshu*. In *LZ* 1:152–55.
"Yu Jiao Ruohou" 與焦弱侯. *Xu Fenshu*. In *LZ* 3:19–20.
"Yu Jiao Ruohou" 與焦弱侯. *Xu Fenshu*. In *LZ* 3:106–7.
"Yu Jiao Ruohou" 與焦弱侯. *Xu Fenshu*. In *LZ* 3:129–31.
"Yu Jiao Ruohou Taishi" 與焦弱侯太史. *Xu Fenshu*. In *LZ* 3:49–55.
"Yu Jiao Yiyuan Taishi" 與焦漪園太史. *Xu Fenshu*. In *LZ* 3:85–94.
"Yu Li Weiqing" 與李惟清. *Fenshu*. In *LZ* 1:148–52.
"Yu Lu Tianpu" 與陸天溥. *Xu Fenshu*. In *LZ* 3:14–18.
"Yu Ma Boshi" 與馬伯時. *Xu Fenshu*. In *LZ* 3:82–83.
"Yu Ma Lishan" 與馬歷山. *Xu Fenshu*. In *LZ* 3:11–14.
"Yu Pan Xuesong" 與潘雪松. *Xu Fenshu*. In *LZ* 3:123–24.
"Yu Ruohou Jiao Taishi" 與弱侯焦太史. *Fenshu*. In *LZ* 3:68–71.
"Yu Wang Dingfu" 與汪鼎甫. *Xu Fenshu*. In *LZ* 3:137.
"Yu Wu Dechang" 與吳得常. *Xu Fenshu*. In *LZ* 3:55–56.
"Yu youren lun wen" 與友人論文. *Xu Fenshu*. In *LZ* 3:21.
"Yu youren shu" 與友人書. *Fenshu*. In *LZ* 1:181–82.
"Yu Zeng Jiquan" 與曾繼泉. *Fenshu*. In *LZ* 1:129–30.
"Yu Zeng Zhongye" 與曾中野. *Fenshu*. In *LZ* 1:127–29.
"Yu Zhou Guiqing" 與周貴卿. *Xu Fenshu*. In *LZ* 3:99–100.
"Yu Zhou Youshan" 與周友山. *Xu Fenshu*. In *LZ* 3:35–37.
"Yu Zhou Youshan" 與周友山. *Xu Fenshu*. In *LZ* 3:46–49.
"Yu Zhou Youshan shu" 與周友山書. *Fenshu*. In *LZ* 1:133–35.
"Yu Zhuang Chunfu" 與莊純夫. *Fenshu*. In *LZ* 1:108–9.
"Yuyue" 豫約. *Fenshu*. In *LZ* 2:96–120.
"Za shuo" 雜說. *Fenshu*. In *LZ* 1:272–76.
"Zaowan shouta" 早晚守塔. *Fenshu*. In *LZ* 2:103–8.
"Zeng Yao'an shou Wenling Li xiansheng zhishi qu Dian xu" 贈姚安守溫陵李先生致仕去滇序. *Fenshu*. In *LZ* 1:189–92.
"*Zhengtu yugong* houyu" 征途與共後語. *Fenshu*. In *LZ* 2:11–13.
"Zhen shi" 真師. *Fenshu*. In *LZ* 1:197–99.
"Zhongcheng dachen" 忠誠大臣. *Cangshu*. In *LZ* 5:88–189.
"*Zhongyi Shuihu zhuan* xu" 忠義水滸傳序. *Fenshu*. In *LZ* 1:301–4.
"*Zhongyi Shuihu zhuan* xu" 忠義水滸傳序. In *Shuihu quanzhuan* 水滸全傳, vol. 4, edited by Zheng Zhenduo 鄭振鐸, 1828–29. Beijing: Renmin Wenxue Chubanshe, 1954. Reprint, Hong Kong: Zhonghua Shuju, 1965.
"Zhou Youshan wei seng Mingyu shu fayu" 周友山為僧明玉書法語. *Fenshu*. In *LZ* 2:26–27.
Zhuangzi jie 莊子解. In *LZ* 14:105–222.

"Zi xu" 自序. *Fenshu*. In *LZ* 1:1–3.
"Zi zan" 自贊. *Fenshu*. In *LZ* 1:356–58.

GENERAL BIBLIOGRAPHY

Ames, Roger, and David Hall. *Dao De Jing: A Philosophical Translation*. New York: 2003.

Araki Kengo 荒木見悟. "Deng Huoqu de chuxian jiqi beijing" 鄧豁渠的出現及其背景. In *Mingmo Qingchu de sixiang yu Fojiao* 明末清初的思想與佛教, translated by Liao Zhaoheng 廖肇亨, 189–214. Taipei: Lianjing Chubanshe, 2006.

———. *Mingmo Qingchu de sixiang yu Fojiao* 明末清初的思想與佛教. Translated by Liao Zhaoheng 廖肇亨. Taipei: Lianjing Chubanshe, 2006.

Bai, Qianshen. "Chinese Letters: Private Words Made Public." In *The Embroidered Image: Chinese Calligraphy from the John B. Elliott Collection*, edited by Robert Harrist and Wen Fong, 380–90. Princeton, NJ: The Art Museum, Princeton University, 1999.

———. *Fu Shan's World: The Transformation of Chinese Calligraphy in the Seventeenth Century*. Cambridge, MA: Harvard University Asia Center, 2003.

Baldrian-Hussein, Farzeen. "Neidan." In *The Encyclopedia of Taoism*, edited by Fabrizio Pregadio, 762–66. 2 vols. London: Routledge, 2008.

Bentley, Tamara Heimarck. *The Figurative Works of Chen Hongshou (1599–1652): Authentic Voices/Expanding Markets*. Surrey, UK: Ashgate, 2017.

Berling, Judith A. *The Syncretic Religion of Lin Chao'en*. New York: Columbia University Press, 1980.

Bernard, Henri. "Li Madou Siduo he dangdai Zhongguo shehui" 利瑪竇司鐸和當代中國社會 (Le P. Matthieu Ricci et la Société Chinoise de son temps), tr. Wang Changshe. In *Li Zhi yanjiu cankao ziliao* 李贄研究參考資料 2:230—32. Fujian: Renmin Chubanshe, 1976.

Billings, Timothy. Introduction to *On Friendship: One Hundred Maxims for a Chinese Prince*, by Matteo Ricci, 1–83. New York: Columbia University Press, 2009.

Birge, Bettine. "Levirate Marriage and the Revival of Widow Chastity in Yuan China." *Asia Major* 8, no. 2 (1995): 107–46.

———. "Women and Confucianism from Song to Ming: The Institutionalization of Patrilineality." In the *Song-Yuan-Ming Transition in Chinese History*, edited by Paul Jakov Smith and Richard von Glahn, 212–40. Cambridge, MA: Harvard University Asia Center, 2003.

Bossler, Beverly. *Courtesans, Concubines, and the Cult of Female Fidelity*. Cambridge, MA: Harvard Asia Center, 2013.

———, trans. "Final Instructions by Yang Jisheng (1516–1555)." In *Under Confucian Eyes: Writings on Gender in Chinese History*, edited by Susan Mann and Yu-Yin Cheng, 119–132. Berkeley: University of California Press, 2001.

———. *Powerful Relations: Kinship, Status, and the State in Sung China (960–1279)*. Cambridge, MA: Harvard University Asia Center, 1998.

Brewitt-Taylor, C. H., trans. *Romance of the Three Kingdoms*. 2 vols. Shanghai: Kelly and Walsh, 1924.

Brokaw, Cynthia. *The Ledgers of Merit and Demerit: Social Change and Moral Order in Late Imperial China*. Princeton, NJ: Princeton University Press, 1991.

Brokaw, Cynthia, and Kai-wing Chow, eds. *Printing and Book Culture in Late Imperial China*. Berkeley: University of California Press, 2004.

Brook, Timothy. *The Confusions of Pleasure: Commerce and Culture in Ming China*. Berkeley: University of California Press, 1998.

———. *Great State: China and the World*. London: Profile, 2019; New York: Harper Collins, 2020.

———. "Li Zhi and Geng Dingxiang: Correspondence." In *A Book to Burn and a Book to Keep (Hidden)*, edited by Rivi Handler-Spitz, Pauline C. Lee, and Haun Saussy, 34–62. New York: Columbia University Press, 2016.

———. *Praying for Power: Buddhism and the Formation of Gentry Society in Late-Ming China*. Cambridge, MA: Harvard University Press, 1993.

———. *The Troubled Empire: China in the Yuan and Ming Dynasties*. Cambridge, MA: Harvard University Press, 2010.

Buck Pearl S., trans. *All Men Are Brothers*. London: Methuen; New York: John Day, 1933.

Carlitz, Katherine. "Printing as Performance: Literati Playwright-Publishers of the Late Ming." In *Printing and Book Culture in Late Imperial China*, edited by Cynthia Brokaw and Kai-wing Chow, 267–97. Berkeley: University of California Press, 2004.

———. "Shrines, Governing-Class Identity, and the Cult of Widow Fidelity in Mid-Ming Jiangnan." *Journal of Asian Studies* 56, no. 3 (1997): 612–40.

Chao Jiong 晁迥. *Zhaode xinbian* 昭德新編. In *Wenyuange Siku quanshu* 文淵閣四庫全書, vol. 849. Taipei: Taiwan Shangwu Shuju, 1983.

Chen Guying 陳鼓應. *Laozi zhushi ji pingjia* 老子註釋及評價. Beijing: Zhonghua Shuju, 1984.

Ch'en, Kenneth. *Buddhism in China: A Historical Survey*. Princeton, NJ: Princeton University Press, 1973.

Chen Xianxing 陳先行 and Bao Yufei 包于飛, eds. *Li Zhuowu pingben Xiyou ji* 李卓吾評本西遊記. 2 vols. Shanghai: Shanghai Guji, 1994.

Chen Xizhong 陳曦鐘, Song Xiangrui 宋祥瑞, and Lu Yuchuan 魯玉川, eds. *Sanguo yanyi huiping ben* 三國演義會評本. 2 vols. Beijing: Beijing Daxue, 1986.

———, eds. *Shuihu zhuan huiping ben* 水滸傳會評本. 2 vols. Beijing: Beijing Daxue, 1981.

Cheng, Pei-kai 鄭培凱. "Continuities in Chinese Political Culture: Interpretations of Li Zhi, Past and Present." *Chinese Studies in History* 17, no. 2 (Winter 1983–84): 4–29.

Cherniack, Susan. "Book Culture and Textual Transmission in Sung China." *Harvard Journal of Asiatic Studies* 54, no. 1 (June 1994): 5–121.

Ch'ien, Edward. *Chiao Hung and the Restructuring of Neo-Confucianism in the Late Ming*. New York: Columbia University Press, 1986.

Ching, Julia, ed. and trans. *The Records of Ming Scholars*. Honolulu: University of Hawaii Press, 1987.

Chou Chih-p'ing. *Yüan Hung-tao and the Kung-an School*. Cambridge: Cambridge University Press, 1988.

Chow, Kai-wing. "The Merging of *Shi* and *Shang* in Travel: Production of Knowledge in Late Ming Books." *Frontiers of History in China* 6, no. 2 (2011): 163–82.

———. *Publishing, Culture, and Power in Early Modern China*. Stanford, CA: Stanford University Press, 2004.

———. "Writing for Success: Printing, Examinations, and Intellectual Change in Late Ming China." *Late Imperial China* 17, no. 1 (June 1996): 120–57.

Clunas, Craig. *Superfluous Things: Material Culture and Social Status in Early Modern China*. Urbana: University of Illinois Press, 1991.

Dai Jingxian (Tai Ching-hsien) 戴景賢. "Li Zhi yu Fojiao: Lun Li Zhi sixiang zhi jiben lichang yu qi huitong Ru Shi zhi qujing" 李贄與佛教: 論李贄思想之基本立場與其會通儒、釋之取徑. *Qinghua xuebao* 清華學報 46, no. 3 (2016): 525–59.

Darnton, Robert. "What Is the History of Books?" *Daedalus* 111, no. 3 (1982): 65–83.

de Bary, William Theodore. "Individualism and Humanitarianism in Late Ming Thought." In *Self and Society in Ming Thought*, edited by Wm. de Bary, 145–247. New York: Columbia University Press, 1970.

———. *The Liberal Tradition in China*. Hong Kong: Chinese University Press, 1983.

———. "Li Chih: Arch-Individualist." In *Learning for One's Self: Essays on the Individual in Neo-Confucian Thought*, 203–70. New York: Columbia University Press, 1991.

———, ed. *Sources of Chinese Tradition*. New York: Columbia University Press, 1999.

de Certeau, Michel. *Heterologies: Discourse on the Other*. Minneapolis: University of Minnesota Press, 1986.

Deng Huoqu 鄧豁渠. *Nanxun lu jiaozhu* 南詢錄校注. Annotated by Deng Hong 鄧紅. Wuhan: Wuhan Keji Daxue Chubanshe, 2008.

Dent-Young, John, and Alex Dent-Young, trans. *The Marshes of Mount Liang*. 5 vols. Hong Kong: Chinese University Press, 1994–2002.

Dryburgh, Marjorie, and Sarah Dauncey, eds. *Writing Lives in China, 1600–2010: Histories of the Elusive Self*. London: Palgrave Macmillan, 2013.

Du Fu 杜甫. *Dushi xiangzhu* 杜詩詳-. Compiled by Qiu Zhao'ao 仇兆鰲. Beijing: Zhonghua Shuju, 1979.

Durrant, Stephen, Wai-yee Li, and David Schaberg, trans. *Zuo Tradition*. 3 vols. Seattle: University of Washington Press, 2016.

Dyer, Svetlana Rimsky-Korsakoff. *Grammatical Analysis of the Lao Ch'i-ta*. Canberra: Australian National University, 1983.

Ebrey, Patricia, trans. *Chu Hsi's Family Rituals*. Princeton, NJ: Princeton University Press, 1991.

———. *Women and the Family in China*. London: Routledge, 2002.

Eichman, Jennifer Lynn. *A Late Sixteenth-Century Chinese Buddhist Fellowship: Spiritual Ambitions, Intellectual Debates, and Epistolary Connections*. Leiden: Brill, 2016.

Elman, Benjamin A. *A Cultural History of Civil Examinations in Late Imperial China*. Berkeley: University of California Press, 2000.

Epstein, Maram. *Competing Discourses: Orthodoxy, Authenticity, and Engendered Meanings in Late Imperial Chinese Fiction*. Cambridge, MA: Harvard University Asia Center, 2001.

———. "Writing Emotions: Ritual Innovation as Emotional Expression." *Nan nü* 11, no. 2 (2009): 155–95.

Fang Xuanling 房玄齡. *Jinshu* 晉書. Beijing: Zhonghua Shuju, 1974.

Fang Yizhi 方以智 and Pang Pu 龐樸, annotators. *Dongxi jun* 東西均. Beijing: Zhonghua Shuju, 2001.

Fei Siyan 費絲言. *You dianfan dao guifan* 由典範到規範. Taipei: National Taiwan University, 1998.

Feng Chen 馮辰. *Li Gong nianpu* 李塨年譜. Beijing: Zhonghua Shuju, 1988.

Foucault, Michel. *The History of Sexuality*. Vol. 3, *The Care of the Self*. Translated by Robert Hurley. New York: Vintage Books, 1986.

Foust, Mathew A., and Sor-hoon Tan, eds. *Feminist Encounters with Confucius*. Leiden: Brill, 2016.

Gao Panlong 高攀龍. *Gaozi yi shu* 高子遺書. Taipei: Shangwu yinshuguan, 1983.

Ge Zhaoguang 葛兆光. *Zhongguo sixiang shi* 中國思想史. 3 vols. Shanghai: Fudan Daxue Chubanshe, 2001–12.

Genette, Gerard. *Paratexts: Thresholds of Interpretation*. Cambridge: Cambridge University Press, 1997.

Geng Dingxiang 耿定向. *Geng Tiantai xiansheng wenji* 耿天臺先生文集. 1598. Reprint, *Siku quanshu cunmu congshu* 四庫全書存目叢書, series 4, vol. 131. Jinan: Qi-Lu Shushe, 1997.

———. *Geng Tiantai xiansheng wenji* 耿天臺先生文集. 4 vols. In *Mingren wenji congkan* 明人文集叢刊, compiled by Shen Yunlong 沈雲龍. Taipei: Wenhai Chubanshe, 1970.

———. "Lizhong san yi zhuan" 里中三異傳. In *Geng Dingxiang ji* 耿定向集, punctuated and annotated by Fu Qiutao 傅秋濤, 2:628–38. Shanghai: Huadong Shifan Daxue Chubanshe, 2015.

———. "Yu Zhou Liutang" 與周柳塘. In *Geng Dingxiang xiansheng wenji* 耿定向先生文集 (Wanli 26 ed., Library of Congress), 3:54b–55b.

Geng Jie 耿介. *Jingshutang wenji* 敬恕堂文集. Zhengzhou: Zhongzhou Guji Chubanshe, 2005.

Goldin, Paul Rakita. "The View of Women in Early Confucianism." In *The Sage and the Second Sex: Confucianism, Ethics, and Gender*, edited by Chenyang Li, 133–162. Chicago: Open Court, 2000.

Goodrich, L. Carrington, and Chaoying Fang, eds. *Dictionary of Ming Biography, 1368–1644*. 2 vols. New York: Columbia University Press, 1976.

Grant, Beata. "*Da Zhangfu:* The Gendered Rhetoric of Heroism and Equality in Seventeenth-Century Chan Buddhist Discourse Records." *Nan nü* 10 (2008): 177–211.

Griffiths, Paul J. *Religious Reading: The Place of Reading in the Practice of Religion*. New York: Oxford University Press, 1999.

Gu Yanwu 顧炎武. *Rizhi lu jishi* 日知錄集釋. Edited by Huang Rucheng 黃汝成. Zhengzhou: Zhongzhou Guji Chubanshe, 1990.

Guo Dongxu 郭東旭. *Songdai fazhi yanjiu* 宋代法制研究. Baoding: Hebei Daxue Chubanshe, 2000.

Guocui xuebao 國粹學報. 13 vols. Taipei: Wenhai Chubanshe, 1970.

Handler-Spitz, Rivi. *Symptoms of an Unruly Age: Li Zhi and Cultures of Early Modernity*. Seattle: University of Washington Press, 2017.

Hawes, Colin. "Mundane Transcendence: Dealing with the Everyday in Ouyang Xiu's Poetry." *Chinese Literature: Essays, Articles, Reviews* 21 (December 1999): 99–129.

He Shouzhuo 何守拙. "Wenshusi beiji" 文殊寺碑記. *Minguo Luquan xianzhi* 民國祿勸縣志, *j.* 13. In *LZ* 26:338–39.

He Xin 何心. *Shuihu yanjiu* 水滸研究. Shanghai: Shanghai Guji, 1985.

He Yan 何晏 et al., eds. *Lunyu Heshideng jijie* 論語何氏等集解. Sibu Beiyao 1. Taipei: Taiwan Zhonghua Shuju, 1966.

He, Yuming. *Home and the World: Editing the Glorious Ming in Woodblock-Printed Books of the Sixteenth and Seventeenth Centuries*. Cambridge, MA: Harvard University Asia Center, 2013.

Hegel, Robert E., and Maria Franca Sibau. "Introduction: *Sanguo zhi yanyi* Chapters 48–49." *Renditions*, nos. 81–82 (2014): 129–37.

Heine, Steven, and Dale S. Wright, eds. *The Kōan: Texts and Contexts in Zen Buddhism*. New York: Oxford University Press, 2000.

Henry, Eric. "The Motif of Recognition in Early China." *Harvard Journal of Asiatic Studies* 47, no. 1 (1987): 5–30.

Hinsch, Bret. "The Emotional Underpinnings of Male Fidelity in Imperial China." *Journal of Family History* 32 (2007): 392–412.

Holmgren, Jennifer. "The Economic Foundations of Virtue: Widow-Remarriage in Early and Modern China." *Australian Journal of Chinese Affairs* 13 (1985): 1–27.

Hou Suping 侯素平. *Chan fei yizhihua: Huangbo Wunian chanshi huayu lu* 禪非一枝花: 黃檗無念禪師話語錄. Beijing: Xinshijie Chubanshe, 2012.

Hsüan Hua. *The Śūraṅgama Sūtra: With Excerpts from the Commentary by the Venerable Master Hsüan Hua*. San Francisco: Buddhist Text Translations Society, 2009.

Hu Shi 胡適. *Zhongguo zhanghui xiaoshuo kaozheng* 中國章回小說考證. Reprint, Hefei: Anhui Jiaoyu, 2006.

Huang, Martin W. "Author(ity) and Reader in Traditional Chinese Xiaoshuo Commentary." *Chinese Literature: Essays, Articles, Reviews* 16 (1994): 41–67.

———. *Literati and Self-Re/presentation: Autobiographical Sensibility in the Eighteenth-Century Chinese Novel.* Stanford, CA: Stanford University Press, 1995.

———. "Male Friendship and *Jiangxue* (Philosophical Debates) in Sixteenth-Century China." *Nan nü: Men, Women and Gender in China* 9 no. 1 (2007): 146–78.

———. "Male Friendship in Ming China: An Introduction." *Nan nü: Men, Women and Gender in China* 9, no. 1 (2007): 2–33.

Huang, Ray. *1587: A Year of No Significance. The Ming Dynasty in Decline.* New Haven, CT: Yale University Press, 1981.

Huang Zhihuang 黃志煌. "Dong Qichang shuxue sixiang jiqi shufa yishu yanjiu" 董其昌書學思想及其書法藝術研究. PhD dissertation. Gaoxiong Shifan Daxue, 2009.

Huang Zongxi 黃宗羲. *Ming Ru xue'an* 明儒學案. Beijing: Zhonghua Shuju, 1985.

———. *Ming Ru xue'an* 明儒學案. Taipei: Huashi chubanshe, 1987.

———. *Ming Ru xue'an* 明儒學案. In *Huang Zongxi quanji* 黃宗羲全集, vol. 7, edited by Shen Shanhong 沈善洪. Hangzhou: Zhejiang Guji Chubanshe, 2005.

———. *Ming Wenhai* 明文海. Bejing: Beijing Zhonghua Shuju, 1987.

Hung Mingshui. *The Romantic Vision of Yuan Hung-tao, Late-Ming Poet and Critic.* Taipei: Bookman Books, 1997.

Idema, Wilt, and Beata Grant, eds. *The Red Brush: Writing Women of Imperial China*. Cambridge, MA: Harvard University Asia Center, 2004.

Jackson, J. H., trans. *The Water Margin.* 2 vols. Shanghai: Commercial Press, 1937.

Jian Ruiyao 簡瑞瑤. *Mingdai funü Fojiao xinyang yu shehui guifan* 明代婦女佛教信仰與社會規範. Banqiao: Daoxiang Chubanshe, 2007.

Jiang Jin. "Heresy and Persecution in Late Ming Society: Reinterpreting the Case of Li Zhi." *Late Imperial China* 22, no. 2 (2001): 1–34.

Jiang Yonglin, trans. *The Great Ming Code*. Seattle: University of Washington Press, 2005.

Jiao Hong 焦竑. "*Xu Cangshu* xu" 續藏書序. *Xu Cangshu* 續藏書. In *LZ* 11:358.

Jones, Charles. "Toward a Typology of *Nien-fo*: A Study in Methods of Buddha-Invocation in Chinese Pure Land Buddhism." *Pacific World* 3 (Fall 2011): 219–39.

———. "Yuan Hongdao 袁宏道 and the *Coral Grove* (Shānhú Lín 珊瑚林): Gentry Buddhist Discourse in the Late Ming Dynasty." Paper presented at the annual meeting of the Association for Asian Studies, Chicago, March 27, 2015.

———. "Yuan Hongdao and the *Xifang helun*: Pure Land Theology in the Late Ming Dynasty." In *Path of No Path: Contemporary Studies in Pure Land*

Buddhism, Honoring Roger Corless, edited by Richard K. Payne, 89–126. Berkeley: Institute of Buddhist Studies and Numata Center for Buddhist Translation and Research, 2009.

Kang Youwei 康有為. *Datongshu* 大同書. Shanghai: Zhonghua Shuju, 1935.

Karlgren, Bernard, ed. *The Book of Odes*. Stockholm: Museum of Far Eastern Antiquities, 1950.

King, Gail. "The Family Letters of Xu Guangqi." *Ming Studies* 31 (1991): 1–41.

Ko, Dorothy. "Pursuing Talent and Virtue: Education and Women's Culture in Seventeenth- and Eighteenth-Century China." *Late Imperial China* 13, no. 1 (June 1992): 9–39.

———. *Teachers of the Inner Chambers: Women and Culture in Seventeenth-Century China*. Stanford, CA: Stanford University Press, 1994.

Kriegel, Blandine, Marc A. LePain, and Jeffrey C. Cohen. *The State and the Rule of Law*. Princeton, NJ.: Princeton University Press, 1995.

Lan, Hua R., and Vanessa L. Fong, eds. *Women in Republican China: A Sourcebook*. Armonk, NY: M. E. Sharpe, 1999.

Lau, D. C., trans. *The Analects*. Harmondsworth, Middlesex, UK: Penguin Books, 1979.

———. *Mencius*. London: Penguin, 1970.

Lee, Pauline C. "Li Zhi (1527–1602): A Confucian Feminist of Late-Ming China." PhD dissertation, Stanford University, 2002.

———. "Li Zhi and John Stuart Mill: A Confucian Feminist Critique of Liberal Feminism." In *The Sage and the Second Sex: Confucianism, Ethics, and Gender*, edited by Chenyang Li, 113–22. Chicago: Open Court, 2000.

———. *Li Zhi, Confucianism, and the Virtue of Desire*. Albany: State University of New York Press, 2012.

Lee, Thomas. "Books and Bookworms in Song China: Book Collection and the Appreciation of Books." *Journal of Sung-Yuan Studies* 25 (1995): 193–218.

Legge, James, trans. *The Chinese Classics*. 5 vols. Hong Kong: Hong Kong University Press, 1960.

———, trans. *The Confucian Analects, The Great Learning, and The Doctrine of the Mean*. Vol. 1 of *Chinese Classics*. Oxford: Clarendon Press, 1893.

———, trans. *The Doctrine of the Mean*. Vol. 1 of *The Chinese Classics*. Hong Kong: Hong Kong University Press, 1960.

———, trans. *Li Chi: Book of Rites*. 2 vols. New Hyde Park, NY: University Books, 1967.

———, trans. *The Sacred Books of China, Part II: The Yi King*. Oxford: Clarendon Press, 1882.

———, trans. *The Shoo King*. Vol. 3 of *Chinese Classics*. Taipei: SMC, 2000.

Lei Menglin 雷夢麟. *Dulü suoyan* 讀律瑣言 1557. Reprint, Beijing: Falü Chubanshe, 2000.

Li, Chenyang, ed. *The Sage and the Second Sex: Confucianism, Ethics, and Gender*. Chicago: Open Court, 2000.

Li Gong 李塨, comp. *Yan Yuan nianpu* 顏元年譜. Edited by Wang Yuan 王源. Beijing: Zhonghua Shuju, 1992.

Li Ruiliang 李瑞良. "Li Zhi nianpu jianbian" 李贄年譜簡編. In *LZ* 26:413–87.

Li Wai-yee. "The Rhetoric of Spontaneity in Late-Ming Literature." *Ming Studies* 1 (1995): 32–52.

———. *Women and National Trauma in Late Imperial Chinese Literature*. Cambridge, MA: Harvard University Asia Center, 2014.

Li Weizhen 李維楨. "Li Weizhen xu" 李維楨序. In *LZ* 11:359–60.

Li, Xiaojiang. "From Modernization to 'Globalisation': Where Are Chinese Women?" *Signs*, 26, no. 4 (Summer 2001): 1274–78.

———. "With What Discourse Do We Reflect on Chinese Women? Thoughts on Transnational Feminism in China." In *Spaces of Their Own: Women's Public Sphere in Transnational China*, edited by Mayfair Mei-Hui Yang, 261–78. Minneapolis: University of Minnesota Press, 1999.

Li Zhi yanjiu cankao ziliao 李贄研究參考資料. Compiled by Fujian sheng Li Zhi zhuzuo zhushi zu Fuzhou xiaozu 福建省李贄著作註釋組福州小組. Fujian: Renmin chubānshe, 1976; Reprinted, Washington, DC: Center for Chinese Research Materials, Association of Research Libraries, 1980.

Li Zhuowu yuan ping Xiuxiang guben Sanguo zhi 李卓吾原評繡像古本三國志. Wujun 吳郡 (Suzhou): Lüyintang 綠蔭堂, ca. 1689. Waseda University copy.

Liezi zhu 列子注. Edited by Zhang Zhan 張湛. Taipei: Taiwan Shangwu Yinshuguan, 1968.

Lin Haiquan 林海權. *Li Zhi nianpu kaolüe* 李贄年譜考略. Fuzhou: Fujian Renmin Chubanshe, 1992.

Lin Jinguang 林縉光, ed. *Huang'an xianzhi* 黃安縣志, 1822.

Lin Shu 林紓. "Zhi Cai Heqing shu" 致蔡鶴卿書. *Gongyan bao* 公言報, March 18, 1919.

Lin Yaling 林雅玲. "Ye Zhou xiaoshuo pingdian xilun: Yi *Li Zhuowu xiansheng piping Zhongyi Shuihuzhuan, Li Zhuowu xiansheng piping Sanguo zhi, Li Zhuowu xiansheng piping Xiyou ji* wei yanjiu zhongxin" 葉晝小說評點析論：以《李卓吾先生批評忠義水滸傳》、《李卓吾先生批評三國志》、《李卓吾先生批評西遊記》為研究中心. In *Chuanbo, jiaoliu yu ronghe—Mingdai wenxue, sixiang yu zongjiao guoji xueshu yantaohui lunwen ji* 傳播、交流與融合——明代文學、思想與宗教國際學術研討會論文集, Nanhua Daxue Wenxuexi, ed., 101–22. Taipei: Xinwenfeng, 2005.

———. *Yu Xiangdou xiaoshuo pingdian ji chuban wenhua yanjiu* 余象斗小說評點及出版文化研究. Taipei: Liren Shuju, 2009.

Ling Lichao 凌禮潮. "Wunian yu Li Zhi" 無念與李贄. *Shoudu shifan daxue xuebao (Shehui kexue ban)* 首都師範大學學報 (社會科學版) 1 (2005): 100–103.

Liu Dongxing 劉東星. "Shu Dao gu lu shou" 書道古錄首. In Li Zhi 李贄, *Dao gu lu* 道古錄. In *LZ* 14:334.

Liu Haiyan 劉海燕. *Ming Qing Sanguo zhi yanyi wenben yanbian yu pingdian yanjiu* 明清《三國志演義》文本演變與評點研究. Fuzhou: Haixia, Fujian Renmin, 2010.

Liu, Lydia H., Rebecca E. Karl, and Dorothy Ko, eds. *The Birth of Chinese Feminism: Essential Texts in Transnational Theory*. New York: Columbia University Press, 2013.

Liu Yiqing 劉義慶 et al. *Shishuo xinyu jianshu* 世說新語箋疏. Annotated by Yu Jiaxi 余嘉錫. Edited by Zhou Zumo 周祖謨 et al. Taipei: Huazheng Shuju, 1984.

Liu Zhiqing 劉芝慶. "Li Zhi de shengsi zhi xue" 李贄的生死之學. *Xin shiji zhongjiao yanjiu* 新世紀宗教研究 10, no. 1 (2011): 101–29.

Lou Zuyi 樓祖詒. *Zhongguo youyi shiliao* 中國郵驛史料. Beijing: Renmin Youdian Chubanshe, 1958.

Lovejoy, Arthur. *The Great Chain of Being*. Cambridge, MA: Harvard University Press, 1964.

Lu Miaw-fen 呂妙芬. *Chengsheng yu jiating renlun: Zongjiao duihua mailuoxia de Ming Qing zhiji Ruxue* 成聖與家庭人倫：宗教對話脈絡下的明清之際儒學. Taipei: Lianjing Chubanshe, 2017.

———. "Du Wenhuan huizong sanjiao" 杜文煥會宗三教. *Mingdai yanjiu* 明代研究 23 (2014): 47–89.

———. "Religious Dimensions of Filial Piety as Developed in Late Ming Interpretations of the *Xiaojing*." *Late Imperial China* 27, no. 2 (2006): 1–37.

———. "Rushi jiaorong de shengren guan: Cong wan Ming rujia shengren yu pusa xingxiang xiangsi chu ji dui shengsi yiti de guanzhu tanqi" 儒釋交融的聖人觀：從晚明儒家聖人與菩薩形象相似處及對生死議題的關注談起. *Bulletin of the Institute of Modern History, Academia Sinica* 32 (1999): 166–207.

———. "Wan Ming *Xiaojing* lunshu de zongjiaoxing yihan: Yu Chuanxi de xiao lun ji qita wenhua mailuo" 晚明《孝經》論述的宗教性意涵：虞淳熙的孝論及其他文化脈絡. *Zhongyang yanjiuyuan jindaishi yanjiusuo jikan* 中央研究院近代史研究所集刊, no. 48 (2005): 1–46.

———. *Xiao zhi tianxia: Xiaojing yu jinshi Zhongguo de zhengzhi yu wenhua* 孝治天下：《孝經》與近世中國的政治與文化. Taipei: Academia Sinica and Lianjing Chubanshe, 2011.

———. *Yangming xue shiren shequn: Lishi sixiang yu shijian* 陽明學士人社群：歷史、思想與實踐. Taipei: Institute of Modern History, Academia Sinica, 2003.

Lu Weijing. *True to Her Word: The Faithful Maiden Cult in Late Imperial China*. Stanford, CA: Stanford University Press, 2008.

Lu Youqin 陸佑勤 et al., eds. *Macheng xianzhi* 麻城縣志, 1882.

Lunyu ji shi 論語集釋. Compiled by Cheng Shude 程樹德. Taipei: Yiwen Yinshu Guan, 1965.

Lunyu yizhu 論語譯註. Edited by Yang Bojun 楊伯峻. Beijing: Zhonghua Shuju, 1980.

Luo Hongxian 羅洪先. *Nian'an wenji* 念庵文集. Taipei: Shangwu Yingshuguan, 1983.

Ma Jinglun 馬經倫. "Yu Dangdao shu" 與當道書. In *Li Wenling waiji* 李溫陵外紀, edited by Pan Zenghong 潘曾紘, 4:167. Taipei: Weiwen Tushu Chubanshe, 1977.

Ma Tiji 馬蹄疾, comp. *Shuihu shulu* 水滸書錄. Shanghai: Shanghai Guji Chubanshe, 1986.

———, comp. *Shuihu ziliao huibian* 水滸資料彙編. Beijing: Zhonghua Shuju, 1980.

Ma Youyuan 馬幼垣 (Y. W. Ma). "Cong pinglinben *Shuihu zhuan* jiacha de shijushi pingyu kan Yu Xiangdou de wenchaogong bense" 從評林本《水滸傳》加插的詩句式評語看余象斗的文抄公本色. In *Chuanbo, jiaoliu yu ronghe—Mingdai wenxue, sixiang yu zongjiao guoji xueshu yantaohui lunwen* ji 傳播、交流與融合—— 明代文學、思想與宗教國際學術研討會論文集, ed. Nanhua Daxue Wenxuexi, 11–22. Taipei: Xinwenfeng, 2005.

MacKinnon, Catherine A. "Substantive Equality: A Perspective." *Minnesota Law Review* 96, no. 2 (2011): 1–27.

———. *Toward a Feminist Theory of the State*. Cambridge, MA: Harvard University Press, 1989.

Mann, Susan. *Precious Records: Women in China's Long Eighteenth Century.* Stanford, CA: Stanford University Press, 1997.

McDermott, Joseph. *A Social History of the Chinese Book: Books and Literati Culture in Late Imperial China*. Hong Kong: Hong Kong University Press, 2006.

McMorran, Ian. "Wang Fu-chih and the Neo-Confucian Tradition." In *The Unfolding of Neo-Confucianism*, edited by Wm. Theodore de Bary, 413–67. New York: Columbia University Press, 1975.

McRae, John. "Encounter Dialogue and the Transformation of the Spiritual Path in Chinese Ch'an." In *Paths to Liberation: The Mārga and Its Transformations in Buddhist Thought*, edited by Robert E. Buswell Jr. and Robert M. Gimello, 339–69. Honolulu: University of Hawaii Press, 1992.

Meng Zhen 孟真. "Wan'e zhi yuan" 萬惡之原. *Xinchao* 新潮 1, no. 1 (January 1, 1919): 124–28.

Ming Shenzong shilu 明神宗實錄. Taipei: Zhongyang Yanjiuyuan Lishi Yuyan Yanjiusuo 中央研究院歷史語言研究所, 1966.

Mingban Jiaxing dazangjing 明版嘉興大藏經. Taipei: Xinwenfeng, 1987.

Mizoguchi Yūzō 溝口雄三. *Zhongguo qianjindai sixiang de quzhe yu zhankai* 中國前近代思想的屈折與展開. Translated by Gong Yin 龔穎. Beijing: Sanlian Shuju, 2011.

Nakagawa Satoshi 中川諭. *Sanguo zhi yanyi banben yanjiu* 《三國志演義》版本研究. Translated by Lin Miaoyan 林妙燕. Shanghai: Shanghai Guji Chubanshe, 2010.

Narayan, Uma. "Contesting Cultures: 'Westernization,' Respect for Cultures, and Third-World Feminists." In *The Second Wave: A Reader in Feminist Theory*, edited by Linda Nicholson, 396–414. New York: Routledge, 1997.

Nietzsche, Friedrich. *Thus Spoke Zarathustra*. In *The Portable Nietzsche*, edited and translated by Walter Kaufmann, 103–439. New York: Penguin, 1976.

Offen, Karen. *European Feminisms,1700–1950: A Political History*. Stanford, CA: Stanford University Press, 1999.

Pan Pingge 潘平格. *Panzi qiurenlu jiyao* 潘子求仁錄輯要. Beijing: Zhonghua Shuju, 2009.

Pan Zenghong 潘曾竑. "Shu *Zuolin jitan*" 書柞林紀譚. *Zuolin jitan* 柞林紀譚. In *LZ* 18:303–4.

Plaks, Andrew H. *The Four Masterworks of the Ming Novel.* Princeton, NJ: Princeton University Press, 1987.

Qian, Nanxiu. *Spirit and Self in Medieval China: The Shih-shuo hsin-yü and Its Legacy.* Honolulu: University of Hawaii Press, 2001.

Qian Qianyi 錢謙益. *Liechao shiji xiao zhuan* 列朝詩集小傳. Edited by Qian Lucan 錢陸燦. In *Mingdai zhuanji congkan* 明代傳記叢刊, compiled by Zhou Junfu 周駿富. Taipei: Mingwen Shuju, 1991.

Qian Xiyan 錢希言. *Yanji* 贗籍. In *Xixia* 戲瑕, vol. 3: In *Jieyue shanfang huichao* 借月山房彙鈔. Reprint, *Baibu congshu jicheng* 百部叢書集成. Taipei: Yiwen Chubanshe, 1967.

Raphals, Lisa. *Sharing the Light: Representations of Women and Virtue in Early China.* Albany: State University of New York Press, 1998.

Ren Guanwen 任冠文. *Li Zhi shixue sixiang yanjiu* 李贄史學思想研究. Guangdong: Guangxi Shifan Daxue Chubanshe, 1997.

Ricci, Matteo. *On Friendship: One Hundred Maxims for a Chinese Prince.* Translated by Timothy Billings. New York: Columbia University Press, 2010.

Roberts, Moss, trans. *Three Kingdoms: A Historical Novel.* Berkeley: University of California Press; Beijing: Foreign Languages Press, 1991.

Rolston, David L. "The Authenticity of the Li Chih Commentaries on the *Shui-hu chuan* and Other Novels Treated in this Volume." In *How to Read the Chinese Novel*, edited by David L. Rolston, 356–63. Princeton, NJ: Princeton University Press, 1990.

———, ed. *How to Read the Chinese Novel.* Princeton, NJ: Princeton University Press, 1990.

———. *Traditional Chinese Fiction and Fiction Commentary: Reading and Writing between the Lines.* Stanford, CA: Stanford University Press, 1997.

Rong Zhaozu 容肇祖. *Ming Li Zhuowu xiansheng Zhi nianpu* 明李卓吾先生贄年譜. Taipei: Shangwu Yinshuguan, 1982.

Ropp, Paul S. "The Seeds of Change: Reflections on the Condition of Women in the Early and Mid Ch'ing." *Signs* 2, no. 1 (Autumn 1976): 5–23.

Rowe, William T. *Crimson Rain: Seven Centuries of Violence in a Chinese County.* Stanford, CA: Stanford University Press, 2007.

Sanguo yanyi huiping ben 三國演義會評本. 2 vols. Edited by Chen Xizhong 陳曦鐘, Song Xiangrui 宋祥瑞, and Lu Yuchuan 魯玉川. Beijing: Beijing Daxue Chubanshe, 1986.

Shapiro, Sidney, trans. *Outlaws of the Marsh.* 2 vols. Beijing: Foreign Languages Press; Bloomington: Indiana University Press, 1981.

Sharf, Robert. "How to Think with Chan Gong'an." In *Thinking with Cases: Specialist Knowledge in Chinese Cultural History*, edited by Charlotte Furth,

Judith T. Zeitlin, and Ping-chen Hsiung, 205–43. Honolulu: University of Hawaii Press, 2007.
Sharma, Arvind, and Katherine K. Young, eds. *Feminism and World Religions*. Albany: State University of New York Press, 1999.
Shen Defu 沈德符. *Wanli yehuo bian* 萬曆野獲編. Preface dated 1619. Reprint, Beijing: Zhonghua Shuju, 1997.
Shen Fu 沈鈇. "Li Zhuowu zhuan" 李卓吾傳. In *LZ* 26:76–77.
Shi Shi 史式. "Cong Mingdai kaishi de minyou" 從明代開始的民郵. *Jiyou* (October 1963): 10–11, 21.
Shi Shouqian 石守謙 and Yang Rubin 楊儒賓, eds. *Mingdai mingxian chidu ji* 明代明賢尺牘集. 3 vols. Taipei: He Chuangshi Shufa Yishu Wenjiao Jijinhui, 2013.
Shields, Anna. *One Who Knows Me: Friendship and Literary Culture in Mid-Tang China*. Cambridge, MA: Harvard University Asia Center, 2015.
Shimada Kenji 島田虔次. "Ijin Tōkatsukyo ryakuden" 異人鄧豁渠略伝. In *Chūgoku shisōshi no kenkyū* 中国思想史の研究, 206–23. Kyoto: Kyoto University Press, 2002.
Shuihu zhuan huiping ben 水滸傳會評本. 2 vols. Edited by Chen Xizhong 陳曦鐘, Hou Zhongyi 侯忠義, and Lu Yuchuan 魯玉川. Beijing: Beijing Daxue Chubanshe, 1981.
Siegert, Bernhard. *Relays: Literature as an Epoch of the Postal System*. Translated by Kevin Repp. Stanford, CA: Stanford University Press, 1999.
Sima Qian 司馬遷. *Shiji* 史記. Beijing: Zhonghua Shuju, 1959.
Sivin, Nathan. "On the Word 'Taoist' as a Source of Perplexity: With Special Reference to the Relations of Science and Religion in Traditional China." *History of Religions* 17 (1978): 303–30.
Skonicki, Douglas. "Getting It for Oneself: An Analysis of Chao Jiong's Conception of the Three Teachings and His Method of Self-Cultivation." *Asia Major*, 3rd series, 28, no. 2 (2015): 77–108.
Smith, Jonathan Z. *Relating Religion: Essays in the Study of Religion*. Chicago: University of Chicago Press, 2004.
Sun Longji 孫隆基. *Weiduannai de minzu* 未斷奶的民族. Taipei: Juliu Tushu Gongsi, 1996.
———. *Zhongguo wenhua de shenceng jiegou* 中國文化的深層結構. Guilin: Guangxi Shifan Daxue, 2011.
Sun Xun 孫遜 and Sun Juyuan 孫菊園. *Zhongguo gudian xiaoshuo meixue ziliao huicui* 中國古典小說美學資料匯粹. Taipei: Da'an Chubanshen, 1991.
Sung, Marina H. "The Chinese Lieh-nü Tradition." In *Women in China: Current Directions in Historical Scholarship*, edited by Richard W. Guisso and Stanley Johannesen, 63–74. Youngstown, NY: Philo Press, 1981.
Suzuki Torao 鈴木虎雄. "Li Zhuowu nianpu" 李卓吾年譜. Translated and edited by Zhu Weizhi 朱維之. In *Li Zhi yanjiu cankao ziliao* 李贄研究參考資料, edited by Xiamen daxue lishixi, 88–175. Fuzhou: Fujian Renmin Chubanshe, 1975.

Szonyi, Michael. *Practicing Kinship: Lineage and Descent in Late Imperial China.* Stanford, CA: Stanford University Press, 2002.

T'ien, Ju-k'ang. *Male Anxiety and Female Chastity: A Comparative Study of Chinese Ethical Values in Ming-Ch'ing Times.* Leiden: E. J. Brill, 1988.

Taishō shinshū Daizōkyō 大正新修大藏經. Comp. Takakusu Junjirō 高楠順次郎, Watanabe Kaigyoku 渡邊海旭, et al. 100 vols. Tokyo: Taishō Issaikyō Kankōkai, 1924–34.

Tang Guizhang 唐圭章, comp. *Quan Song ci jianbian* 全宋詞簡編. Shanghai: Shanghai Guji Chubanshe, 1986.

Taylor, Charles. *The Ethics of Authenticity.* Cambridge, MA: Harvard University Press, 2018.

Tong, Rosemarie. *Feminist Thought: A More Comprehensive Introduction.* Boulder, CO: Westview Press, 1998.

Van Overmeire, Ben. "Encounter Dialogue: The Literary History of a Zen Buddhist Genre." PhD dissertation, University of California, San Diego, 2016.

Vitiello, Giovanni. *The Libertine's Friend: Homosexuality and Masculinity in Late Imperial China.* Chicago: University of Chicago Press, 2011.

Waley, Arthur, trans. *The Analects of Confucius.* New York: Vintage, 1938.

Waltner, Ann. "Widows and Remarriage in Ming and Early Qing China." In *Women in China: Current Directions in Historical Scholarship,* edited by Richard W. Guisso and Stanley Johannesen, 129–46. Youngstown, NY: Philo Press, 1981.

Wang Fansen 王汎森. *Ming mo Qing chu de yi zhong daode yange zhuyi* 明末清初的一種道德嚴格主義. Taipei: Zhongyang Yanjiuyuan Jindaishi Yanjiusuo, 1998.

———. *Wan Ming Qing chu sixiang shi lun* 晚明清初思想十論. Shanghai: Fudan Daxue Chubanshe, 2004.

Wang Ji 王畿. *Longxi Wang xiansheng quanji.* 龍谿王先生全集 Tainan: Zhuang Yan Wenhua Shiye Chuban Gongsi, 1997.

———. *Wang Ji ji* 王畿集. Edited by Wu Zhen 吳震. Nanjing: Fenghuang Chubanshe, 2007.

Wang Shihuai 王時槐. *Tangnan Wang xiansheng youqingtang hegao.* 塘南王先生友慶堂合稿 Tainan: Zhuangyan Wenhua Shiye Chubanshe, 1997.

Wang Yangming 王陽明. "Da Luo Zheng'an Shaozai shu" 《答羅整庵少宰書》. In *Wang Yangming Chuanxi lu xiangzhu jiping* 傳習錄詳註集評, edited by Wing-tsit Chan 陳榮捷, 247–56. Taipei: Xuesheng Shuju, 1992.

———. "Letter in Reply to Vice-Minister Lo Cheng-an." In *Instructions for Practical Living and Other Neo-Confucian Writings by Wang Yangming,* 157–65. Translated by Wing-Tsit Chan 陳榮捷. New York: Columbia University Press, 1963.

———. *Wang Yangming quanji* 王陽明全集. Edited by Wu Guang 吳光, Qian Ming 錢明, and Dong Ping 董平. Shanghai: Shanghai Guji Chubanshe, 1992.

Wanxu zangjing 卍續藏經. Taipei: Xinwenfeng, 1983.

Watson, Burton, trans. *The Analects of Confucius*. New York: Columbia University Press, 2007.

———, trans. *Records of the Grand Historian*. Vol. 2. New York: Columbia University Press, 1961.

Wei An 魏安 (Andrew West). *Sanguo yanyi banben kao* 三國演義版本考. Shanghai: Shanghai Guji Chubanshe, 1996.

Wu Jen-shu 巫仁恕. *Pinwei shehua: Wan Ming de xiaofei shehui yu shidaifu* 品味奢華: 晚明的消費社會與士大夫. Taipei: Academia Sinica, 2007.

Wu, Jiang. "Discipline and Enlightenment: Hanyue Fazang 漢月法藏 and the Spread of the Triple Platform Ordination Ceremony in Seventeenth-Century China." Paper presented at the conference Vinaya Revival in 20th Century China and Taiwan, Taipei, December 20–21, 2017.

———. *Enlightenment in Dispute: The Reinvention of Chan Buddhism in Seventeenth-Century China*. New York: Oxford University Press, 2008.

———. *Leaving for the Rising Sun: Chinese Zen Master Yinyuan and the Authenticity Crisis in Early Modern East Asia*. New York: Oxford University Press, 2015.

Wu, Pei-yi. *The Confucian's Progress: Autobiographical Writings in Traditional China*. Princeton, NJ: Princeton University Press, 1990.

Wu, Yinghui 吳穎慧. "Commentary, Illustration, and Cross-Generic Writings in Paired Editions of *Xixiang ji* and *Pipa ji*." PhD dissertation, Washington University, 2014.

Wu Yu 吳虞. "Ming Li Zhuowu biezhuan (wei wan)" 明李卓吾別傳(未完). *Jinbu zazhi* 進步雜誌 9, no. 3 (1916): 19–24.

———. *Wu Yu wenlu* 吳虞文錄. 1927. *Minguo congshu* 民國叢書, series 2, vol. 96. Reprint, Shanghai: Shanghai Shudian, 1990.

Wu Ze 吳澤. *Rujiao pantu Li Zhuowu* 儒教叛徒李卓吾. Shanghai: Huaxia Shudian, 1949.

Xie Wenjian 謝文洊. *Xie Chengshan ji.* 謝程山集 Tainan: Zhuangyan Wenhua Shiye Chubanshe, 1997.

Xu Jianping 許建平. *Li Zhi sixiang yanbianshi* 李贄思想演變史. Beijing: Renmin Chubanshe, 2005.

———. *Li Zhuowu zhuan* 李卓吾傳. Beijing: Dongfang Chubanshe, 2004.

Xu Shuofang 徐朔方. "Qianyan" 前言. In *Li Zhuowu pingben Xiyou ji* 李卓吾評本西遊記, edited by Chen Xianxing 陳先行 and Bao Yufei 包于飛, 1:1–6. Shanghai: Shanghai Guji Chubanshe, 1994.

Yan Dunyi 嚴敦易. *Shuihu zhuan de yanbian* 水滸傳的演變. Shanghai: Gudian Wenxue; Beijing: Zuojia Chubanshe, 1957.

Yan Jun 顏鈞. *Yan Jun ji* 顏鈞集. Edited by Huang Xuanmin 黃宣民. Beijing: Zhongguo Shehui Kexue Chubanshe, 1996.

Yan Kejun 嚴可均. *Quan shanggu sandai Qin Han sanguo liuchao wen* 全上古三代秦漢三國六朝文. Shijiazhuang: Hebei Jiaoyu Chubanshe, 1999.

Yan Lieshan 鄢烈山 and Zhu Jianguo 朱健國. *Li Zhi zhuan* 李贄傳. Beijing: Shishi Chubanshe, 2000.

Yan Yuan 顏元. "Juyou yujian" 居憂愚見. In *Xizhai jiyu* 習齋記餘, 162–68. Reprint, Beijing: Zhonghua Shuju, 1985.

Yang Bojun 楊伯峻. *Chunqiu Zuozhuan zhu* 春秋左傳注. 4 vols. Beijing: Zhonghua Shuju, 1990.

Yang Jisheng 楊繼盛. *Yang Zhongmin gong yibi* 楊忠愍公遺筆. *Congshu jicheng* edition. Shanghai: Shangwu Yingshuguan, 1939.

Yang Qiyuan 楊起元. *Taishi Yang Fuso xiansheng zhengxue bian* 太史楊復所先生證學編. Tainan: Zhuangyan Wenhua Shiye Chubanshe, 1995.

Ye Lang 葉朗. "Ye Zhou pingdian *Shuihu zhuan* kaozheng" 葉晝評點水滸傳考證. In *Zhongguo xiaoshuo meixue* 中國小說美學, 280–302. Beijing: Beijing Daxue, 1982.

Ying Huiqian 應撝謙. *Xingli dazhong* 性理大中. Haikou: Hainan Chubanshe, 2001.

Yong Rong 永瑢. *Siku quanshu zongmu* 四庫全書總目. Taipei: Shangwu Yingshuguan, 1983.

Yu, Anthony C., trans. *Journey to the West.* Rev. ed. 4 vols. Chicago: University of Chicago Press, 2012.

Yu Jinfang 余晉芳. *Minguo Macheng xianzhi qianbian* 民國麻城縣志前編. In *Zhongguo difangzhi jicheng* 中國地方誌集成, edited by Zheng Zhong 鄭重. Nanjing: Jiangsu Guji Chubanshe, 2001.

Yu, Li. "A History of Reading in Late Imperial China, 1000–1800." PhD dissertation, Ohio State University, 2003.

Yu Xiangdou 余象斗. *Beiyou ji: Beifang Zhenwu zushi Xuantian shangdi chushen zhizhuan* 北遊記：北方真武祖師玄天上帝出身志傳. Jianyang, Fujian: Shuangfengtang, 1602. Reprint as vol. 71 of *Guben xiaoshuo jicheng* 古本小說集成. Shanghai: Shanghai Guji Chubanshe, 1990.

———. *Nanyou ji: Ke quanxiang Wuxian lingguan dadi Huaguang tianwang zhuan* 南遊記：刻全像五顯靈官大帝華光天王傳. Jianyang, Fujian: Changyuantang 昌遠堂, 1571? Reprint as vol. 70 of *Guben xiaoshuo jicheng* 古本小說集成. Shanghai: Shanghai Guji Chubanshe, 1990.

———, ed. *Wanyong zhengzong* 萬用正宗. Jianyang, 1599.

Yu Ying-shi 余英時. "Shi-shang hudong yu Ruxue zhuanxiang: Ming Qing shehuishi yu sixiangshi zhi yi mianxiang" 士商互動與儒學轉向：明清社會史與思想史之一面相. In *Rujia lunli yu shangren jingshen* 儒家倫理與商人精神. In *Jinshi Zhonggguo zhi chuantong yu tuibian (Liu Guangjing Yuanshi qishiwusui zhushou lunwenji)* 近世中國之傳統與蛻變 (劉廣京院士七十五歲祝壽論文集), edited by Hao Yanping 郝延平 and Wei Xiumei 魏秀梅, 1:3–35. Taipei: Zhongyang Yanjiuyuan Jindaishi Yanjiusuo, 1998.

———. *Zhongguo jinshi zongjiao lunli yu shangren jingshen* 中國近世宗教倫理與商人精神. Taipei: Lianjing Chubanshe, 2004.

Yuan Guangyi 袁光儀. *Li Zhuowu xinlun.* 李卓吾新論. Shanxia: Taipei University Press, 2008.

Yuan Hongdao 袁宏道. *Yuan Hongdao ji jianjiao* 袁宏道集箋校. Shanghai: Shanghai Guji Chubanshe, 2008.
Yuan Mei 袁枚. *Xiaocang shanfang shiwenji* 小倉山房詩文集 Shanghai: Shanghai Guji Chubanshe, 1988.
Yuan Zhongdao 袁中道. *Kexuezhai ji* 珂雪齋集. 3 vols. Edited by Qian Bocheng 錢伯城. Shanghai: Shanghai Guji Chubanshe, 1989.
———. "Li Wenling zhuan" 李溫陵傳. In *LZ* 26:157–61.
———. *Zuolin jitan* 柞林紀譚. In *LZ* 18:299–328.
Yuan Zongdao 袁宗道. *Yuan Boxiu xiaopin* 袁伯修小品. Edited by Zhao Botao 趙伯陶. Beijing: Wenhua Yishu Chubanshe, 1996.
Zhang Dai 張岱. "Li Zhi, Jiao Hong liezhuan" 李贄、焦竑列傳. In *Shikui shu* 石匱書, annotated by Luan Baoqun 欒保群, 9:205.2985–90. Beijing: Gugong Chubanshe, 2017.
Zhang Jianye 張建業, ed. "Li Zhi yanjiu ziliao huibian" 李贄研究資料匯編. In *LZ* 26:1–356.
Zhang, Ying. *Confucian Image Politics: Masculine Morality in Seventeenth-Century China.* Seattle: University of Washington Press, 2016.
———. "Politics and Morality during the Ming-Qing Transition, 1570–1670." PhD dissertation, University of Michigan, 2010.
Zheng Zhenduo 鄭振鐸, ed. *Shuihu quanzhuan* 水滸全傳. 4 vols. Beijing: Renmin Wenxue Chubanshe, 1954. Reprint, Hong Kong: Zhonghua Shuju, 1965.
Zhou Qun 周群. *Yuan Hongdao pingzhuan: Fu Yuan Zongdao, Yuan Zhongdao pingzhuan* 袁宏道評傳: 附袁宗道, 袁中道評傳. Nanjing: Nanjing Daxue Chubanshe, 1999.
Zhou Rudeng 周汝登. *Dongyue zhengxue lu* 東越證學錄. Taipei: Wenhai Chubanshe, 1970.
Zhou, Yiqun. "The Hearth and the Temple: Mapping Female Religiosity in Late Imperial China, 1550–1900." *Late Imperial China* 24, no. 2 (2003): 109–55.
Zhu Changwen 朱長文. *Qin shi* 琴史. Taipei: Taiwan Shangwu Shuju, 1983.
Zhu Xi 朱熹. *Shi jizhuan* 詩集傳. Edited by Li Jingde 黎靖德. Shanghai: Zhonghua Shuju, 1958.
———. *Sishu zhangju jizhu sizhong* 四書章句集注四種. In *Guoxue jiben congshu* 國學基本叢書. Compiled by Wu Zhizhong 吳志忠. Annotated by Wu Ying 吳英. Taipei: Taiwan Shangwu Yinshuguan, 1968.
———. *Zhuzi yulei* 朱子語類. Edited by Li Jingde 黎靖德. Taipei: Huashi Chubanshe, 1987.
Zhuangzi jishi 莊子集釋. Edited by Wang Xiaoyu 王孝魚. Compiled by Guo Qingfan 郭慶藩. 3 vols. Beijing: Zhonghua Shuju, 1995.
Zi, Xin. "Strolling in 'Coral Grove': Yuan Hongdao's *Shan Hu Lin* and the Revival of Chan Buddhism in the Wanli Period (1573–1620)." MA thesis, University of Arizona, 2013.

Ziporyn, Brook. *Evil and/or/as the Good: Omnicentrism, Intersubjectivity and Value Paradox in Tiantai Buddhist Thought*. Cambridge, MA: Harvard University Asia Center for the Harvard-Yenching Institute, 2000.

Zuo Dongling 左東岭. *Li Zhi yu wan Ming wenxue sixiang* 李贄與晚明文學思想. Tianjin: Tianjin Renmin Chubanshe, 1997.

Zwicker, Steven N. "The Reader Revealed." In *The Reader Revealed*, compiled and edited by Sabrina Alcorn Baron et al., 11–18. Washington, DC: Folger Library; Seattle: University of Washington Press, 2001.

CONTRIBUTORS

TIMOTHY BROOK is professor of history at the University of British Columbia. His publications include *The Confusions of Pleasure: Commerce and Culture in Ming China*, *The Troubled Empire: China in the Yuan and Ming Dynasties*, *Vermeer's Hat: The Seventeenth Century and the Dawn of the Global World*, *Praying for Power: Buddhism and the Formation of Gentry Society in Late-Ming China*, and numerous edited volumes.

KAI-WING CHOW is professor of East Asian studies and history at the University of Illinois, Urbana-Champaign, and curator of the Spurlock Museum. His publications include *Printing, Culture, and Power in Early Modern China*, *The Rise of Confucian Ritualism in Late Imperial China: Ethics, Classics and Lineage Discourse*, and several edited volumes.

MARAM EPSTEIN is professor of Chinese literature at the University of Oregon. She is the author of *Competing Discourses: Orthodoxy, Authenticity, and Engendered Meanings in Late-Imperial Chinese Fiction* and *Orthodox Passions: Narrating Filial Love during the High Qing.*

RIVI HANDLER-SPITZ is associate professor in the Department of Asian Languages and Cultures at Macalester College. She is the author of *Symptoms of an Unruly Age: Li Zhi and Cultures of Early Modernity* and a coeditor, along with Pauline C. Lee and Haun Saussy, of *A Book to Burn and a Book to Keep (Hidden): Selected Writings of Li Zhi.*

ROBERT E. HEGEL is the Liselotte Dieckmann Professor Emeritus of Comparative Literature in Arts and Sciences at Washington University in St. Louis. His publications include *The Novel in Seventeenth Century China*, *Reading Illustrated Fiction in Late Imperial China*, and several edited and translated volumes.

MARTIN W. HUANG is professor of East Asian studies at the University of California, Irvine. His publications include *Negotiating Masculinities in Late Imperial China* and *Intimate Memory: Gender and Mourning in Late Imperial China*.

PAULINE C. LEE is associate professor of Chinese religions and cultures at Saint Louis University and the author of *Li Zhi, Confucianism, and the Virtue of Desire*. With Rivi Handler-Spitz and Haun Saussy, she is a coeditor of *A Book to Burn and a Book to Keep (Hidden): Selected Writings of Li Zhi*.

WAI-YEE LI is the 1879 Professor of Chinese Literature at Harvard University. Her publications include *Enchantment and Disenchantment in Chinese Literature, The Readability of the Past in Early Chinese Historiography, Women and National Trauma in Late Imperial Chinese Literature*, and several translations and edited volumes.

MIAW-FEN LU is the director of Academia Sinica's Institute for Modern History and the author of *Ruling All under Heaven with Filial Piety: The Xiaojing in Late Imperial China, Becoming a Sage and Family Ethics: Ming Qing Confucianism in the Tradition of Religious Dialogue, The Wang Yangming School during the Ming Dynasty: History, Thought, and Practice* (all in Chinese), and several edited volumes.

HAUN SAUSSY is University Professor at the University of Chicago. His books include *The Problem of a Chinese Aesthetic, Great Walls of Discourse and Other Adventures in Cultural China, The Ethnography of Rhythm: Orality and Its Technologies, Translation as Citation: Zhuangzi Inside Out*, and several edited volumes.

JIANG WU is professor of East Asian studies and the director of the Center for Buddhist Studies at the University of Arizona. His books include *Leaving for the Rising Sun: Chinese Zen Master Yinyuan and the Authenticity Crisis in Early Modern East Asia, Spreading Buddha's Word in East Asia: The Formation and Transformation of the Chinese Buddhist Canon*, and *Enlightenment in Dispute: The Reinvention of Chan Buddhism in Seventeenth-Century China*.

YING ZHANG is associate professor of history at the Ohio State University and the author of the monograph *Confucian Image Politics: Masculine Morality in Seventeenth-Century China* and a short volume, *Religion and Prison Art in Ming China (1368–1644): Creative Environment, Creative Subjects*.

INDEX

Asterisks indicate works translated in part or in full in *A Book to Burn and A Book to Keep (Hidden).*

CPSIA information can be obtained
at www.ICGtesting.com
Printed in the USA
BVHW071632081220
594491BV00003B/6

9 780295 748382